GENDERED JUSTICE

Gendered Justice

Addressing Female Offenders

Edited by

Barbara E. Bloom

Carolina Academic Press

Durham, North Carolina

ISBN 0-89089-123-0
LCCN 2002117307

CAROLINA ACADEMIC PRESS

700 Kent Street
Durham, North Carolina 27701
Telephone (919) 489-7486
Fax (919) 493-5668
www.cap-press.com

Printed in the United States of America

This book is dedicated with gratitude and affection to Peter Graham Cohn who has devoted his life to the struggle for justice and who has inspired me to do likewise.

CONTENTS

FOREWORD

The Gender and Justice series responds to two of the most profound changes in criminal justice over the last quarter-century, one well-known, the other almost unrecognized.

The well-known change is the introduction of gender into the study of crime and its consequences. In the early 1970s, scholars and practitioners began to realize that gender—the social effects of being men and women—has an enormous impact on both the kinds of crimes men and women commit and the ways in which social systems respond to those offenses. Studying the effects of gender is necessarily an ongoing project, partly because gender roles themselves are in a constant state of flux, partly because scholars are constantly uncovering new facets of gendered existence—new historical meanings of gender and previously overlooked variations in gender by age, ethnicity and nationality, sexuality, and social class. To explore the ramifications of gender in the arena of crime and justice is, then, one goal of this series.

A second, barely recognized though equally profound change in criminal justice over the last twenty-five years lies in ways of conceptualizing *justice*. Citizens of democracies like to think that the concept of justice is unchangeable—that justice has always meant equal treatment under the law. But it is not so. Ideas of justice, like ideas of gender, change over time. In the 1970s, many criminal justice officials assumed that Black and Hispanic prisoners should be segregated and provided with fewer resources than white prisoners; similarly, nearly everyone assumed that women prisoners should be treated differently than their male counterparts. While differential treatment by race has been rejected, many people continue to advocate differential treatment by gender, at least during some stages of criminal justice process. If we aim at treating men and women the same, the reasoning goes, we in fact use a masculine model and draw on assumptions developed in reaction to men, who have always outnumbered women as offenders and convicts.

Figuring out whether justice should result in the same or different treatment is, then, another ongoing process. To explore the evolving meanings of justice as it relates to gender—to investigate ways in which people try to achieve gender equity in an unfair world—is, then, a second objective of this series.

Barbara Bloom's *Gendered Justice: Addressing Female Offenders* confronts these debates in the context of corrections, an arena in which the meaning of justice is currently hotly contested. Thirty years ago, few questioned the assumption that women offenders were less important than male offenders and that their institutions should be funded last. By the 1980s, however, advocates were demanding equal treatment, which many defined as identical treatment of men and women offenders. Jurisdictions throughout the Western world embraced that ideal, and policy-makers and practitioners today try to achieve it. Yet, for reasons explained in *Gendered Justice*, the goal is now starting to seem ill-advised as well as perhaps impossible to achieve. Bloom's book exposes the flaws of the justice-as-equality ideal, providing a trenchant and wide-ranging critique. As Bloom shows, today there is a new consensus emerging on the need to respond differently to male and female offenders, a consensus accompanied by renewed interest in correctional treatment and rehabilitation.

The burgeoning interest in gender-specific treatment of offenders is the topic of Bloom's book. Chapters by leading authorities analyze innovative efforts to develop gender-sensitive correctional programs in the United States and Canada. Addressing major theoretical as well as practical concerns, this book provides an international overview and evaluation of cutting-edge strategies for achieving gendered justice.

Nicole Hahn Rafter
Gender and Justice Series Editor
Northeastern University

ABOUT THE AUTHORS

Joanne Belknap, Ph.D. received a Ph.D. in Criminal Justice and Criminology from Michigan State University in 1986. She is currently a Professor in Sociology at the University of Colorado. Dr. Belknap has numerous scholarly publications, most of which involve violence against women and female offenders. She has also served on state advisory boards for female offenders and women in prison. She is currently working on research projects assessing the court processing of woman battering cases, on delinquent girls, and a second edition of her book *The Invisible Woman: Gender, Crime, and Justice.* Dr. Belknap is the recipient of the 1997 national award "Distinguished Scholar of the Division on Women and Crime" of the American Society of Criminology and the University of Colorado teaching award for 2001.

Barbara E. Bloom, Ph.D. is an Assistant Professor in the Department of Criminal Justice Administration at Sonoma State University. Her research and policy interests include women and girls under criminal justice supervision and gender-responsive interventions and services. Among her publications are several national studies: *Why Punish the Children? A Reappraisal of the Children of Incarcerated Mothers in America,* and a National Institute of Corrections sponsored study, *Female Offenders in the Community: An Analysis of Innovative Strategies and Programs.* She is the Project Director of the National Institute of Corrections' *Gender-Responsive Strategies: Research, Practice and Guiding Principles for Women Offenders* Project. She received an MSW from San Francisco State University in 1981 and a Ph.D. in Sociology from the University of California, Riverside in 1996. She is a past President of the Western Society of Criminology.

Bonnie K. Cady is a client Manager/Parole Officer for the Colorado Division of Youth Corrections. She is also a drug and alcohol counselor who has worked with offenders since 1978. She has a background in program development as well as assessment, case management and direct service. Her background spans adult and juvenile offenders, both male and female, with particular expertise with female offender populations. She is considered a "Gender Expert" in regard to juvenile justice/corrections in Colorado.

Meda Chesney-Lind, Ph.D. is Professor of Women's Studies at the University of Hawaii at Manoa. She has served as Vice President of the American Society of Criminology and President of the Western Society of Criminology. Nationally recognized for her work on women and crime, her books include *Girls, Delinquency and Juvenile Justice, The Female Offender: Girls, Women and Crime,* and *Female Gangs in America.* Her most recent book is a co-edited volume that examines the social consequences of mass imprisonment entitled *Invisible Punishment.* She recently received the Bruce Smith, Sr. Award "for outstanding contributions to Criminal Justice" from the Academy of Criminal Justice Sciences in April, 2001. She was named a fellow of the American Society of Criminology in 1996.

Stephanie S. Covington, Ph.D. has over twenty years of experience in the design, development and implementation of treatment services for women. She is recognized for her work on gender-responsive services in both the public and private sectors. Her twelve years of experience in the criminal justice system include training, speaking, writing, and consulting with varied national, state and local corrections agencies in the U.S. and Canada. Dr. Covington has published extensively. She developed a comprehensive, integrated, gender-responsive treatment model for criminal justice settings entitled *Helping Women Recover: A Program for Treating Substance Abuse,* and she provides training and speaks regularly at national conferences. Dr. Covington is the lead consultant on the National Institute of Corrections' *Gender-Responsive Strategies: Research, Practice, and Guiding Principles for Women Offenders* Project. Dr. Covington holds a Masters degree in Social Work from Columbia University and a Ph.D. in Psychology from the Union Institute.

Kelly Hannah-Moffat, Ph.D. is an Assistant Professor in the Departments of Criminology and Sociology, University of Toronto. She worked as a researcher and policy advisor for the *Commission of Inquiry into Certain Events at the Prison for Women in Kingston.* She is a past President of the Toronto Elizabeth Fry Society, a halfway house and organization that works for and on behalf of all women in conflict with the law. Her publications and research focus on sociology of punishment, governmentality, feminist criminology, parole and social policy. Her publications include *Punishment in Disguise: The Governance of Canadian Women's Federal Imprisonment,* University of Toronto Press; and "Prisons that Empower: Neoliberal Governance in Canadian Women's Prisons" in *British Journal of Criminology (2000)* for which she received the *Radzinowicz Memorial Prize*; and *An Ideal Prison: Critical Essays on Women's Imprisonment in Canada* co-edited with M. Shaw.

Kathleen Kendall, Ph.D. is a sociologist in the School of Medicine at the University of Southampton, United Kingdom. She has lectured in both Canada and the United Kingdom. Kathleen has worked for the Correctional Service of Canada variously as a program evaluator, researcher and special advisor on female offenders. She has written extensively on issues related to female prisoners in Canada and was recently consulted by the Canadian Human Rights Commission with regard to her work on the mental health of female prisoners. Currently she is conducting research on human experimentation in Canadian prisons with Dorothy Proctor and is involved in a qualitative study of depression funded by the British Medical Research Council.

Elizabeth Dermody Leonard, Ph.D. is Associate Professor of Sociology at Vanguard University where her course offerings include Family Violence, Criminology, and Sociology. She received her Ph.D. in 1997 from the University of California, Riverside. Her research on incarcerated battered women has been used by legislators, legal scholars, and advocates for women in prison. Her publications include *Convicted Survivors: The Imprisonment of Battered Women Who Kill* (2002 SUNY Press); journal articles in the Prison Journal, Journal of Criminal Law & Criminology, Caribbean Journal of Criminology and Social Psychology, Women, Girls, & Criminal Justice and Journal of Interpersonal Violence; and book chapters in Analyzing Social Problems: Essays and Exercises, and Social Problems.

Scott K. Okamoto, Ph.D. is an Assistant Professor in the School of Social Work at Arizona State University, Main Campus. His research areas include child and adolescent mental health, juvenile delinquency, practitioner issues, and barriers to effective practice with high-risk youth. His recent publications have focused on the feelings and perceptions of youth-serving practitioners, and culturally-informed social work practices. He has experience working with children, adolescents, and families in residential, shelter-based, and school-based programs.

Barbara Owen, **Ph.D.** is a Professor of Criminology at California State University, Fresno. Receiving an NIJ Graduate Research Fellowship in 1982, she earned her Ph.D. in Sociology from UC Berkeley in 1984. In 2002, she was awarded the Provost Award for Excellence in Research from her university. A former Senior Researcher with the Federal Bureau of Prisons, Barbara Owen is the author of over 12 articles and two books, including *In the Mix: Struggle and Survival in a Women's Prison* (SUNY Press, 1998). As an ethnographer, she continues to work in the areas of feminist criminology, substance abuse treatment and prison culture.

Shoshana Pollack is an Assistant Professor in the Faculty of Social Work, Wilfrid Laurier University, Waterloo, Ontario. She teaches clinical social work courses, anti-oppression theory and practice, and gay/lesbian/bisexual issues. Shoshana worked as a psychotherapist in women's prisons for five years. Her research interests are in the areas of women in prison, evaluation of male batterer's programs, women's mental health and violence against women.

Myrna S. Raeder, J.D. is a Professor at Southwestern University School of Law in Los Angeles, California, a past chair of the American Bar Association's Criminal Justice Section, and a nationally known expert on Gender and Sentencing. She has written extensively and lectured to varied groups of lawyers and judges on this topic and is an advocate on behalf of women offenders and their children. Professor Raeder is also a 2002 recipient of the Margaret Brent Women Lawyers of Achievement Award given by the A.B.A.'s Commission on Women in the Profession.

Christine E. Rasche, Ph.D. is Associate Professor of Criminal Justice and Sociology at the University of North Florida. In addition to university teaching and research, she consults with state and federal correctional departments and provides training for prison staff on the specialized supervision of female offenders. She is also active in women's affairs in her community, chairing the Mayor's Sexual Assault Advisory Council and serving on the Advisory Board of Hubbard House, the local battered women's refuge.

Margaret Shaw, Ph.D. is Director of Analysis and Exchange at the International Centre for the Prevention of Crime (ICPC) in Montreal. She is a sociologist and criminologist who has worked as a research and policy analyst in the Home Office, England, and for the federal and provincial governments in Canada. She taught in the Department of Sociology & Anthropology at Concordia University, Montreal for the past ten years. She has a long-standing interest in prisons and prison reform, women's involvement in lawbreaking, crime prevention, treatment and program evaluation and restorative justice. Her recent published work includes a number of studies on women's imprisonment. With Kelly Hannah-Moffat she edited *An Ideal Prison? Critical Essays on Women's Imprisonment in Canada* (Fernwood, 2000), and completed a study of the use of classification in women's prisons in Canada *Taking Risks: Incorporating Gender and Culture into the Classification & Assessment of Federally Sentenced Women in Canada* (Status of Women Canada, 2001).

Erica L. Winter formerly worked with institutionalized delinquent girls and is currently a doctoral student in Sociology at the University of Colorado.

Acknowledgments

My deepest appreciation goes to the contributors to this volume. They are internationally recognized scholars in the study of gender and justice and it has been my honor to include their work in this book.

The initial impetus for this book came from my colleague and friend, Stephanie Covington, to whom I am most grateful. She said simply, but emphatically, "Barbara, you really need to do this book." And with her encouragement and support, I did.

I am thankful to Nicky Rafter, Editor of the Carolina Academic Press Gender and Justice Series, who has inspired so many of us along the way, and who was instrumental in every stage of the development of the book. Her support and encouragement are greatly appreciated.

There have been many women who have inspired my work over the years, Joanne Belknap, Meda Chesney-Lind, Joy Pollock, and Nicky Rafter to name a few. Barbara Owen, my research partner with whom I have collaborated on a number of projects and publications, has remained steadfast in her dedication to enhancing research and scholarship on behalf of women and girls in the justice system. In the fifteen plus years that we have worked together, she has continued to be a supportive and reliable colleague and good friend.

The National Institute of Corrections has been a leader in terms of women offender initiatives, including the Gender-Responsive Strategies: Research, Practice, and Guiding Principles for Women Offenders Project (Bloom, Owen, & Covington, 2002). Phyllis Modley, Andie Moss, and Mary Scully Whitaker are to be applauded for their commitment to raising the visibility of gender issues in U.S. corrections.

Many thanks to my former student, Correne Testa, for her editing assistance, Linda Cepeda, for doing the final edits, and to Robin Button for her attention to detail in preparing the manuscript.

Finally, this book is dedicated to the girls and women who have experienced the justice system first-hand and whose voices and life stories have informed my research and advocacy. You have inspired me to continue my struggle for gender and justice.

INTRODUCTION

Barbara E. Bloom

A focus on gender and gender difference is not simply a focus on what some scholars term 'women's issues.' It is a far more encompassing enterprise, raising questions about how gender organizes the disciplines of criminology and sociolegal studies (Chesney-Lind & Bloom, 1997).

Many feminists now argue that women themselves must determine when difference is relevant so that they can be both the same and different across situations and individuals. The goal is not equality but equivalence, not sameness for individual men and women but parity for women as a sex or for groups of women in their specificity (Martin & Jurik, 1996).

This volume evolved from a panel entitled *Gendered Justice: Programming for Women in Correctional Settings* that I chaired at the American Society of Criminology Annual Meeting in San Francisco, November 2000. It was a provocative and lively session and, as is often the case, we did not have enough time to fully explore the content of the excellent papers that were presented. Subsequently, some of the panelists revised their papers into chapters contained in this book. This volume represents a rich diversity of contemporary research, theory and perspectives on gender-appropriate policy and programming from the U.S., Canada, and the United Kingdom. All of the authors included in this book are on the cutting edge of the research that is being conducted on gender and justice and they are widely acclaimed for their work.

This book should be of interest to a wide audience including criminal justice policy makers and practitioners, as well as researchers who are interested in looking at the ways in which gender influences correctional policy and practice. In addition, this book should be relevant to academics and students in sociology, psychology, criminology, criminal justice, and women's and gender studies. This volume should also be of value internationally to jurisdictions that are interested in re-examining their policies and practices regarding female offenders.

Female offenders[1] have experienced a history of neglect in the development and implementation of correctional programming targeted to their circumstances. Historically, programs for female offenders were based on male program models without consideration of their appropriateness for women and girls. Often by default, practices designed for male offenders were viewed as the norm. The significant increase in women and girls under correctional supervision has called attention to their status in the justice system and the particular circumstances they encounter within the system.

This book addresses the complex questions that arise regarding female offenders and criminal justice policy. It raises serious questions about current criminal justice policy and practice which ignore gender as well as practices that have been widely accepted by mainstream criminologists, policy makers, and practitioners without regard for their implications for women and girls. This book discusses the special circumstances faced by female offenders and the "equal treatment" tradition that has guided criminal law and practice for the past century and has generated the phenomenon known as 'vengeful equity'. It challenges mainstream policies of "gender neutrality" in terms of their implications for women and girls in conflict with the law. With the dramatic rise of women and girls in the criminal justice system, gender-based issues are now receiving attention in the U.S., Canada, the United Kingdom, and elsewhere.

There are a number of global themes that are addressed in this volume including the following:

Gender Matters

The central theme of this book is that crime is gendered and that gender matters significantly in shaping patterns of offending as well as the criminal justice system's response to criminal offending and to offenders. Gendered differences in female pathways to crime and incarceration, their offense patterns, and their behavior and needs while incarcerated, all suggest a need for gender-responsive policies and practices. In order to sufficiently explain women and girls' criminality, it is important to recognize the significance of gender in defining as well as prescribing behavior and how gender interacts with race and class. Race and class are important risk factors in being processed through the criminal justice system. Racial disparity is a factor in the arrests, pretrial treatment, and sentencing of female offenders. Women of color, especially

---

1. The term female offender is used to describe both women and girls under correctional supervision.

African-Americans, are disproportionately incarcerated in U.S. prisons and jails.

In her book, Women and Punishment (2002), Pat Carlen asks if gendered justice is viable? She states:

> The notion of a 'gendered justice' persists because there is ample evidence that at operational levels it is indeed alive and well. Whether or not they should be, women are already punished differently to men because sentencing policies impact differently on different age, ethnic and gender groups (pp. 11-12).

Gender is also important in examining the differential effects of current policies. For example, in the U.S. much of the increase in criminal justice control rates for women is a result of the war on drugs. Inadvertently, the war on drugs became a war on women, particularly poor women and women of color (Bloom, Chesney-Lind, & Owen, 1994). The emphasis on punishment rather than treatment has brought many women and girls into the criminal justice system. Female offenders who in past decades would have been given community sanctions are now being sentenced to prison. Mandatory minimum sentences for drug offenses coupled with federal sentencing guidelines intended to reduce racial, economic, and other disparities in sentencing males, have distinctly disadvantaged females. These so-called "gender-neutral" sentencing laws fail to recognize the distinction between major players in drug organizations and minor ancillary players.

While most of the attention on the impact of the war on drugs has focused on the criminal justice system, policy changes in welfare reform, housing and other social policy arenas have combined to create a disparate and adverse impact on women who have been convicted of drug offenses and their families. Women are often the custodial parent with major responsibilities for their children. Frequently caught in the cross-fire of the war on drugs, women and their families pay an enormous price.

Is Equal Treatment, Fair Treatment?

There is an emerging awareness that women and girls who are involved in the correctional system present different issues than their male counterparts. However, an appropriate recognition of these differences fuels debate regarding concepts of 'justice-as-equality' or 'justice-as-parity'. In the 1980s, the equal treatment model (which was translated as identical treatment) was embraced by justice systems around the globe and according to some scholars, this model led to "vengeful equity" (Bloom & Chesney-Lind, 2003).

Today, some criminal justice organizations are beginning to re-examine their policies and programs in terms of gender with an acknowledgment that 'parity' differs conceptually from equality and stress the importance of *equivalence* rather than *sameness*. For example, the American Correctional Association's Policy Statement suggests that "correctional systems should be guided by the principle of parity. Female offenders must receive the equivalent range of services available to male offenders, including opportunities for individual programming and services that recognize the unique needs of this population" (ACA, 1995, p. 2).

Gender-Responsive Policy and Practice

While the Canadian "what works" literature[2] has provided a foundation for a renewed interest in correctional treatment and rehabilitation, the research in this volume raises critical issues regarding the applicability of the assumptions upon which it is based. The "what works" body of research continues a male-oriented focus and ignores gender and culturally responsive treatment. While this literature has had an enormous impact on correctional treatment in Canada, the U.S. and elsewhere, the question of whether or not findings, such as the importance of identifying criminogenic risks and needs, can be generalized to women and girls as well as persons of diverse racial and ethnic backgrounds is still unanswered. In a previous publication, I questioned whether women's offending relates to criminogenic risks and needs or is but one factor in the complex interconnection of race, class, gender, abuse, trauma, addiction, or a combination (see, for example, Bloom, 2000, p. 122). Chapters 3 and 4 offer further insight into these issues.

In Chapter 1, *Gendered Justice: Women in the Criminal Justice System*, Stephanie Covington and I discuss the need to develop effective gender-responsive programming for women that is based on their life circumstances and pathways to crime. We discuss how gender makes a critical difference in terms of its impact on standard correctional procedures. We provide an

---

2. The "What Works" Literature refers to the work of Don Andrews, James Bonta, and Paul Gendreau. This work emphasizes criminogenic risks, needs, and responsivity as factors that should be considered in correctional treatment.

overview of contemporary issues relating to criminal justice practices impacting women, such as bail, sentencing, classification, programming, management strategies, and transition to the community. The chapter concludes with a framework for developing gender-responsive policy, procedures, and programs for women offenders that addresses four primary areas: prevention, harm reduction, gender-responsive services and community support.

In Chapter 2, *Differences with a Distinction: Women Offenders and Criminal Justice Practice*, Barbara Owen describes how few jurisdictions have developed appropriate policies on the management and supervision of female prisoners and parolees. As a result, female prisons are managed based on policies and procedures developed for the management of the male offender. These issues include classification, program development, training and operational procedures. Owen states that the gendered differences in women's pathways to incarceration, offense patterns, their behavior while imprisoned and their needs before, during, and after incarceration must be considered in planning for appropriate correctional policy.

Adding insight into the utility of risk assessment, Chapter 3, *The Meaning of Risk in Women's Prisons: A Critique*, by Kelly Hannah-Moffat and Margaret Shaw discusses the fact that, during the past ten years, correctional professionals have become increasingly concerned with the risk and needs assessment. This is particularly true of federal corrections in Canada and related government-based correctional research. The proliferation of risk assessment techniques is one of several characteristics of an increasingly technocratic and calculated system of penal governing. The desire or "need" for risk assessment in current correctional practice is pressing. However, there is often little consensus on the meaning or type of risk, such as the risk of re-offending or the risk of danger to the public, to be predicted and managed. This chapter summarizes the findings of a two-year study that examined some of the theoretical, methodological, and practical difficulties linked to current efforts to create gender and ethno-culturally sensitive risk assessment tools for Canadian federally sentenced women. Hannah-Moffat and Shaw argue that, while the methods used for male populations for assessing risk may also be of concern, especially in relation to ethno-cultural diversity, mental heath and social disadvantage, they should not be generically incorporated into women's corrections. Furthermore, in spite of existing legislative criteria, it remains questionable as to whether or not a risk-based approach to the management of the female offender is the most suitable.

Building on the research described in the previous chapter, Chapter 4, *Cognitive Behavioralism in Women's Prisons: A Critical Analysis of Therapeutic Assumptions and Practices*, by Kathleen Kendall and Shoshana Pollack makes the case, that within corrections, cognitive behavioral approaches are gaining global currency. According to the authors, cognitive behavioralism is a term applied to a range of interventions derived from three psychological theories: behaviorism, cognitive theory and social learning theory. When applied to corrections, a cognitive behavioralist approach generally assumes that offenders have failed to develop particular cognitive skills and have learned inappropriate ways of behaving. Programs are designed to target "criminal thinking" and teach offenders new coping strategies and ways of controlling their behavior. The chapter discusses the efficacy of Dialectical Behavioral Therapy (DBT), a cognitive behaviorist approach used widely in Canadian women's prisons. The authors conclude that all therapeutic services delivered within prison risk being co-opted and made integral to the prison system. Further, they suggest that mental health services to women are best delivered by community providers outside of, rather than inside of, prison.

In Chapter 5, *Stages of Gendered Disadvantage in the Lives of Convicted Battered Women*, Elizabeth Leonard compellingly explores the gender-specific nature of violence against female partners which produces a series of criminalizing events for women seeking nothing more than safety for themselves and their children. When individual and/or institutional efforts fail to protect battered women from life-threatening danger, some women resort to lethal force to save their own lives and the lives of their children. When that occurs, these women face another sequence of profound gendered disadvantages as the criminal justice system aggressively responds to their actions. Drawn from interviews with 42 women, this chapter graphically describes a series of gendered difficulties encountered by battered women who kill abusive partners as their paths take them from victims to convicted survivors.

In Chapter 6, *Cross-Sex Supervision of Incarcerated Women and the Dynamics of Staff Sexual Misconduct*, Christine Rasche traces the historical demise of cross-sex supervision of female offenders in the late nineteenth and early twentieth centuries and the legal changes of the 1970s and 1980s which prompted its return. She describes the methodological difficulties of investigating this phenomenon which also help to explain why some cases of custodial sexual misconduct do not come to light until they explode into scandal. The focus of this chapter is on the forms and dynamics of staff sexual abuse of female inmates in cross-sex supervision situations and on remedies which correctional authorities may wish to consider to alleviate these exploitive practices.

In Chapter 7, *Gendered Implications of Sentencing and Correctional Practices: A Legal Perspective*, Myrna Raeder focuses on the innumerable ways in which there are gendered consequences of sentencing and correctional practices that are supposedly gender-neutral. She explores the legal ramifications of such issues which include a comprehensive overview of the current case law as well as a sound legal framework to challenge practices that disadvantage female offenders. Individual topics include the effects of sentencing guidelines and mandatory minimums on women, child-related issues in custodial and community settings, access to programs, services and facilities, staff sexual misconduct, and privacy.

The next two chapters focus specifically on girls and delinquency. They raise important insight into juvenile justice professionals' assessment of pertinent issues regarding delinquent girls and trends in the treatment of girls. These chapters also provide descriptions of promising interventions with girls.

In Chapter 8, *Professionals' Assessments of the Needs of Delinquent Girls: The Results of a Focus Group Study,* Joanne Belknap, Erica Winter, and Bonnie Cady discuss the findings of focus groups with professionals who work with delinquent girls across the state of Colorado. In particular, the authors were interested in determining what these individuals believe to be the primary issues in responding appropriately to girls. The authors were interested in finding out how best to assess the unique needs of delinquent girls and to improve the ways in which the juvenile justice system responds to these needs. They also discuss the major, themes, challenges, and rewards of effectively working with delinquent girls.

In Chapter 9, *Gender Matters: Patterns in Girls' Delinquency and Gender Responsive Programming,* Meda Chesney-Lind and Scott Okamoto reveal that while girls in the juvenile justice system were once "dubbed" "the forgotten few" (Bergsmann, 1989), that construction of female delinquency has rapidly faded as increases in girls' arrests have dramatically outstripped those of boys for most of the last decade. Girls now account for one out of four arrests and attention is being called to the fact that their arrests for non-traditional offenses are among those showing the greatest increases. These shifts and changes bring into sharp focus the need to better understand the dynamics involved in female delinquency and the need to tailor responses to the unique circumstances of girls growing up in the new millennium.

In the concluding Chapter 10, *A New Vision: Gender-Responsive Principles, Policy, and Practice,* I propose a call to action for policy reform that considers the gendered differences in women and girls' lives and the need for approaches that are responsive to these differences. This chapter, which reflects research sponsored by the National Institute of Corrections (Bloom, Owen, & Covington, 2002) identifies guiding principles, general strategies and steps for implementation of a gender-responsive justice system.

The ultimate challenge is to carefully and critically examine our priorities. While creating a gender-responsive criminal justice system is an important goal, the ultimate goal should be reducing women and girls' incarceration, halting the unnecessary expansion of correctional facilities for females, expanding the use of community alternatives, and preventing the pattern of continued imprisonment for generations to come.

References

American Correctional Association (1995). *Public correctional policy on female offender services*. Lanham, MD: Author.

Bergsmann, I.R. (1989). The forgotten few: Juvenile female offenders. *Federal Probation, LIII*(1), 73–78.

Bloom, B. (2000). Beyond recidivism: Perspectives on evaluation of programs for female offenders in community corrections. In M. McMahon (Ed.), *Assessment to assistance: Programs for women in community corrections* (pp. 107–138). Lanham, MD: American Correctional Assocation.

Bloom, B., & Chesney-Lind, M. (2003). *Women in prison: Vengeful equity*. In R. Muraskin (Ed.), *It's a crime: Women and justice*, third edition (pp. 175–195). Upper Saddle River, NJ: Prentice Hall.

Bloom, B., Chesney-Lind, M., & Owen, B. (1994). *Women in California prisons: Hidden victims of the war on drugs*. San Francisco: Center on Juvenile and Criminal Justice.

Bloom, B., Owen, B. & Covington, C. (2002). *Gender-responsive strategies: Research, practice, and guiding principles for women offenders*. Washington, DC: National Institute of Corrections.

Carlen, P. (2002). *Women and punishment: The struggle for justice*. Devon, United Kingdom: Willan Publishing.

Chesney-Lind, M. & Bloom, B. (1997). Feminist criminology: Thinking about women and crime. In B. MacLean & D. Milovanovic (Eds.), *Thinking critically about crime* (pp. 45–55). Vancouver, Canada: Collective Press.

Martin. S., & Jurik, N. (1996). *Doing justice, doing gender: Women in law and criminal justice occupations*. Thousand Oaks, CA: Sage Publications.

GENDERED JUSTICE

CHAPTER 1

Gendered Justice: Women in the Criminal Justice System

Stephanie S. Covington and
Barbara E. Bloom

Introduction

In recent decades, the number of women under criminal justice supervision has increased dramatically. In 1990, there were approximately 600,000 women in prisons or jails, on probation, or on parole in the United States; in 2001, the figure had risen to more than one million women. Although the current rate of incarceration for women continues to be far lower than the rate for men (58 of 100,000 women versus 896 of 100,000 men), the number of women imprisoned in the United States since 1980 has increased at a rate nearly double the rate for men. Nationally, the number of women in state and federal prisons increased nearly eightfold between 1980 and 2001, from 12,300 to 93,031 (Bureau of Justice Statistics, 2002; National Institute of Justice, 1998).

Despite these figures, there does not appear to be a corresponding increase in women's criminality. In 1998, nearly two-thirds of women in state prisons were serving sentences for nonviolent offenses (Bureau of Justice Statistics, 1999). Women are arrested and incarcerated primarily for property and drug offenses, with drug offenses representing the largest source of the increase (36%) in the number of women prisoners in 1998. Interestingly, the proportion of women imprisoned for violent crimes has continued to decrease. The rate at which women commit murder has been declining since 1980, and the per capita rate of murders committed by women in 1998 was the lowest recorded since 1976. Of the women in state prisons in 1998, 28 percent had been incarcerated for a violent offense (Bureau of Justice Statistics, 1999).

Many of the violent crimes committed by women are against a spouse, ex-spouse, or partner, and the women committing such crimes are likely to report having been physically and/or sexually abused, often by the person they assaulted.

The increased incarceration of women appears to be the outcome of larger forces that have shaped U.S. crime policy. These include the war on drugs; the shift in legal and academic realms toward a view of lawbreaking as individual pathology, ignoring the structural and social causes of crime; government policies that prescribe simplistic and punitive enforcement responses to complex social problems; federal and state mandatory sentencing laws; and the public's fear of crime even though crime in the United States has been declining for nearly a decade.

Although there is agreement among criminal justice professionals that few women pose a risk to public safety, current sentencing models assume that everyone charged with or convicted of a crime poses such a risk. Current sentencing laws are based on male characteristics and male crime and thus fail to take into account the reality of women's lives, characteristics, responsibilities, and roles in crime.

Until recently, criminological theory and research focused on explaining male criminality, with males seen as the normal subjects of criminology. Historically, theories of female criminality have ranged from biological to psychological and from economic to social. Two approaches may be observed in the literature. In the first, theorists have attempted to explain female criminality individually, without recourse to theories of male criminality. Unfortunately, many such theorists employ assumptions about the female psyche that are blatantly sexist and without empirical support.

The second approach applies traditional theories, developed to explain male criminality, to women. This creates the "generalizability problem" (see Daly and Chesney-Lind, 1988). In addressing this problem, criminologists have tested theories derived from all-male samples to see whether these also apply to girls and women (Cernkovich & Giordano, 1979; Datesman & Scarpitti, 1980; Warren, 1981; Zietz, 1981). Others have borrowed from existing theories (e.g., Moyer, 1985, on conflict theory) or have recast the logic of a theory altogether (e.g., Schur, 1984, on labeling).

Many feminist scholars have described the extent to which science has been tainted by characteristically male approaches to social reality. As Cain (1990) explains, "[W]omen and girls exist as other: that is to say, they exist only in their difference from the male, the normal." The results of such critiques have increased attention to women and girls in criminological theory and research, and a re-analysis of basic assumptions, research interests, and theoretical frameworks. This re-analysis goes beyond just "adding women and stirring" in the empirical study of law and legal institutions, and it is not simply a matter of focusing on "women's issues." The re-analysis is a far more encompassing enterprise that raises questions about gender and about the disciplines of criminology and sociolegal studies (Chesney-Lind & Bloom, 1997). Recent research has contributed to our understanding of women's lives in ways that constitute far more than simple contrasts between the lives of women and men.

Is Equal Treatment
Fair Treatment?

Numerous feminist writers have demonstrated and documented the patriarchal nature of our society and the variety of ways in which patriarchal values serve masculine needs (de Beauvoir, 1968; Friedan, 1963; Millett, 1970). In creating appropriate services for women in the criminal justice system, it is critical that we first acknowledge and understand the importance of gender differences, as well as the gender-related dynamics inherent in any society: "Despite claims to the contrary, masculinist epistemologies are built upon values that promote masculine needs and desires, making all others invisible" (Kaschak, 1992, p. 11). Women are often invisible in the many facets of the criminal justice system, and this invisibility can act as a form of oppression.

Where sexism is prevalent, one of the gender dynamics frequently found is that something declared genderless or gender neutral is, in fact, male-oriented. The same phenomenon occurs in terms of race in a racist society, where the term "race neutral" generally means white (Kivel, 1992). The stark realities of race and gender disparity touch the lives of all women and appear throughout the criminal justice process (Bloom, 1996).

Racial disparity is a factor in the arrests, pretrial treatment, and sentencing of female offenders. Women of color, especially African-Americans, are disproportionately incarcerated in the United States. In 1999, African-American women were nearly eight times more likely to be incarcerated than white women (Bureau of Justice Statistics, 2000a). The rising number of incarcerated women of color is a key factor in the population explosion in women's prisons.

It is also important for us to understand the distinction between sex differences and gender differences. While sex differences are biologically determined, gender differences are socially constructed: they are assigned by society, and they relate to expected social roles. They are neither innate nor unchangeable. Gender is about the reality of women's lives and the contexts in which women live (Covington, 2002).

Pollock (1994) asks whether women are receiving more equal treatment in the criminal justice system today than was the case in years past. If equal treatment means equal incarceration, the answer is a definite yes. Many more women offenders are likely to be incarcerated now than at any previous time in U.S. history, and the criminal justice system appears to be more willing to imprison women (Bloom & Chesney-Lind, 2000).

There is continuing debate about whether equality under the law is necessarily good for women (see Chesney-Lind & Pollock-Byrne, 1995; Chesney-Lind & Bloom, 1997). Some argue that the only way to eliminate the discriminatory treatment and oppression that women have experienced in the past is to push for continued equalization under the law—that is, to champion equal rights amendments and to oppose any legislation that treats men and women differently. This group argues that, although equal treatment may hurt women in the short run, it is the only way to guarantee in the long run that women will ever be treated as equal partners in economic and social realms. MacKinnon (1987) states, "For women to affirm difference, when difference means dominance, as it does with gender, means to affirm the qualities and characteristics of powerlessness" (pp. 38–39). Even those who do not view the experience of women as one of oppression conclude that women are victimized by laws that were created from "concern and affection" and that were designed to protect them (Kirp, Yudof, & Franks, 1986).

The opposing argument maintains that because women are not the same as men, the use of a male standard to measure equality means that women will always lose. Recognition of the different or "special" needs of women is thus called for. This would mean that women and men would receive differential treatment, as long as such treatment did not put women in a more negative position than the absence of such a standard.

Yet another position points out that both the equal treatment and special needs approaches accept the domination of male definitions. For example, equality for women is defined as rights equal to those of males, and differential needs are defined as needs different from those of males. In this position, women are the "other" under the law; the bottom line is a male one (Smart, 1989). Eisenstein (1988) writes, "Difference in this instance is set up as a duality: woman is different from man, and this difference is seen as a deficiency because she is not man" (p. 8).

While these and other scholars are identifying the limitations in law of a model for equal treatment, that model is the basis for sentencing reforms throughout the United States. These "gender-neutral" sentencing reforms aim to reduce sentencing disparity by punishing like crimes in the same way. By emphasizing parity and then utilizing a male standard, we ensure that more women lose their freedom (Daly, 1994).

As a result of prisoners' rights litigation based on the parity model (see Pollock-Byrne, 1990), women offenders are being swept up in a system that appears to be eager to treat women equally, which actually means *as if they were men*. Since this orientation does not change the role of gender in prison life or corrections, female prisoners receive the worst of both worlds.

For example, boot camps have become popular as alternatives to prison for juvenile and adult offenders. New York State implemented a boot camp for women that was modeled on boot camps for men, including the use of uniforms, shorn hair, humiliation for disrespect of staff, and other militaristic approaches. Chain gangs for women have also become acceptable, as is the case in Maricopa County, Arizona (Atwood, 2000).

As mentioned, the current model of justice—called the "equalization" approach—emphasizes parity and then utilizes a male standard. Therefore, increased incarceration of women takes the place of alternatives to prison (Daly 1994). "Gender-blind" mandatory sentencing statutes, particularly for drug law violations, contribute to the rising numbers of women in prison. This is what Lahey (1985) calls "equality with a vengeance." Under the male model of justice, the ideal may be fair treatment. However, as Heidensohn (1986) points out, equal treatment may not be fair treatment, since the social reality is that women may have different economic needs, may have been victimized, and may in other ways be in different situations than male defendants.

"Doing Time": Women's Experiences in the Criminal Justice System

Gender makes a difference in terms of its impact on standard correctional procedures. There are numerous areas in which day-to-day practice in the criminal justice system ignores behavioral and situational differences between female and male offenders. The pages that follow present examples of women's gendered experience in the correctional system.

Bail

The original concept regarding bail was to provide public protection. Nevertheless, women who commit less serious crimes still have to post bail in order to stay out of jail. The task of making bail is different for men and women. Most female offenders are poor, undereducated, and unskilled, with sporadic employment histories. A survey of female jail inmates in the United States found that nearly two-thirds were unemployed when arrested, while fewer than one-third of male inmates were unemployed (Collins & Collins, 1996). Women become disadvantaged due to their overall lower socioeconomic status. Unlike men, few women have partners who might post bail for them.

In a study of female pretrial jail detainees, the majority of subjects were nonviolent offenders who had been jailed because they could not post bail for misdemeanors (Teplin, Abram, & McClelland, 1996). Another study found that, of the women who had been employed before incarceration, many were on the lower rungs of the economic ladder, with only 37 percent working at a legitimate job. In addition, the U.S. Census Bureau reports that women in the U.S. earn 74 percent of what men earn for similar jobs. For African-American women, the figure is even lower, at 67 percent (U.S. Census Bureau, 1996). When bail is set equally for women and men, it is thus actually more difficult for women to make bail than it is for men.

Sentencing Policies

Mandatory minimum sentencing statutes for drug offenses have significantly increased the numbers of women in state and federal prisons. Women offenders who in past decades would have been given community sanctions are now being sentenced to prison. Between 1995 and 1996, female drug arrests increased by 95 percent, while male drug arrests increased by 55 percent. In 1979, approximately one in every ten women in U.S. prisons was serving a sentence for a drug conviction; in 1999, this figure was approximately one in three (Bureau of Justice Statistics, 2000a).

Inadvertently, the war on drugs became a war on women (Bloom, Chesney-Lind, & Owen, 1994). Nationwide, the number of women incarcerated for drug offenses rose by 888 percent between 1986 and 1996 (Mauer, Potler, & Wolf, 1999). From 1986 to 1995, drug offenses accounted for 91 percent of the increase in the number of women sentenced to prison in New York State, 55 percent in California, and 26 percent in Minnesota. Although the war on drugs has significantly affected the incarceration of all women, African-American women have experienced the greatest increase in the percentage of offenders incarcerated for drug offenses. According to the Sentencing Project, between 1986 and 1991 the population in state prisons for drug offenses increased by 828 percent for African-American women, 328 percent for Latinas, and 241 percent for white women (Mauer & Huling, 1995).

The passage of harsh mandatory minimums for federal crimes, coupled with sentencing guidelines intended to reduce racial, economic, and other disparities in the sentencing of men, have distinctly disadvantaged women. Twenty years ago, nearly two-thirds of the women convicted of federal felonies were granted probation; in 1991, only 28 percent of women were given straight probation (Raeder, 1993). Female drug couriers can receive federal mandatory sentences ranging from fifteen years to life for their first felony arrests. These gender-neutral sentencing laws fail to recognize the distinction between major players in drug organizations and minor or ancillary players. In sentencing, women are indeed experiencing equal opportunities to their detriment (Merlo & Pollock, 1995).

Studies show that in state prisons, 40 percent of women versus 32 percent of men report drug use at the time of their offenses, while alcohol use was higher among the male inmates (Bureau of Justice Statistics, 1999). Women in prisons used more drugs than men did and used them more frequently (National Institute of Justice, 1998). Women are more likely than men to have committed crimes in order to obtain money to purchase drugs. Although it is commonly assumed that female addicts will most likely engage in prostitution to support their drug habits, it is even more common for these women to be involved in property crimes.

Classification

Valid and equitable classification is critical for women because it impacts decisions regarding programming, housing, work, and the perceptions of staff (see Chapter 2, Owen, for further discussion). The current "gender-neutral" classification systems, based on security and custody, incorrectly label and house women at higher levels than is necessary (Nesbitt, 1994). Actuarial tools are used to classify prisoners in terms of security risks as well as in terms of criminogenic needs. There is confusion both in the literature and in practice between needs and risks. Hannah-Moffat (2000) argues that:

> The blending of risk and need creates an interesting paradox. It combines two quite different elements: traditional security concerns, which are generally associated with danger and the prevention of harm to others, and a more recent emphasis on need, which by contrast implies that a prisoner is lacking something and entitled to resources (p. 36). (For further discussion, see Chapter 3, Hannah-Moffat & Shaw).

In a national survey of women's programs in the criminal justice system conducted by Morash and Bynum (1999), respondents mentioned classification, screening, and assessment as critical management problems, noting that these did not provide needed information, were not adapted to women, and were not useful in matching women's needs for programming. Van Voorhis and Presser (2001) found that gender differences were often ignored:

> Although many respondents discussed differences between men and women offenders in terms of needs and risks to institutional and public safety, few states have incorporated these differences in objective classification instruments (p. vi).

Needs often become relabeled risks. Criminogenic needs are defined as problems that influence the chances of recidivism (Hannah-Moffat & Shaw, 2001). Several other factors could replace risk assessment as the organizing principle of inmate classification—for example, safety, treatment, consistency, fairness, least-restrictive custody, rehabilitation, or reintegration needs. Medical and hospital classification systems provide an alternative model that is focused on acuity and service needs and, that at the same time, is highly concerned with the overall "safety" of the patient (Brennan, 1998).

Programming

Because of the historical lack of services for women, both the U.S. Congress and the courts have mandated that female offenders be given access to services of the same quality and quantity as those provided for males (Collins & Collins, 1996). Litigation involving what are known as "parity cases" has increasingly exposed the lower quality of services available to female offenders. However, parity and fairness do not mean simply providing women with copies of men's programs.

Historically, correctional programming for female offenders has been based on profiles of male criminality or pathways to crime. The research literature on "what works" in terms of correctional treatment tends to continue this male-oriented focus. Programs, policies, and services that focus on the overwhelming number of men in the criminal justice system often fail to identify options that are gender-responsive and culturally responsive in terms of women's needs.

For example, one aspect of the "what works" literature is the focus on cognitive theory and behaviorism. Gendreau, Andrews, Bonta and others in the "Ottawa School" have developed a theory they call the "psychology of criminal conduct" (Andrews, Bonta, and Hoge, 1990). However, an important shift has been taking place in the theory of human psychology. In recent years, there has been a move from cognitive, behaviorist, humanistic, and psycho-analytic psychology, which postulate the individual as primary, to relational psychology (Stacey, 1999). Relational psychology focuses on connections, in-terdependence, changing patterns, and the understanding that individuals cannot develop outside a web of relationships (Covington, 1998a). In de-signing programs for women, the core theoretical approach ought not to be the cognitive and rational-emotive approach, as this makes artificial divisions in women's experiences (Kaschak, 1992). This approach also ignores the com-plexity of human experience and its interrelatedness (For further discussion, see Chapter 4, Kendall & Pollack).

Over the past twenty years, much knowledge concerning women's services has been gained in the fields of mental health, substance abuse, and trauma treatment. However, this knowledge has yet to be applied in the majority of programs serving women in the criminal justice system. Further, few correc-tional administrators have a clear understanding of what elements of their cur-rent programs promote successful outcomes for women. Most criminal jus-tice professionals who are not familiar with the criteria for female-responsive interventions, do not understand the ways in which effective female-respon-sive services differ from effective services in general (Covington, 1999). Cor-rectional administrators and program providers need to have gender-respon-sive curricula and training programs that incorporate this knowledge.

Mother-Child Contact

The Bureau of Justice Statistics (2000b) reports that in 1997, 65 percent of the women in state prisons and 59 percent of the women in federal prisons had minor children. The number of children with a mother in prison nearly doubled between 1991 and 1999 (Bureau of Justice Statistics, 2000b); in 1999, an estimated 126,000 children in the U.S. had a mother in prison. In a 1995 study of female prisoners in California, 80 percent of the respondents were mothers (Owen & Bloom, 1995). The majority were single mothers with an average of two children; prior to their arrests, these women had been the cus-todial parents (Bloom & Steinhart, 1993; Bureau of Justice Statistics, 2000b).

Separation from children is considered to be among the most damaging as-pects of imprisonment for women (Baunach, 1985; Bloom & Steinhart, 1993). The difficulties of separation are exacerbated by a lack of contact. In some cases, the forced separation between parent and child results in permanent termination of the parent-child relationship (Genty, 1995). The 1997 Adop-tion and Safe Families Act (ASFA) now mandates termination of parental rights once a child has been in foster care for fifteen or more of the preceding twenty-two months; incarcerated women serve an average of eighteen months (Jacobs, 2001).

In a 1993 study, *Why Punish the Children? A Reappraisal of the Children of Incarcerated Mothers in America,* 54 percent of children were found to have *never* visited their incarcerated mothers (Bloom & Steinhart, 1993). According to the Bureau of Justice Statistics (2000b), 54 percent of mothers in state prisons reported not having had visits with their children since admission. Geographical distance from the prison and the prisoner's relationship with the child's caregiver are the reasons cited most often for infrequent visits.

Management Strategies

The standard procedures used in correctional settings (e.g., searches, restraints, and isolation) can have profound effects on women with histories of abuse, trauma and mental illness. Female inmates are more than three times as likely as male inmates to report having experienced physical or sexual abuse at some time in their lives. Standard correctional procedures often act as "triggers" to retraumatize women who have post-traumatic stress disorder (PTSD). According to a 1994 study of women in U.S. jails, approximately 22 percent of the women had been diagnosed with PTSD, and 14 percent of women in jails had been diagnosed with major depression. (Veysey, 1997).

Another study found that nearly 80 percent of women prisoners had experienced some form of abuse, either as children or as adults (Bloom, Chesney-Lind, & Owen, 1994). Pollock (1998) points out that female offenders have histories of sexual and/or physical abuse that appear to be "instigators of delinquency, addiction, and criminality." The diagnosis of PTSD is often evidence of an experience common to many women, especially those in correctional facilities—that of repeated, severe, and/or long-term physical and sexual abuse. These findings clearly have implications for service providers, corrections administrators, and staff.

Gender also plays a role in how disciplinary procedures are applied. McClellan (1994) examined disciplinary practices at two Texas prisons housing female inmates and compared these to practices found in a Texas prison for males. She found gender-related differences in treatment, in that women were cited more frequently for disciplinary infractions and punished more severely than male inmates. McClellan notes that the wardens of the women's prisons stated that they demand total compliance with every rule and punish violations using official mechanisms. McClellan also found a higher level of surveillance at the female institutions. This suggests that gender bias may influence the number of infractions for which women are cited, especially less serious infractions, such as "violation of a written or posted rule" or "refusing to obey an order" (p. 76).

Transition to the Community

Women who are returning to their communities from correctional facilities must often comply with conditions of probation or parole, achieve financial stability, access health care, locate housing, and try to reunite with their families. They must find employment (often with few skills and a sporadic work history), find safe and drug-free housing, and, in many cases, maintain recovery from addiction. However, many women find themselves either homeless or in environments that do not support sober living. Without strong support in the community to help them navigate the multiple systems and agencies, many women fall back into a life of substance abuse and criminal activity.

The majority of women in the correctional system are mothers, and a major consideration for them is reunification with their children. This adds what Brown, Melchior, and Huba (1999) refer to as an additional "level of burden," as the requirements of these women for safe housing, economic support, medical services, and so on include the needs of their children.

There is little or no coordination among the systems a reentering woman must navigate in the community, and there are often conflicting expectations that increase the risk of relapse and recidivism (Covington, 2002).

Assisting Women Offenders: What Is the Work?

As noted, a major theme in the criminal justice literature is the question "What works?" However, because female offenders have been invisible in much of the research, we suggest that another question must be addressed first, and that is "What is the work?" (Covington & Bloom, 1999). The following is our proposed response to this question.

Prevention

We need to create a community response to the issues that impact women's lives and increase their risk of incarceration. A series of focus groups were conducted with women in the criminal justice system for the

National Institute of Corrections Gender-Responsive Strategies: Research, Practice, and Guiding Principles for Women Offenders Project (Bloom, Owen, & Covington, 2002). One of the questions was "How could things in your community have been different to help prevent you from being here?" The respondents identified a number of basic needs that, if unmet, put them at risk for criminal justice involvement. These needs were housing, physical and psychological safety, education, job training and opportunities, community-based substance-abuse treatment, economic support, positive female role models, and a community response to violence against women. These needs are the critical components of a gender-responsive prevention program.

Girls in troubled home situations or in juvenile justice facilities are at risk of becoming women in the criminal justice system. We need to look at the specific needs of girls at risk in order to develop prevention strategies. A number of interconnected risk factors must be considered, including the following:

- family factors
- sexual and/or physical abuse
- school problems
- early sexual activity
- association with delinquent peers and gangs
- substance abuse
  (Girls Incorporated, 1996)

Women in the U.S. correctional system are mostly young, poor, and undereducated women of color, with complex histories of trauma and substance abuse. Their greatest needs are for multifaceted drug abuse and trauma recovery treatment and for education and training in job and parenting skills (Bloom & Covington, 1998). It is critical that all of these factors be addressed if we are to reduce and prevent the continuing increase in female incarceration.

Do No Harm

We need to create alternatives to secure custody. A controlled environment such as a prison by its nature fosters dependence and powerlessness, which are two of the factors that lead women into the criminal justice system in the first place. Furthermore, rules and regulations based on those used in male prisons are often harmful to women. As Girshick (1999) notes:

The prison becomes the punitive parent, regulating the child through rules and sanctions. Keeping female prisoners in the status of dependent children makes them easier to control, and the women themselves feel infantalized (p. 78).

Most correctional officers are not provided with appropriate training in how to supervise and communicate with women offenders, and it is often stated that correctional officers and other staff members do not want to work with women offenders (Bloom, Owen, & Covington, 2002). We need to develop a culture within correctional settings that promotes respectful attitudes, communication, and behavior on the part of correctional staff.

As stated previously, standard policies and procedures in correctional settings (e.g., searches, restraints, and isolation) can have far-reaching effects on women with histories of abuse, trauma, and mental illness and such practices often act as triggers to retraumatize women who have PTSD. These issues clearly have implications for service providers, correctional administrators, and staff.

Custodial misconduct has been documented in many forms, including verbal degradation, rape, sexual assault, unwarranted visual supervision, denial of goods and privileges, and the use or threat of force (Amnesty International USA, 1999; General Accounting Office, 1999; Human Rights Watch Women's Rights Project, 1996). For example, women prisoners are generally strip-searched after prison visits and at other times, and these searches can be used arbitrarily and punitively. A large percentage of incarcerated women have been sexually abused, making strip searches even more likely to be traumatic personal violations. Also, many state prisons require that pregnant women be shackled while being transported to hospitals to give birth. This procedure can be traumatic to a woman who is experiencing the pains of labor, and the risk of escape in such a situation is minimal.

Sexual misconduct by staff is a serious issue in women's prisons (for further discussion see Chapter 2, Owen, Chapter 6, Rasche, and Chapter 7, Raeder). Corrections departments should deem any abuse of women prisoners by staff unacceptable and culpable. Reviewing the situation of women incarcerated in five states—California, Georgia, Michigan, Illinois, and New York—and the District of Columbia, Human Rights Watch (1996) concluded:

> Our findings indicate that being a woman prisoner in U.S. state prisons can be a terrifying experience. If you are sexually abused, you cannot escape from your abuser. Grievance or investigatory procedures, where they exist, are often ineffectual, and correctional employees continue to engage in abuse because they believe that they will rarely be held accountable, administratively or criminally. Few people outside the prison walls know what is going on or care if they do know. Fewer still do anything to address the problem (p.1).

In her study of imprisoned battered women who have killed their abusers, Elizabeth Leonard (2002) notes the overuse of psychotropic drugs such as tranquilizers, which she refers to as "chemical restraints," as a means of institutional social control. Leonard also states that many of her interviewees reported that psychotropic drugs directly interfered with their ability to participate in the preparation of their defense cases. The use of psychotropic drugs is ten times higher in women's prisons than in men's prisons (Culliver, 1993). (For further discussion see Chapter 5, Leonard).

Create Gender-Responsive Services

We need to provide women in the system with services that, in both context (structure and environment) and content, are comprehensive and relate to the realities of their lives. Programs need to take into consideration the larger social issues of poverty, abuse, race, and gender inequalities, as well as individual factors that impact women in the criminal justice system (Bloom, 1996). Services also need to be responsive to the cultural backgrounds of women (Bloom & Covington, 1998). Culture may be defined as a framework of values and beliefs and a means of organizing experience. Being culturally sensitive means being sensitive to differences in ethnicity—including differences in language, customs, values, and beliefs—in order to create a sense of inclusivity.

Context refers to everything in the environment: work, family, class, culture, race, obligations, the likelihood of experiencing violence and discrimination, access to health care and education, legal status, and so on (Tavris, 1992). Typically, women have less in terms of income, power, access to medical and legal treatment, and the like, while having more family and household obligations than men (Epstein, 1988). Only women experience pregnancy and childbirth, and the overwhelming majority of parental caretakers are women. Low-income women are often the sole caretakers of their children and of elderly family members. These contextual factors create the realities of women's lives and many of the differences in needs, behaviors, and experiences between women and men.

The consideration of context also means the environment in which the service is provided. The culture of corrections (i.e., the environment created by the criminal justice system) is often in conflict with the culture of treatment. As mentioned, the corrections culture is based on control and security. Treatment, however, is based on the concern for safety and on change (Covington, 1998b). Creating effective gender-responsive services must include creating an environment through site selection, staff selection, and program development that reflects an understanding of the realities of women's lives and addresses the specific issues of participants (Bloom & Covington, 2000).

Content includes the breadth of services that should be provided. These services should also be trauma informed, meaning that services provided for problems other than trauma should incorporate knowledge about violence against women and the impact of trauma, thereby increasing their effectiveness. Trauma-informed services need to do the following:

1. Take the trauma into account.
2. Avoid triggering trauma reactions and/or traumatizing the individual.
3. Adjust the behavior of counselors, other staff, and the organization to support the individual's coping capacity.
4. Allow survivors to manage their trauma symptoms successfully so that they are able to access, retain, and benefit from the services. (Harris & Fallot, 2001)

Build Community Support

There is a critical need to develop a system of support within communities to provide assistance to women who are returning to their communities. Assistance is needed in the areas of housing, job training, employment, transportation, family reunification, child care, drug and alcohol treatment, peer support, and aftercare. Women transitioning from jail or prison to the community must navigate a myriad of systems that often provide fragmented services; this can be a barrier to successful reintegration. In addition, the planning process for reentry into the community must begin *as soon as the woman begins serving her sentence*, not conducted only in the final thirty to sixty days.

A further point is that female offenders are frequently good candidates for community-based corrections. Because women commit far fewer serious or violent offenses, they pose less risk to public safety than do male offenders. When deemed appropriate, the least restrictive alternative to incarceration should be considered for a female offender.

Wraparound models and other integrated and holistic approaches can be very effective, because these address multiple goals and needs in a coordinated way and facilitate access to services (Reed & Leavitt, 1998). Wraparound models are based on the concept of "wrapping necessary resources into an individualized support plan" (Malysiak, 1997, p. 12). Both client-level and system-level linkages are stressed in the wraparound model. The need for wraparound services is highest for clients who have multiple complex needs that cannot be addressed by limited services from a few locations in the community.

Community-based wraparound services can be particularly useful for the following reasons:

- A higher percentage of female than male offenders are the primary caregivers of young children. These children have needs of their own and require other caregivers if their mothers are incarcerated. Support for parenting, safe housing, and a family wage level are crucial when the welfare of children is at stake.
- Women have been socialized to value relationships and connectedness and to approach life within interpersonal contexts (Covington, 1998a). Approaches to service delivery that are based on ongoing relationships, that make connections among different life areas, and that work within women's existing support systems are especially congruent with female characteristics and needs.

Effective gender-responsive and culturally responsive programming must emphasize support. Service providers need to focus on women's strengths, and they must recognize that a woman cannot be treated successfully in isolation from her social support network—her relationships with her partner, children, family, and friends.

Coordinating systems that link substance abuse, criminal justice, public health, employment, housing, and child welfare will promote a continuity-of-care model. Such a comprehensive approach would provide sustained continuity of treatment, recovery, and support services, with provision of all services beginning at the start of a jail or prison sentence and continuing throughout transition to the community.

Conclusion

As this chapter asserts, gender plays a critical role throughout the criminal justice process. A review of women's life circumstances and of the backgrounds of female offenders in the system makes clear that there are more effective ways to prevent and address women's criminality than are currently in use. Criminal justice practice could be improved by addressing women's pathways into the criminal justice system, their differences in offense patterns from the patterns of male offenders, their experiences in the criminal justice system, and their responses to programs.

It is important to reexamine the gendered effects of public policies that criminalize substance abuse, which often result in the overrepresentation of women in U.S. jails and prisons. Mandatory minimum-sentencing statutes for drug offenses have had a devastating effect on women and have unfairly punished them as well as their children.

Standard gender-neutral correctional procedures have also disadvantaged women in that such procedures do not take into account the histories of abuse of many female offenders. The criminal justice system must become trauma-informed in order to provide effective interventions and services for women.

At present, both the availability of programming for women offenders and the types of services offered fall short of what is needed. For example, because women in treatment find recovery complicated by trauma, child-care issues, inadequate social support systems, and lack of financial resources, programming for women must take these issues into account. Additionally, it is critical that programs provide appropriate screening and assessment of the needs (not risks) of individual clients, along with a range of services designed to meet those needs.

In creating appropriate services that truly take into account and respond to gender and cultural factors, we need first to reexamine our current criminal justice policies. We can then work to adjust those policies so that the response to women's offending is one that emphasizes human needs, specifically those that reflect the realities of women's lives. Rather than focusing solely on punitive sanctions, we can begin to systematically consider the least restrictive appropriate alternatives to incarceration. The savings to society from a reduction in women's imprisonment and from improved reintegration of female offenders into the community will benefit not only the women themselves but also generations to come.

References

Amnesty International USA. (1999). *Not part of my sentence: Violations of the human rights watch in custody.* New York: Author.

Andrews, D., Bonta, J., & Hoge, R. (1990). Classification for effective rehabilitation: Re-discovering psychology. *Criminal Justice and Behavior, 17,* 19–52.

Atwood, J. (2000). *Too much time: Women in prison.* New York: Phaidon Press.

Baunach, P. (1985). *Mothers in prison.* New York: Transaction Books/Rutgers University Press.

Bloom, B. (1996). *Triple jeopardy: Race, class, and gender as factors in women's imprisonment.* Unpublished doctoral dissertation. University of California, Riverside.

Bloom, B., & Chesney-Lind, M. (2000). Women in prison: Vengeful equity. In Roslyn Muraskin (Ed.), *It's a crime: Women and justice.* Upper Saddle River, NJ: Prentice Hall.

Bloom, B., Chesney-Lind, M., & Owen, B. (1994). *Women in California prisons: Hidden victims of the war on drugs.* San Francisco: Center on Juvenile and Criminal Justice.

Bloom, B., & Covington, S. (1998, November). *Gender-specific programming for female offenders: What is it and why is it important?* Paper presented at the 50th Annual Meeting of the American Society of Criminology, Washington, DC.

Bloom, B., & Covington, S. (2000, November). *Gendered justice: Programming for women in correctional settings.* Paper presented at the 52nd Annual Meeting of the American Society of Criminology, San Francisco, CA.

Bloom, B., Owen, B. & Covington, S. (2002). *Gender-responsive strategies: Research, practice, and guiding principles for women offenders.* Washington, DC: National Institute of Corrections.

Bloom, B., & Steinhart, D. (1993). *Why punish the children? A reappraisal of the children of incarcerated mothers in America.* San Francisco: National Council on Crime and Delinquency.

Brennan, T. (1998). Institutional classification of females: Problems and some proposals for reform. In R. Zaplin (Ed.), *Female offenders: Critical perspectives and effective interventions.* Gaithersburg, MD: Aspen Publishers.

Brown, V., Melchior, L., & Huba, G. (1999). Level of burden among women diagnosed with several mental illness and substance abuse. *Journal of Psychoactive Drugs, 31*(1).

Bureau of Justice Statistics (1999). *Women offenders.* Washington, DC: U.S. Department of Justice, Office of Justice Programs.

Bureau of Justice Statistics (2000a). *Prisoners in 1999.* Washington, DC: U.S. Department of Justice, Office of Justice Programs.

Bureau of Justice Statistics (2000b). *Incarcerated parents and their children.* Washington, D.C.: U.S. Department of Justice, Office of Justice Programs.

Bureau of Justice Statistics (2002). *Prisoners in 2001.* Washington, DC: U.S. Department of Justice, Office of Justice Programs.

Cain, M. (1990). Towards transgression: New directions in feminist criminology. *International Journal of the Sociology of Law, 18* (1), 1–18.

Cernkovich, S., & Giordano, P. (1979). Delinquency, opportunity and gender. *Journal of Criminal Law and Criminology, 70,* 141–151.

Chesney-Lind, M., & Bloom, B. (1997). Feminist criminology: Thinking about women and crime. In B. MacLean & D. Milovanovic (Eds.), *Thinking critically about crime* (pp. 45–55). Vancouver, Canada: Collective Press.

Chesney-Lind, M., & Pollock-Byrne, J. (1995). Women's prisons: Equality with a vengeance. In J. Pollock-Byrne & A. Merlo (Eds.), *Women, law and social control* (pp. 155–175). Boston: Allyn and Bacon.

Collins, W., & Collins, A. (1996). *Women in jail: Legal issues.* Washington, DC: National Institute of Corrections.

Covington, S. (1998a). The relational theory of women's psychological development: Implications for the criminal justice system. In Ruth T. Zaplin (Ed.), *Female offenders: Critical perspectives and effective interventions* (pp. 113–131). Gaithersburg, MD: Aspen Publishers.

Covington, S. (1998b, September). *Creating gender-specific treatment for substance-abusing women and girls in community correctional settings.* Paper presented at the Annual Conference of the International Community Corrections Association, Arlington, VA.

Covington, S. (1999). *Helping women recover: A program for treating substance abuse* (special edition for the criminal justice system). San Francisco: Jossey-Bass.

Covington, S. (2002). *A woman's journey home: Challenges for female offenders.* Washington, DC: Urban Institute.

Covington, S., & Bloom, B. (1999, November). *Gender-responsive programming and evaluation for females in the criminal justice system: A shift from what works? to what is the work?* Paper presented at the 51st Annual Meeting of the American Society of Criminology, Toronto, Canada.

Culliver, C. (1993). Females behind prison bars. In C. Culliver (Ed.), *Female criminality: The state of the art.* New York: Garland.

Daly, K. (1994). *Gender, crime and punishment.* New Haven, CT: Yale University Press.

Daly, K. and Chesney-Lind, M. (1988). Feminism and criminology. *Justice Quarterly,* 5 (December), 497–538.

Datesman, S., & Scarpitti, F. (1980). *Women, crime and justice.* New York: Basil Blackwell, Inc.

de Beauvoir, S. (1968). *The second sex.* New York: Bantam.

Eisenstein, Z. (1988). *The female body and the law.* Berkeley, CA: University of California Press.

Epstein, C.F. (1988). *Deceptive distinctions: Sex, gender, and the social order.* New Haven, CT: Yale University Press.

Friedan, B. (1963). *The feminine mystique.* New York: Norton.

General Accounting Office. (1999). *Women in prison: Sexual misconduct by correctional staff.* United States General Accounting Office.

Genty, P. (1995). Termination of parental rights among prisoners: A national perspective. In K. Gabel & D. Johnston (Eds.), *Children of incarcerated parents* (pp. 167–182). New York: Lexington Books.

Girls Incorporated. (1996). *Prevention and parity: Girls in juvenile justice.* Washington, DC: U.S. Department of Justice, Office of Juvenile Justice and Delinquency Prevention.

Girshick, L. (1999). *No safe haven: Stories of women in prison.* Boston: Northeastern Unversity Press.

Hannah-Moffat, K. (2000). Reforming the prison, rethinking our ideals. In K. Hannah-Moffat & M. Shaw (Eds.). *An ideal prison? Critical essays on women's imprisonment in Canada.* Halifax, Nova Scotia: Fernwood Publishing.

Hannah-Moffat, K., and Shaw, M. (2001). *Taking risks: Incorporating gender and culture into the classification and assessment of federally sentenced women in Canada.* Ottawa: Status of Women Canada, Policy Research Fund.

Harris, M. and Fallot, R.D. (2001). *Using trauma theory to design service systems.* San Francisco: Jossey-Bass.

Heidensohn, F.M. (1986). Models of justice: Portia or Persephone? Some thoughts on equality, fairness and gender in the field of criminal justice. *International Journal of the Sociology of Law, 14,* 287–298.

Human Rights Watch. (1996). *All too familiar: Sexual abuse of women in U.S. state prisons.* New York: Human Rights Watch.

Jacobs, A. (2001). Give'em a fighting chance: Women offenders reenter society. *Criminal Justice Magazine 45* (Spring).

Kaschak, E. (1992). *Engendered lives.* New York: Basic Books.

Kirp, D., Yudof, M., & Franks, M. (1986). *Gender justice.* Chicago: University of Chicago Press.

Kivel, P. (1992). *Men's work: Stopping the violence that tears our lives apart.* Center City, MN: Hazelden.

Lahey, K. (1985).Until women themselves have told all they have to tell. *Osgoode Hall Law Journal, 23*(3), 519–541.

Leonard, E. (2002). *Convicted survivors: The imprisonment of battered women who kill.* New York: State University of New York.

MacKinnon, C. (1987). *Feminism unmodified: Discourse on life and law.* London: Harvard University Press.

Malysiak, R. (1997). Exploring the theory and paradigm base for wraparound fidelity.*Journal of Child and Family Studies, 7*(1), 11–25.

Mauer, M., & Huling, T. (1995). Young black Americans and the criminal justice system: Five years later. Washington, DC: The Sentencing Project.

Mauer, M., Potler, C., & Wolf, R. (1999). *Gender and justice: Women, drugs, and sentencing policy.* Washington, DC: The Sentencing Project.

McClellan, D. (1994). Disparity in the discipline of male and female inmates in Texas prisons. *Women and Criminal Justice, 5*(2), 71–97.

Merlo, A., & Pollock, J. (1995). *Women, law, and social control.* Boston: Allyn and Bacon.

Millett, K. (1970). *Sexual* politics. Garden City, NY: Doubleday.

Morash, M. & Bynum, T. (1999). *The mental health supplement to the national study of innovative and promising programs for women offenders.* Washington, DC: National Institute of Justice.

Moyer, I. L. (1985). *The changing role of women in the criminal justice system.* Prospect Heights, IL: Waveland Press.

National Institute of Justice (1998, August). *Women offenders: Programming needs and promising approaches* (Research in Brief). Washington, DC: U.S. Department of Justice, Office of Justice Programs.

Nesbitt, C. (1994). *The female offender in the 1990s is getting an overdose of parity.* Unpublished paper. Longmont, CO: National Institute of Corrections Information Center.

Owen, B. & Bloom, B. (1995). Profiling women prisoners: Findings from national surveys and a national sample. *The Prison Journal, 75*(2), 165–185.

Pollock, J. (1994). *The increasing incarceration rate of women offenders: Equality or justice?* Paper presented at the Prisons 2000 Conference, Leicester, England.

Pollock, J. (1998). *Counseling women offenders.* Thousand Oaks, CA: Sage.

Pollock-Byrne, J. (1990). *Women, prison and crime.* Pacific Grove, CA: Brooks/Cole.

Raeder, M. (1993). Gender and sentencing: Single moms, battered women and other sex-based anomalies in the gender-free world of federal sentencing guidelines. *Pepperdine Law Review, 20*(3), 905–990.

Reed, B.G., & Leavitt, M. (1998, September). *Modified wraparound and women offenders: A community corrections continuum.* Paper presented at the International Community Corrections Annual Research Conference, Arlington, VA.

Schur, E. (1984). *Labeling women deviant: Gender, stigma, and social control.* New York: McGraw-Hill.

Smart, C. (*1989*). *Feminism and the power of law.* London: Routledge and Kegan Paul.

Stacey, R. (1999). Complexity: The problem with the notion of the autonomous individual. *Complexity and the group matrix.* Draft.

Tavris, C. (1992). *The mismeasure of women: Why women are not the better sex, the inferior sex, or the opposite sex.* New York: Simon and Schuster.

Teplin, L., Abram, K., & McClelland, G. (1996). Prevalence of psychiatric disorders among incarcerated women. *Archives of General Psychiatry, 53,* 505–512.

U.S. Census Bureau (1996). www.now.org/nmt/05-98/wagegap.html

Van Voorhis, P. & Presser, L. (2001). *Classification of women offenders: A national assessment of current practice.* Washington, DC: National Institute of Corrections.

Veysey, B. (1997). *Specific needs of women diagnosed with mental illnesses in U.S. jails.* Del Mar, NY: The GAINS Center.

Warren, M. (1981). *Comparing female and male offenders.* London: Sage.

Zietz, D. (1981). *Women who embezzle or defraud: A study of convicted felons.* New York: Praeger.

CHAPTER 2

DIFFERENCES WITH A DISTINCTION: WOMEN OFFENDERS AND CRIMINAL JUSTICE PRACTICE

Barbara Owen

Introduction

Gender is an often-ignored aspect of criminal justice practice. Traditional correctional policy is typically male-based, without due consideration of gender-based differences that shape individual behavior related to coming to, and living in, prison. With few exceptions, correctional systems have been designed to manage the behavior and the characteristics of male offenders. This chapter discusses selected aspects of operational policy and practice within women's prisons and the ways in which gender has been ignored in these areas. In identifying the impact of gender-based differences on the supervision and management of women in institutional settings, the chapter argues that gender-based differences require a distinct, gender-appropriate response. Much of this discussion is drawn from a report to the National Institute of Corrections (NIC), *Gender-Responsive Strategies: Research, Practice and Guiding Principles for Women Offenders* (Bloom, Owen, & Covington, 2002). In this report, several data collection strategies were used: 1) national focus groups and interviews with experts representing various criminal justice agencies, as well as with women in the criminal justice system 2) written documents that included official and technical reports concerning women offenders, policies and procedures, and existing academic research were then collected and analyzed and 3) a Practitioner Advisory Group, representing community corrections, jail, prison, and parole professionals at all levels of the criminal justice system, reviewed these findings. Analysis of the available data found that the differences between women and men in correctional settings have distinct implications for criminal justice policy and practice.

Two key findings emerged from this examination. First, because of the overwhelming number of male offenders, the issues relevant to women are often overshadowed. For example, in a discussion of legal issues concerning women in jail, Thigpen suggests that "ignoring problems relating to female inmates on the basis of comparative numbers, or pushing those issues to the back burner in order to focus on issues involving male inmates, increases exposure to litigation and liability" (in Collins & Collins, 1996, p. iv). Second, the criminal justice system often has difficulty applying to women offenders policies and procedures that have been designed for male offenders. Differences in the behavior of women offenders—behavior that brings them into corrections and their behavior while under correctional supervision—may render policies and practices based on male behavior ineffective, and in some cases, damaging to the female prisoner.

Differences in women's pathways to the criminal justice system, women's behaviors while in custody, and the realities of women's lives in the community should have a significant bearing on the practices of the criminal justice system. There is persuasive evidence that proves responses of women to community supervision, incarceration, treatment, and rehabilitation are different from those of men. Differences between men and women offenders have been documented in terms of the following:

- levels of violence and threats to community safety in their offense patterns
- responsibilities for children and other family members
- relationships with staff and other offenders
- vulnerability to staff misconduct and revictimization
- differences in programming and service needs while under supervision and in custody, especially in terms of health, mental health, substance abuse, recovery from trauma, and economic/vocational skills
- differences in reentry and community integration
  (Bloom, Owen, & Covington, 2002).

A number of questions emerge when gender differences are raised. How can prison policy address the gendered nature of the differences in criminal behavior and institutional behavior between female and male prisoners? What do we know about the differences in female and male prisoners that can assist in improving post-release outcomes? How should knowledge about the gendered pathways to incarceration shape operational practice?

This chapter considers some of these questions and argues that these gender-based differences require a distinct, gender-based response. These areas

of difference have traditionally been ignored in correctional policy and practice, shaping a system that is unresponsive and ineffective for women. A consideration of the real differences in levels of violence, degree of harm created
by the bulk of female criminality, women's response to correctional supervision and the rehabilitative and re-integration requirements of women would
lead to a system distinct from that designed for men.

A review of the enormous increase in the population of women's prisons and
the effect of drug law policy since the mid-1980s also provides a context for discussing policy and practice. In 1980, 12,300 women were imprisoned in state and
federal institutions, rising to 44,065 in 1990 and to 75,000 women in 1996. By
1998, this number had risen to 84,427, an almost four-fold increase in just under
twenty years. In addition, approximately 64,000 women were incarcerated in
local jails and over 700,000 were on probation, parole, or community supervision. In total, nearly 850,000 women are under some form of criminal justice supervision in the United States (Bureau of Justice Statistics, 1999a; 1999b). In California alone, the female prison population rose dramatically from 1,316 in 1980,
to almost 12,000 in 1999, leveling out to just over 10,000 in 2002. In the Federal
system, the women's prison population increased from 5,011 in 1990 to 11, 281
in 2002. Most observers agree that women have been channeled into prison in
these ever-increasing numbers due to the 'war on drugs' and related changes in
legislation, law enforcement practices and judicial decision-making that has fueled this remarkable increase in the punishment and incarceration of women
(Human Rights Watch, 1996). A gendered difference is found in comparing the
population increases in female and male prisons in the last decade: Between 1990
and 1998, the number of women in United States prisons has increased 92 percent compared to a 67 percent increase in the number of men (BJS, 1999a).

As a result of the misguided drug war and its punitive consequences,
women have become increasingly punished as the United States continues to
stiffen criminal penalties through mandatory sentencing and longer sentence
lengths. While men too have suffered as the United States continues its imprisonment binge (Austin & Irwin, 2000), it is clear that women have suffered
disproportionately to the harm their drug behavior represents. Mauer, Potler
and Wolf (1999) measured the gender-based difference in the rates of this increase. They argued that drug policy affects women differently because women
are more likely than men to commit drug offenses. In examining the overall
rise in prison population between 1986 and 1995, they found that drug offenses account for about one-third of the rise in male prison population, but
fully half of the increase in the female prison population. During this period,
the number of women incarcerated for drug offenses rose an amazing 888 percent; the number of women incarcerated for other crimes rose 129 percent.

This difference is particularly marked in states with serious penalties for drug offenses. In New York, they argue, the notorious Rockefeller drug laws account for 91 percent of the women's prison population increase, in California, drug offenses account for 55 percent and in Minnesota, a state committed to limiting incarceration to very serious offenses, only 26 percent. This difference is most apparent among women of color. Compared to white women, women of color are also more likely to be arrested, convicted, and incarcerated at rates higher than their representation in the freeworld population (Mauer, Potler & Wolf, 1999).

This population increase has resukted in some attention to the issue of managing female prisoners—something that prison systems were able to ignore for decades. Women's prisons and related management issues were isolated from the more pressing concerns of the system, such as dealing with the problems of male prisons with their overwhelming numbers and higher levels of violence. While women's issues have garnered increased attention, systemic change has not occurred. As Van Voorhis and Presser suggest (2002), in their study of classification systems for women, "it is noteworthy that few states have designed systems that started with women in mind. Most map existing male-based assumptions regarding goals and purposes of corrections onto women and the systems that classify them" (p. x). Interestingly, some systems have acknowledged the importance of gender without making the necessary changes in their policy and practice. In the national assessment conducted by Van Voorhis and Presser, respondents in fifteen states indicated that the following correctional goals were more central to women offenders:

- habilitation and rehabilitation, particularly programs targeted to meet needs unique to women
- transitional programming pertinent to parenting and family issues
- moving women who have committed minor offenses to lower custody levels and out of the system as soon as possible, to serve more women in community facilities rather than institutions (p. 13)

Van Voorhis and Presser (2002) conclude by suggesting that if we started with women, we might expect to see classification systems that focused more attention on factors that seem key to women's reintegration—their children, relationships, abuse, mental illness, and job skills (p. 24). With these real differences identified, the next step is obvious: developing correctional policy and practice that incorporates gender difference in managing and serving women prisoners.

Given these huge increases in the populations of imprisoned women and the new attention to this issue, why the delay in the development of gender-responsive policy and practice? There are many justifications—and not all of them unreasonable. First, one might argue that the tyranny of the numbers has focused policy attention and resource distribution on the male prison population. Even though the rate of increase has been far greater in the female prison population, the male population continues to outnumber the women's by an overwhelming ratio of about nine to one in most systems. These absolute numbers have compelled correctional systems to respond to the needs and behavior of male prisoners. Second, men in prison present more immediate problems to prison management chiefly due to higher rates of violence against each other and against prison staff. For example, classification systems have been male-based because of the inadvisability of housing men of different classifications together (particularly the "predators" and "vulnerable inmates"), the gang and clique antagonisms and other practical concerns rising from their inability to peacefully co-exist within a heterogeneous population. This greater propensity to violence has specific implications for classification and other operational issues such a staff training and recruitment, staffing patterns, program and architectural design, and, equally important, attitudes shaping styles of communication and relating to prisoners. As one example, the image of the prison as a place of confinement for the male—specifically the violent male—offender has implications for staff recruitment. Most potential employees (male and female) come to the job expecting to work with men and may be unprepared to work in female institutions (Pollock, 1986). As another, program development has historically been directed at men and their specific needs in terms of educational and vocational programs, visiting regulations and recreational opportunities, for example. The specific conditions that propel women into criminality suggested by the pathway perspective are often ignored in program design.

The Pathways Perspective

Lynne Goodstein (2001) summarizes the current state of feminist criminology:

> Much more is known today than even 20 years ago about women and crime. Traditionally, criminology as a discipline has focused on male offending—street crime, violent crime, organized crime and white-collar crime. Most theories of crime have been developed to explain why men commit crime with little focus on the different dynamics that might affect women as criminals. Yet there are some very sub-

stantial differences between male and female criminality that virtually scream out for interpretation (p.3).

A critical component of managing women in prison is an understanding of women's pathways to incarceration. Feminist criminology argues that this understanding begins with an investigation of the context of their lives prior to imprisonment. As I have written previously, three central issues shape the lives of women prior to imprisonment: multiplicity of abuse in their pre-prison lives; disrupted family and personal relationships, particularly those relating to male partners and children; and drug use. Given this background, spiraling marginality and subsequent criminality is a common result (Owen, 1998). Combined with a public policy that criminalizes drug-using behavior, the outcome is ever-increasing rates of imprisonment for women.

Research on women's pathways to prison shows that gender matters significantly in shaping criminality. Steffensmeier and Allan (1998) note that the "profound differences" between the lives of women and men shape their patterns of criminal offending. Among women, the most common pathways to crime are based on survival (of abuse and poverty) and substance abuse. Belknap (2001, p. 402) has found that the pathway perspective incorporates a "whole life" perspective in the study of crime causation. Recent research establishes that because of their gender, women are at greater risk of experiencing sexual abuse, sexual assault, domestic violence, and single-parent status. Pathway research has identified such key issues in producing and sustaining female criminality as histories of personal abuse, mental illness tied to early life experiences, substance abuse and addiction, economic and social marginality, homelessness, and relationships (Bloom, Owen, & Covington, 2002).

Existing Policy

Many systems lack a written policy on the management and supervision of female defendants, probationers, inmates or parolees. In a 1998 survey of current issues in the operation of women's prisons, the National Institute of Corrections (NIC) identified the following policy areas that may affect female and male inmates differently:

- pat-search and strip search procedures
- commissary items, particularly health and beauty items
- allowable personal property
- transportation and restraint policies for pregnant women

In focus group interviews, many managers and line staff reported that they often have to manage women offenders based on policies and procedures developed for the male offender. They also reported difficulties in modifying these policies to develop a more appropriate and effective response to women's behaviors within the correctional environment. The American Correctional Association (ACA, 1995) policy on female offenders also raises this issue, stating:

> Departments of corrections should ensure that their written policies and procedures address both female and male offenders. Historically, manuals or policies and procedures have been written from the point of view of the male offenders. For example, official lists of "clothing to be issued," "permissible personal items," and "rules of probation" have overlooked the needs of the female offender; policies on hygiene, recreation, paid employment, and visitation with children are often inappropriate for female offenders or else do not exist (p. 1).

Morash and Bynum (1998) have found that at the policy and system level, the reality of managing a women's institution is often ignored or dismissed. They report that institutional-level managers often feel that their superiors fail to recognize these gender distinctions, as noted in this statement: "The higher administration in this state does not understand us. When we try to bring up issues related to women offenders, they don't want to be bothered by us" (p. 33). A commitment to improving operations and procedures for women offenders acknowledges these important distinctions and devotes resources to addressing them.

The Effects of Gender on Current Criminal Justice Practice

Gender differences between male and female prisoners have been documented in several studies of prison populations (Belknap, 2001; Owen, 1998; Pollock, 2002). These differences are summarized below:

- There are far fewer women than men in jails and prisons.
- Women, as a group, commit crimes that are less violent, and are also less violent in custody.
- Drug offenses account for a greater proportion of the imprisonment of women than of men.
- Children play a more significant role in the lives of incarcerated women than men.

- Trauma and victimization histories, substance abuse histories, and mental and physical health profiles are different for female and male prisoners.
- Educational, vocational, and treatment programs are typically less available to female than male prisoners.
- Staff training traditionally ignores female offender issues.

From the beginning, prisons in the United States were designed to punish men, with little consideration of women and their specific realities. Although the numbers of women in prison continues to grow, the imprisoned women remain neglected in most policy and practice. Analysis of available materials has identified numerous areas in which day-to-day practice in probation, jail, prison and parole is made problematic and rendered ineffective by ignoring behavioral and situational differences between female and male offenders. The following discussion is offered as a starting point for examining the ways in which correctional agencies respond to female offenders. This section examines gender and its effects on current criminal justice practice in the following selected areas:

- classification and assessment procedures
- women's services and programs
- staffing and training
- staff sexual misconduct

Prison Classification Studies

As with previous studies of assessment and classification procedures for women (Burke & Adams, 1991; Morash & Bynum, 1998; Harer & Langan, 2001), Van Voorhis and Presser (2002) found that differences between women and men and their institutional behavior were not considered in developing and applying classification policy. In a national survey of women's programs in the criminal justice system conducted by Morash and Bynum (1998), classification, screening, and assessment were mentioned as critical management problems because they did not provide needed information, were not adapted to women, and were not useful in matching women's needs for programming.

Additional concerns have been raised, particularly by Canadian researchers, regarding the reliability and validity of risk assessment and classification instruments as they relate to women and to people of color (Hannah-Moffat,

2000; Kendall, 1994; McMahon, 2000). Most risk-assessment instruments are developed and validated for white males, and the use of these tools with women and nonwhite offender populations raises empirical and theoretical questions about their utility (Hannah-Moffat, 2000).

In correctional institutions, classification systems are designed to make housing and programming assignments within the available range of options. In assessing the current state of women's prison classification systems, Van Voorhis and Presser (2002) conducted a national assessment of state and Federal classification practices for female offenders. They found that some states see classification of women and men in different lights, voicing a desire for classification models that would better support gender-responsive programming and that would move less serious offenders through the system more quickly (p. iv). Central findings from this study include these:

- Most policymakers recognize that as a group, women offenders are less dangerous than male offenders.
- Women have different needs than men do, but these needs are seldom considered by institutional needs-assessment systems.
- Existing classification systems in many states over-classify women offenders.
- Many states do not use the classification system to assign women offenders to institutional or housing areas.
- Only about twenty states have validated their systems on samples of women.

Current debate in this area centers on the question of appropriate classification systems for women and the lack of empirically validated classification instruments for them (Harer & Langan, 2001; Van Voorhis & Presser, 2002). In smaller systems, the lack of multiple facilities often makes the question of housing assignments moot. Morash and Bynum (1998) noted that states with only one women's facility were challenged to "manage women who span all custody levels and address their needs whether it is aging, mental health, medical issues, or lengthy sentences" (p. 18).

The problem of overclassification of female offenders is also a critical issue. (Harer & Langan, 2001; Van Voorhis & Presser, 2002). With risk-assignment scores based on male behavior, women are often given scores that do not match their actual levels of violence or escape potential. The overprediction or overclassification problem results in useless scores that are often overridden in actual practice. Overclassification can result in unwarranted assignment to higher security levels and to exclusion from community corrections placements (Van Voorhis & Presser, 2002).

As Nancy Stableforth, Deputy Commissioner for Women, Correctional Service of Canada, asserts:

> There are respected and well-known researchers who believe that criminogenic needs of women offenders is a concept that requires further investigation; that the parameters of effective programs for women offenders have yet to receive basic validation; that women's pathways to crime have not received sufficient research attention; and that methodologies appropriate for women offender research must be specifically developed and selected to be responsible not only to gender issues, but also to the reality of the small number of women (Stableforth, 1999, p. 5).

Additionally, most classification systems tend to use a woman's offense as a primary predictor of risk, however, research indicates that a woman's offense often has little relationship to her adjustment to prison and is also a weak predictor of success following release to the community (Shaw & Dubois, 1995). Instead of criminogenic factors, women's risk for re-offending may be tied to a lack of transitional programs and support systems that could help them reintegrate into their communities.

Women's Services and Programs

The salient features that propel women into crime include family violence and battering, substance abuse, and the struggle to support themselves and their children (Pollock, 2002; Belknap, 2001; Owen, 1998; Chesney-Lind, 1997). Harris (2001) argues that there is significant evidence that rehabilitative programs for women offenders are often based on generic programs that make no gender distinctions. For example:

- Program staff may have little knowledge of gender differences in behavioral, cognitive, moral, and emotional development.
- Most correctional interventions do not address the effects of early physical, sexual and emotional abuse and the resulting trauma.
- There is still a common perception that nothing works with women offenders because this is an intractable population.
- Placement of women in lower-risk groups may result in the belief that they are inappropriate targets of intervention.
- Various entities in the criminal justice system, the social services system, and the treatment realm continue to operate as independent entities; full

integration of the planning and delivery of treatment services seldom occurs.

Services and Programs in Jails

In their study of exclusively women's jails, Stohr and Mays (1993) suggest that women are often denied the same recreational, social, and programming opportunities that men have traditionally been afforded. They also found that women's medical and familial needs are not met in jails designed to incarcerate men. In our national focus group interviews, one mixed-jail administrator stated:

> There is no question that different programming is needed for female offenders, particularly in a jail. In pre-trial incarceration, the transition to incarceration is difficult for all inmates, but particularly females. Many were arrested and incarcerated at the same time as their spouse or significant other and so received few visits or had no one on the outside. Many were dealing with issues of sexual or physical abuse, and others were left with working out arrangements for children, as well as dealing with financial issues, family separation, and other issues.

In a 1996 review of legal issues involving female jail inmates, Collins and Collins suggest that the Equal Protection Clause of the Fourteenth Amendment requires jail officials to explain and justify differences in housing, privileges, and programming for male and female inmates. They state that female jail inmates are without many of the programs and services available to men due to their smaller numbers and the resulting limited resources allocated to them (Collins & Collins, 1996, pp. 2–4). Collins and Collins (1996) and Gray, Mays and Stohr (1995) found that work programs were much less common for women in jail, sometimes resulting in fewer opportunities for earned good time and work release.

Vocational programs were found to be inadequate both in number and in the ability to prepare women for career-oriented training. Health-related resources, particularly those relating to gynecological and obstetric needs, were also found to be lacking. Johnston (2001), Veysey (1997), Teplin, Abram, McClellan (1996), and Singer, Bussey, Song, & Lughofer (1995) all found that mental health problems among jail populations were particularly significant and were typically not addressed in the jail environment. Pregnant inmates, argue Collins and Collins (1996), present particular challenges to the jail health care system. As in the prison setting, staff sexual harassment was identified as a problem in jails, but one with little documentation at the time of the report. Family concerns, they assert, are magnified for women in jail, since women are often both the sole caretakers and source of financial support for their children. Other problems identified in women's jails were obstacles to visiting and access to legal resources that provide assistance in the area of parental rights.

Services and Programs in Prisons

The national survey of prison administrators conducted by Morash and Bynum (1998) found that about 40 percent of the states surveyed indicated that providing programs and services for women offenders (including resources) was their most serious operational problem. Research on prison programs for women has consistently established the following:

- Male prisons typically provide a greater variety of educational and vocational programs and training for more skilled (and better compensated) occupations.
- Women were offered a narrow range of stereotypical job-training programs for conventionally "female" occupations, such as cosmetology and low-level clerical work.
- Women in prison receive fewer institutional work assignments and lower rates of pay than male inmates, and men have greater access to work-release programs (derived from Belknap 2001; Pollock, 2002; Morash, Harr & Rucker, 1994).

Attention to the gender differences that maximize successful outcomes and rehabilitation for women has been minimal. In order to better address female criminality, services and programs must be developed that take into account the histories, backgrounds, and experiences that promote female criminal behavior. One approach to increasing both the attention given to these issues and the availability of women's services was suggested by many focus group participants and some of the written policies: criminal justice agencies and systems should make the planning, funding, and administration of women's services an integral part of executive decision-making. Through the development of a department of women's services, or the creation of a high-level administrative position, women's services and programs could receive the appropriate level of support within a system dominated by the male offender.

Services and Programs at Re-entry

In an examination of re-entry needs for women, Richie (2001) argues for comprehensive and wraparound services in the community. A case management approach has been found to work effectively with women in that it addresses their multiple treatment needs in a comprehensive, gender-responsive way. Richie argues that childcare, transportation, safety from abusive partners, and access to staff beyond business hours are critical elements of successful reintegration. She suggests that policy should address community needs as well as individual needs to improve outcomes for women. In concluding her series of in-depth interviews with women, Richie (2001) states:

> [Women] need families that are not divided by public policy, streets and homes that are safe from violence and abuse, and health and mental health services that are accessible. The challenges women face must be met with expanded opportunity and a more thoughtful criminal justice policy. This would require a plan for reinvestment in low-income communities in this country that centers around women's needs for safety and self-sufficiency (p. 386).

The challenges to successful reentry for women offenders also parallel those facing men, but, again, there is often a gender-based distinction to this process. While both genders confront a range of reintegration needs, the gender difference in responsibilities for children and other family members creates an additional "level of burden" (Brown, Melchior, and Huba, 1999) for these women, as their requirements for safe housing, economic support, medical services, and other needs include the ability to take care of others. Some important points concerning these women are as follows:

- A majority of incarcerated mothers expect to take responsibility for their children once they are released and rarely receive any financial or emotional support from the fathers.
- Families who have taken care of the children of imprisoned women often expect the paroled woman to take immediate custody of her children following release.
- Reunification with children is an important but often elusive goal of released mothers.
- If a child has been placed in foster care or state custody while the mother has been incarcerated, it is especially difficult for the released mother to demonstrate to state agencies that she is able to take care of and provide for her child adequately.

- Many women released from prison have lost touch with their families and thus face greater adjustment problems in reintegrating into the community (Bloom, Owen, & Covington, 2002, p.25).

Staffing and Training

Issues of staffing and training are critical at each stage within the criminal justice system. The national focus groups conducted for the NIC report revealed a need for gender-specific training within each segment of the system. Respondents mentioned that the lack of training also contributed to the perception that female offenders were much more difficult to work with than male offenders. A participant in a jail focus group noted, "None of the jail staff have received any gender-specific training. We had to learn on the job. We need training in communication skills, sensitivity training, available community resources, and how to handle the emotions and manipulations of the female inmate."

While the Morash and Bynum study (1998) found that at the institutional level, most administrators report staffing and training as a high priority, Rasche (2000) stated that a 1998 national survey of forty prison systems found that more than half did not have specialized training on the female offender. Rasche also suggests that specialized training for those working with female offenders is justified, based on the real differences between male and female offenders along three dimensions: demographics, needs, and personalities.

Morash and Bynum (1998) also suggested that the education of central office management in the nature of these differences is important. Preparing staff to work with female offenders requires increased knowledge about women to develop constructive attitudes toward female offenders and the interpersonal skills necessary for working with women, and to establish guidelines for appropriate interaction with women under correctional supervision.

National surveys (Morash & Bynum, 1998), research (Rasche, 2000; Pollock, 1986) and our national focus group interviews have identified negative attitudes and cultural stereotypes about the female as major obstacles to supervising women and providing services for them. In the prison setting, Rasche (2000) refers to these attitudes as "the male inmate preference" and suggests that it is found among both male and female correctional officers at all ranks (p. 238). Pollock (1986) notes that "there is an informal agreement among correctional personnel that female offenders are somehow 'harder to work with' than male offenders" (p.84). Pollock also found that both male and female officers defined women inmates as more demanding, more complaining, and more likely to refuse orders.

Training is a core issue in the appropriate management and supervision of women in the criminal justice system. Those responsible for managing programs and facilities, as well as line staff, have not been provided with the appropriate information, attitudes, skills, and guidelines for behavior that would allow them to work competently and professionally, acknowledging salient differences between female and male offenders.

Staff Sexual Misconduct

In the last ten years, the problems of staff sexual misconduct have been given significant attention by the media, the public, and many correctional systems (Smith, 2001; General Accounting Office, 1999). Moss (1999) offers a definition of sexual misconduct as "sexual behavior directed toward inmates, including sexual abuse, sexual assault, sexual harassment, physical contact of a sexual nature, sexual obscenity, invasion of privacy and conversations or correspondence of a romantic or intimate nature" (p. 189). The potential abuse of power inherent in staff-inmate relationships is at the core of staff sexual misconduct. It is this inherent difference in power between staff and inmates that makes any consensual relationship between staff and inmates impossible.

Misconduct can take many forms, including inappropriate language, verbal degradation, intrusive searches, sexual assault, unwarranted visual supervision, denying of goods and privileges, and the use or threat of force (Human Rights Watch, 1996). Misconduct includes disrespectful, unduly familiar, or threatening sexual comments made to inmates or parolees. It is also important to note that female officers have also been found to be involved in this serious misconduct, although the more publicized pattern appears to involve male staff with female inmates.

The problem can be aggravated by poor grievance procedures, inadequate investigations, and staff retaliation against inmates or parolees who "blow the whistle." Such operational concerns as the isolation of post assignments, the overuse of overtime, inadequate facility design for privacy, extended inmate work assignments, poor transportation practices, and an absence of teamwork among security staff and civilian staff can also contribute to the inadequacies of the environment in systemically addressing staff sexual misconduct. One focus group respondent noted that, in the final analysis, staff sexual misconduct should be defined as a security issue, in that such behavior damages the safety and security of everyone, staff and inmate alike.

Major Reports

Human Rights Watch (1996) reviewed the situation of women incarcerated in five states—California, Georgia, Michigan, Illinois, and New York—and the District of Columbia and made recommendations concerning training, legislation, and policy (Smith, 2001). Amnesty International (1999) also researched this issue and made similar recommendations. Smith (2001, p. 32) summarizes these overlapping recommendations as:

- same-sex supervision for female inmates
- more explicit policies and laws prohibiting sexual abuse of inmates
- stronger mechanisms for investigating and prosecuting sexual abuse
- appropriate supportive services and redress for sexual abuse
- greater protection from retaliation for inmates reporting sexual misconduct

The Government Accounting Office (1999) also examined this issue through a review of staff sexual misconduct policy in selected jurisdictions. Recommendations contained in this report focused on problems in monitoring, tracking, and reporting incidents.

Conclusion

A review of the evidence strongly suggests that systems and agencies encounter problems and minimize success by not acknowledging gender differences and integrating them into their operational and management practices. Addressing the implications of gender within the criminal justice system is grounded in a simple assumption: responding to the differences between women and men in criminal behavior and to their antecedents is consistent with the goals of all correctional agencies. These goals are the same for all offenders, whether they are male or female. Across the criminal justice continuum, the goals of the system typically involve sanctioning the initial offense, controlling behavior while the offender is under its jurisdiction, and, in many cases, providing interventions, programs, and services to decrease the likelihood of future offending. At each stage in the criminal justice process, the differences between female and male offenders affect behavioral outcomes and the ability of the system to address the pathways to offending and thus achieve its goals. Without policy attention to the specifics of women's lives and the gender differences between female and male prisoners, correctional systems will continue to miss the mark in developing appropriate policy and practice for women prisoners. By attending to women's pathways to prison, their behaviors while in custody and their lives outside of prison, correctional practice can become more gender-responsive and thus increase the chances of improved outcomes in terms of the lives of women offenders and the systems which manage them.

References

American Correctional Association. (1995). *Public correctional policy on female offender services.* Latham, MD: Author.

Amnesty International USA. (1999). *Not part of my sentence: Violations of the human rights watch in custody.* New York, NY: Author.

Austin, J. & Irwin, J. (2000). *It's about time: America's imprisonment binge.* Belmont,CA: Brooks Cole.

Belknap, J. (2001). *The invisible woman: Gender, crime, and justice.* Belmont, CA: Wadsworth.

Bloom, B. (1996). *Triple jeopardy: race, class and gender as factors in women's imprisonment.* Riverside, CA: Department of Sociology, UC Riverside.

Bloom, B., Owen, B., & Covington, S. (2002). *Gender-responsive strategies: Research, practice and guiding principles for women offenders.* Washington, DC: National Institute of Corrections.

Brown, V., Melchior, L. & Huba, G. (1999). Level of burden among women diagnosed with severe mental illness and substance abuse. *Journal of Psychoactive Drugs, 31* (1), 31–40.

Bureau of Justice Statistics. (1999a). *Correctional populations in the United States, 1996.* Washington, DC: U.S. Department of Justice.

Bureau of Justice Statistics. (1999b). *Special report: Women offenders.* Washington, DC: U.S. Department of Justice.

Burke, P. & Adams, L. (1991). *Classification of women offenders in state correctional facilities: A handbook for practitioners.* Washington, DC: National Institute of Corrections.

Chesney-Lind, M. (1997). *The female offender: Girls, women and crime.* Thousand Oaks, CA: Sage Publications.

Collins, W. & Collins, A. (1996). *Women in jail: Legal issues.* Washington DC: National Institute of Corrections.

General Accounting Office. (1999). *Women in prison: Sexual misconduct by correctional staff.* United States General Accounting Office.

Goodstein, L. (2001). Introduction: Women, crime, and criminal justice—An overview. In C. M. Renzetti & L. Goodstein (Eds.), *Women, crime, and criminal justice* (pp. 1–12). Los Angeles, CA: Roxbury Publishing Company.

Gray, T., Mays, G. L. & Stohr, M. K. (1995). Inmate needs and programming in exclusively women's jails. *The Prison Journal, 75* (2), 186–202.

Hannah-Moffat, K. (2000). Reforming the prison: Rethinking our ideals. In K. Hannah-Moffat & M. Shaw (Eds.), *An ideal prison? Critical essay on women's imprisonment in Canada* (pp. 30–40). Halifax, Nova Scotia: Fernwood Publishing.

Harer, M. D. & Langan, N.P. (2001). Gender differences in predictors of prison violence: Assessing the predictive validity of a risk classification system. *Crime & Delinquency, 474* (4), 513–536.

Harris, K. (2001, December). Assessing existing operations and programming for gender responsivity. *National Institute of Corrections "Improving community responses to women offenders" Project seminar.* Memphis, TN.

Human Rights Watch Women's Rights Project. (1996). *All too familiar: Sexual abuse of women in U.S. state prisons.* New York, NY: The Ford Foundation.

Johnston, D. (2001, November). *Jailed mothers.* Testimony to the California Legislative Women's Caucus, Dana Point, CA.

Kendall, K. (1994). Therapy behind prison walls: A contradiction in terms? *Prison Service Journal, 96,* 2–11.

Mauer, M., Potler, C., & Wolf, R. (1999). *Gender & justice: Women, drugs & sentencing policy.* Washington DC: The Sentencing Project.

McMahon, M. (2000). *Assessment to assistance: Programs for women in community corrections.* Latham, MD: American Correctional Association.

Morash, M. & Bynum, T. (1998). *Findings from the national study of innovate and promising programs for women offenders.* Washington, DC: National Institute of Justice.

Morash, M., Haarr, R. N. & Rucker, L. (1994). A comparison of programming for women and men in U.S. prisons. *Crime & Delinquency, 40* (2), 197–221.

Moss, A. (1999). Sexual misconduct among staff and inmates. In P. Carlson & J. Garrett (Eds.), *Prison and jail administration, practice and theory* (pp. 185–195). New York: Aspen Publishers.

Owen, B. (1998). *In the mix: Struggle and survival in a women's prison.* Albany, NY: State University of New York Press.

Pollock, J. (1986). *Sex and supervision: Guarding male and female inmates.* New York, NY: Greenwood Press.

Pollock, J. (1998). *Counseling women in prison.* Thousand Oaks, CA: Sage Publications.

Pollock, J. (2002). *Women, prison and crime.* Pacific Grove, CA: Brooks/Cole.

Rasche, C. E. (2000). The dislike of female offenders among correctional officers: Need for special training. In R. Muraskin (Ed.), *It's a crime: Women and justice* (pp. 237–252). Upper Saddle River, NJ: Prentice Hall.

Richie, B. (2001). Challenges incarcerated women face as they return to their communities: Findings from life history interviews. *Crime & Delinquency, 47* (3), 368–389.

Shaw, M. & Dubois, S. (1995). *Understanding violence by women: A review of the literature.* Ottawa, Ontario: Correctional Service of Canada.

Singer, M., Bussey, J., Song, L., & Lunghofer, L. (1995). The psychosocial issues of women serving time in jail. *Social Work, 40* (1), 103–113.

Smith, B. V. (2001). Sexual abuse against women in prison. *Criminal Justice, 16* (1), 30–38.

Stableforth, N. L. (1999). Effective corrections for women offenders. *Forum on Correctional Research, 11*(3), 3–5.

Steffensmeier, D. & Allan, E. (1998). *The nature of female offending: Patterns and explanations*. In R.T. Zaplin (Ed.), *Female offenders: Critical perspectives and effective interventions* (pp. 5–29). Gaithersburg, MD: Aspen Publishing.

Stohr, M. K. & Mays, G. L. (1993). W*omen's jails: An investigation of offenders, staff,* administration *and programming*. Las Cruces, NM: New Mexico State University, Department of Criminal Justice.

Teplin, L. A., Abram, K. M., & McClellan, G. M. (1996). Prevalence of psychiatric disorders among incarcerated women. *Archives of General Psychiatry, 53* (6), 505–512.

Van Voorhis, P & Presser, L. (2002). *Classification of women offenders: A national assessment of current practice*. Washington, DC: National Institute of Corrections.

Veysey, B. M. (1997). *Specific needs of women diagnosed with mental illnesses in U.S. jails*. Delmar NY: National GAINS Center, Policy Research Inc.

CHAPTER 3

The Meaning of 'Risk' in Women's Prisons: A Critique

Kelly Hannah-Moffat and
Margaret Shaw[1]

Introduction

In recent years correctional authorities in a number of countries have become increasingly concerned with assessing the risks and needs which prisoners present, and a number of assessment tools have been developed. This trend toward risk/needs assessment is a contemporary manifestation of two older concerns: predicting dangerousness or re-offending, and determining "what works" and "what is needed" in terms of correctional program interventions. However, the research behind these assessment tools rarely considers the gendered, racialized, or stratified characteristics of risk and need. It embodies white, middle-class moral assumptions, and generalizes knowledge about (white) men to women and to diverse ethno-cultural groups. It implies that these tools can adequately assess the needs or risks of such groups.

The assessment of women prisoners' needs and risks has typically relied on male-based methods of assessment and classification. Most correctional jurisdictions use gender-neutral systems that do not differentiate between women and men. A few use modified systems that append gender-specific items to standard male-derived assessment tools. In spite of the rapidly grow-

1. We are grateful to Status of Women, Canada, for funding this research project, and the participants at the Interdisciplinary Workshop in May 1999. None of them is responsible for our views or errors.

ing literature on gender and diversity, which demonstrates the considerable differences among correctional populations, such differences are rarely reflected in classification and assessment instruments. This can result in inequitable practices of classification and risk/need management for women and minorities, compared with men and majority populations, and in systemic discrimination ranging from over-classification, to lack of attention to program and service needs.

A number of Western correctional systems, including the federal system in Canada, are currently reviewing the classification of women prisoners. It is now more widely argued that in order to develop effective program interventions which match the needs of women, and ultimately reduce their risk of reoffending, we need to consider the demographics and the history of such populations, and how various life factors impact their offending (Bloom & Covington, 1998; Abbott & Kerr, 1995; Farr, 2000). What has received *less* attention, however, are some of the theoretical and practical challenges faced by reformers and bureaucrats attempting to create more gender and ethno-culturally appropriate systems of assessment and classification.

Drawing on the findings of a two-year research project funded by Status of Women, Canada, this chapter outlines some of the challenges associated with the creation of a women-centered system of assessment. It identifies some of the theoretical, methodological, and practical difficulties linked to *generic* methods of classification, and to Canadian attempts to create *gender and culturally sensitive* risk assessment tools for federally[2] sentenced women. While the women's prison system in Canada is unique, it provides an opportunity to examine the principles and problems underlying classification and assessment more generally. Thus, the purpose of the chapter is not to propose solutions, but to generate a thoughtful debate about the theory and practice of risk/need assessment as it relates to female and ethno-cultural correctional populations.

This chapter gives a brief outline of the context and purpose of the project and some of its main findings, and discusses some of their implications. First, it reviews the intrinsic limitations of using classification techniques developed and validated on male populations, for female populations. Second, it explores some of the operational difficulties associated with reform initiatives that attempt to integrate our knowledge of women's crime with deeply entrenched

---

2. Federally sentenced women refers to women incarcerated for a period of two years or more. Those serving less than two years are confined in provincial prisons.

hegemonic correctional techniques. Finally, it examines how the increased reliance on, and appeal of, actuarial-based risk and need assessments obscures
the highly subjective aspects of assessment, and the realist assumption that
risks and needs are *knowable* and *calculable* phenomenon.

The Context for the Study

In 1990, the federal government in Canada, which is responsible for all
those sentenced to imprisonment for periods of two years or more, accepted
the report of the Task Force on Federally Sentenced Women entitled, *Creating Choices*. *Creating Choices* (1990) recommended the closure of the only
federal women's penitentiary, Prison for Women (P4W) and its replacement
with five new regional facilities, including an Aboriginal Healing Lodge.[3]
This report was the culmination of over 150 years of concern with the conditions under which the small population of federal women served their sentences compared with men, as well as, much more recently, recognition of
the considerable difficulties experienced by Aboriginal women. Federally
sentenced women represent only 2 percent of the federal population, around
360 women, compared with some 12,600 men. Aboriginal women are heavily over-represented and constitute up to 25 percent of the federal female
population, yet they represent only 1 percent of the Canadian population as
a whole.

The most significant aspect of the report was its acceptance of a feminist,
or women-centered philosophy of women's corrections, which recognized the
specific needs and experiences of women. *All* aspects of the new regimes, from
buildings, facilities, programs and services, to staff recruitment and training,
were to reflect the different needs of women compared with men prisoners.
All federally sentenced women were to be housed in these facilities, with vary-
ing degrees of staff support. And unlike men, women were to be *assessed*
rather than classified, since they were generally seen to constitute little risk
within prison or to society, but to have high and often overlapping needs. The
existing Correctional Service of Canada (CSC) process for assessing treatment
needs and supervision was also criticized for prioritizing 'types of need' rather
than seeing women's needs as interrelated and holistic. The report recommended that holistic individual treatment plans be developed for each woman

---

3. For a more detailed account and discussion of this history see Shaw (1993) and
Hannah-Moffat & Shaw (2000).

by a team of correctional staff and community workers, as well as the woman herself.[4]

Over the past ten years, many, but not all, of the recommendations of the report have been implemented, and four new regional prisons and the Healing Lodge opened between 1996 and 1998. A number of events at the old penitentiary and the new regional prisons, as well as changes in the public climate concerning risk and violence in Canada, have led to further deviations from the original task force plans, and to a concern with the *risks* which a small minority of women present. These included a series of events at P5W which led to a commission of inquiry (Arbour, 1996), disturbances in the new prisons resulting in internal and external inquiries, the construction of fences, increases in perimeter security and secure accommodation, and the exclusion of women classified as maximum security from the new prisons (Hannah-Moffat & Shaw, 2000; Hannah-Moffat, 2000). From 1997, such women were housed in separate units in men's penitentiaries.[5]

Parallel to these developments, CSC was developing an extensive actuarial classification and risk assessment system on the basis of its male population. The Offender Intake Assessment system (OIA) was launched in 1994 and was subsequently extended to the entire federal prison system.

The Study

Given this history of a strong commitment to the special status of women, and the parallel implementation of a complex actuarial risk assessment system within the Canadian federal correctional service, the current research was an exploratory study which sought to *understand* and examine the *practices* of classification and assessment being used for all federally sentenced women. Specifically, it questioned how they were supposed to work, and how they were

---

4. The process was to ensure: planning is based on the needs of the individual, not driven by resource availability in the correctional setting; aggressive recruitment or creation of new resources to meet an individual's needs; a comprehensive initial assessment for each individual addresses socio-economic and psychological context; work in equal partnership with each woman; the individual planning approach is an integral aspect of the institutional operational plan, not a minor function; case management remains focused on people rather than paper; case management is actively oriented towards release; and that case management is based on a holistic approach.

5. In 2000, CSC announced plans to build new maximum security accommodation in each of the new regional prisons, as well as separate houses for women with mental health needs.

actually working. The overall purpose of the study was to critically assess the underlying assumptions and current practice of classification and assessment in federal women's prisons in Canada, and to contribute to the development of more gender-specific and culturally sensitive approaches.[6]

This analysis required an examination of practices at the new regional prisons, as well as those used for maximum-security women in men's penitentiaries. The methodology of the study included review of the literature on classification in relation to gender and diversity; consultations with corrections administrators and researchers, and external stakeholders; an interdisciplinary workshop on the theoretical, legal, methodological and practical issues relating to classification and assessment; and site visits and interviews with 70 staff associated with classification and assessment in eight institutions housing federally sentenced women and one men's penitentiary.

Findings

It was evident that during the 1990s there had been a number of attempts to develop an assessment system for women to meet the goals set by the task force. This had included a security management system adapted from one used at Shakopee Women's Prison in Minnesota (Correctional Service of Canada, 1995). This allocated women to levels of security on the basis of both their offense history and their behavior in the institution, and contained categories that were women-specific. A Women-Centered Assessment (WCA) system was developed at one prison. This was to be completed by women prisoners themselves, and incorporated approaches used in family therapy, as well as in the Aboriginal culture. It was intended to help women think about both positive and negative aspects of their lives.

Nevertheless, when the new regional prisons opened, the male-derived classification and assessment system including the OIA was put in place. The OIA contains some 200 questions related to factors on seven domain scales: employment, marriage/family, associates, social interaction, substance abuse, community functioning, personal/emotional orientation, and attitude. None of these domains accounted for gender or minority concerns. An early guide to the use of the OIA with women was prepared in 1996 (Correctional Service of Canada, 1996). This encouraged staff to add textual information relating

---

6. See Hannah-Moffat & Shaw (2001) for a detailed account of the study and its findings.

to women's lives, and to code childcare, for example, as employment. However, by the time of the study, very few staff undertaking classification or assessment had seen the guide, heard about it or used it. The WCA was still in use in one prison, as a supplement to actuarial tools, but the original security management system was not in use. Staff turnover, lack of specific training relating to women's assessment, a continuing emphasis within CSC as a whole on the need for uniformity in decision-making and the reduction of overrides, and a continuing emphasis on gender-neutrality, contributed to this situation. There also appeared to have been continual changes and additions to the tools themselves and to staff responsibilities relating to classification and assessment.

Training varied considerably within regions and between regions, and primarily meant that staff from the women's prisons attended sessions on classifying men. In the view of many staff, these were neither appropriate nor relevant to the needs of women. Some of the tools were difficult to use and the items inappropriate, while other relevant information was not included. Not surprisingly, there were considerable differences between the prisons in how they completed the assessment process. In some cases long, open-ended interviews were held with women over a series of days to elicit information to complete the OIA. In other cases, staff asked direct questions and entered the responses onto the computer screen. None of this is to suggest that staff were not sensitive to the very different needs of women, but to underline the managerial framework within which they had to work.

Staff expressed a need for specific training on the classification and assessment of women, whom they saw as very different from men in terms of their needs, behavior and reactions to prison. It was also clear that there needed to be greater managerial support from outside individual prisons (both within regions, but also from national headquarters) to support the specific requirements of women's prisons. The other outcome of the classification and assessment process was that the tools identified needs as criminogenic, or as "dynamic predictors of criminal conduct" (Andrews & Bonta, 1998, p. 84), requiring women to complete specific programs before reductions in security levels, day releases or parole could be considered. This issue is explored later in the chapter.

In accepting the report of the Task Force, CSC had undertaken to operationalize a women-centered and culturally sensitive model of correctional policy that recognized the differences between men and women and responded to women's needs on an individual basis. It had accepted the replacement of the male model of static security with a more individual dynamic security one, and placed a priority on treatment needs.

In practice, however, women's prisons had succumbed to the external pressures of bureaucratic continuity and universal assessment protocols. The feminist concept of needs identification, which was meant to provide a viable alternative to risk assessment was appropriated, and a system designed to meet the management and training needs of the much larger male population imposed.

Limitations

It is clear from the literature that from the late 1970s onward, many prison classification systems have focused on *risk* and its management (e.g., of escape, risk to the public, to other prisoners, to staff, to institutions, to self) rather than just security or sentence length. Earlier methods of assessing and predicting risky behavior[7] using clinical checklists and assessments have come to be seen as subjective and discretionary. In their place, a series of objective tools to measure risk, using actuarial measurements and based on research on large population samples have been created (Gottfredson & Tonry, 1987; Dallao, 1997). These actuarial tools have an intuitive political appeal because they are seen to reduce ad-hoc decision-making and result in greater uniformity and fairness in decisions. They are viewed as more *efficient* in fitting individuals to appropriate institutional settings, and to service and program delivery. They also satisfy accountability and management concerns for correctional staff.

Thus a good classification scheme is one that is reliable and valid, based on a representative sample, relevant to large populations, and easy to administer. However, these systems rely on large-scale prediction studies. The problem for small populations such as women is that many of those requirements cannot easily be met. If the primary requirement of a system is based on expectations about the majority population, this may be inappropriate for minority populations with diverse backgrounds and experiences, and where there is greater heterogeneity (Hannah-Moffat, 1997). Actuarial risk prediction is now a prominent feature of many Western prison systems including Canada and the USA, England and Wales (Clark, Fisher, & McDougall, 1993; Ditchfield, 1997; Mair, 1999); and Australia (Brown, 1996; Daley & Lane, 1999; Dawson, 1999).

In the 1990s, actuarial tools have expanded to assess not only the *risks*, which prisoners present, but also their "criminogenic" *needs*. Much of this work has been developed in Canada by psychologists working in the correctional field (Andrews, Bonta, & Hoge, 1990; Andrews, Zinger, Hoge, Bonta,

---

7. These followed the development of parole and sentencing guidelines.

Gendreau, & Cullen, 1990). It is closely tied to their view that only specific types of treatment (based in cognitive psychology), and targeted to particular groups of offenders, can reduce re-offending. Risk/need classification and assessment is now used in Canadian federal prisons to determine security classification and placement, and to allocate type of treatment or supervision. Risks are commonly referred to as *static* unchangeable factors (such as age or offense history) and needs as *dynamic* factors, which are capable of being modified by treatment programs. As noted by Andrews and Bonta (1998):

> ...the term *need* is used for the practical reason that with it the hope that criminogenic need factors are reduced, the chances of criminal conduct will decrease. However, our use of the term *need* is a highly specific one. We do not imply that all *unpleasant* conditions represent criminogenic need factors, not that any or all covariates of crime are in any way *bad* or *unpleasant* on their own, Risk factors and need factors are simply predictors of future criminal conduct...(p. 84).

Criminogenic needs[8] thus are explicitly defined as problems, which if left untreated, will increase the likelihood of recidivism, rather than a statement of entitlements (Hannah-Moffat, 1999).

Problems with Risk

Numerous reservations have been raised about this emphasis on risk and the use of actuarial risk-profiling tools. A major concern is how risk is defined. The concept of "risk" focuses on characteristics of individuals and ignores broader situational and environmental factors. It leads to oversimplified categorization, and overlooks wider systemic factors, which affect individual behavior. Prison staff, for example, may contribute to the risk category allotted to individual prisoners by their reactions and treatment towards them. It has been argued that the *climate* of an institution is just as important as the characteristics of individuals, but is rarely taken into account in risk assessment (McHugh, 1997). As Haggerty has pointed out (1999) risk assessment tools presume "that there is an objective degree of riskiness posed by...offenders which can be captured" yet they ignore "the role of the tools themselves in constituting thresholds of risk" (p. 73).

---

8. In the Canadian literature, not all needs are seen as criminogenic, only those predictively linked to reoffending.

A second series of concerns relates to the relevance of tools designed and tested almost exclusively on majority populations, for other correctional sub-populations. Rarely are the theoretical assumptions that support these tools re-examined when used for populations such as women, or ethno-cultural minorities, although in the 1980s, there had been some concern about their use in sentencing or parole decision-making.[9] It is clear that many studies and discussions of classification and risk prediction throughout the 1990's have failed to consider gender or diversity.[10] Given the inherent limitations of generic assessments, in the following section we explore the gendered and racialized aspects of risk, arguing that the assessment and classification of women *must* reflect our knowledge of women and ethno-cultural populations.

Gender Differences and Pathways to Offending

There *is* a significant and very rapidly growing literature that addresses the qualitative and quantitative gender differences in the pathways to crime, in types of crimes, and in custodial and in post-custodial experiences. Such literature is able to demonstrate the very different backgrounds, security and program needs of men and women prisoners. For example, a study comparing men and women in three U.S. states concluded that a significant proportion of women should be decarcerated because they have less serious criminal histories, lower levels of institutional misconduct, greater child and family responsibilities and connections, specific medical requirements, low vocational and educational levels, and high levels of substance and physical and sexual abuse (Acoca & Austin, 1996).[11] The theoretical literature on female crime, including the literature on social learning (Morash, 1999), which is central to Canadian correctional assessment models, increasingly and clearly shows how crime is gendered.

---

9. Some researchers warned that rigid and mechanical applications of assessment tools could lead to inequitable and unjust decisions for minorities, particularly black American males (Petersilia & Turner, 1987), or that actuarial tools could institutionalize minority disadvantage (Gottredson, 1987).

10. Some do not distinguish women from men; others fail to even mention the gender of their (male) subjects (e.g. Dhaliwal, Porporino, & Ross, 1994; Clement, 1996; Holt, 1996; Aubrey & Hough, 1997; Quinsey, Harris, Rice, & Cormier, 1998).

11. The findings of this study are typical of many similar studies of women in prisons in the United States and elsewhere.

Current evidence also suggests that the nature of women's offending is *qualitatively* different from men's even if the charges are similar.[12] Briefly, the research on women's crime demonstrates that it is a highly gendered activity, and that motivations for crime, the context of offending and access to criminal opportunities are shaped by differences in men and women's lives. These problems are magnified for non-white women. There is a significant, but less extensive literature, addressing ethno-cultural differences among offenders. A number of researchers have pointed to the inequalities experienced by minority populations such as Aboriginal communities and prisoners, for example. In the Canadian context such disadvantages include: racism, residential school experiences, high unemployment rates, illiteracy, alcoholism, conflicting cultural demands, and wide differences between the local conditions, histories and social structures of Aboriginal and non-Aboriginal communities. This problem affects both the court process and other justice decision-making stages including security classification, risk assessment, penitentiary placement and parole (Monture-Angus, 2000, p. 57). This makes the use of generic tools questionable. Monture-Angus (2000, p. 56), for example, argues that individualized risk assessments rarely account for the significance of colonial oppression in the lives of Aboriginal men and women and on their communities and nations. Such devices reflect the individualized nature of law, which obscures systemic and structural factors.

Recent work has argued strongly that "risk" is *gendered* as well as *racialized* (Stanko, 1997; Dawson, 1999; Hannah-Moffat, 1999; Bhui, 1999). At a minimum, future research and attempts to create assessment tools *must* consider the extensive literature on gender (and diversity) in order for them to be "valid." While the same or similar variables may seem intuitively valid for women and various ethno-cultural populations, the gendered and racialized context of those variables must be taken into consideration.

Integrating Knowledge of Women's Crime with Correctional Practice

Integrating specific knowledge about women's crime may "improve" correctional practices, and such integration is preferable to failing to recognize difference, nevertheless, gender—appropriate classifications and assessments

---

12. A detailed list and synopsis of this literature is available in Hannah-Moffat & Shaw, 2001.

remain problematic. The content of classifications and assessments is contingent upon forms of expert knowledge. The knowledge used to assess women's risk is typically linked to male normative standards, and stereotyped constructions of femininity. Such practices utilize structural principles of binary opposition. They are concerned with differentiating and identifying high need/low need, high risk/low risk, recidivists/non-recidivists, treatable/untreatable, responsible/irresponsible (Cohen, 1985; Haggerty, 1999; 2001). Such oppositions are central to correctional bureaucracies. Further, as previously noted, in most risk-based research, definitions of risks are statistical and reflect characteristics of adult male *populations* and not individuals. The research used to construct given variables as "risky" is not based on the female population or our knowledge of female crime. This is a crucial observation if one accepts that most forms of risk governance are based on the identification of characteristics common to a particular population, and that the characteristics of female and ethno-cultural populations are different from the white male correctional population.

Can Gender and Culture Be Added to the Generic Mix?

In spite of the guidelines developed by Burke & Adams (1991), work on classification systems for female prisoners has been limited to adapting generic male-based systems (Maine Department of Corrections, 1991; Austin, Chan, & Elms, 1993; Forcier, 1995; Cook County, 1997). Attempts to modify classification systems designed for managing male correctional populations (or simply adjust through the use of over-rides) has revealed several distinct problems. An Indiana study, for example, found the new objective tools required excessive uses of over-rides, to avoid over-classifying women (Austin et al., 1993).[13]

Other researchers have concluded that adapted tools based on male risk and behavioral norms are still not validated for women, or have very poor predictive validity, tend to over-classify, and do not adequately assess or meet the treatment needs of women (Brennan & Austin, 1997; Brennan, 1998). They often fail to account for differences between male and female crime, such as

---

13. Another review of the classification of women in U.S. jails lists as continuing problems lack of standardization, excessive use of overrides, inadequate assessment for and provision of community programs, over-classification, invalid (male-based) risk factors, inappropriate policy priorities, legal challenges, and a general lack of research on women (Brennan & Austin, 1997).

the much lower levels of violence by women in and out of prison. Farr (2000) who summarizes recent trends in the United States[14] concludes, as before, that women present little risk, risk predictors for men are invalid for women, and that current classification systems have led to an excessive use of over-rides for women. She similarly stresses the importance of a needs-based classification system for women, and an emphasis on the differences evident in women's pathways to crime.

Classification systems specifically designed on and for women are rare.[15] Morash, Bynum and Koons (1998) found male-based systems in use for women in prisons in 39 states within the United States, and within these states, classification instruments were adapted to women in seven states, and only three states had a special instrument. In jails, 50 of the 54 surveyed used the same instrument for men and women. Classification and assessment were the most common management problems mentioned by staff since systems in use were unrelated to women's risk profiles or circumstances, or to housing and program needs.

Adding in gender specific variables or slightly modifying pre-existing assessment tools is now becoming a more common practice in correctional jurisdictions. A few studies of risk have begun to pay attention to individual or group differences in pathways to crime, or to how risk and protective factors may vary from group to group. In an Australian study, for example, Homel, Lincoln, and Herd (1999), argue that for women and minority ethnic groups, "the nature, meaning, and impact over the life course of risk protective factors may be quite different from the mainstream" (p. 183). Yet even while recognizing this difference, the response has generally been to attempt to construct a culturally specific set of risk predictors that can be added to standard lists (Homel et al., 1999; Bonta, Pang, & Wallace-Capretta, 1997). For example, risk assessment instruments are sometimes adjusted in areas like employment to account for differences in childcare and elder care responsibilities, but other areas of assessment remain unmodified.

Much of the research in this area, particularly in Canada, attempts to validate male-derived tools[16] on female populations, or to identify specific crite-

---

14. A project to examine classification systems for women and the development of some innovative pilot projects has just begun. This is a two-year study funded by the National Institute of Corrections, conducted by Dr. Patricia Van Voorhis, University of Cincinnati.

15. Outside the prison system risk assessment and strength/needs assessment tools for girls have been developed (e.g., Cook County, 1997).

16. The phrase "male derived tool" referred to assessment instruments normed on male populations and validated for use on a male population, with little or no consideration of gender differences. Much of the research conducted in the research di-

ria that should be added to a male-derived tool to improve its predictive validity for females (Loucks & Zamble, 1999; Motiuk & Blanchette, 1998;
Blanchette, 1997a; 1997b; 1997c; Motiuk, 1997; Couslon, Ilacqua, Nutbrown,
Giulekas, & Cudjoe, 1996). A wide range of methodological difficulties has
plagued much of that research.

Methodological Problems

The acknowledgment of difference in research on risk and need assessment
scales is welcomed. Nevertheless, we argue that the general practice of "validating" pre-existing scales based on research and theories about men's crime
as applied to women is theoretically and empirically problematic. Being able
to define the variables under study accurately (conceptualization), and to
transform those definitions into indicators that reliably measure the concepts
(operationalization), are particularly important when the purpose of the research is to make causal or predictive statements about a specific group of people, in this case, female and minority offender populations.[17]

While some of these gender-neutral tools may be considered "valid and reliable" as a result of such exercises, some wider methodological and theoretical concerns about "validity" are overlooked. The broader literature on gender and cultural diversity and scale construction argues that *predictive* validity
is not the same as *content* validity. A tool may score well in terms of its ability to predict risk to reoffend, but that does not necessarily mean that it has
content validity in that it is capturing gender or cultural variations[18] in recidivism. For example, variables like unemployment cannot discriminate
within indigenous populations in terms of re-offending, if levels of unemployment in their communities are much higher in comparison to the majority population (Dawson, 1999; Howells, Day, Byrne, & Byrne, 1999).

In Canada, the *validation* of existing tools on women is also problematic
because of the small size of the federal women's population and its hetero-

---

vision of the Correctional Service of Canada attempts to fulfill this objective. See various issues of the *Forum on Corrections Research*.

17. For example, it is often assumed that the category "Native" or "Aboriginal" is
homogeneous and that the term "non-Native" refers to Caucasian without considering other cultural, racial, or ethnic differences. Many studies make the assumption
that gender and biological sex are substantively equivalent.

18. See the literature that examines some of the difficulties associated with the
measurement of gender and cultural differences in terms of social economic status.

geneity. Much of the Canadian research on women's classification and assessment is based on small non-random samples of between 50–150 women. The use of convenience samples, or extrapolation from other populations is also questionable. As noted by Atchison (2000), the samples obtained are often subdivided in order to make comparisons between groups of substantive interest. While this itself is not a problem, when subdivision results in comparison groups that are very small or disproportionate, reliable statistical comparisons cannot be made.[19]

Further, there is a general tendency among researchers in this area to compare a randomly selected sample of males with a convenience sample of females. While such comparison has descriptive utility, when the goal of the research is to generalize, or to determine predictive validity, such techniques produce statistically unreliable results. As Burke & Adams (1991) argued, a population of at least 1000 is necessary in order to undertake the appropriate statistical analysis needed to develop and validate classification tools. Recent Australian studies have raised similar concerns about small samples, which limit the testing of variables in relation to Aboriginal heritage (Daly & Lane, 1999). Dawson (1999) similarly warns about the methodological problems arising from the appropriation of tools developed in other countries (primarily Canada and the United States) for use on Australian Aboriginal prisoners.

The Spiral of Classification

In the specific case of women's assessment, therefore, there are two main options: either you choose to use a basic tool developed for men and modify it for women, or you begin from the ground up as many feminist researchers would advocate. As the previous discussion has suggested, the first approach has many disadvantages. The second requires the development of a gendered and ethno-culturally sensitive method of assessment that is based on contextual and empirical research about women's crime and women offenders' experiences, and that also takes account of both quantitative and qualitative differences.

The focus on gender goes beyond simply adding another variable to a risk scale or needs assessment. Gender bias is not necessarily eliminated by the adap-

---

19. See C. Kruttschnitt (1996) for a discussion of the measurement problems associated with crime and gender-based comparisons.

tation of male-derived actuarial measures. Simply adjusting risk and need as-sessment scales based on white male behavioral norms to include gendered cri-teria does not accurately reflect the extent of differences between men and women, or among women. It takes for granted that all but a few assessment cri-teria are the "same" for men and women, without challenging the gendered and racialized components of empirical data on which the scale was originally con-structed.

There is a further problem, however, in attempting to create more gen-der and ethno-culturally appropriate tools. This relates to the creation of an "amplifying spiral of classifications" as new sub-populations are singled out for their own risk profiles (Haggerty, 1999, p. 74). Such a situation will occur as identifiable segments of the correctional population (eg., socio-eco-nomic, geographical, cultural, sexual orientation, etc.) claim that risk-pro-filing tools are unfair in that they do not adequately or appropriately cap-ture distinctive attributes. As Haggerty (1999) notes, claims that the aggregate fails to capture the specific and defining properties of smaller groups is a standard critique of any statistical tool. This raises important questions about the value of constructing increasingly refined risk-profiling tools for more discrete sub-populations such as women and minority groups.

Focusing on Needs

In keeping with this logic, one of the other options often proposed for women's classification has been to replace the central emphasis on risk pre-diction with an emphasis on women's program needs. Brennan (1998), among others, has argued for this approach:

> Achieving equal validity may require the use of additional or differ-ent risk factors that are objectively and statistically demonstrated to be salient for females. Additionally, if 'risk prediction' is technically impossible, given the very low base rates for women offenders, then we may conclude that this approach may be simply less relevant for females than males. It may thus be arguably misguided to impose this unworkable goal as the central purpose when classifying female of-fenders (p. 198).

While this position implicitly links needs to recidivism in much the same way as risks, it reclaims the category of need by defining it as *distinct from* risk.

In contrast, as earlier discussion indicates, the recent focus on risk in Canadian correctional research is clearly linked to a wider strategy of reaffirming rehabilitation by demonstrating "what works" in terms of program intervention. The proliferation of risk-based technologies is integrally linked to the reaffirmation of rehabilitation. Actuarial tools are now being used to classify prisoners in terms not just of their security *risks*, but also in terms of their criminogenic *needs*. The analysis of risk factors is linked to the identification of *criminogenic* factors[20] that have a role in preventing offending rather than simply predicting offending. Risk assessment tools are seen as playing a central role in matching "levels of treatment service to the risk level of the offender"(Andrews et al., 1990). This is combined with the assertion that only specific types of treatment (primarily those based in cognitive psychology) can reduce re-offending when they are targeted to particular groups of offenders.

Notwithstanding the scepticism within criminology and other social sciences about our ability to make accurate and reliable predictions of dangerousness and recidivism, Canadian correctional researchers in particular have maintained that there is a consistent relationship between the type and number of needs offenders present, and the likelihood of recidivism. They also argue that the combined assessment of risk and needs will improve our ability to predict who is likely to reoffend, and who is not (Motiuk, 1993). Calls for an increased emphasis on women's needs should be carefully considered in light of these claims and recent developments.

Women's Needs Redefined— Hybridization

This recent trend reflects a hybridization of risk and rehabilitation. It is a "mixed model of government,"[21] wherein traditional rehabilitative strategies are reaffirmed and deployed to minimize and reduce risk. It re-establishes a place for rehabilitative regimes in correctional institutions. This mixed model of governance has resulted in a substantial slippage between the concepts of risk and need. This obscures the distinctions made by the critics of risk as-

---

20. This construction of the criminogenic factor is similar to what O'Malley (1999) calls a protective factor.

21. See O'Malley (1999) for a more elaborate discussion of the "mixed models of governance" that occur through the blending of risk and punishment, risk and restorative justice, and risk and rehabilitation.

sessment, and proponents of need assessment. It seems that where there is an unsatisfied need there is a potential risk factor. In some cases, the two are indistinguishable. The blending of risk and need creates an interesting paradox. It combines two quite different elements: traditional security concerns, which are generally associated with danger and the prevention of harm to others, and the more recent emphasis on need, which by contrast implies that a prisoner is lacking something and entitled to resources. This is likely to have significant consequences for women, and the quest for a woman-centered risk assessment raises another potential difficulty which has been discussed elsewhere but is worth restating (Hannah-Moffat, 1999).

It has been argued that the enterprise of 'risk' assessment is inappropriate for women, yet it must be recognized that in most jurisdictions it is a required, and inevitable, correctional practice.[22] In the recent Canadian literature on classification (particularly for women prisoners) the hybrid term *risk/need* is often used and certain offender characteristics are identified as both risks and needs. Some of the characteristics defined as criminogenic needs include dependency, low self-esteem, poor educational and vocational achievement, parental death at an early age, foster care placement, constant changes in the location of foster care, residential placement, living on the streets, prostitution, suicide attempts, self-injury, substance abuse, and parental responsibilities (Correctional Service Canada, 1994, p 5). More recently, an adult history of abuse victimization and self-injurious behaviors have been constructed as risk factors for female offenders (Bonta, Pang, & Wallace-Capretta, 1995; Blanchette, 1997a, 1997b). The resulting hybridization of risks and needs can lead to the identification of "a multitude of unrelated risk factors that in and of themselves provide no foundation for systemic rehabilitative interventions" (O'Malley, 1999, p. 18). The term *need* then is both vacuous and enabling. It is a category that can be deployed to either extend the arm of the state or to reinstate welfare-based techniques of rehabilitation, which have an extensive history of medicalizing and pathologizing women's deviance (Kendall, 2000). Seemingly benevolent needs-based interventions directed at "empowering" or

---

22. In Canada, for example, the legislation governing the administration of corrections, the *Corrections and Conditional Release Act*, requires that all offenders be given a classification of maximum, medium, or minimum security. This also reflects the rigidity of penal institutions, with their history of categorization and separation (Cohen, 1985; Foucault, 1977; Haggerty, 1999). As Haggerty (1999) notes: "There is a mania about classification in corrections. Each new classification is yet another instance of an apparently unending effort to sort, differentiate, and assess the prison population" (p. 72).

"curing" women can be as problematic as more overt masculinist risk management strategies (Duguid, 2000; Hannah-Moffat, 2001).

The Morality of Risk and Need Assessment

Much of the work on women's classification discussed in the previous section has been conducted by or for correctional systems. While it recognizes the need to change or adapt systems for women, there is little questioning of the underlying assumptions on which classification is based or its objectivity, nor of the concept of risk itself. This section of the chapter situates the technical practice of risk and need assessment in a larger debate about how we govern prisoners. It identifies some of the pitfalls of not questioning the underlying assumptions of research on risk and its potential impact on correctional practice.

The concept of risk (and to some extent need) mobilized in most criminological discourse and practice is a largely "taken for granted" phenomenon. It is often assumed that "criminogenic risks/needs" are real, knowable, calculable, and quantifiable, and that expert knowledge and techniques like actuarial risk/need assessment are useful in identifying "risks and needs" and in devising prescriptions for their management. This approach to risk overlooks a number of structural and systemic issues of longstanding importance to critical criminologists, feminist criminology and critical race studies. We argue that risk and need assessments are highly subjective and moralistic enterprises even though they are often portrayed as objective, efficient and non-biased, and that most risk/need assessments avoid analysis of significant structuring factors in recidivism (e.g., poverty or program availability).

Risk and need are socio-cultural constructs. Ewald (1991) contends that "nothing is a risk in itself; there is no risk in reality. But on the other hand, anything *can* be a risk; it all depends on how one analyzes the danger, considers the event" (p. 191). Of interest then is not the nature of risk itself, but how forms of knowledge and dominant discourses and expert techniques and institutions render risk and needs calculable and knowable. The socio-cultural constructions of risk/need embedded in actuarial and/or quasi actuarial risk/need assessments are moralistic, gendered, racialized, stratified and contingent upon subjective judgments.

Evaluations of such criteria seen to be indicative of "risk" are clearly discretionary and rely heavily on clinical as well as non-clinical judgments about an offender.[23] These scales require assessors to make a host of moral judgments about the offenders' past and probable future conduct. For instance, tools like the OIA require assessors to evaluate subjectively the leisure habits (or lack of socially accepted leisure habits), the quality of relationships, and the attitude of the offender, employment stability and educational success.[24] These evaluative criteria represent white middle class moral and social standards. The failure to conform to such standards implies an unacceptable deviation from the norm. For example, variables used to evaluate community functioning and social interactions respectively include participation in organized activities (sports teams, clubs and church groups), and unattached to community groups (charitable, Big Brothers, athletic). Such categorizations require normative evaluations of leisure habits, which many law-abiding citizens do not fulfill.

In short, the calculative rationality of risk is discretionary and subjective, and it creates only an illusion of objectivity, consistency and efficiency. While risk factors may appear to be amoral, *neutral statistical realities* uncovered through rigorous scientific research, such factors also reflect highly moralistic views of the social world. While those who construct risk assessment scales may differ with practitioners who apply their tools, the use and interpretation of tools is fundamental to understanding the intricacies of risk-based governance, which is implicitly moralistic. With few exceptions, analyses of risk-based governance have not fully explored the class-specific, gendered and ethno-cultural aspects of the social construction of risk and practices of risk management. While criminological discourses generally accept that gender, race, and social position are structural factors that influence our interpretations and management of crime and criminality, correctional risk management techniques invoke white, heterosexual, male normative criteria.

Wider sociological understandings of social stratification, sexism, racism, and discretionary applications of rules are rarely incorporated into correctional knowledge and statistical calculations of risk. Consequently, social-structural disadvantages as well as gender and ethno-culturally based stereotypes can often be discretely institutionalized and reproduced. Although risk/need and the enterprise of risk/need management appear on the surface to be amoral, efficient, objective and non-discriminatory, they are not.

---

23. See S. Kirk & H. Kutchins (1992) for a discussion of the DSM and its construction and use.

24. Examples used here are taken from the "Offender Intake Assessment and Correctional Plan User's Manual" produced by the Correctional Service of Canada.

Conclusions

What is emerging is a complex relationship between risk, need and social policy. Current methods of assessment in Canada and elsewhere do not adequately address gender or diversity, and the wisdom of creating new assessments processes requires thought. Reflecting upon our current state of reform, Haggerty (1999) has argued that:

> each new classification is yet another instance of an apparently unending effort to sort, differentiate and assess the prison population. [...] analysts would have to view the world through rose-colored glasses of a remarkably strong prescription to believe that this classificatory enterprise has resulted in a series of improvements to the material conditions of inmates or to their reform. Hence, I am inclined to be wary of proposals that would enshrine yet another set of classifications in the correctional complex (p. 1).

There remains, however, a practical desire (and in Canada a legal requirement) among correctional officials to identify and sort prisoners and to prescribe and justify interventions. There are legitimate concerns about limiting and structuring the discretion of therapists, classification officers, program administrators, social workers and a host of well-meaning others. Consequently, the demand for and appeal of assessment tools will persist. What remains to be seen is whether or not Canada, in keeping with the philosophy of *Creating Choices*, can reclaim and redefine the assessment of women prisoners, and more significantly if women's corrections can establish a distinct space and develop a truly woman-centered alternative. Attempts to do this over the past ten years have been thwarted by external pressures of bureaucratic continuity, universal assessment, staff turnover, and gender neutral training on overarching correctional procedures that are at times in direct conflict with the wider goal of achieving a woman-centered correctional model.

Thus far there has been little reflection on the kind of information individuals use and trust in developing their risk logics, or on how structuring factors such as gender, age, ethnicity, and social class, and different social contexts (leisure, work) influence risk logics. Risk and need cannot be accepted as unproblematic facts, nor are they phenomena that can be isolated from their social, historical and cultural contexts. Risk knowledge is used to inform correctional practices. While risk factors are statistical artifacts that reflect certain population characteristics, these factors are often ascribed to individuals and used to legitimate a wide range of interventions, including the responsibilization of offenders. The ascription of risk to individuals occurs through the development of assessment tools and through the administration and interpretation of these tools. Our observations of this process have revealed some disturbing trends that call for more critical evaluations of the criteria used in risk/need assessments and the proposed methods of risk reduction. Researchers and practitioners who advocate risk technologies often define risk from the standpoint of white middle class morality. What kinds of information do risk or need assessments offer, and how can or should this information be used in the management of offenders?

References

Abbott, B., & Kerr, D. (1995). *Substance abuse program for Federally sentenced women.* Ottawa, Ontario: Correctional Service of Canada.

Acoca, L., & Austin, J. (1996). *The crisis: Women in prison. Women offender sentencing study.* San Francisco, CA: National Council on Crime & Delinquency.

Andrews, D., & Bonta, J. (1998). *Psychology of criminal conduct* (2nd ed.). Cincinnati, Ohio: Anderson Publishing.

Andrews, D., Bonta, J., & Hoge, R. D. (1990). Classification for effective rehabilitation. *Criminal Justice and Behavior, 17,* 19–52.

Andrews, D., Zinger, I., Hoge, R. D., Bonta, J., Gendreau, P., & Cullen, F. T. (1990). Does correctional treatment work? A clinically relevant and psychologically informed meta-analysis. *Criminology, 28* (3), 369–404.

Arbour, L. (1996). *Report of the commission of inquiry into the prison for women in Kingston.* Ottawa, Ontario: Public Works and Government Services.

Atchison, C. (2000). Methodological and statistical problems with existing offender classification studies. In K. Hannah-Moffat & M. Shaw (Eds.), *Taking risks: Incorporating gender and culture into the classification and assessment of federally sentenced women in Canada.* Ottawa, Ontario: Status of Women.

Aubrey, R., & Hough, M. (1997). *Assessing offenders' needs: Assessment scales for the probation service* (Home Office Research Study 166). London: Home Office.

Austin, J., Chan, L., & Elms, W. (1993). *Indiana department of corrections women classification study.* San Francisco: National Council on Crime & Delinquency.

Bhui, H. S. (1999). Racism and risk assessment: Linking theory to practice with black mentally disordered offenders. *Probation Journal, 46* (3), 171–181.

Blanchette, K. (1997a). *Risk and need among federally sentenced female offenders: A comparison of minimum, medium and maximum-security inmates.* Ottawa, Ontario: Research Division Correctional Service Of Canada.

Blanchette, K. (1997b). Classifying Federal female offenders for correctional interventions. *Forum on Corrections Research, 9* (1), 36–41.

Blanchette, K. (1997c). Comparing violent and non-violent female offenders on risk and need. *Forum on Corrections Research, 9* (2), 14–18.

Bloom, B., & Covington, S. (1998). Gender specific programming for female offenders: What is it and why is it important? Paper presented at the 50th Annual Meetings of the American Society of Criminology, Washington, DC.

Bonta, J., Pang, B., & Wallace-Capretta, S. (1995). Predictors of recidivism among incarcerated female offenders. *Prison Journal, 75* (2), 135–164.

Bonta, J., Pang, B., & Wallace-Capretta, S. (1995). Predictors of recidivism among incarcerated female offenders. *The Prison Journal, 75* (3), 227–293.

Bonta, J., Pang, B., & Wallace-Capretta, S. (1997). Risk prediction and re-offending: Aboriginal and non-aboriginal offenders. *Canadian Journal of Criminology,* 127–144.

Brennan, T. (1998). Institutional classification for females: Problems and some proposals for reform. In R. T. Zaplin (Ed.), *Female offenders: Critical perspectives and effective interventions* (pp. 179–204). Gaithersburg, MD: Aspen Publishers Inc.

Brennan, T. & Austin, J. (1997). *Women in jail: Classification issues.* Washington, DC: U.S. Department of Justice, National Institute of Corrections.

Brown, M. (1996). Refining the risk concept: Decision context as a factor mediating the relation between risk and program effectiveness. *Crime and Delinquency, 42* (3), 435–455.

Burke, P., & Adams, L. (1991). *Classification of women offenders in state correctional facilities: A handbook for practitioners.* Washington, DC: National Institute of Corrections.

Clark, D. A., Fisher, M. J., & McDougall, C. (1993). A new methodology for assessing level of risk in incarcerated offenders. *British Journal of Criminology, 33* (3), 436–448.

Clement, G. (1996). *Care, autonomy, and justice: Feminism and the ethic of care.* Boulder, CO: Westview Press.

Cohen, S. (1985). *Visions of social control.* New York: Polity.

Cook County. (1997). *Cook county juvenile female offender project—female youth strengths and needs assessment and risk assessment.* Illinois Probation and Court Services.

Correctional Service of Canada. (1994). *Literature review: Federally sentenced women's program.* Ottawa, Ontario.

Correctional Service of Canada. (1995). *Security Management System.* Federally Sentenced Women's Program. Ottawa, Ontario.

Correctional Service of Canada. (1996). *FSW facilities offender intake assessment content guidelines.* Ottawa, Ontario.

Coulson, G., Ilacqua, G., Nutbrown, V., Giulekas, D., & Cudjoe, F. (1996). Predictive utility of the LSI for incarcerated female offenders. *Criminal Justice Behavior, 23* (3), 427–439.

Dallao, M. (1997). Keeping classification current. *Corrections Today,* 86–88.

Daly, D., & Lane, R. (1999). Actuarially based 'on line' risk assessment in Western Australia. *Probation Journal, 46* (3), 164–170.

Dawson, D. (1999). Risk of violence assessment: Aboriginal offenders and assumption of homogeneity. Paper presented to the Australian Institute of Criminology and Department of Correctional Service for S.A., Best Practice Interventions in Corrections for Indigenous People Conference, Adelaide, Australia.

Dhaliwal, G. K., Porporino, F., & Ross, R. R. (1994). Assessment of criminogenic factors, program assignment, and recidivism. *Criminal Justice and Behavior, 21*(4), 454–467.

Ditchfield, J. (1997). Actuarial prediction and risk assessment. *Prison Service Journal, 113,* 8–13.

Duguid, S. (2000). *Can prison work: The prisoner as object and subject in modern corrections.* Toronto: University of Toronto Press.

Ewald, F. (1991). Insurance and risk. In G. Burchell, C. Gordon, & P. Miller (Eds.), *The Foucault effect studies in governmentality* (pp. 197–210). Chicago: University of Chicago Press.

Farr, K. (2000). Classification for female inmates: Moving forward. *Crime and Delinquency, 46* (1), 3–17.

Forcier, M. 1995. *Development of an Objective Classification System for Female Offenders.* Final Report. (Massachusetts). Washington, DC: National Institute of Corrections.

Foucault, M. (1977). *Discipline and punish.* New York: Vintage Books.

Gottfredson, D. M., & Tonry, M. (Eds.). (1987). Prediction and classification. *Crime and Justice, 9.* Chicago: University of Chicago Press.

Gottfredson, S. D. (1987). Prediction: An overview of selected methodological issues. In D. M. Gottfredson & M. Tonry (Eds.), Prediction and classification. *Crime and Justice, 9.* Chicago: University of Chicago Press.

Haggerty, K. (1999). *Correctional risk classifications: Pragmatic cautions and theoretical reflections.* Paper presented at the workshop on Risk Gender and Diversity for the Status of Women, Toronto.

Haggerty, K. (2001). *Making crime count.* Toronto: University of Toronto Press.

Hannah-Moffat, K. (1997). From christian maternalism to risk technologies: Penal powers and women's knowledge in the governance of female prison. Unpublished doctoral dissertation, University of Toronto.

Hannah-Moffat, K. (1999). Moral agent or actuarial subject: Risk and Canadian women's imprisonment. *Theoretical Criminology, 3* (1), 71–94.

Hannah-Moffat, K. (2000). Re-forming the prison-rethinking our ideals. In K. Hannah-Moffat & M. Shaw (Eds.), *An ideal prison? Critical essays on women's imprisonment in Canada* (pp. 30–40). Halifax: Fernwood.

Hannah-Moffat, K. (2001). *Punishment in disguise: Governance in Canadian women's prisons.* Toronto: University of Toronto Press.

Hannah-Moffat, K., & Shaw, M. (2000). *An ideal prison? Critical essays on women's imprisonment in Canada.* Halifax, Nova Scotia: Fernwood Publishing.

Hannah-Moffat, K., & Shaw, M. (2001). *Gender, diversity, risk assessment and classification with federally sentenced women.* Ottawa, Ontario: Status Of Women Canada.

Holt, N. (1996). *Inmate classification: A validation study of the California system.* Sacramento, CA: California Department of Corrections.

Homel, R., Lincoln, R., & Herd, B. (1999). Risk and resilience: Crime and violence prevention in aboriginal communities. *Australian and New Zealand Journal Of Criminology, 32* (2), 182–196.

Howells, K., Day, A., Byrne, S., & Byrne, M. (1999, October). *Risk needs and responsivity in violence rehabilitation: Implications for programs with indigenous offenders.* Paper presented at the Best Practice Interventions in Corrections for Indigenous People Conference for the Australian Institute of Criminology and Department of Correctional Services, Adelaide, South Australia.

Kendall, K. (2000). Psy-ence fiction: The moral regulation of female prisoners through psychological sciences. In K. Hannah-Moffat & M. Shaw (Eds.), *The ideal prison:*

Critical essays on women's imprisonment in Canada. Halifax, Nova Scotia: Fernwood Publishing.

Kirk, S., & Kutchins, H. (1992). *The selling of the DSM: The rhetoric of science in psy-chiatry.* New York: Aldine de Gruyter.

Kruttschnitt, C. (1996). Contributions of quantitative methods to the study of gen-
der and crime, or bootstrapping our way into the theoretical thicket. *Journal Of Quantitative Criminology, 12* (2), 135–61.

Loucks, A. & Zamble, E. (1999, February). Predictors of recidivism: In serious female offenders—Canada searches for predictors common to both men and women. *Corrections Today, 26–32.*

Maine Department of Corrections. (1991). *Female offenders: An afterthought.* Report of the task force on female offenders, Augusta.

Mair, G. (1999). A man's man's man's world. Paper presented at the workshop on Risk Gender and Diversity for the Status of Women, Toronto.

McHugh, M. (1997). Risk assessment and management of suicides in prison. *Prison Service Journal, 111,* 4–8.

Monture-Angus, P. (2000). Aboriginal women and correctional practice: Reflections on the task force on federally sentenced women. In K. Hannah-Moffat & M. Shaw (Eds.), *The ideal prison: Critical essays on women's imprisonment in Canada* (pp. 52–60). Halifax, Nova Scotia: Fernwood Publishing.

Morash, M. (1999). A consideration of gender in relation to social learning and social structure: A general theory of crime and deviance. *Theoretical Criminology, 3* (4), 451–462.

Morash, M., Bynum, T. S., & Koons, B. A. (1998). *Women offenders: Programming needs and promising approaches.* Research in Brief. Washington, DC: National Institute of Justice.

Motiuk, L. (1993). Where are we in our ability to assess risk? *Forum of Corrections Research, 5* (2), 14–18.

Motiuk, L. (1997). Classification for correctional programming: The offender intake assessment process. *Forum of Corrections Research,* 9(1), 18–22.

Motiuk, L., & Blanchette, K. (1998). Assessing female offenders: What works? Paper presented at the International Community Corrections Association for the Correctional Service of Canada Research Division, Arlington, Virginia.

O'Malley. P (1999). The risk society implications for justice and beyond. Report Commissioned For The Department Of Justice, Victoria, Australia.

Petersilia, J., & Turner, S. (1987). Prediction and racial minorities. In D. M. Got-
tfredson & M. Tonry (Eds.), Prediction and Classification. *Crime and Justice,* 9. Chicago: University of Chicago Press.

Quinsey, V. L., Harris, G. T., Rice, M. E., & Cormier, C. A. (1998). *Violent offenders: Ap-
praising and managing risk.* Washington, DC: American Psychological Association.

Shaw, M. (1993). Reforming Federal women's imprisonment. In E. Adleberg & E. Currie (Eds.), *In Conflict with the Law* (pp. 50–75). Vancouver, BC: Press Gang Publishers.

Stanko, E. (1997). Safety talk: Conceptualizing women's risk assessment as a Technology of the soul. *Theoretical Criminology, 1* (4), 479–499.

Task Force on Federally Sentenced Women. (1990). *Report on the task force on federally sentenced women—Creating choices.* Ottawa Ministry of the Solicitor General.

CHAPTER 4

Cognitive Behavioralism in Women's Prisons: A Critical Analysis of Therapeutic Assumptions and Practices

Kathleen Kendall and
Shoshana Pollack

Introduction

This chapter reflects a conversation between us that is almost ten years old. We met while working at the Prison for Women, which at the time, was the only federal women's prison in Canada. Kathleen, a sociologist, was hired under contract by the Correctional Service of Canada to carry out an evaluation of therapeutic services within the prison (Kendall, 1993). Shoshana completed her social work degree by serving an internship with the psychology department, counselling prisoners and continued to work as a therapist there for the next four years (1993). We came from different perspectives but shared a feminist vision of women's emancipation. Now, about a decade later, from our respective academic positions, we continue our research and reflection on the effect of therapeutic services in women's prisons.

The basic tension that we encountered when we first embarked on this exercise, and now continue to struggle with, is how to reconcile our belief that women in prison deserve to have mental health services with a recognition that therapeutic services typically become a part of the punitive prison regime. While acknowledging that all mental health practices have the potential to be repressive, we continually ask ourselves whether this means we should avoid implementing alternative feminist forms of prison services and/or working inside of prisons altogether.

This chapter illustrates our conundrum with one example, the use of Dialectical Behavior Therapy (DBT) in Canadian women's prisons. It begins by contextualizing the use of DBT within the cognitive behavioralist framework which currently underpins all programming adopted by the Correctional Service of Canada (CSC). We critically examine the rise to dominance and key assumptions of this correctional cognitive behavioralism. Next, we provide a brief definition and examination of borderline personality disorder (BPD), the raison d'être of DBT. Following this discussion we consider the evolution of DBT and provide a critique of its use both outside of and inside prison. We contend that, like so many other deficit-based treatment models, the use of DBT in prisons is harmful and its use should be reconsidered. However, we conclude that it is necessary to continue feminist work with women prisoners. Toward this end, we provide some suggestions for practice that acknowledge the punitive prison environment and help to challenge the individualization of women's struggles. Ultimately, all therapeutic services delivered within prison risk being co-opted and made integral to the prison regime. This is the reason that we ultimately suggest that mental health services are best delivered outside of prison.

We have chosen to begin each section with brief reflections by each of us in order to illustrate the uncertainties, tensions and experiences that inform our work. Research, from its conception through to its writing-up, is a very messy and complex process. However, it is usually presented as if it occurs in a straightforward, seamless and linear fashion such that the complexities, contradictions and doubts are stripped away. Aldridge (1993) calls this process the "textual disembodiment of knowledge." She argues that it is the more personal aspects and experiences of researchers that are most often disembodied from texts. This practice gives the impression of a neutral, detached and objective body of work.

Yet, how we conduct, interpret and report our research is contingent upon our social location, assumptions, knowledge and experience. While we can take measures to limit our biases and ensure that our work is rigorous, it nonetheless will remain influenced by our own past and present intellectual and material circumstances. However, by making visible the positions we occupy as well as the assumptions, and reservations we hold, we can become more accountable for the products of our research and encourage readers to critically engage with us (Maynard & Purvis, 1994; Stanley, 1990; Stanley & Wise, 1990)

Such self-reflexivity seems particularly crucial for penal research with strong policy implications. As Hannah-Moffat (2001; 1995) has demonstrated, feminist prison reforms can be just as oppressive as the practices they seek to replace. By being more open about what we do, how we do it, and the ambiguities embedded in both our knowledge and practice, we hope that the implications of our work will become more evident.

Cognitive Behavioralism: The Foundation of Dialectical Behavior Therapy

Kathleen: For six months I worked at CSC National Headquarters as a Special Advisor on Female Offenders. It was here where I realized how central cognitive behaviouralism was to correctional programming. When I raised critical questions about this approach with some of my co-workers, I typically was met with the simple response that CSC officially adopted the model and therefore we had to work within it. There was little effort to defend it or even engage in further discussion. I thought that this was ironic given that CSC was claiming to teach offenders how to think critically. Yet, I soon found myself constricted by the cognitive behavioural framework, either bending other perspectives to fit inside the model or even failing to consider alternatives. The official adoption of cognitive behaviouralism by CSC precludes other ways of thinking about female prisoners. My recent research on human experimentation within Canadian federal penitentiaries has further served to confirm my concerns about prison programs, particularly those intending to change "criminal personalities" (Proctor & Kendall, 2001). While abuses of the past are now evident, how do we know that what we're currently doing will not be met with the same kind of horror in fifty or even ten years time? How do we avoid becoming immobilized by such fears?

Shoshana: I worked on contract at the Kingston Prison for Women as a psycho-therapist for five years. The team with whom I worked predominantly identified themselves as feminist therapists whose central job was to support and advocate on behalf of the women prisoners. However, despite the fact that our theoretical approach and practice agenda was at odds with those of the prison system, prison operations and discourses often undermined our practices and at times positioned us as part of the overall prison machinery. This dichotomy, attempting "empowering" therapeutic work within a disempowering environment, informs my understanding of the potential risks inherent in prison treatment programs.

During the 1970s, a great deal of scepticism surrounded both the effectiveness and ethics of correctional rehabilitation programs in the United States,

Canada and the United Kingdom (UK) (Martinson, 1974; Mitford, 1973). However, while such criticism contributed to the decline of a rehabilitative philosophy in the United States, it has continued to endure, and indeed strengthen, in Canada. This is due, in great measure, to the efforts of a group of Canadian psychologists strongly affiliated with the CSC and closely working with one another (Andrews, Bonta, & Hoge, 1990; Andrews, Zinger, Hoge, Bonta, Gendreau, & Cullen, 1990; Gendreau & Ross, 1987; 1979). The Canadian work has also been acknowledged as having a great influence on the revival of rehabilitation in the UK (Vanstone, 2000; Vennard, Sugg, & Hedderman, 1997) as well as upon some programs in the US (Sharp, 2000). Faith in the rehabilitation model has remained alive in Canada, to a large degree, because of the ability of the Canadian psychologists to take advantage of a policy shift established in the wake of disrepute surrounding rehabilitation.

In the 1980s, an "opportunities model" was introduced to replace the rehabilitation model. The rehabilitation framework assumes that prisoners are sick due to a potentially correctable pathology and therefore they cannot ultimately be held responsible for their actions. In contrast, the opportunities framework asserts that offenders are accountable for their actions. Therefore, they are offered program opportunities to change their behavior. If inmates fail to take up the offer or recidivate following their program involvement, they (and perhaps the program) are held accountable. However, this model has not in fact replaced the rehabilitation philosophy. Rather, it has been grafted onto it. Cognitive behavioralism, the approach championed by a core group of Canadian psychologists working with CSC, nicely bridges the rehabilitative and opportunities models (Gamberg & Thomson, 1994; Duguid, 2000).

Cognitive behavioralism does not consist of one single method or theory, but is a term applied to a range of interventions derived from three psychological theories: behaviorism, cognitive theory, and social learning. During the 1970s, these were integrated "into a new approach to understanding the complex dynamic relationships between thoughts, feelings and behavior" (McGuire cited in Vennard et al., 1997, p. 6). When applied to corrections, a cognitive behavioralist approach generally assumes that offenders have failed to develop particular cognitive skills and have learned inappropriate ways of behaving. Because it is acknowledged that cognitive deficits and undesired behaviors are learned, programs are designed "to teach offenders to face up to what they have done, to understand their motives and to develop new coping strategies and ways of behaving" (Vernnard, et. al., 1997, p. 6). Since cognitive behavioralism still aims to rehabilitate prisoners but does this by targeting their thinking, conceptualized as a learned and therefore mutable process for which they are held accountable, it links the rehabilitative and opportunities models. Cognitive behavioralism also fits with the broader neo-liberal or advanced liberal political climate which emphasizes responsibility, choice and enterprise (Hannah-Moffat, 2001; Kemshall, 2002). In this way, cognitive behavioralism has flourished within Canadian corrections.

Perhaps unsurprisingly, cognitive behavioral programs have been designed by some of the same Canadian researchers who conducted the research discovering their effectiveness. In particular, the Reasoning and Rehabilitation Program developed by Robert Ross and Elizabeth Fabiano and its more recent manifestation, the Living Skills Program, has been a core component of programming within CSC (Ross & Ross, 1995; Fabiano, Porporino, & Robinson, 1990; Ross, Fabiano & Ewles, 1988; Ross & Fabiano, 1985; Fabiano & Ross, 1983). This program is also central to the Correctional Program Strategy for Federally Sentenced Women guiding the development of all CSC programming for women prisoners (Correctional Service of Canada, 1994). Simply stated, the Living Skills Program attempts "to address criminogenic factors (those factors which played a role in criminal behavior) so that the offender's likelihood of re-offending has been reduced" (Solicitor General Canada, 1998, p. 7). In a rather bold tautology, cognitive behavioral programs are claimed to be the only effective means of addressing criminogenic factors (Bonta, 1997; Gendreau & Goggin, 1996; Gendreau, Little, & Goggin, 1996).

More recently, it has been posited that cognitive behavioral programs are the most effective intervention with female offenders (Andrews & Dowden, 1999; Loucks & Zamble, 1999; Blanchette, 1997; Blanchette & Motiuk, 1995). Cognitive behavioralism has gained an even stronger foothold in Canadian corrections through the program accreditation strategy adopted by CSC. One of the criteria for accreditation is that programs must target criminogenic needs. Other criteria require demonstrations as to how the program will achieve this (Correctional Service of Canada, 1999a). Since cognitive behavioral programs are said to be the only programs, which effectively target criminogenic needs, they are almost guaranteed to be the only programs granted accreditation. However, these accreditation criteria have not yet been approved for women's programs partly because their appropriateness for women was challenged by some members of a "panel of experts."[1]

The cognitive behavioral model currently guiding prison programming in Canada is probably best described in the book *The Psychology of Criminal Conduct* (1998) by Don Andrews and James Bonta. These two psychologists have

---

1. These 'experts' included Kathleen and other contributors to this book: Barbara Bloom, Stephanie Covington and Margaret Shaw. All accredited programs must first be approved by a panel of experts (Correctional Service of Canada, 1999a).

carried out a great deal of the research, which was cited earlier, and they have been very influential in correctional program and policy development in Canada and elsewhere. In sum, they argue the following:[2]

1. There is a general criminal personality that typifies offenders, regardless of gender, race, ethnicity or class.
2. This personality type has been discovered through psychological research embracing the scientific method. Therefore, the research is neutral, objective, generalizable, empirical and rational. Quantitative methods are privileged. Meta-analysis, in particular, is considered to be the 'gold standard'. Here, different quantitative studies are combined to produce summary statistics regarding the overall "effect size" of different program treatments upon recidivism. This approach is compared to sociological research, which is considered to be qualitative, unscientific, value-laden, un-generalizable, non-empirical, and irrational.
3. Criminal personalities are characterized by cognitive inadequacies or thinking deficits.
4. These thinking deficits are anti-social and "criminogenic." That is, they are statistically associated with crime. As such, they must be "targeted" in order to reduce recidivism and ultimately prevent crime.
5. Programs should therefore be designed to teach offenders to think differently or "pro-socially."
6. It is largely a waste of time to address social structural and systemic issues. Andrews and Bonta (1998) warn: "Do not get trapped in arguments with primary prevention advocates who believe that a society-wide focus on unemployment, sexism or racism will eliminate crime" (p. 363). They encourage the "neutralization" and "self destruction"of explanations which embrace such a focus. Class, gender, and race are considered relevant only as co-variants with little explanatory power.
7. Dissenters are accused of engaging in "knowledge destruction." Here, Bonta and Andrews undermine methodological criticisms against their own work by claiming such fault finding to be groundless and actually rooted in personal, professional and/or ideological bias.

As Andrews and Bonta (1998) demonstrate, the cognitive behavioral model adopted by the CSC individualizes crime and pathologizes prisoners. It blatantly disregards the structural aspects of crime. Racism, sexism, classism, and

---

2. For other critiques of Canadian correctional cognitive behavioral programs see Kendall, 2002; Hannah-Moffat & Shaw, 2000; Shaw, 1997. For a description of some American correctional cognitive behavioral programs see Sharp, 2000.

poverty are dismissed as largely irrelevant, since their statistical association with crime is said to be weak or insignificant. Furthermore, challenges to the model are undermined through accusations of bias. Yet, the strict reliance on quantitative measures to determine criminogenic needs and program effectiveness *is* problematic because it not only ignores the context within which programs are delivered, but also within which people generally live. Additionally, very little research and evaluation has included females[3] (Gorman, 2001; Hannah-Moffat & Shaw, 2001; Duguid, 2000; Kendall, 1998; Pawson & Tilley, 1997).

Central to the cognitive behavioralist model is the belief that prisoners are characterized by deficit or faulty thinking. Yet, who decides *what* to think and *how* to think it? Those involved in the design of cognitive behavioral programming have been mostly white, middle-class men. As we stated in the introduction, all researchers bring their own social locations, knowledge and experience to their practices. The research and program material designed by Andrews, Bonta, and others will therefore reflect their own norms and values as well as those of the CSC. Indeed, it has been argued that the CSC programmatic tools, instruments and manuals are rife with moral judgements incorporating class, race/ethnic, and gender bias (Hannah-Moffat & Shaw, 2001).

LSD, ECT, sensory deprivation, aversive therapy and other harmful practices were used in Canadian prisons throughout the 1960s and early 1970s in an attempt to rehabilitate the "criminal mind" (Proctor & Kendall, 2001; Somerville & Gilmore, 2000; Correctional Service of Canada, 1998; Gilmore & Somerville, 1998). At the time, it was claimed that such practices were informed by current scientific knowledge and implemented for prisoners' "own good." More recently, the Grandview Training School for Girls in Ontario, where Robert Ross drew his inspiration for the Living Skills Program (Ross & Fabiano, 1986; Ross & McKay, 1979) has been at the center of abuse allegations. A 1976 investigation into abuses contributed to the School's closure. However, the subsequent report was never released. Eight former employees, including Ross, have since been accused of physical, sexual and psychological abuse against former inmates. While Ross has been acquitted of some of the charges, and others were withdrawn, eleven remain stayed. Two guards were convicted. In November 1999, the Ontario government issued a formal apology to former inmates as part of a compensation package (Globe & Mail, 1999; Laframboise, 1997; Grandview Agreement Between the Grandview Sur-

---

3. For a more general feminist critique of cognitive behavioral therapy, see Kantrowitz and Ballou, 1992.

vivors Support Group and the Government of Ontario, 1994). These examples demonstrate the need for vigilance because of the great potential for harm institutional programs contain.

An environment that is de-humanizing fosters abuse. Numerous studies demonstrate how prisons and other total institutions de-humanize inmates through extreme power imbalances and the stripping away of their identities (Eaton, 1993; Toch, 1992; Goffman, 1961). In this way, prisoners are a vulnerable population. Such vulnerability is exacerbated by cognitive behavioralism which emphasizes their "otherness." For example, in talking about the success of cognitive skills training, Lucie McClung, current Canadian Commissioner of Corrections is quoted as saying: "The criminal mind does not operate like yours and mine. What would work for you in terms of deterrence will not work for the offender" (cited in Stewart, 2001, p. 38). As countless wars have illustrated, atrocities are easier to commit if victims are stripped of their humanity, and if their differences are exaggerated or invented (Glover, 1999). Prisons exacerbate this situation even further because of the intrinsic obedience to authority expected from prisoners and lower-ranking fellow correctional staff (Conover, 2000; McMahon, 1999). In light of this, we find it particularly disturbing that the CSC cognitive behavioral programs are teaching offenders what and how to think! We imagine that the dissonance created by programs claiming moral superiority while advocating morally questionable notions is not lost on prisoners.

As upsetting as this paradox is, it is unsurprising. Notions of the "criminal other" are necessary to support and justify correctional discipline and rehabilitation (Garland, 1996). Within this framework, criminal identities are further reliant upon de-contextualized understandings of crime which cognitive behavioralism embodies (Fox, 2001). In this way, cognitive behavioralism serves to legitimate incarceration.

No matter how far individual program deliverers/facilitators attempt to distance themselves from cognitive behavioralism, it nevertheless underpins all programming within the CSC (Solicitor General Canada, 1998). Furthermore, despite conflicting with the Task Force for Federally Sentenced Women's recommendation that programming reflects women's realities, cognitive behavioral programming for women has been instituted through the *Mental Health Strategy for Women Offenders* (Laishes, 1997), and the *National Strategy for High Need Women Offenders in Correctional Institutions* (Correctional Service of Canada, 1999b). The influence of cognitive behavioralism is particularly evident in the first of these, which aims to "understand and transform the thoughts and behaviors that are the source of the women's problems" (Laishes, 1997, p. 10).

We will now consider one particular variant of cognitive behavioralism, Dialectical Behavioral Therapy (DBT). This treatment model was designed specifically for women and is currently provided in Canadian, British and American prisons. DBT has recently been used with some male prisoners but is still generally delivered to women. Since it was created specifically to treat women diagnosed with borderline personality disorder (BPD), we will first provide a brief definition and critique of this diagnosis.

Borderline Personality Disorder

Kathleen: One of the things I really struggle with is how to acknowledge women's distress and their own violence without pathologizing them. For example, while carrying out the evaluation at the Prison for Women, some women claimed to hear malevolent voices inside their heads and others maintained that they had multiple personalities which caused them great difficulties. A few women had self-inflicted scars covering most of their bodies. One woman was in fear of being attacked by other prisoners after threats were made against her. These women stated that they wanted help. However, understandings of the women's problems and the kind of help on offer was—and is—constrained by institutional interpretations and services which ultimately pathologize the women. While the women can ask for help, they do so under conditions not of their choosing.

Shoshana: Most of the women I worked with had received psychiatric diagnoses even before arriving in prison. Often, women had been diagnosed with various disorders, accumulating at times seven or eight different diagnostic labels. Inevitably, Borderline Personality Disorder was one of these labels, especially if the woman had a history of frequent suicide attempts and/or self-injurious behavior. I remember most clearly after working with a woman for three years, attempting to connect her with a therapist in the community to which she was getting released, as she wanted to continue the work she had started with me. This therapist had seen this woman prior to her arrest and remembered her well. He asked me if she still had active symptoms of BPD, and although I told him she had made great progress in this regard, he abruptly interrupted to tell me he had to go and that he would call me back the next day. He didn't call back.

Borderline Personality Disorder (BPD) is an official psychiatric diagnosis characterized by extreme emotionality, impulsivity, aggressive behavior, dichotomous thinking, 'confused' identity, self-injurious behavior and suicidal ideation. Although not officially designated a "female" mental illness, about 75 percent of those who receive this diagnosis are women (Wirth-Cauchon, 2001). A high percentage of those with this diagnosis have a history of childhood trauma. Definitions of BPD have changed over time, but it takes its name from the notion that individuals with these characteristics fit neither into the diagnostic categories of *psychotic* nor *neurotic* but are somewhere in between, on the *"borderline"* of the two categories (Stone, 1986).

In the mental health field it is commonly felt that people with BPD are extremely difficult for therapists to deal with in that change is slow, resistance to therapy is strong and patients are angry, aggressive, and manipulative. Many mental health workers are reluctant to work with women diagnosed with DBT, as they are often thought to be untreatable and unpleasant. Warner (1998) states that professionals are often "frustrated and feel hopeless in their efforts to help [individuals with BPD] address their problems, and as a result they may eventually be denied treatment or refused admission to psychiatric inpatient units" (p. 77). Similarly, Kutchins and Kirk (1997) quoting a therapist, argue: "Borderline is a wastebasket diagnosis; the diagnosis given to patients who therapists don't like, or are troublesome or hard to treat" (p. 199). Furthermore, in warning of the potential abuse, they cite examples in which psychiatrists have used BPD to justify their own sexual abuse of patients. Sam Warner (1996) suggests that this label is applied to women who do not fit into gender role stereotypes and that it is "a new name for an old 'problem,' disorderly women" (p. 65). In addition to the pejorative nature and abusive potential of the BPD label, many researchers question its very existence (Wirth-Cauchon, 2001; Kutchins & Kirk, 1997; Warner, 1996). Among numerous problems with BPD, critics cite a lack of empirical evidence, invalid and unreliable diagnostic criteria, as well as vague and shifting definitions that encourage distortion and subsume ever-increasing numbers of female patients.

Furthermore, some contend that many women given a diagnosis of BPD actually suffer from Post Traumatic Distress (Armstrong, 1993; Cauwels, 1992; Hamilton & Jensvold, 1992). Here it is argued that symptoms associated with BPD are in fact responses to external, abusive events rather than indicators of a personality disorder. In fact, most women diagnosed with BPD have histories of abuse (Wirth-Cauchon, 2001; Zanarini, Frankenburg, Reich, Marino, Haynes & Gunderson, 1999; Kutchins & Kirk, 1997; Warner, 1996). Finally, gays and lesbians have received a BPD diagnosis because of problems with "identity formation" (Dworkin, 2000). Such labelling implies that one's sexuality is pathological, rather than the surrounding homophobic environment.

Along with these criticisms, there is much disagreement about what causes BPD. Nonetheless, the dominant explanation is a bio-medical one, which maintains that BPD results from a combination of biological predisposition and environmental factors (Linehan, 1993a, 1993b; Linehan & Heard, 1992). That is, BPD is understood as rooted in a biological inability to regulate emotions under stressful circumstances. The dysfunctional family is seen as an especially common trigger for those biologically predisposed toward BPD. Families characterized by the invalidation of negative emotions such as anger and sadness and where children receive mixed messages (where what is *said* to them is incongruent with what is *done* to them) are particularly likely to precipitate BPD.

What Is Dialectical Behavior Therapy (DBT)?

Kathleen: DBT has become an industry. Program books, manuals, workshops, videos, trainers and so on are all available at a cost. Other correctional programs are similarly marketed. It seems distasteful to me that money is being made and reputations established off the backs of prisoners' pain. Yet, in some ways, to differing degrees, all of us who work in this area are doing so as well. In what ways are we compromised by pressures to obtain research grant money and to publish?

Shoshana: In reviewing the practice literature about DBT it became clear to me that the strength of this model lies in its support for practitioners. In addition, at a recent conference a participant also showed how DBT helps to maintain the stability of the women's prison by teaching women cognitive behavioral skills that decrease the likelihood that they will "act out". So, the question for me becomes, for whom is DBT developed?

Dialectical Behavior Therapy (DBT) is currently being used by the CSC as a treatment for BPD (Blanchette, 2002; McDonagh, 2002). Invented by Marcia Linehan, it is described by her as an integrative *cognitive-behavioral* treatment (1993a, 1993b). Since its development, DBT has become somewhat of an industry. In fact, the CSC hired Linehan's own company, the Behavioral Technology Transfer Group based in Seattle to train correctional staff (referred to as coaches) in this method of treatment. DBT has a reputation for being the only treatment that works with BPD patients. As mentioned earlier, the treatment method is based upon a cognitive-behavioral model incorporating biological factors. Such an approach is said to be appropriate for this group because they are thought to fail at more psycho-therapeutic oriented models.

The focus of DBT is to change patients' thoughts and feelings, and ultimately, their behavior. As DBT was developed for women with BPD diagnosis, the problematic behaviors targeted are such things as suicide attempts, self-injury and angry outbursts. The therapeutic goals of changing how women cope with their emotions and distorted thought processes are in the service of eliminating these problematic behaviors. Treatment involves both group and individual therapy as well as pharmacotherapy (drug treatment).

However, there is very little research on this treatment model and even less empirical evidence validating its effectiveness (Scheel, 2000). Linehan herself and those she has trained, have conducted some research on their own programming, but with inconclusive results (Scheel, 2000). They suggest that DBT may be useful for decreasing suicidal and self-harming behavior while in treatment. However, a noted limitation in the research thus far is that no long-term studies have been conducted to determine whether DBT provides lasting changes (Scheel, 2000). One study has also found that patients who were treated with DBT strategies actually experienced an *increase* in symptoms (Springer, Lohr, Buchtel, & Silk, cited in Turner, 2000). Turner (2000) writes that this finding is likely due to the fact that rather than implementing the standardized treatment model as originally conceived, the study modified some of the DBT strategies. Therefore, he argues that the failure should not be attributed to the DBT model per se, but rather to the inappropriate use of its components. However, this possibility should render us all the more cautious, since DBT prison programs adapt selected aspects of the model, rather than deliver it as originally conceived. Indeed, some modification is necessary due to the constraints of the prison environment.

Despite the lack of empirical evidence regarding its short- and long-term effectiveness, and the use of DBT across different populations, as well as in different settings, DBT has been enthusiastically welcomed and implemented by a wide variety of mental health professionals (Swenson, 2000). This appears largely due to several factors, none of them related to evidence that this treatment method actually works.

First, as Swenson (2000) points out, DBT is extremely cost effective. In the United States, insurance companies, research funding bodies, and hospital administrators, have embraced DBT for its promise of reducing the financial and resource costs of treating women with BPD. Second, from the point of view of clinicians, DBT seems to be extraordinarily attractive because of two factors: it provides hope to a disillusioned mental health community that there may exist a treatment that works for BPD and it offers a structured practice methodology towards this end. BPD is conceptualized as a deep characterological disorder, for which there exists no cure. As such, it is conceived as a problem that "permeates all the way down to a person's soul" (Solicitor General Canada, 1998, p. 45). Such a conceptualization contributes to the sense of futility many clinicians feel in working with this population and is a likely reason why so many whole-heartedly embrace DBT—it holds the promise of treatment that helps clinicians feel less frustrated and powerless. Third, one of the core components of this model is built in support and supervision for DBT therapists. As this population tends to challenge clinicians in that they often exhibit "therapy interfering behaviors" and worse, do not seem to change their behavior, therapist support is much needed. In fact, the appeal of DBT may well be the relief it provides for mental health professionals rather than any real evidence that it helps those diagnosed with BPD.

Those who employ and/or adapt this treatment model and even those who are cautious about its use, however, do not appear to seriously question DBT's underlying assumptions or clinical strategies. Sometimes these are masked by rhetoric. For example, in describing the population of women prisoners for whom DBT is designed, CSC has recently shifted from using the term BPD to 'high-risk/high-need' (McDonagh, 2002). Here, need and risk refer to criminogenic characteristics or factors statistically associated with recidivism as well as to problems associated with institutional management. Hannah-Moffat (2000) has written elsewhere how semantic shifts can give the illusion of a more progressive, less pathologizing model but in reality be even more punitive. As we discuss below, this slippage in language occurs easily because the same presuppositions underpin both labels. Thus, although the terminology has changed from BPD to high-risk/high-need CSC continues to regard a particular group of troublesome women prisoners as having a biological predisposition towards emotional dysregulation and of being mentally disordered. Essentially, CSC has put "old wine into a new bottle."

In the next section, we focus in more detail upon some problematic aspects of DBT' as applied to women prisoners. We acknowledge that our critique is limited because it is largely theoretical and reliant upon information released into the public arena. Unfortunately, most DBT program material is not accessible to those outside the prison program and/or prison service. Furthermore, we have only spoken informally to program providers and not at all to prisoners who have taken a DBT program. Research with these people is crucial to a deeper and more complete understanding of DBT.

DBT in Prisons

Kathleen: I was recently at a conference where I met two women who run DBT at one of the institutions. I found these women very commit-

ted and honorable in their intentions, as were the therapists at the Prison for Women where I carried out the evaluation. Likewise, many of my colleagues at National Headquarters worked very hard for women prisoners. In critiquing programs like DBT, I am attempting to highlight the institutional demands which impose upon, and limit, the work that can be done. Nonetheless, I feel that my writing may be regarded as an attack against individuals working within the system and that I am therefore somehow betraying them. At the same time, I believe that there are others whose motivations are questionable and who do abuse their position of power. How can we ensure that the former, and not the latter, work with women prisoners?

Shoshana: Models with the inherent assumption that women prisoners are deficient and sick fit very comfortably within the correctional context. Perhaps this is why corrections has whole-heartedly embraced DBT. Imagine the different response should we suggest that women's actions may be rational responses to unjust circumstances. Or imagine the assertion that many groups of women are socially positioned through systemic marginalization, to be constantly "in conflict with the law"? With these understandings in mind, who benefits from constructing such women as mentally disordered?

DBT is now being used at in least five Canadian institutions with federally sentenced female prisoners.[4] Its implementation followed a recommendation by Alan Warner (1998), who saw DBT as the treatment of choice for this population. Yet, as far as we have been able to determine, there are no published studies demonstrating the effectiveness of its use in correctional facilities for women.[5]

----

4. These institutions include: the Burnaby Correctional Center for Women in British Columbia, the Regional Psychiatric Center and Saskatchewan Penitentiary in Saskatchewan, as well as Springhill and Truro institutions both in Nova Scotia.

5. We were, however, able to obtain two unpublished, undated studies from the behavioral Technology Transfer Group: McCann, Ball and Ivanoff and Trupin, Stewart, Boesky, McClung, and Beach. The first of these studies involved the delivery of DBT to a mostly male inpatient forensic population but included no evaluation. The paper by Trupin et al. evaluated the delivery of DBT to incarcerated female offenders in Washington state. DBT was delivered to 22 young women with significant behavioral problems in a mental health cottage and to 23 adolescents in a general population cottage. While the first group demonstrated a decrease in behavioral problems during the 10 months of the study, there was no decrease compared to the year prior to the implementation of DBT. The second group showed no reduction in behavioral

However, the prison profile fits nicely with the target population of DBT. That is, the majority of imprisoned women are said to have mental disorders such as BPD. For example, *The Mental Health Strategy for Women Offenders* reports that 74 percent of women incarcerated at Burnaby Correctional Center have a personality disorder (Laishes, 1997). Furthermore, a central assumption of the BPD diagnosis is that these women are emotionally labile and given to extreme feelings, identities, relationships and behavior. This results in an inability to cope or manage one's own emotions. Women's inability to cope or to be managed is also a central theme in the literature on women in prison. It is particularly evident in CSC's description of women labelled as high-risk/high-need (Laishes, 1997; Laishes & Lyth, 1996; Blanchette, 2002; McDonagh, 2002). Thus assumptions about BPD and DBT again coincide with established thinking about women offenders (Pollack, 2000a).

In fact, the entire model of DBT is consistent with notions of criminalized women. Women classified as BPD and female offenders (particularly those classified as high-risk/high-need) are constructed as groups whose cognitions, emotions and behaviors are out of control, extreme and dangerous (Wirth-Cauchon, 2001; Kendall, 2000; Jimenez, 1997). Given that the DBT treatment model conforms to correctional cognitive behavioralism and more specifically, to constructions of female prisoners, it is unsurprising that it has found a welcome home in women's prison programming. As with cognitive behavioralism more generally, DBT attempts to persuade women into internalizing notions of criminal identities, which are then transformed into reformed selves (Fox, 2001). However, this process paradoxically requires inherently pathological selves to self-recover. As Fox (2001) has stated elsewhere, the goal of producing healthy prisoners conflicts with the assumption that their very souls are defective. This contradiction is managed by DBT through its incorporation of *dialectics.*

Originating in classical philosophy, dialectics entails a logical debate between two opposing views. One perspective is presented (the thesis), a conflicting standpoint is posited (antithesis) and out of this process, a shared understanding is reached (synthesis). This method is proposed as being appropriate for women with BPD since they are characterized as having rigid

---

problems but staff became more punitive toward prisoners. CSC is currently undertaking a program evaluation of DBT, using a multi-method approach. However, the evaluation doubles as a clinical assessment and the program facilitators are given back the results for each individual prisoner (Blanchette, 2002). We have serious ethical and methodological concerns about this evaluative model. For example, how forthright can an inmate be when they know that their responses will determine whether or not they receive a positive assessment?

dichotomous thinking, and an inability to synthesize contradictory events, perspectives or feelings. Irrational behavior, such as suicide attempts and/or explosive anger, is understood to be the result of this cognitive deficiency. DBT thus adopts a dialectical approach whereby patients are taught about inter-relatedness, synthesis and change. For the facilitators, this means accepting women where they are, while simultaneously demanding that they change; validating and confronting them at the same time. Through this process, patients purportedly learn "that judgments of 'good versus bad' and 'right versus wrong' fail to reflect the nature of life, and that instead a continuous process of balancing or integrating conflicting elements must occur" (Linehan & Heard, 1992. p. 50).

Such a process, while potentially liberating, may also have invidious consequences, particularly inside prisons, which are rife with conflicting messages. In her research at the Prison for Women, Kathleen also found that the women identified a contradiction between programs purporting to heal them, and the prison regime, which undermined attempts to do so (Kendall, 1993). Women were also sometimes punished for practicing skills taught in their programs, such as self-assertiveness. While DBT encourages a rejection of simplistic dichotomies rooted in right versus wrong, there are in fact, very clear rules about right and wrong and good and bad within the prison setting. Here, the message of DBT is itself contrary to institutional expectations and conduct.

DBT further incorporates dialectics into the therapeutic relationship. Since women with BPD are viewed as being unable to maintain stable, reciprocal relationships, DBT encourages the establishment of such associations through the therapist's own modelling of appropriate behavior, coping techniques and dialectical thinking. For example, one of the strategies that DBT therapists are instructed to use is called "irreverent communication" (Linehan & Heard, 1992, p. 260). As with all the strategies for DBT therapists, it represents one-half of a dyad that is to be employed in combination with another technique. Irreverent communication refers to "sarcastic" and "indifferent" therapeutic responses designed to "introduce a new viewpoint" and "temporarily unbalance" the patient. It is to be used in conjunction with such strategies as validation, understanding and empathy. Linehan and Heard (1992) provide an example of this therapeutic method, which seeks to respond to a patient who says she is thinking about killing herself with the comment: "That would make it difficult to come to therapy" (p. 260).

Although such an approach may be appropriate under very specific and unusual circumstances, we feel it has great potential for misuse and misunderstanding, particularly for women in prison who so often have their feelings, behavior and words misconstrued and dismissed. Irreverent communication is supposed to be used in conjunction with therapeutic strategies of "sincerity, responsiveness and warmth" (Linehan & Heard, 1992, p. 260). It is the combination, the dialectic, of these two strategies that is thought to be an effective means of promoting "the patient's cessation of thinking and behaving in the extreme" (Linehan & Heard, 1992, p. 260). However, validation strategies in this model are constructed as techniques rather than as sincere and appear disingenuous in their motivation. This is underscored by Linehan and Heard's (1992) statement that validation is accomplished by searching "for the nugget of gold in the pail of sand, so to speak" (p. 261).

The limitations and falsity of validation as conceptualized by DBT is apparent in another of its components—distress tolerance. Essentially, distress tolerance is the process of "learning to bear pain skillfully" by "tolerating and surviving crises" and "accepting life as it is in the moment" (Linehan, 1993b, p. 96). Teaching distress tolerance to prisoners has odious implications. Not only may it encourage women to accept and internalize their oppression, it could furthermore serve to thwart their legitimate protest against the prison regime. When added to this is the fact that prisoners are a discredited group by virtue of their criminalized status, and those with labels of BPD or high-risk/high-need even more so, the potential for abuse is great. In fact, a recent Commission of Inquiry into the Prison for Women (1996) found that the CSC adopted a "deplorable defensive culture" and that "too often, the approach was to deny error, defend against criticism, and react without a proper investigation of the truth" (*Commission of Inquiry into Certain Events at the Prison for Women*, 1996, p. 173). The Commissioner concluded that there was a "disturbing lack of commitment to the ideals of justice on the part of the correctional service" (p.198). Given this, the systematic promotion of distress tolerance is cause for great concern.

Not only may DBT serve to discredit legitimate prisoner protest, it could encourage staff to blame prisoners for the failures and problems of the penal regime. This is evident in the CSC Intensive Healing (Mental Health) program designed for women with personality disorders in need of an enhanced level of treatment services (Laishes & Lyth, 1996). The program is essentially a modified version of DBT, which conceptualizes prisoners as manipulative and divisive:

> These individuals often split their internal world into "all good" or "all bad" and this situation may be replicated in the external environment of the institution. Some staff members are idealized and seen as "all good" whereas others are regarded with contempt and seen as useless or "all bad". These two groups of staff members are treated differently by these individuals, so polarization and splitting occurs among staff. This can lead to those staff who are idealized feeling that the "bad" staff simply do not understand the woman, and

those staff who are regarded as "bad" view the "good staff" as having been conned by the manipulative behavior of the woman. If these individuals are to engage in certain behaviors such as splitting, the entire institution may be disrupted as a result. (Laishes & Lyth, 1996, p. 2).

By encouraging a simple acceptance of the oppositions, tensions, and incongruities embedded within prisons, critical analysis and understanding is discouraged. Fundamentally, the failings of the prison regime are framed as rooted within prisoners' pathology. This way, the institution becomes legitimized while prisoners are discredited. As stated earlier, mixed-messages and an invalidating environment are claimed to trigger BPD. Prisons, therefore, maintain and reproduce the very conditions thought to provoke BPD and DBT becomes self-sustaining.

Two final and related problematic aspects of the DBT model of concern to us here are the techniques of "autobiography" and "behavioral chain analysis." Each of these is subsumed under "behavioral analysis," a fundamental component of DBT. Behavioral analysis is designed to "figure out what the problem is, what is causing it, what is interfering with the resolution of the problem, and what aids are available to help solve the problem" (Linehan, 1993b, p. 254). It does this essentially by getting women to, in detail, recount their past behavior and monitor their current behavior. However, the women are expected to do so in accordance with the institutional construct of the criminal woman. Writers such as Foucault (1977), Rose (1999), and Fox (2001), have argued that this process of self-reflection and self-construction is a form of covert social control through which prisoners learn to exercise discipline over themselves and ultimately become self-governing.

The Intensive Treatment Program at Burnaby,[6] for example, requires prisoners to create an "autobiography," written and then verbally presented, which summarizes their lives and describes their psychosocial development from birth to the present. This overview is to include such things as abuse and trauma history, family dynamics, sexual history, self-destructive behavior, drug and alcohol use and criminal history. This history is then meshed with

---

6. We have focused upon the DBT program at the Burnaby Correctional Center for Women here because it is the only one for which we were able to obtain a detailed program manual. We commend the program facilitators for making the manual freely available and hope that others will follow their lead. Although public access to program details makes programs somewhat vulnerable it encourages integrity, transparency and accountability. This is particularly important when programs are delivered to vulnerable populations such as prisoners.

a "criminal behavior cycle" in which participants identify "a repetitive cycle of cognitive, emotional, and behavioral events that lead to offending and self-destructive behavior, and to discover and practice appropriate interventions to change this cycle" (Saidman & Chato-Manchuk, p. 16). In this way, the social context of women's actions is in fact stripped away, so that the women's history and behavior is reduced to faulty cognitions and emotions.

The consent form states that the women's completed Criminal Behavior Cycle will be part of the official file and furthermore, that "facilitators are required to report any significant previously undisclosed information about past or present criminal behavior that comes to their attention" (p. 24). Thus, prisoners are required be honest and open in their participation in DBT but are not guaranteed confidentiality. In fact, some prisoners enrolled in DBT programs or programs where DBT is a component, contacted the Canadian Association of Elizabeth Fry Societies (CAEFS) reporting that information they provided as a compulsory aspect of their program involvement, was used against them in terms of privileges and parole.

Not only is there a contradiction between confidentiality and security, it is questionable how appropriate it is for prisoners to be discussing very personal and often distressing aspects of their lives, when they may not otherwise choose to, especially in such a public place. This is particularly so within a coercive environment where the possibility of voluntary participation and informed consent are doubtful and where women's own understandings are disqualified, reinterpreted, or silenced by the privileged discourse.

Thus, although DBT is heralded for stripping BPD of its pejorative implications by viewing such things as suicide attempts and self-injury as coping strategies rather than as manipulative (Scheel, 2000), the DBT strategies and presuppositions of its incorporation in Canadian prisons suggest otherwise.

Summary

We hope that we have made the potential problems of cognitive behavioralism and DBT as they operate within prisons apparent. A cognitive behavioral model, which individualizes crime and pathologizes prisoners, informs all programming within the CSC, including DBT. This model serves to support and legitimize prisons. DBT was specifically designed to treat BPD, a biologically rooted mental disorder purportedly affecting mainly women. However, the status of BPD is highly contested. Not only have critics questioned its validity, reliability, and disparaging tone, they have challenged its very existence. We are furthermore anxious about the ways in which DBT constructs and reinforces notions of "criminal women," invalidates their legitimate protests and blames them for failures of the prison regime. Furthermore, anecdotal evidence suggests that information provided during DBT is used to deny women prisoners' privileges and parole. Although some women may benefit from the program and others resist it, or even use it to their advantage, we question the ability of any program to effectively support women while they are literally locked into the contradictions and pressures inherent in prisons. Such tensions need to be challenged, not tolerated.

Future Directions

Kathleen: Now for the really difficult part. I have been accused of being an ivory tower 'radical intellectual' (Pollock, 1998, pp. 198–199). That is, while I deconstruct prison programming, I offer nothing in its place. Similarly, while I argue that alternatives to imprisonment must be our goal, this will not happen overnight. While waiting for the revolution, what will happen to the women inside? In fact, this dilemma is something I continually struggle with. Unfortunately, I don't think that there are any easy answers. There is no panacea. Prison work is full of paradoxes and dilemmas. Shoshana and I have had numerous discussions and debates over such issues. This chapter, and particularly our conclusion below, is the result of these. No doubt that some will be disappointed by our lack of a clear direction. To me, however, the important thing is to keep asking difficult questions, being self-reflective, and encouraging dialogue. Perhaps such a task is more comfortable for me than those working on the front-line. Yet like other academics, I am reliant upon grant money to carry out my work as well as the cooperation of prison officials to gain access to prisons and prisoners. When our work becomes too critical, we find ourselves denied funding and more importantly, we are refused entry into prisons. We are then criticised for not understanding what is going on inside. How then, can we remain critical and ensure that prisoners' voices be represented in our research?

Shoshana: As a social worker, I don't find the contradictions of providing therapy in women's prisons all that much different from social work practice in general. As my students have often said, the tensions between being a helper and being an agent of social control are endemic to social work. The goal as practitioners is to be constantly vigilant and self-reflective, to make practices as transparent as possible to our clients, and to be clear about in whose interest we are ultimately working. This is not easy, but in order to be accountable to our clients, whether they are in the prison system, welfare system, or child protection system, we must engage in ongoing self-scrutiny and honesty. This chapter is an example of this sort of deconstructive project.

The struggle between offering support services to women in prison and the very real possibility that these services will be complicit in perpetuating the regulation of women prisoners is a challenging one. However, this challenge is not unique to prison work: the social control/helping dichotomy is integral to the helping professions, such as social work, and is a tension that must be consistently grappled with by practitioners (Townsend, 1998). As Rossiter (2000) argues, when working with and for marginalized populations, all our practices take place within power relations and oppressive social structures. There is therefore no "place of innocence" when doing this type of work. Although there are serious and multiple obstacles to offering support services within prisons without becoming part of the overall agenda of social control, the decision to abandon this project and therefore, the women inside, is not an option for many of us. In order to do this, however, we must challenge how women prisoners are constructed and modify our practices so that they not only acknowledge the contradictions of therapy within prisons, but also actively challenge the individualization and pathologization of women's behaviors.

As stated above, women inmates are typically constructed as emotional, angry, needy, irrational and poor decision makers. In Canada, these same constructions have been framed within a "woman-centered" perspective that purports to locate the experiences of female offenders within women's social context of being marginalized and oppressed (Task Force on Federally Sentenced Women, 1990). However, rather than de-individualizing women's lawbreaking, this "woman-centered" analysis has merely reconstructed the same deficit based understandings within a victimization and low self-esteem discursive frame (Pollack, 2000a). Therefore, when we advocate the need for feminist approaches to working with women in prison, we do so with the full awareness that feminist therapeutic models are also vulnerable to individualizing and de-politicizing women's lives (Hannah-Moffat, 2001; Kendall, 1994).

We need to understand the multi-dimensional aspects of those factors which bring women into conflict with the law—that racial, class, and gender oppression intersect at individual, interpersonal, and systemic levels in ways that limit choices for many women. The task of progressive mental health services for this population is to counter constructions of women offenders as having personality disorders, thinking deficits, or risks and needs that render them incapable of rational and reasonable behavior. Rather, we need to draw upon feminist, anti-oppression, post modern and multi-cultural mental health approaches that recognize the impact of oppression on the availability of choices, on decision-making, identity development and behavior. This also means moving from a deficit model to one that emphasizes women's strengths and acknowledges their varied and skillful modes of coping.

We also must to devise creative practices that operationalize the above assumptions within the prison environment. It is important for anyone attempting to work within the prison to recognize that the environment replicates the abusive dynamics many women offenders have experienced and that it presents serious obstacles to therapeutic practice (Pollack, 2000b; Covington, 1998; Heney & Kristiansen, 1998; Kendall, 1993). With this recognition as the starting point, and with Rossiter's (2000) argument that we are never located outside of power relations in mind, such programs as prisoner facilitated peer support programs (Boudin, 1998; Pollack, 1994) multi-cultural models (Pope-Davis & Coleman, 1997) and a feminist post-structuralist approach (Warner, 2001) may be helpful. In addition, those working inside must also function as advocates for the women and actively seek linkages and resources with community advocates and service providers.

Ultimately we contend, in terms of therapeutic services, that women should be afforded the opportunity to utilize community mental health services. In fact, this was the spirit of *Creating Choices*, the 1990 Canadian women's prison reform document, which emphasized community resources and connections. In practice, however, women are rarely permitted passes to attend programming in the community. Sometimes community services are brought into the prison, to operate within the confines of institutional mandates. Community programming that is feminist in orientation, such as that provided by Sexual Assault Crisis Centers, has a tremendous opportunity here to provide non-oppressive services or at least potentially less-oppressive ones. However, not all communities, particularly smaller and rural areas such as in the Canadian Atlantic provinces, have feminist community services available.

Inevitably the question arises, particularly from those committed to helping change prison conditions and the lives of those living inside them, about the best place to challenge prison practices. Unfortunately, these discussions all too often assert that one form of feminist challenge is better than another. The issue at the crux of the debate is an important one: are feminists better placed to have serious impact on the criminal justice system from within the system or from outside of it? Although the question is important, it is also problematic in how it is structured. The obvious answer to us is that we need challenges from both inside and outside the prison walls. In addition, there needs to be solid linkages between those pressuring for change outside and those doing the work from within. Pitting the two against each other and insisting that one method is somehow "better" than another, defeats our overall purpose: combating the social structural factors underlying women's oppression, developing community supports, improving conditions for women inmates and challenging the use of prisons.

References

Aldridge, J. (1993). The textual disembodiment of knowledge in research account writing. *Sociology, 27* (1), 53–66.

Andrews, D. A., & Bonta, J. (1998). *The psychology of criminal conduct* (Rev. ed.). Cincinnati, OH: Anderson Publishing Company.

Andrews, D., Bonta, J., & Hoge, R. D. (1990). Classification for effective rehabilitation. *Criminal Justice and Behavior, 17,* 19–52.

Andrews, D., & Dowden, C. (1999). A meta-analytic investigation into effective correctional intervention for female offenders. *Forum on Corrections Research, 11* (3), 18–21.

Andrews, D., Zinger, I., Hoge, R. D., Bonta, J., Gendreau, P., & Cullen, F. T. (1990). Does correctional treatment work? A clinically relevant and psychologically informed meta-analysis. *Criminology, 28* (3), 369–404.

Armstrong, L. (1993). *Rocking the cradle of sexual politics: What happened when women said incest.* Reading, MA: Addison-Wesley.

Blanchette, K. (2002) An evaluation framework for Dialectical Behaviour Therapy (DBT) in Canadian women's federal correctional facilities. Paper presented at the XXVIIth International Congress on Law and Mental Health, Amsterdam, The Netherlands, July 12.

Blanchette, K. (1997). Classifying female offenders for correctional interventions. *Forum on Corrections Research, 9* (1), 36–41.

Blanchette, K., & Motiuk, L. (1995). Female offender risk assessment: The case management strategies approach. Paper presented at the Annual Convention of the Canadian Psychological Association, Charlottetown, P.E.I.

Bonta, J. (1997). *Offender rehabilitation: From research to practice.* Ottawa, Ontario: Ministry of the Solicitor General of Canada.

Bonta, J. (1995). The responsivity principle and offender rehabiliation. *Forum on Corrections Research, 7* (3), 34–37.

Boudin, K. (1998). Lessons from a mother's program in prison: A psychosocial approach supports women and their children. In J. Harden & M. Hill (Eds.), *Breaking the rules: Women in prison and feminist therapy* (pp. 103–125). Binghamton, New York: The Haworth Press.

Cauwels, J. (1992). *Imbroglio: Rising to the challenges of borderline personality disorder.* New York: W. W. Norton.

Commission *of Inquiry Into Certain Events at the Prison for Women in Kingston, Canada.* (1996). Ottawa, Ontario: Public Works and Government Services.

Conover, T. (2000). *Holding the key: My year as a guard at Sing Sing.* London: Scribner.

Correctional Service of Canada. (1999a). Consultation on Possible Accreditation for Women Programs. January 6–7. Ottawa, Ontario: Author.

Correctional Service of Canada. (1999b). News Release. 'Backgrounder-What is the Strategy? September 3, 1999. Ottawa, Ontario: Author.

Correctional Service of Canada. (1998). Board of investigation into allegations of mistreatment by a former inmate at the prison for women between March 22, 1960–August 1, 1963. Ottawa, Ontario: Author.

Correctional Service of Canada. (1994). Correctional program strategy for federally sentenced women. Ottawa, Ontario: Author.

Covington, S. (1998). Women in prison: Approaches in the treatment of our most invisible population. In J. Harden & M. Hill (Eds.), Breaking the rules: Women in prison and feminist therapy (pp.141–155). Binghamton, New York: Haworth Press.

Duguid, S. (2000). Can prisons work? The prisoner as object and subject in modern corrections. Toronto: University of Toronto Press.

Dworkin, S. (2000) Individual therapy with Lesbian, Gay, and Bisexual Clients. In Perez, R., & DeBord, K., & Bieschke, K (Eds). Pp: 157–181. Handbook of Counseling and Psychotherapy With Lesbian, Gay, and Bisexual Clients. Washington, DC: American Psychological Association

Eaton, M. (1993). Women after prison. Buckingham, England: Open University Press.

Fabiano, E., & Ross, R. (1983). The cognitive model of crime and delinquency: Prevention and rehabilitation. Toronto: Planning and Research Branch of the Ontario Ministry of Correctional Services.

Fabiano, E., Porporino, F., & Robinson, D. (1990). Rehabilitation through clearer thinking: A cognitive model of correctional intervention (Research Brief No. B-04). Ottawa, Ontario: Research and Statistics Branch, Correctional Service of Canada.

Foucault, M. (1977). Discipline and punish: The birth of the prison. New York: Vintage.

Fox, K. (2001). Self-change and resistance in prison. In J. Gubrium & J. Holstein (Eds.), Institutional selves: Troubled identities in a postmodern world (pp.176–192). Oxford, England: Oxford University Press.

Gamberg, H., & Thomson, A. (1994). The illusion of prison reform: Corrections in Canada. New York: Peter Lang.

Garland, D. (1996) The limits of the sovereign state: strategies of crime control in contemporary society' British Journal of Criminology, 36 (4), 445–471.

Gendreau, P., & Goggin, C. (1996). Principles of effective programming with offenders. Forum on Corrections Research, 8 (3), 38–40.

Gendreau, P., Little, T., & Goggin, C. (1996). A meta-analysis of the predictors of adult offender recidivism: What works! Criminology, 34 (4), 575–607.

Gendreau, P., & Ross, R. R. (1987). Revivication of rehabilitation: Evidence from the 1980s. Justice Quarterly, 4 (3), 349–408.

Gendreau, P., & Ross, R. R. (1979). Effective correctional treatment: Bibliotherapy for Cynics. Crime & Delinquency, 25 (4), 463–489.

Gilmore, N., & Somerville, M. (1998). A review of the use of LSD and ECT at the prison for women in the early 1960s. Ottawa, Ontario: Correctional Service of Canada.

Globe and Mail. (1999, November 17). Ontario apologizes for grandview abuse, 3.Glover, J. (1999). Humanity: A moral history of the twentieth century. London: Jonathan Cape.

Goffman, E. (1961). *Asylums.* Garden City, NY: Anchor Books.

Grandview Agreement Between the Grandview Survivors Support Group and the Government of Ontario. June 30, 1994.http://www.grandviewsurvivors.on.ca/ga1.html July 8, 2002.

Gorman, K. (2001). Cognitive behaviorism and the holy grail: The quest for a universal means of managing offender risk. *Probation Journal, 48* (1), 3–9.

Hamilton, J., & Jensvold, M. (1992). Personality, psychopathology and depression in women. In L. Brown & M. Ballou (Eds.), *Personality and psychopathology: Feminist Reappraisals* (pp. 116–143). London: The Guilford Press.

Hannah-Moffat, K. (2002) Creating choices: reflecting on choices. In P. Carlen (Ed.) *Women and punishment. The struggle for justice* (pp.199–219). Cullompton, Devon, England: Willan.

Hannah-Moffat, K. (2001). *Punishment in disguise. Penal governance and federal imprisonment of women in Canada.* Toronto: University of Toronto Press.

Hannah-Moffat, K. (2000) Re-forming the prison-rethinking our ideas. In K. Hannah-Moffat and M. Shaw (Eds.), *An Ideal Prison? Critical Essays on Women's Imprisonment in Canada* (pp.30–40). Halifax: Fernwood.

Hannah-Moffat, K. (1995). Feminine-fortresses: Women-centred prisons? *The Prison Journal, 75* (2), 135–164.

Hannah-Moffat, K., & Shaw, M. (2001). *Taking risks: Incorporating gender and culture into the classification and assessment of federally sentenced women in Canada.* Ottawa, Ontario: Status of Women Canada.

Hannah-Moffat, K., & Shaw, M. (2000). Thinking about cognitive skills? Think Again! *Criminal Justice Matters, 39,* 8–9.

Heney, L. & Kristiansen, C. (1998). An analysis of the impact of prison on women survivors of childhood sexual abuse. In J. Harden & M. Hill (Eds.), *Breaking the rules: Women in prison and feminist therapy* (pp. 29–44). New York: Haworth Press.

Jimenez, M. A. (1997). Gender and psychiatry: Psychiatric conceptions of mental disorders in women, 1960–1994. *Affilia, 12* (2), 154–175.

Kantrowitz, R., & Ballou, M. (1992). A feminist critique of cognitive-behavioral therapy. In L. Brown & M. Ballou (Eds.), *Personality and psychopathology: Feminist Reappraisals* (pp. 70–87). London: The Guilford Press.

Kemshall, H. (2002) Effective practice in probation: an example of 'advanced liberal' responsibilities? *The Howard Journal, 41* (1), 41–58.

Kendall, K. (2002) Time to think again about cognitive behavioural programmes. In P. Carlen (Ed.) *Women and punishment. The struggle for justice* (pp.182–198). Cullompton, Devon, England: Willan.

Kendall, K. (2000). Psy-ence fiction: Inventing the mentally disordered female prisoner. In K. Hannah-Moffat & M. Shaw (Eds.), *An ideal prison? Critical essays on women's imprisonment in Canada* (pp. 82–93). Halifax, Nova Scotia: Fernwood Publishing.

Kendall, K. (1998). Evaluation of programs for female offenders. In R. Zaplin (Ed.), *Female offenders: Critical perspectives and effective interventions* (pp. 361–379). Gaithersburg, MD: Aspen Publishers.

Kendall, K. (1994). Therapy behind prison walls: A contradiction in terms? *Prison Service Journal, 96,* 2–11.

Kendall, K. (1993). *Program evaluation of therapeutic services at the prison for women.* Ottawa, Ontario: Correctional Service of Canada.

Laframboise, D. (1997, November 8). Who's the victim now? *Globe and Mail,* D3.

Laishes, J. (1997). *Mental health strategy for women offenders.* Ottawa, Ontario: Correctional Service of Canada.

Laishes, J., & Lyth, S. (1996). *Intensive healing (mental health) program.* Ottawa, Ontario: Correctional Service of Canada.

Linehan, M. (1993a). *Cognitive-behavioral treatment of borderline personality disorder.* New York: The Guilford Press.

Linehan, M. (1993b). *Skills training manual for treating borderline personality disorder.* New York: The Guilford Press.

Linehan, M., & Heard, H. (1992). Dialectical behavior therapy for borderline personality disorder. In J. Clarkin, J, Marziali, E., & Munroe-Blum, H. (Eds.), *Borderline personality disorder: Clinical and empirical perspectives* (pp. 248–267). New York: The Guilford Press.

Loucks, A., & Zamble, E. (1999). Predictors of recidivism: In serious female offenders. Canada searches for predictors common to both men and women. *Corrections Today,* February, 26–32.

McCann, R., Ball, E., & Ivanoff, A. (no date). DBT with an inpatient forensic population: The CMHIP forensic model. Unpublished paper.

McDonagh, D. (2002) The Correctional Service of Canada's correctional/forensic adaptation of dialectial behaviour therapy. Paper presented at the XXVIIth International Congress on Law and Mental Health, Amsterdam, The Netherlands, July 12.

McMahon, M. (1999). *Women on guard, discrimination and harassment in corrections.* Toronto: University of Toronto Press.

Martinson, R. (1974). What works? Questions and answers about prison reform. *Public Interest, 35,* 22–54.

Maynard, M., & Purvis, J. (1994). Doing feminist research. In M. Maynard & J. I. Purvis (Eds.), *Researching women's lives from a feminist perspective* (pp. 1–9). London: Taylor and Francis.

Mitford, J. (1973). *Cruel and unusual punishment.* New York: Random House.

Pawson, R., & Tilley, N. (1997). *Realistic evaluation.* London: Sage.

Pollock, J (1998) *Counseling women in prison.* Thousand Oaks, California: Sage.

Pollack, S. (1993) Opening the window on a dark day: A program evaluation of the peer support team at the Kingston prison for women. Unpublished master's thesis. Carleton University School of Social Work, Ottawa, Ontario.

Pollack, S. (1994). Opening the window on a very dark day: A program evaluation of the peer support team at the Kingston prison for women. *Forum on Correctional Research, 6* (1), pp. 36–38.

Pollack, S. (2000a). Reconceptualizing women's agency and empowerment: Challenges to self-esteem discourse and women's lawbreaking. *Women and Criminal Justice, 12* (1), 75–89.

Pollack, S. (2000b). *Outsiders inside: The social context of women's lawbreaking and imprisonment.* Unpublished doctoral dissertation, University of Toronto, Toronto, Ontario.

Pope-Davis, D., & Coleman, H. (1997). *Multicultural counselling competencies: Assessment, education and training, and supervision.* Thousand Oaks: Sage.

Proctor, D., & Kendall, K. (2001). Experimentation on prisoners. Paper presented at the Women's Resistance: From Victimization to Criminalization Conference, Ottawa, Ontario.

Rose, N. (1999). *Governing the soul. The shaping of the private self* (2nd ed.). London: Free Association Books.

Ross, R., & Ross, R. (1995). *Thinking straight. The reasoning and rehabilitation program for delinquency prevention and offender rehabilitation.* Ottawa, Ontario: Air Training and Publications.

Ross, R., & Fabiano, E. (1985). *Time to think: A cognitive model of delinquency prevention and offender rehabilitation.* Johnson City, TN: Institute of Social Sciences and Arts.

Ross, R., Fabiano, E. and Ewles, C.D. (1988) Reasoning and Rehabilitation. *International Journal of Offender Therapy and Comparative Criminology, 32,* 29–36.

Ross, R, & Fabiano (1986) Female Offenders: Correctional Afterthoughts. Jefferson: North Carolina: McFarland.

Ross, R. & McKay, H.B. (1979) *Self-Mutilation.* Toronto: Lexington Books.

Rossiter, A. (2000). The postmodern feminist condition: New Conditions for Social Work. In Barbra Fawcett, Brid Featherstone, Jan Fook, & Amy Rossiter (Eds), *Practice and research in social work: Postmodern feminist perspectives* (pp. 24–37). New York: Routledge.

Saidman, L., & Chato-Manchuk, F. (No date). *Intensive treatment program for female offenders.* Burnaby, British Columbia: Burnaby Correctional Centre for Women. Unpublished document.

Scheel, K. (2000). The empirical basis of dialectical behavior therapy: Summary, critique, and implications. *Clinical Psychology, 7* (1), 68–86.

Sharp, B.(2000) *Changing criminal thinking: a treatment program.* Lanham, Maryland: American Correctional Association.

Shaw, M. (1997). *Conflicting agendas: Evaluating feminist programs for women offenders.* Unpublished doctoral dissertation, University of Nottingham, England.

Solicitor General Canada. (1998). *Women offenders: The corrections and conditional release act five years later. Toward just, peaceful and safe society.* Ottawa, Ontario: Solicitor General Canada.

Somerville, M., & Gilmore, N. (2000). *A report on research on inmates in federal penitentiaries.* Ottawa, Ontario. Prepared for the Correctional Service of Canada.

Stanley, L., & Wise, S. (1990). Method, methodology and epistemology in feminist research processes. In L. Stanley (Ed.), *Feminist praxis* (pp. 20–60). London: Routlege.

Stewart, B. (2001). Not a country club. *Macleans,* April 9, 34–38.

Stone, M. (Ed.). (1986). *Essential papers on borderline disorders.* New York: New York University Press.

Swenson, C. (2000). How can we account for DBT's widespread popularity? *Clinical Psychology, 7* (1), 87–91.

Task Force on Federally Sentenced Women (1990) *Creating Choices. The report of the task Force on Federally Sentenced Women.* Ottawa: Ministry of the Solicitor General.

Toch, H. (1992). *Mosaic of despair: Human breakdowns in prison* (Rev. ed.). Washington, DC: American Psychological Association.

Townsend, E.(1998) *Good intentions over ruled.* Toronto: University of Toronto Press.

Trupin, E., Stewart, D., Boesky, L., McClung, B., & Beach, B. (no date). Effectiveness of a dialectical behavior therapy program for incarcerated female juvenile offenders. Unpublished manuscript.

Turner, R. (2000). Understanding dialectical behavior therapy. *Clinical Psychology, 7* (1), 95–98.

Vanstone, M. (2000). Cognitive-behavioral work with offenders in the United Kingdom: A history of influential endeavour. *The Howard Journal, 39*(2), 171–183.

Vennard, J., Sugg, D., & Hedderman, C. (1997). Part I: The use of cognitive-behavioral approaches with offenders—Messages from the research. In Home Office Research and Statistics Directorate (Ed.), *Changing offenders' attitudes and behavior: What works?* (Home Office Research Study 171), 1–35. London: Home Office Research and Statistics Directorate.

Warner, A. (1998). *Implementing choices at regional facilities: Program proposals for women offenders with special needs.* Ottawa, Ontario: Correctional Service of Canada.

Warner, S. (1996). Visibly special? Women, child sexual abuse and special Hospitals. In C. Hemingway (Ed.), *Special women? The experience of women in the special hospital system* (pp. 59–76). Aldershot, Hants England: Avebury.

Warner, S. (2001). Disrupting identity through visible therapy: A feminist post-structuralist approach to working with women who have experienced child sexual abuse. *Feminist Review, 68* (Summer), 115–139.

Wirth-Cauchon, J. (2001). *Women and borderline personality disorder.* New Brunswick, New Jersey : Rutgers University Press.

Zanarini, M., Frankenburg, F., Reich, D., Marino, M., Haynes, M., & Gunderson, J. (1999). Violence in the lives of adult borderline patients. *The Journal of Nervous and Mental Disease, 187* (2), 65–71.

CHAPTER 5

Stages of Gendered Disadvantage in the Lives of Convicted Battered Women

Elizabeth Dermody Leonard

Introduction

A battered woman is somebody that is abused, used, talked down to, treated like she's less than a human, a sub-species. She's somebody that someone else can get a nut off of abusing and hitting and pounding on, watching her bleed, watching her teeth knocked loose or out, looking at her face looking like hamburger, that controls the situation. Basically that's the whole thing; that's the key. It's a control. Running someone else's life, someone else having the power over you to dominate, to put you down, to make you grovel, make you show fear. I wished many times that somebody would just pull the trigger and blow my head off. I wouldn't have to deal with it. But that is what a battered woman is to me—you have no self-esteem, you don't like yourself, you don't love yourself, you don't know who you are, you are a shadow of this "wonderful" man, you don't count. You are Mrs. whatever. You don't have an identity. I thought my name was 'bitch' until I came here." [In 1977, Ellen received a 7 year-to-Life sentence and remains in prison with no parole date. Her two male co-defendants (including a son age 14 when he shot his father) were both released in the mid-1980s[1]

---

1. The quotes in this chapter are from women serving some form of life sentence or life without the possibility of parole for the death of abusive partners. Interviews

No one knows how many convicted survivors like Ellen currently live out their lives behind the walls of America's female prisons—women held criminally responsible for the death of abusive male partners. These formerly battered women exist, close to invisible, as they negotiate and survive the multilayered gendered realities of our society. Their status as female in a male-dominated society lessens their relevance and credibility. As battered women, they are silenced and isolated socially by their abusers and by the shame they feel as a result of ongoing victimization. When they respond to their mates' lethality by using deadly force, prosecutors, judges, and juries ignore their self-protective motivations. Convicted battered women are then incarcerated by the same criminal justice system that largely ignored their cries for help. According to various estimates, 800 to 2,000 women serve prison sentences for killing their abusers. However, these estimates may be conservative (Leonard, 2002). The number of convicted survivors remains unknown for several reasons: criminal justice agencies do not collect systematic data on victim-offender relationships in all homicide cases; trial transcripts of battered women who kill often are devoid of evidence of abuse; correctional files rarely reveal which women killed abusive partners; after incarceration, many women do not reveal the context of the homicide, nor do they always identify themselves as domestic violence survivors. Thus, their invisibility continues.

Ellen's experiences as a survivor of severe domestic violence and as a woman convicted in the death of her husband mirror those of many other women living out their lives in U. S. prisons. While each woman's life has its own distinctiveness, closer examination of their experiences reveals shared patterns and processes—patterns and processes structured around the gendered nature of our society. Throughout these violent relationships, gender norms and expectations dictate the actions and responses of violent men, traumatized women, family and friends, the criminal justice system, communities of faith, and other social institutions. The patriarchal legacy has shaped a society stratified by gender, which continues to facilitate and enable intimate violence against women with its myriad destructive consequences, while it overpunishes those women who defend themselves with lethal force. This chapter describes the difficulties encountered by battered women who kill abusive partners as their paths take them from victim to prisoner. The voices of convicted survivors at one California prison provide vivid examples of gender-systematic disadvantages many women confront along this pathway.

---

were conducted in the course of the author's doctoral research (See Convicted Survivors: The Imprisonment of Battered Women Who Kill, 2002, State University of New York Press).

I talked to one minister and I was told, "Oh, you're not loving him enough. Just love him a little harder." Then I went to a psychiatrist and he told me it was all our fault. It was all women's fault because we are always trying to castrate the man. So I figured, this man has gone through years of schooling, he's a psychiatrist, he works in Beverly Hills with all the others getting big bucks, I figured he knew what he was doing. I figured it must be my fault. I was just told it was. So I stopped trying to figure out what was wrong, because it was all my fault.

Women and Intimate Violence

To understand what makes this form of violence against women so common and how a society can allow so many relationships to move from dating to death, it is essential to examine domestic violence, woman/wife battering, or intimate partner violence within its broader historical, political, cultural, and socioeconomic conditions. Around the world, gender specific violence is a major social and health problem for women. Lori Heise's (1994) summary of 35 studies from 24 countries finds that up to one-half of the women surveyed reported physical abuse and even more reported ongoing emotional and psychological abuse. In most countries, rape and sexual abuse by intimates is not considered a crime and women victims often do not define forced sex with a husband or cohabitant as rape (United Nations Children's Fund, 2000). Social norms, laws, policies, and sheer physical strength systematically have given men more power than women. Therefore, explanations of domestic violence that assert gender neutrality assume an equality of power in heterosexual relationships and ignore centuries of male-dominated social systems and structures.

Despite nearly four decades of increasing awareness, policy improvements, and resource development, violence against women by their intimate partners continues to permeate American society. While intimate relationships are expected to act as a shield against the violence that exists in the public arena, with alarming regularity, the relationship itself poses the greatest risk for the health, well-being, and lives of women. American women are most vulnerable to assault and injury not on the job or on the nation's highways and city streets, rather, women are in greatest danger in their own homes at the hands of men who claim to love them.

In the United States, women are more likely to be attacked, injured, raped, or killed by a current or former male partner than by all other types of assailants combined (Browne, 1992; Maguire & Pastore, 1996; Violence Against Women Grants Office, 1997). Male intimates inflict more injuries on women than auto accidents, muggings, and rape combined (Hart, 1990a; Jones, 1996; McLeer & Anwar, 1989; Stark, 1990). A female assault victim is more likely to need medical care if her attacker is an intimate rather than a stranger—injuries occur nearly twice as often when the offender is an intimate (Bachman, 1994). In 1994, women accounted for nearly 40 percent of hospital emergency room visits for violence-related injuries and represent the vast majority of individuals (84 percent) treated for injuries inflicted by intimates (Greenfeld, Rand, Craven, Klaus, Perkins, Ringel, Warchol, Maston, & Fox, 1998). In contrast, men are at greatest risk of being physically assaulted by a stranger (Tjaden & Thoennes, 2000). Violence by an intimate partner accounts for about 2 percent of the violence sustained by males (Greenfeld et al., 1998).

The National Crime Victimization Survey (NCVS) estimates that, in over 90 percent of domestic violence incidents, the victim was female; women experience over 10 times as many violent episodes by an intimate than males (Buzawa & Buzawa, 1996). Overall, a woman is four times more likely than a man to be raped, assaulted, and/or stalked by a current or former intimate partner (64 percent compared to 16 percent) (Tjaden & Thoennes, 2000).

While research shows that the battering of female partners crosses all socioeconomic levels, all racial, ethnic, religious, and age groups (Collins, Schoen, Joseph, Duchon, Simantov, & Yellowitz, 1999; Bachman & Saltzman, 1995; Silverman, Raj, Mucci, & Hataway, 2001), younger women with fewer economic and educational resources, and who are divorced or separated appear to be at increased risk (Healey, Smith, & O'Sullivan, 1998). While the private nature of domestic violence keeps the actual rates of occurrence unknown, rates of incidence and prevalence in the United States suggest that it permeates all levels of society. At least 1.8 to 4.8 million American women are abused in their homes each year (Diaz, 1996; Hofford & Harrell, 1993; Tjaden & Thoennes, 2000). Conservatively, at least 20 percent to 25 percent of adolescent girls have experienced physical or sexual violence from a dating partner (Silverman et al., 2001; James, West & Deters, 2000; Makepeace, 1999). Approximately 1 million women are stalked each year, most often by a current or former intimate partner (Tjaden & Thoennes, 2000). Three out of four women who are raped and/or physically assaulted are victimized by current or former husbands, cohabiting partners, or dates (Tjaden & Thoennes, 1998). Campbell (1995) reports that up to 45 percent of battered women are being raped on an ongoing basis by their partners; when the rapist is a current or former partner the risk of injury increases (Tjaden & Thoennes, 2000). Of women who seek prenatal care, approximately 25 percent are abused by their partners, resulting in fetal injury, miscarriage, hemorrhage, and low birthweight (American Medical Association, 1992). Partner violence has been linked to many of the suicide attempts made by females (Flitcraft, 1995; Silverman et al., 2001).

Women are more likely to be killed by an intimate partner than by a combination of all other categories of assailants (Moracco, Runyan, & Butts, 1998). Approximately one-third to one-half of female murder victims are killed by their intimate partners (Healey & Smith, 1998; Rennison & Welchans, 2000). In 1998, nearly three out of four homicides by intimates had a female victim (Rennison & Welchans, 2000). The actual percentage may be even higher—a Florida mortality review found that of 321 domestic homicides, the state's Department of Law Enforcement had identified correctly only 72 percent or 230 deaths as domestic fatalities (Johnson, Li, & Websdale, 1998). While the last two decades have seen an overall decline in intimate homicides, men have benefited from this decrease much more than their female counterparts. Between 1976 and 1997, the number of male victims among blacks dropped by 77 percent, while female victims declined by 46 percent; among whites, the number of male victims decreased by 55 percent compared to a 14 percent drop in female victimization (Fox & Zawitz, 1999). Disturbingly, between 1997 and 1998, the number of white female victims increased 15 percent; white women are the only category of victims for whom intimate partner homicide has not decreased substantially since 1976 (Rennison & Welchans, 2000). At present, women are eight times more likely than men to be killed by an intimate (Rennison & Welchans, 2000). In their discussion of conjugal jealousy and violence around the world, Wilson and Daly (1992) report that American women are at an especially high risk for partner homicide:

> Women in the United States today face a statistical risk of being slain by their husbands that is about five to ten times greater than that faced by their European counterparts, and in the most violent American cities, risk is five times higher again. It may be the case that men have proprietary inclinations oward their wives everywhere, but they do not everywhere feel equally entitled to act upon them (p. 96).

In sum, violence against women occurs predominantly in the context of intimate partner violence. Whether a woman is raped, beaten, and/or stalked, her current or former husband, boyfriend, or lover, is the most frequent and most dangerous assailant. The same pattern does not hold for males. Dobash and Dobash (1979) observe: "The home is a dangerous place for women (and children) and markedly less dangerous for men" (p. 20). Clearly, intimate partner violence is a social problem structured by gender and rooted in gender inequality.

Violent Women?

A major debate in the discourse on intimate abuse is the question of "mutual combat" and the related claim that women are as violent as men in intimate relationships. While both men and women can be verbally or physically aggressive, evidence clearly shows that when abuse of intimate partners occurs, the victim of the most severe and most frequent physical abuse is much more likely to be a wife or girlfriend rather than a husband or boyfriend. Bonnie Campbell, former director of the U.S. Department of Justice's Violence Against Women Office, argues that assertions of women battering men to the degree that men batter women are part of a backlash:

> The more success we have as a society in highlighting violence against
> women, the more of a backlash we get...I view a lot of this talk about
> battered men as a significant part of the backlash (Crary, 2001, p. 1).

Men are sometimes physically and psychologically abused by their wives or girlfriends, but compared to most women, they have many more options to prevent or escape the violence. The vast majority of men are not physically or economically restrained from walking out the front door to never return should their wives become abusive. In most, though certainly not all cases of female-to-male violence, her violence is self-defensive in nature.

Those studies that report mutual combat, or high rates of female-to-male abuse, most often derive their findings from a survey instrument widely used in domestic violence research, the Conflict Tactics Scale (CTS). This scale has been criticized widely by those who challenge the instrument's inherent assumption of gender equality, which ignores the very real physical, symbolic, social, economic, sexual, and power differences between women and men (Dobash & Dobash, 1988; Ferraro, 2001; Pagelow, 1985; Stark & Flitcraft, 1996). The scale, for example, fails to measure intent, injury, or fear, opting to make simple counts of specific acts, such as hits, kicks, or attempts to hit or kick. When decontextualized in this manner, a woman's self-defensive reactions become the equivalent of her male partner's brutal and coercive acts. Further, claims that men and women are equally violent in relationships fail to consider the prevalence and impact of marital rape, or sexual assault in intimate relationships, virtually all of which are perpetrated by men. Thus, studies using the CTS routinely produce findings that support the idea of violent women and mutual combat. Further, the issue of husband battering as a serious problem appears to be limited to the United States. Dobash and Dobash (1992) explain this exclusivity as the result of "a narrow and restricted approach to the research and an unswerving reliance on a seriously flawed data collection instrument" (p. 275).

In addition, gender-blind analyses ignore the role that perceptions of risk play on a victim's responses and choices. A huge disparity exists in the prospect of serious bodily harm from being kicked, punched, or raped by a typical unarmed man versus a typical unarmed woman. On average, men are larger and physically stronger than women, so they can easily do greater bodily harm than is done to them, they can use nonviolent means to protect themselves from harm, or they can leave the scene without being physically restrained. Both parties are well aware of these physical differences—physical threat is a powerful dynamic in male to female abuse. Undoubtedly there are violent wives and some battered husbands, but the proportion of systematically abused husbands to abused wives is relatively small, and certainly the phenomenon does not amount to a "syndrome" as popularly reported. Where female to male abuse does exist, Kantor and Jasinski (1998) observe, "available evidence suggests that women's physical violence is less injurious and less likely to be characterized as motivated by attempts to dominate or terrorize the partner" (p. 10). When we take into account criminal justice data, medical data, field research, and surveys that use other methods of data collection than the CTS, it appears that when family violence researchers claim than women are as violent as men, they base their opinions on faulty data and flawed assumptions about gender and the family. Evidence fails to support a large-scale "syndrome" that begins to compare to the widespread, serious, and systematic abuse of intimate violence against women. Therefore, omitting analysis of gender and power from domestic violence research misrepresents the full reality of this form of interpersonal violence and leaves women at a disadvantage.

> It would have been different if I would have been six foot two and him five foot seven. Mutual combat is between two men in a bar. It's an antiquated term. It doesn't apply to women. And I know there's a lot of women out there with the Tae Bo and all that stuff that I see on TV, but that's just not how it was.

The Question

Inevitably, the question that arises in the minds of many, if not most people who hear about intimate violence is the question: Why doesn't she just leave? That this question is routinely asked in the absence of the more relevant questions: Why is he hitting her? Why doesn't he stop beating her? Why doesn't he leave? Why won't he let her leave? reveals the widespread gender bias of our society. The question why doesn't she leave? assumes her behavior, rather than his, is unusual and in need of explanation. The question makes the woman, rather than the abusive man, responsible for stopping the violence. This bias suggests an implicit acceptance of the abuser's actions as falling within a normative range of male behavior. Furthermore, the question assumes:

1. **Leaving is easy or simple**—when abusers restrict their partners' access to finances and outside social support; some men sabotage cars, rip telephones off walls, threaten, and go to other extreme measures to ensure women stay.
2. **The woman has not made attempts to leave**—when some women do leave, batterers locate and threaten them or their children; restraining orders are not enforced, and abusers force their return.
3. **The woman has not left**—when half or more do leave, they continue to be stalked and harassed.
4. **Leaving stops the violence**—when, in fact, separation often escalates the violence.

Furthermore, women who leave are at a substantially higher risk of being killed by their abusers than those who stay (Block & Christakos, 1995; Hart, 1988; Wilson & Daly, 1992), and they remain at increased risk for at least two years (Walker, 1992).

> *I knew Norman would find me. He's found me before. I'd always left him when my daughter was out of state. I knew he couldn't get to her. That was always in the summer. I would leave and not tell anyone I had left. And he always found me. I don't know how it happened, because I'd go someplace and be a prisoner in that place because I wouldn't go outside. I'd hide in the car, do something. I'd think I did it all right. I'd go somewhere there's a kitchenette to stock up and hide for a while. The last time I made it all the way to Arizona, Route 66. I was hiding in one of these little hotels, no phones in the hotel, no nothing. I was hoping he'd think I went on the main drags, not the tacky old ones. And he found me. I took the cottage in the back, didn't use my real name. He found me somehow; I came around the building, and I froze. I'd just gone two buildings down to a little market. I came back and there he was, leaning against his car. But from that day, I lost it. I became a prisoner in my own home. Couldn't go anywhere. If he'd call and the phone was*

busy, then he'd get mad because I was on the phone. If he called and I answered the phone, he'd get mad because I answered the phone. I couldn't even go grocery shopping without him, and if I did, I had a time limit. I was a prisoner. These bars mean nothing. These fences, they're nothing. I'm freer in here than I was out there with him.

Actually, many women do leave and go on to healthy, satisfying relationships with non-abusive men. In fact, they leave at high rates. And their leaving is often an act of courage because it means having to cope with enormous fear as well as financial insecurity. But there is nothing wrong with or odd about those who remain in abusive relationships. For some women, staying with an abuser is a strategy for survival. The reality is that it is much easier to get into an abusive relationship than it is to get out of one.

Many factors, highly gendered in nature, interact to keep a woman in a relationship with an abusive mate, despite the likelihood that the violence will increase in frequency and severity over time. Women are socialized to invest themselves in their relationships and taught to derive their identities from them. Many female victims feel responsible for the abuse and make every attempt to resolve conflicts and create peace in hopes of avoiding future violence. Many women believe or hope that abusive partners can or will change. A battered woman may view her abusive partner as "sick" and dependent on her for survival. Romantic ideology that insists, "the course of true love never runs smooth" and "true love conquers all" socializes women to "stick it out" and "stand by your man" at their own peril. Abusive events occur at intervals around otherwise ordinary interactions and the emotional attachment a woman feels for her partner can be difficult to overcome. Religious ideologies frequently elevate the institution of marriage above the safety of women, often leaving victims with the idea that they must choose either their faith or their lives and safety. Traditional beliefs, reinforced by family and friends, often work against a victimized woman's departure from the home and her mate.

I prayed a lot, fasted a lot, cried a lot. It made it even worse, him being a pastor and all. I wore glasses and my hair was long, so I'd fix my hair so people at church couldn't see. I was always protecting him. I thought he'd get himself together. I was very confused. I couldn't figure out why I was going through what I was going through because all I'd ever been for him was a helpmate. And I'd picked him up so much. So many times I was in his corner. I just didn't know what to do. I was very submissive to him. I said little because I thought if I said much it would make him worse. But it didn't help me at all. I tried so hard to do the right thing within my marriage, with my husband. My situation was: "God will work it out."

Over time, most abusers isolate their partners from outside social support, leaving women with few alternatives to staying in a violent home. While shelters and safe houses provide vital support services for battered women and their children, they have not been able to keep up with the need. Women with children may stay with an abuser out of fear of losing custody of their children, either in the divorce settlement or through later kidnapping by the man. In general, the batterer maintains sole control over family finances restricting his partner's access to funds that could enable her to leave. The woman often fears for the economic well-being of her children if she leaves; current studies on homelessness estimate that about 50 percent of homeless women and children are homeless because they are fleeing violent men (U.S. Conference of Mayors, 1998). Fear of retaliation, generated by the batterer's actual threats of suicide, his threats against her, the children, and/or family and friends, causes many women to remain in abusive relationships. In addition, researchers and practitioners cite the lack of help given to battered women by the police and other criminal justice representatives among the factors that keep women trapped in abusive relationships. Despite these complex multiple forces that make it so difficult for abused women to leave, "those who are battered and who remain in battering relationships are regarded as more pathological, more deeply troubled, than the men who batter them" (Schneider, 2000, p. 23).

> *I had surgery to repair damage and the pain I'd been living with from his assaults. It was a matter of, "Well, how do we know you didn't do this to yourself?" I think about it now and I'm like, if the [police] scenario and their opinion was, "You expect us to believe that this man could go to work and function at work and yet come home and be an animal?" I'm like, "Yeah." Then they turn around and, "How do we know you didn't do this to yourself?" So it's okay if he can. It's impossible to believe that he can do this but it's okay to think I could be so sick?*

Domestic Violence and the Law

Historically, religion, law, traditional family structure, the economy, and other social institutions routinely supported the authority of men over women. Marital traditions and laws have given husbands the right to control their wives, by force if necessary. Roman law allowed husbands to "chastise, divorce, or kill their wives for engaging in behavior that they themselves engaged in daily" (Dobash & Dobash, 1979, p. 37). Napoleon decreed that women must be legal minors their entire lives. English jurist Sir Edward Coke (1552–1634) captured male household supremacy with the still familiar saying, "a man's home is his castle." British common law permitted wife beating but restricted the size of the husband's punishment device to a "rod not thicker than his thumb" (Dobash & Dobash, 1977; U.S. Commission on Civil Rights, 1982). "Coverture," a British legal doctrine, declared a husband and wife a single legal entity—marriage suspended her legal identity and right to own property, and marital rape was not considered a crime. Under British common law,

> To become a wife meant to take on a special legal status, a status that excluded the woman from the legal process, placed her in the same category as children and servants, demanded surrender and obedience, and elevated her husband to the position of lawmaker, judge, jury, and executioner (Dobash & Dobash, 1979, p. 61).

Under the same legal system, if a man killed his wife, his action was classified as a homicide; if a woman killed her husband, her action was classified as an act of treason and she would be drawn (i.e. disemboweled) and burned alive (Dobash & Dobash, 1979). These laws and others like them codified a married woman's inferior social and legal status as well as her loss of identity and autonomy.

American law, directly influenced by British legal tradition, supported a husband's right to discipline his wife. In the mid-nineteenth century, courts found acceptable "moderate" forms of wife assault, declaring only the more serious forms illegal (Gagne, 1998). In 1871 the state of Alabama withdrew a husband's legal right to beat his wife; a North Carolina court, following suit three years later, softened the repeal:

> If no permanent injury has been inflicted, nor malice, cruelty nor dangerous violence shown by the husband, it is better to draw the curtain, shut out the public gaze, and leave the parties to forget and forgive (U.S. Commission on Civil Rights, 1982, p. 2).

Twentieth century reforms revoked the right of an American husband to beat his wife, but the domestic curtain shows little sign of disintegration. For example, while many batterers rape their female partners, often causing serious physical and psychological damage,[2] defining rape within marriage as

---

2. Physical effects of marital rape include: bruising, vaginal and anal injuries, broken bones, knife wounds, burns, miscarriages, sexually transmitted diseases; psycho-

a crime continues to be controversial. According to the National Research Council,

> A few states have completely eliminated the marital exemption from their law; others have enacted legislation that makes some rapes within marriage a crime; and in other states court actions have essentially overturned the marital exemption (Crowell & Burgess, 1996, p. 127).

Currently, thirty-three states uphold exemptions that shield husbands from rape prosecution, evidence that the majority of states view rape in marriage as a lesser crime than other forms of rape (Bergen, 1999).

> *The sexual abuse didn't start until the last two years. He had a video machine. He had started getting into the triple X-rated movies. He wanted reenactments. If they weren't done to perfection, it was punishment. The sexual abuse got worse and worse. He started using foreign objects. He used a gun on me rectally. A loaded gun. [The night he died] he ripped the nightgown off of me then and started raping me, with the handgun, again. He beat me with the butt end of the gun before he used it on me. He called me names, dirty names…I wished I was dead. I remember begging him to pull the trigger so I wouldn't have to suffer anymore. He said that was too easy. Told me it was too easy.*

Gender-biased ideology results in a pattern of victim-blaming when a man assaults his female intimate. Capturing the seemingly no-win situation abused women encounter, Barbara Hart (1996) reports:

> Unlike other victims of violent crime, battered women are often viewed by the police, the prosecutor, judges, jurors, and probation/parole staff as responsible for the crimes committed against them — responsible either because battered women are believed to "provoke" the perpetrator into violence or because they are believed to have the power to avoid the criminal assault through accommodating the perpetrator's demands. Other victims of violent crime are not seen as culpable for the crimes inflicted on them, but battered women frequently report that criminal justice system personnel appear to consider them "unworthy victims" who are clogging up the courts with unimportant family matters (p. 101).

---

logical effects include: depression, intense fear, suicidal ideation, post-traumatic stress disorder, eating and sleeping disorders, and sexual dysfunction (Bergen, 1999).

The police, every time I called them, they were usually there about 30 minutes or so, but by the time they left, they had me believing I had done something to him to cause it.

Clearly, American law has been resistant to labeling as criminal the actions of men who assault their wives and girlfriends. Consequently, abusive men tend to face little punishment for their violence against women, and female victims receive little protection from them. However, even when particular acts are defined as illegal, and even when policies call for particular responses, there is no guarantee that law enforcement personnel will enforce those laws or consistently follow departmental policies (Belknap, 1995; Caringella-MacDonald, 1997; Ewing, 1997; Gillespie, 1989; Miller, 1993; O'Dell, 1996). Despite recent reforms, Marvin (1997) observes, "law enforcement still does not address domestic violence in the same way it addresses other violent crimes" (p. 65). Police are significantly less likely to arrest in an intimate partner assault compared to a non-intimate partner assault (Eigenberg, Scarborough, & Kappeler, 1996). In a review of arrests in a police department with a pro-arrest policy, of 1,870 domestic violence reports,

Less than one third of the domestic violence cases (28.8 percent)... ended in arrest. Even cases in which the violence was serious enough to charge someone with aggravated or sexual battery often did not end in arrest. These results indicate that the pro-arrest policy used in the police department being studied may not have been forcefully or consistently enacted... [P]olice officers may still have a great deal of discretion in whether or not to make an arrest in domestic violence cases (Bourg & Stock, 1999, pp. 29–30).

Victims' requests for arrests were ignored in 75 percent of the cases examined by Buzawa, Austin, and Buzawa (1995). Along with reluctance to arrest, police are disinclined to enforce domestic violence restraining orders, leaving women at even greater risk of violence (Belknap, 2001). Female officers are more likely to view domestic violence as a serious crime (National Center for Women and Policing, 2001), however, only about 10 percent of police officers in the United States are women (Belknap, 2001).

How many times did I call? Hundreds. How many times did someone show up? If it was women officers on, more. If it was men officers, they'd come an hour, two hours later. Maybe half the times I called, they showed up. Maybe they took him from the home four, three times....

He'd just tried to shoot me earlier... in the afternoon. I called the police.
"What do you want us to do, lady? It's his house. We can't get him out."

While the percentage of women who report domestic violence crimes to police has increased, nearly half still do not report their victimization (Rennison & Welchans, 2000). Most women do not report their victimization because they believe the police can do nothing about it and because they believe that the police would not believe them (Tjaden & Thoennes, 2000). Additional reasons women give for non-reporting include: belief that the incident is a private matter, fear of reprisal, protection of the offender, and police bias (Rennison & Welchans, 2000). In reality, fear of reprisal renders battered women six times more likely not to report the crime than women victims of stranger-perpetrated violent crimes (Zawitz, 1994).

I never called the police. He was brought up in gangs. He told me, "No one ever snitches on anyone." He would tell me some of the things that they would do to snitches in jail. I knew not to call the cops on him because he would get out anyway. If I had called, it would at least have allowed him to know that he had done the wrong thing. You can't get away with continuing to do this. What's funny is, not only did I not call the police, but a minister was next door and he could hear me screaming. He heard everything breaking. He knew Rick was beating me up because it had happened so many times before, yet he didn't call the police. So we put him on the witness stand. "Why didn't you call the police?" "Well, I didn't want to get involved. I didn't want him to come hurt me and my family." No one ever called the police.

Studies show that many who enforce the law hold the same stereotypical views[3] as the general public about battered women and family disputes, stereotypes, which undermine police effectiveness in dealing with both batterer and victim (Andersen, Boulette, & Schwantz, 1991; Ferraro, 1989; Gibbs, 1997). In general, the tendency persists for officers to view women claiming to have been abused as non-credible and unworthy of police time (Belknap, 1995; Hart, 1992). An additional disturbing factor is noted by the National Center for Women and Policing (2001): up to 40 percent of police officer families may

---

3. Common stereotypes include: battered women could leave abusive relationships if they wanted to; women provoke the attack and probably deserve to be hit; women will drop charges against their abusers; domestic violence is a private problem not a criminal issue and is not as serious as violence outside the home; domestic violence is a way of life for some people; the man is the sole head of the household and the wife should obey him.

be experiencing domestic violence, a rate four times higher than the general population.

> *When everything started getting really bad we were living on the base. Unfortunately he was the police. He was a military policeman.*
> *I weighed 80 pounds. He was six foot four and 250 pounds. I saw him as my protector—he was a policeman…I filed 46 different complaints from his assaults and got a restraining order…The neighbors heard me screaming and called the police. When they arrived, Robert went out to meet them, shook hands, talked. He knew them all from work. After that the police just left.*

Battered women not only encounter law enforcement who are reluctant to arrest their attackers, they also confront an increased risk of being arrested themselves if they use physical force to defend themselves (Buzawa & Buzawa, 1993; Ferraro, 1997). Only about 2 percent of women arrested for domestic violence are actually the primary physical aggressors (Healey et al., 1998). Another growing trend further jeopardizes women's help-seeking actions— women victimized by intimates have increasingly found themselves charged with failing to protect their children, even their fetuses, from exposure to domestic violence (Jacobs, 1998; Roth, 2000; Schneider, 2000; Sengupta, 2000).

Police response to domestic violence may be influenced by other components of the criminal justice system as well. If law enforcement experience or perceive a lack of support from prosecutors and judges, they may hesitate to use their full discretionary power in domestic violence situations (Marcus, 1981). As Hofford and Harrell (1993) observe, "Without a policy of strong prosecution, efforts by law enforcement agencies have little impact" (p. 7).

Historically, prosecutors have not been known for their aggressive pursuit of domestic violence offenders (Fagan, 1996; Hart, 1990b; U.S. Commission on Civil Rights, 1982) and these patterns from the past routinely resurface (Caringella-MacDonald, 1997). Prosecution rates vary widely by jurisdiction and where practice does not support criminal justice interventions, the rate of prosecution has been low (Crowell & Burgess, 1996). In many communities, prosecution rates remain low, less than 10 percent for misdemeanor cases (Fagan, 1996). Aggressive prosecution policies are being adopted by many jurisdictions (Freidman & Shulman, 1990), yet, in practice, that may not always work in favor of victims—in some districts, a woman who refuses to testify against her partner may be charged with contempt of court and be incarcerated (Ferraro, 1993).

Buzawa and Buzawa (1996) report that domestic violence crimes often are not treated as seriously as they might deserve in the prosecution process and that, in the limited instances of convictions, sentences are quite lenient. Frequently, bail is set low enough to allow the abuser to be released from custody until a preliminary hearing. It is not uncommon for a man to be released on bail or on his own recognizance almost immediately, allowing him to return home and intimidate or assault his partner.

In many jurisdictions, whether or not to file charges against the batterer is left in the hands of the victim, rather than the district attorney, thus leaving her at increased risk of harm. Making the woman responsible for the batterer's prosecution encourages him to place all the blame for his legal problems on her rather than on his own actions. Prosecution rates are high in jurisdictions where prosecutors pay special attention to battering cases (Crowell & Burgess, 1996), and the vast majority of injured parties cooperate in the pursuit of prosecution (Marcus, 1981). Furthermore, as Zorza (1997) points out:

> The same prosecutors who have refused to go forward without a victim's cooperation when she is alive have no problem prosecuting her abuser without her assistance after the abuser has killed her (p. 7).

Judges exert influence over police and prosecution practices as well as the behaviors of defendants and victims (Goolkasian, 1986). The history of judicial response to domestic violence, however, corresponds to that of law enforcement and prosecutors. While recent statutory and policy changes have produced improvements (Rebovich, 1996), all too often, courtroom decisions reveal leniency for batterers (Bannister, 1993), dismissed or downgraded charges (Hart, 1996; Jacobson & Gottman, 1998), acceptance of stereotypes of women as emotional and unreliable witnesses, and victim-blaming (Hofford & Harrell, 1993). In its recommendation to integrate domestic violence issues into legal education, the American Bar Association Commission on Domestic Violence cites these disturbing examples of judicial failures:

> In Maryland, for example, a victim was killed by her intimate partner after a judge refused to grant her a civil protection order. Recently, another judge expunged a batterer's criminal record for wife abuse in order to allow him to join a country club; the judge reversed his ruling only in response to public outcry. Still another judge modified a custody order and awarded custody of the child to the child's father, despite the fact that the father had abused the child's mother, and had been convicted of killing his first wife (Goelman & Valente, 1997, p. I-5).

Research on courtroom gender bias shows that the judiciary systematically minimizes the violent behavior of men against their female intimates and often blames women for their victimization (Schafran, 1990; Welling, Biren, John-ston, Kuehl, & Nunn, 1990). The Judicial Council of California survey of 425 judges found that nearly half believed many domestic violence allegations are exaggerated and some expressed actual antagonism towards victims of do-mestic violence. The Council's report states:

> Again and again, this committee heard testimony that police officers, district and city attorneys, court personnel, mediators, and judges— the justice system—treated the victims of domestic violence as though their complaints were trivial, exaggerated, or somehow their own fault.... The committee found that *gender bias* contributes to the judicial system's failure to afford the protection of the law to victims of domestic violence (emphasis added)(Welling, et al., 1990, p. 5).

Several decades of legislative reforms have produced an increase in arrests and requests for restraining orders, thus many court systems have had to ad-just procedures and practices to handle the increase (Hofford & Harrell, 1993). While more jurisdictions are making it easier for women to obtain restrain-ing orders, violations of these orders are routinely ignored or not punished seriously (Belknap, 2001; Schafran, 1991).

> *We were separated and I told the lawyer about the abuse. The lawyer told me that it would be best if I got a restraining order. So I went down, and after I typed it all out and took it to the lady, she said I had to pay $125. I didn't have it. She told me that if I had to I could go and take the kids to a shelter for battered women. I said, "No, I don't need that because I don't fit that." She didn't give me any information then about battered women. I didn't get anything to read about battered women until I was in CWAA.[4] A restraining order wouldn't have made any dif-ference anyway, even if I'd gotten one.*

Despite these ongoing inequities, some localities have created specialized domestic violence courts and more jurisdictions consider victims' needs and preferences in regard to sentencing of offenders. However, due to the com-plex nature of domestic violence cases, police, prosecutors, and judges will likely continue to experience frustrations—frustrations with the sheer volume of cases, fearful victims who recant, reluctant witnesses, serial offenders, lack

---

4. Convicted Women Against Abuse (CWAA) is an inmate-led support group for battered women at the California Institution for Women. CWAA was initiated in 1989 by women convicted for the death of their abusive partners.

of treatment programs, child custody issues, and so on (Hofford & Harrel, 1993). The American Bar Association reports:

> The increasing intolerance for lawyers or judges who commit or con-
> done domestic violence suggests that the legal system has begun to
> treat violence against intimate partners as a criminal matter. Despite
> this shift, however, many legal professionals have not been trained
> adequately on appropriate legal interventions for domestic violence
> (Goelman & Valente, 1997).

Recent reforms notwithstanding, women beaten and terrorized by male intimates systematically have been and continue to be disadvantaged and routinely left to their own devices for self-rescue. The gendered social system,
through tradition and ideologies, teaches women and girls to submit and obey,
work it out, invest themselves above all in their relationships, stay for the sake
of the children, and a woman is incomplete without a man to give her an identity and ensure her survival. Additionally, battered women learn to hide and
minimize the violence, to blame themselves for being attacked, and to protect
abusive partners. When victimized women seek help, the gendered norms and
practices that suffuse the criminal justice system perpetuate the same messages. After all, as they hear repeatedly, it's only a domestic dispute.

When the levels of violence and coercive control have gone beyond en-
durance, when attempts to end the relationship have resulted in stalking,
forced return, death threats, and near-lethal assaults, when the legal system
has failed to protect her, a woman may become convinced that her death is
certain. She may see no possible way of escape from the terror and conclude
that only death will end the relationship. In such cases, spousal homicide may
be the culmination of an escalating trajectory of domestic violence. Battering
is the most frequently recurring antecedent to homicide by intimate partners
(Campbell, 1995).

Intimate Homicide and
Convicted Survivors

Gendered Homicide

As in other dimensions of domestic violence, intimate homicide follows
gendered patterns. In general, women are much less likely than men to commit homicide. Males are over nine times as likely than females to commit murder, and women are more likely to be the victims in intimate homicide cases

(Fox & Zawitz, 1999). When women kill, they usually act alone, and their killings are likely to be unplanned, intersexual, intraracial, and intrafamilial (Mann, 1992). While not all homicides by women are related to domestic violence (Brownstein, Spunt, Crimmins, Goldstein, & Langley, 1994; Mann, 1992), between 40 to 93 percent of female-perpetrated spousal homicides involve the killing of an abusive mate (Browne, 1987; Campbell, 1992; Totman, 1978; Wolfgang, 1967).

Spousal homicide studies consistently show striking gender differences in circumstances and outcomes. Wolfgang (1957) introduced the term "victim-precipitated" to describe a killing provoked by the initial aggressive actions of the victim and reported that husbands, much more often than wives, were likely to precipitate their own deaths. Duncan and Duncan (1978) observe:

> Victim-precipitated homicide is significantly associated with mate slayings wherein the husband is the victim…When the husband is the perpetrator, the mate slaying…is frequently unusually brutal (p. 179).

Casenave and Zahn (1992) report the following gender differences in spousal homicides:

1. Only male offenders beat or strangle their victims while women, on the other hand, are more likely to stab or shoot their victims once.
2. When the eventual offenders are women, men tend to be the aggressor in the lethal interaction.
3. When men kill their partners, their actions tend to be more violent than their female counterparts.
4. When women kill, they kill men with whom they cohabit.
5. Men kill their female cohabitants, but they also kill their estranged spouses and their girlfriends.

The deadly assaults on a large proportion of female victims of intimate homicide concern their attempts to leave the relationship (Casenave & Zahn, 1992; Gillespie, 1989; Wilson & Daly, 1992). Even so, Dobash and Dobash (1992) note one factor that appears in both male and female intimate homicides—they both occur in the context of male violence. Steffensmeier and Allan (1998) summarize:

> Wives are far more likely to have been [spousal] victims, and turn to murder only when in mortal fear, after exhausting all their alternatives. Husbands who murder wives, however, have rarely been in fear for their lives. Rather, they are more likely to be motivated by rage at suspected infidelity, and the murder often culminates a period of pro-

longed abuse of their wives. Some patterns of wife killing are almost never found when wives kill husbands: murder-suicides, family massacres, and stalking (p. 22).

Intimate Homicide and Legal Processes

The very legal system that largely failed to respond to their cries for help zealously prosecutes battered women who kill, despite their lack of criminal histories (Browne, 1987; Leonard, 2001; O'Shea, 1993; Walker, 1989). Rarely receiving leniency or compassion (Bannister, 1991), women who kill abusive partners are routinely charged with murder or manslaughter and plead self-defense (Ewing, 1990; Osthoff, 1991). Most, up to 80 percent, are convicted or accept a plea, and many receive long, harsh sentences (Belknap, 2001; Diaz, 1996; Gagne, 1998; Jones, 1994; Osthoff, 1991). In Leonard's (2000; 2002) study of 42 convicted survivors, only two received determinate sentences, the remaining sentences ranged from 7-to-life to 35-to-life, while six women received life without parole. This was the first violent offense for all of these women.

Following the broader pattern of gender bias encountered by females in juvenile and adult justice systems (American Bar Association/National Bar Association, 2001; Bloom, Chesney-Lind, & Owen, 1994; Chesney-Lind & Shelden, 1998; Richie, 1996), ample research documents gender inequities in the indictment, prosecution, and sentence determination of women who kill abusive intimates. Women are more frequently charged with such crimes than men would be (Bannister, 1991; Gillespie, 1989; O'Shea, 1993; Schneider & Jordan, 1981). Women are punished more severely than men for killing their partners (Bannister, 1991; Diaz, 1996; Stout & Brown, 1995). An examination of women on death rows reveals that almost half have a history of abuse, and they are there for the murder of an abusive spouse or lover. Further, women are more likely than men to be sentenced to death on a first offense (O'Shea, 1993).

> I kept telling [the public defender] about the abuse. I kept telling him about the cops coming out to the house and he says, "Well, I could subpoena those records but for every record I could subpoena, for everybody that you tell me that I can call, they'll just have somebody else. I don't think we can do anything here. The only hope I can see for you is either the death penalty or life without parole unless you take a plea bargain." I was never offered a plea bargain. It was always life without or the death penalty.

Conversely, in an analysis of spousal murder defendants, Langan and Dawson (1995) report shorter prison sentences for women than for men. Inexplicably, despite the likelihood of severe sentences for women offenders (Belknap, 2001; Bannister, 1996; Diaz, 1996; Gagne, 1998; Jones, 1994; Osthoff, 1991) this comparison excludes life or death sentences. Yet they also found that wives were not significantly less likely than husbands to receive life sentences. The report further states that four times more wife defendants than husband defendants had been assaulted by their spouse at or around the time of the murder, suggesting victim-precipitation as a common scenario in cases of women who kill. This analysis fails to address the significant gender differences in the circumstances and outcomes of spousal homicide and fails to fully compare sentencing patterns, rendering such comparisons questionable in their explanatory power.

While Missouri may or may not be typical of other states in its sentencing patterns, Stout and Brown's (1995) analysis of prison terms for spousal homicide offenders in Missouri reveals startling inequities, especially when considering the usual circumstances surrounding such incidents. Sixteen of the 18 women had been physically abused by their male partners, but only five were permitted to present evidence in court about the past abuse; nine women received life without the possibility of parole, or life without the possibility of parole for fifty years; four of the women received life with the possibility of parole; the remaining five received sentences of 7 to 19 years. Amazingly, none of the 21 men received sentences of life without parole, or life without possibility of parole for fifty years; half of the men were given a life sentence with the possibility of parole; and 7 men received sentences ranging from 12 to 35 years. Hence, the modal sentence for women in Missouri was more severe than that for men.

Bannister (1991) suggests that judges show lenience toward male spousal homicide offenders because they perceive that "the woman goaded the husband into the act of killing her" (p. 406). Stanko (2001) explains:

> Female criminals...are [seen as] dangerous because the crime they commit is proof of their ability to step beyond what is considered to be the ordinary range of behavior of "real" women....[They] are treated as dangerous because they endanger thinking about women's passivity....[M]ale lawbreakers or deviants are only acting like real men (pp. 15–17).

A battered wife who kills is at a particular disadvantage before the bench if, like most married partners, the couple carried life insurance—she is charged with killing for "financial gain."

Women are punished severely for using a weapon against so-called defenseless husbands or boyfriends. Repeatedly, batterers use their hands, fists, and feet; they choke, smother, and stomp their victims. The average female has neither the training nor sufficient body strength to fend off such an attack. A weapon may be her only recourse to protect herself from the lethal assault, yet the laws of self-defense consider that to be "excessive force," systematically leaving women at a disadvantage. Male-defined laws of self-defense are based largely on assumptions that apply best to situations of adult males fighting adult males (Belt & McDonald, 2000; Dressler, 1997; Schneider, 2000). Castel (1990) argues that the legal requirements for self-defense pleas discriminate against women who kill their abusive partners. Wilson (1993) agrees:

> The requirements of immediate danger, necessary force, reasonable belief and the duty to retreat present almost insurmountable barriers to a self-defense claim in the wife-battery situation (p. 50).

Consequently, Schneider (2000) reports, "Many courts have now accepted the view that there is gender bias in the law of self-defense" (p. 33).

Along with the problematic self-defense paradigm, a number of factors combine to complicate the legal outcomes of what some term "homicidal self-help" (Gagne, 1998; Jones, 1994; Marcus, 1981). Often juries never hear of the pattern of escalating violence as abusive men refuse to let their partners leave or end the relationship. Exculpatory information fails to enter the adjudication process due to the actions of defense attorneys, prosecutors, and judges, as well as the law itself. These legal actors often accept cultural myths and stereotypes about battered women.

> *The DA made a comment to the judge that "the sole purpose of a woman is to satisfy her husband, no matter how bad he treats her." Judge _____ said, "Don't ever say that in front of my wife!"*

According to Gagne (1998), all too often lawyers who represent women defendants have

> *little understanding of the dynamics of wife abuse or the psychological response to chronic violence...Defense attorneys are often unfamiliar with the dynamics of crimes resulting from abuse and know little about defense strategies that could help introduce a defendant's life experiences into evidence (pp. 40–41).*

Moreover, because batterers typically isolate, humiliate, and terrorize their partners behind closed doors, the violence can be hidden from others outside the home (Gibbs, 1997), making it difficult for defense attorneys to produce corroborating evidence of ongoing victimization. Further shrouding the truth, women often find it too painful and humiliating to report sexual violence to male defense attorneys and investigators.

> *I couldn't talk to the lawyer or the police about the rapes and the sexual abuse because they were all males. Maybe if there had been a woman to talk to…*

Prosecutors exercise broad discretion as to what charges, if any, they file (Siegel, 1998). When prosecutors choose to charge women for killing abusive partners, they may do so because they expect it to be an easy conviction—battered women usually admit to the killing. If evidence of domestic violence by the deceased is admitted into evidence, rather than supporting a self-defense argument, it can become a motive for the woman's crime of revenge—she is hysterical and out-of-control or she is cold-blooded and calculating (Gillespie, 1989). In the minority of cases that occur in a non-confrontational or preemptive circumstance, such as hiring someone to kill the man, or shooting him while he sleeps following a prolonged assault or his death threats, prosecutors claim it signals "anarchy" or "open season" on men (Gagne, 1998). In explaining the high rate of convictions, Gillespie (1989) writes:

> The trial courtroom provides a forum for a biased or cynical prosecutor to trot out every myth and stereotype and misconception about women that could conceivably inflame a jury against the defendant and that could encourage the jurors to ascribe the worst possible motive to her actions (p. 23).

> *When the trial was so obviously going in my favor, the DA brought in photos and letters that had nothing to do with the trial but were allowed in to simply "dirty me up," which it did. The judge that I went before did not believe in battered women syndrome. He said, "Battered women syndrome shmendrome." He told me at the very end of my trial that he felt like I was battered far worse and for a longer period of time by [my husband] than by [my boyfriend who died] and that I didn't kill [my husband].*

According to the U.S. Department of Justice et al. (1996), "expert testimony on battering and its effects has now been admitted in all 50 states and the District of Columbia, although considerable variation among and within states remains" (p. iii). Frequently, expert testimony involves the use of the "battered women syndrome (BWS)." BWS, a sub-category of Post Traumatic Stress Disorder (American Psychiatric Association, 1994), is used increasingly as a part of a justification defense and not, in most cases, as a mental health defense

(Walker, 1992). All too often, however, this legal strategy has functioned as reinforcement for old stereotypes of female incapacity and passivity "rather than explaining homicide as a woman's necessary choice to save her own life" (Schneider, 2000, p. 80). Moreover, courts may use BWS as the standard by which a woman's behavior is evaluated. Schuller and Hastings (1996) report, "courts have found the BWS testimony irrelevant on the grounds that the particular battered woman at trial did not fit all aspects of the syndrome" (p. 70). Problematically, the term "syndrome," implying an illness or disorder, and psychopathologizes the woman's behavior (Schuller & Hastings, 1996), behavior that is quite reasonable in the context of her particular situation. For these and other reasons, many experts have raised concerns "that the word 'syndrome' may be misleading...and preferred to refer to evidence or expert testimony 'on battering and its effects' and urged the adoption of this terminology as the standard phrase of reference" (U.S. Department of Justice et al., 1996, p. vii).

Many battered women defendants who remain in jail awaiting and undergoing the adjudication of their cases encounter an additional and unexpected stumbling block that silences them—the misuse or overuse of psychotropic medications. Like women in the general population (Lott, 1994), women prisoners receive antidepressants, sedatives, and tranquilizers at alarmingly high rates compared to their male counterparts (Auerhahn & Leonard, 2000; Culliver, 1993; Genders & Player, 1987; McCorkel, 1996). Under the rubric of "treatment," yet without medical or psychological evaluations, female inmates are routinely drugged with medications such as Elavil, Sinequan, Desyrel, Vivactil, Haldol, Mellaril, Stelazine, Lithium, and Thorazine (Auerhahn & Leonard, 2000; Leonard, 2002). In her autobiographical book on Canadian lifers, Bonny Walford (1987) warns:

> Prison doctors...will prescribe tranquilizers or perhaps sleeping pills...Be sure that your lawyer makes the jury aware that you are on strong tranquilizers, otherwise members of the jury will look at you sitting there relaxed, calm and unemotional, and think, "Well! Isn't she the cold-hearted one!" (p. 118).

A study of convicted survivors at one California prison (Leonard, 2002) reveals a high level of jail-prescribed drugs, in some cases, over the women's objections. These drugs seriously impaired the defendants' ability to effectively participate in their own cases.

11 months of being on Sinequan, and during the trial I took Mellaril four times a day. I fell asleep seven times during the trial. You're not com-

prehending, you're not real aware of what's going on. I'm not in la-la land but I was just mellow, you know, and I didn't know what was going on. I never realized what the seriousness was.

The jail staff…decided I had to be on Mellaril, Lithium, Elavil, Sinequan, Vistaril. I didn't want to take it. I was on all of it during the trial.

During the trial I was on both a tranquilizer and an anti-depressant. I was not able to testify well—I was a zombie. They said I was cold and remorseless, not showing any emotion. I'm articulate—a college graduate with a graduate degree—the meds made me inarticulate.

The counselor or the jail nurse put me on Vistaril and Elavil. I was told to take them and I did. I wanted to and I didn't want to. They kept me on them during the trial. It lasted two months. I stopped the day I came to prison.

I'd seen girls on that medication [Thorazine]…. They were telling me they were going to lock me up if I didn't take them. I said, "I'm not taking them." But it wasn't the judge ordering them, it was just Sybil Brand [LA County Jail]. I think it made a difference that I was a woman.

One California woman prisoner began an advocacy group, Women Prisoners Convicted by Drugging, after being forced by jail staff to take a combination of Valium, Vistaril, Robaxin (a muscle relaxant), Elavil, Benadryl, Phenargan (a sedative), and Tylenol with codeine, dispensed four times daily (Auerhahn & Leonard, 2000). When medications cause muddled thinking, forgetfulness, excessive sleepiness, and flattened affect, a woman's right to present a full self-defense is seriously jeopardized and her civil and human rights are violated (Amnesty International, 1999). Systematically, the battered woman defendant's voice, once silenced by her batterer, is silenced by legal strategies and judicial decisions, and silenced by the mood-altering drugs dispensed in jail.

Post-Conviction Realities

Convicted survivors arrive dazed, terrified, and some have the added burden of sudden withdrawal from psychiatric medications. They are patted down and their bodies searched by predominantly male correctional officers. While this can be humiliating and traumatic for any woman, it may generate flashbacks and severely retraumatize battered women. Women make up about one-fourth of county correctional officers, less than 20 percent of state prison guards, and 11 percent of federal correctional officers (cited in Jurik & Martin, 2001).

I'll never forget when I came through these gates and that door slammed. It was like, "I'm never going to get out of here again and I'll never see my baby again." I'll never forget when I was booked in, they made us strip down. There's men officers walking all over. Stripped down, making us bend over and cough. Putting some lice stuff on us or something. Making us take showers. Talking to us like we were nothing, like we're animals. I'll never forget that. These officers just talk to you like you're nothing. That's very humiliating what they did to me. They still do the same things to you. The men officers sit like in the back while the girls are stripping and stuff.

Many women are able to build networks of support where the healing process can begin. In numerous cases, women, long-silenced, find their voices again. Those who receive indeterminate sentences begin to look to parole in the hopes of returning to their children and families. The majority of women are mothers and their children are forced to "serve time" as well.

How can the system think that the abuse and the crime ended with our guilty conviction? It is just the beginning for our children and loved ones. Our children are left without the physical presence of a parent, they are alone with the feelings of isolation, to cope with the guilt, the shame, the abandonment, the hurt. They're suddenly different, they don't fit in. We try to continue our relationship from behind bars, but we cannot be there physically when they need us, at the precise moment when they need to be held, to wipe away the tears, to give them a hug, to share, to comfort, to laugh, to play—and to see that look in their eyes when they yearn for love and acceptance. They have to make an appointment to see mom to make sure they are home and the phone is free for that one single fifteen minute phone call. They have to put their feelings on hold, waiting for their scheduled visiting day. I find it so sad that so few understand that the suffering continues throughout our incarceration, into the next generation, our grandchildren.

The increasingly punitive nature of the criminal justice system reduces the likelihood of release for convicted battered women with indeterminate sentences. Since the mid-1970s, rates of discretionary parole release have declined significantly (Stinchcombe & Fox, 1999). Legislation designed to keep violent male felons behind bars for longer periods of time inadvertently and unfairly nets these one-time, situational women offenders.

Just as women who use lethal force against their abusers receive disproportionately severe sentences compared with men...women who kill their abusers are treated more harshly by parole boards as well (Diaz, 1996, p. 7).

This phenomenon is even more unwarranted when research shows that violent female offenders are less likely to recidivate than violent male offenders (Steffensmeier & Broidy, 2001).

When convicted survivors appear before predominantly male parole boards, at best, it seems to many like an exercise in futility—at worst, a reenactment of the battering relationship. Typically, parole board hearings simply rehash their trials and plea bargains. During one of Ellen's[5] parole hearings, a Commissioner stated, "So, you let this man abuse you for 16 years, then you manipulated your teenage son into killing his father so you could collect the life *insurance!*"

> *What's it like at Board? Like I am a pile of shit. You get talked to like you're an animal. You have no feelings, you're a cold-blooded murderer. To hear them talkin' I'm worse than Charlie Manson and the whole Family, the Hillside Strangler and Son of Sam, all rolled into one. [After that] your guts are chewed up, you have nightmares, you have flashbacks, your insides are just in total turmoil, it takes you a month or longer to get anything, you know, back in normalcy without just spacing out. All kinds of horrid, horrid memories are back in your life, you're talked down to, you're abused. Don't ever say or think that they are not abusive, they are trained in abuse! It's horrible. They act like you have no feelings, you just literally set out to be the most horrid person in the world. They treat you like you're stupid. They treat you like you have no feelings, emotions, common sense, or anything else. You are everything that your husband told you, plus some.*

Board members routinely dismiss a woman's attempt to add to the record any newly recalled information, or newly gained insights to her situation. Prison psychiatrists, predominantly male, conduct psychiatric evaluations on prisoners and prepare a report for the parole board's review. A woman who has endured years of coercive control at the hands of her male partner is likely find it difficult to discuss intimate traumatic experiences with male authority figures, psychiatrists and parole commissioners alike. She may find it especially difficult to express herself freely and clearly when scrutinized by a particularly stern or authoritarian male.

> *I had no problem with my first evaluation done by Dr. ___. She knew me. [It was] a good evaluation. Later when [the governor]got tough on lifers paroling, only psychiatrists could do evaluations and they brought in ___.*

---

5. See opening quote.

He's the only psychiatrist who has done the evaluations…He interrogated me. There is no other word for it. He would cut me off as I was trying to express myself.…I felt he was trying to confuse me. I stumbled over my words. I had a hard time following him and he couldn't follow me. I found him to be arrogant and very intimidating. I feel I was not quoted accurately and some of the things he says, he didn't even ask me. Some of the women have complained that the interviews should be taped because the women are not being quoted accurately. This is a common complaint.… I complained to his supervisor…Nothing ever came of my complaints…

To seek redress for the undue severity of sentences, adjudication errors, and lack of paroles, legal activists in at least 34 states actively campaign on behalf of incarcerated women survivors for gubernatorial clemency (Gagne, 1998).

Conclusion and Recommendations

In the beginning, when Prince Charming reveals himself to be a type of Marquis de Sade, women believe in and seek help from whatever social systems are available to them—family, the law, religious resources, friends, mental health practitioners, etc. These systems, in the end, fail many women and their children, resulting in futile self-help and escape attempts. As a result, some women die and some women cause their abusers to die. When women use deadly self-defense, women who have been attacked and terrorized by male partners, they find it difficult, or impossible, to discuss the painful, traumatic, and humiliating details of intimate assault with male police officers, male attorneys, and male psychologists, regardless of the men's sensitivity levels. While female victims are well aware of the gendered character of physical and sexual battering, many lawyers and investigators fail to adjust their approach to better fit the experiences of women. As a result, potentially exculpatory information is not investigated, crucial evidence remains unused, and women are left with no real defense. In some cases, an attack on the personal character of a woman defendant, or her immaterial, past behavior overwhelms even ample evidence of abuse.

Some accused women take the offered plea bargains to protect their children, to spare their families, to avoid the death penalty threatened by prosecutors, or to speed up what they see as the inevitable guilty verdict. Other women go to trial because they believe in the fairness of the system, because they are ready to fight for themselves, because they feel they have nothing to lose, or because they follow the instructions of their attorneys.

Despite the relationship between domestic violence and spousal homicide, criminal justice representatives routinely decontextualize intimate homicides. Systematically, investigators, attorneys, and judges disconnect the woman's deadly action from the batterer's ongoing, escalating violence and threats. Prosecutorial and defense strategies and judicial decisions prevent women from presenting their full stories and deny them the opportunity to offer evidence to support their claims of self-defense. The adjudication process for convicted survivors produces incomplete, distorted, or confusing pictures of events.

Repeatedly, battered women encounter a pattern of gender insensitivity and gender bias in the responses of authorities and institutions. What can be done to reduce the likelihood that other women will experience the same pattern of abuse and the same pathway to prison? While the past three decades have seen improvements in services for victims of domestic violence, it is clear that there remains a need for further changes in public policies and attitudes that act upon private lives.

Gender

The gender-specific nature of violence against women by intimate partners calls for policies and approaches that demonstrate awareness and responsiveness to gender dynamics. More women need to be involved at all levels of the criminal justice process. Whether the issue is domestic assault or homicide, battered women are better able to describe their experiences and explain their actions to female investigators, especially when it involves sexual abuse or torture. Frequently, women have the impression that male authorities are sympathetic toward abusive men rather than to the female victims; they feel that the men asking the questions do not believe them, are insensitive to the women's emotional and physical injuries, and blame women for men's violence.

Recommendation:

Ongoing gender-sensitive, domestic violence education is recommended for all representatives of the criminal justice system. All jurisdictions need specially trained units, generously staffed with females, comprised of officers, counselor-advocates, and prosecutors to handle domestic violence cases. Similar relevant resources need to be available for battered women charged in the death of their abusers.

Domestic Violence Arrest and Prosecution

Mandatory arrest policies continue to generate debate among researchers and practitioners. Interestingly, domestic violence appears to be the only violent crime for which arrest is applied so begrudgingly. Yet, the higher the social and legal price batterers are forced to pay, the greater the likelihood of a cessation or reduction of violence among chronic and sporadic abusers (Ellis & DeKeseredy, 1997). When mandatory arrest policies are part of a broader strategy of intervention—not the sole response—they reduce the overall rates of domestic violence by deterring recidivism and communicating societal condemnation of battering (Stark, 1996). The systematic arrest of batterers is a critical symbol of society's opposition to the abuse of women. Assault on women by male partners must be viewed as a crime, not simply a "domestic" or personal problem.

Recommendation:

Law enforcement should arrest all abusers not acting in self-defense. When implemented by well-trained personnel in a coordinated effort, mandatory arrest, aggressive prosecution, and increased penalties for batterers grant women greater freedom from abuse and retaliation while holding abusers accountable for their behavior.

Medical Reporting

Domestic violence is a critical health problem of staggering proportions as well as a serious crime of violence. However, despite the increased attention given to the issue, many primary care clinicians still grossly underestimate the prevalence of domestic violence, fail to ask about domestic violence when examining injured patients, and fail to attend educational programs on domestic violence (Sugg, Thompson, Thompson, Maiuro, & Rivara, 1999). The vast majority of domestic abuse victims are not likely to self-identify as battered women; they minimize the violence they have endured sometimes even when that violence becomes severe and life threatening. Abusive partners maintain their power and control whether they hover over victims in a hospital emergency room or remain at a distance. Until women are free from fear and coercive control, until they gain understanding of the dynamics of abusive relationships, until they have time to place their private experiences in the context of gender-based violence, the responsibility for rescue cannot rest solely on their own shoulders. Medical documentation of domestic violence-related injuries provides important legal evidence for the prosecution of batterers as well as for the defense of women who kill their abusers. Convicted survivors report frustration with medical personnel who fail to intervene when they were unable to report or to specify the nature of the situation themselves (Leonard, 2002).

Recommendation:

Medical and nursing schools must prepare future health care professionals to respond to victims of domestic violence, not merely stitch up their wounds. Mandated reporting of abuse in medical settings is recommended. All medical personnel should have ongoing domestic violence education and learn to use protocols to identify and treat the physical and emotional consequences of intimate partner violence. Medical offices, clinics, and institutions should have brochures and pamphlets clearly displayed and readily available to the public as well as to their clients.

Resources

Batterers frequently prevent their female partners from gaining economic independence and limit or prevent a woman's access to family or shared funds. When the limited number of shelters (about 1200 in the United States per Crowell and Burgess, 1996) do have space available, desperate women seeking to escape violence discover that the length of stay is seldom longer than 90 days (Hamby, 1998). However, the current number of shelters is woefully inadequate to match the level of domestic assault against women. Domestic violence is a major cause of homelessness for women and children (U.S. Conference of Mayors, 1998). Browne and Williams (1989) report a marked decline in female-perpetrated homicides as legal and extralegal resources become increasingly available.

Recommendation:

More shelters with expanded resources must be established and linked to transitional housing programs and out-of state placement where needed. Public assistance programs must take into account the immediate and long-term needs of abuse victims and work toward women's economic autonomy. Enhanced job skills and job placement are essential for long-term solutions for women and their children. Faith communities need to provide material as well as spiritual support for domestic violence survivors in their congregations and to address the issue publicly. States should help women who leave abusers to protect the confidentiality of their new addresses by granting substitute or false addresses for mail and all public purposes.

Restraining Orders

Orders of protection increase a woman's sense of self-empowerment and control over her situation while documenting the abuse and her efforts to end it. Many victims seek a restraining order as an act of desperation after experiencing extensive problems, and these orders are routinely violated (Tjaden & Thoennes, 2000). For many abused women, obtaining a restraining order can be very difficult. All too often, filing fees, transportation problems, childcare challenges, qualifying restrictions, daylong waits, and slow-moving and confusing bureaucratic procedures may combine to prevent a victim from obtaining an order of protection. Further, restraining orders do little more than create a paper trail when judges refuse to sanction men who violate them.

Recommendation:

Procedures for obtaining orders of protection need to be simplified and standardized, fees must be lowered or waived, and accessibility must be facilitated. Any female who seeks a restraining order against a current or former intimate should be provided with information on battering relationships, safety plans, and shelters along with referrals to counseling and legal services. Automatic arrest is the appropriate first response to any violation of a restraining order, followed by strict judicial sanctioning.

Homicide Prosecution

When a woman finds no legal way to stop life-threatening violence, she may determine that the only option left is the death of the abuser or her own death. When women use their own agency to put a final end to the violence, the criminal justice system punishes them severely. Their lethal actions can be understood only when placed within the context of her ongoing victimization and the lack of outside help and support. Yet, time and again, trials and plea bargains exclude evidence and testimony of their injuries and fear as well as their partners' violence, stalking, and threats. This produces an inaccurate picture, which fails to reflect the self-defensive motivation of women's actions. Thus, battered women who kill are placed in the same category as drive-by shooters and other dangerous criminal offenders, although these women are highly unlikely to have any history of criminal or violent behavior (Browne,

1987; Leonard, 2000; 2002). When prosecutors file homicide charges, abused women's self-protective acts become criminalized. Further, judges, juries, prosecutors, and sometimes defense attorneys do not believe women who are positive that they took a life only to save their own lives and/or the lives of threatened loved ones. Women are found guilty even when they sustain serious injuries in the incident that led to the homicide (Leonard, 2002). Prosecutors and juries display a single-minded interest in the sexist question, "Why didn't she just leave?" When judges disallow evidence of past victimization and instruct juries in ways that give them little option but to convict, women become double victims, once again controlled and silenced, once again told that the violence they endured was insignificant.

Recommendation:

When severe abuse precipitates deadly self-defense, prosecutors need to differentiate career criminals from one-time situational offenders who pose no danger to society. If the prosecutor pushes the case forward, manslaughter is the charge that best fits the battered woman's experience, rather than the widespread first- and second-degree murder indictments. All officers of the court should be required to attend in-depth, continuing education programs on domestic violence as a follow-up to mandatory law school courses on the subject. Juries need to be better educated on the dynamics and consequences of ongoing abuse through the use of expert testimony, and they need to hear all available exculpatory evidence and testimony. Jury instructions must allow jurors to consider the lethality of male violence. Further, battered women held criminally responsible for the death of abusive partners should be exempt from the death penalty.

Legal Assistance

In the vast majority of cases, police officers arrive on the scene of a homicide committed by a battered woman to find a traumatized and terrified individual who willingly cooperates with their investigation. Women who are convinced that they acted in self-defense believe once they tell authorities what transpired, everything would be all right—surely police and prosecutors would understand that they were left with no alternative but to kill or be killed. Women assume they will be able to stay with and comfort their children. To their horror, women find that their accounts, given without legal counsel or protection, are used against them as authorities construct their own version of what occurred in order to secure a successful prosecution (Bannister, 1993). By the time a woman acquires an attorney it may be too late. The socially constructed "official" version becomes the objective account and is nearly impossible for accused women to refute. All too often, women seldom see their attorneys, are not informed about plea negotiations, and are allowed little or no input on their defense cases.

Recommendation:

Female advocates, lay or professional, with knowledge and experience in domestic violence and spousal killing, need to be assigned to each battered woman homicide case to assist the traumatized woman as she negotiates the confusing and intimidating adversarial system of criminal justice. Advocates can assist women defendants to construct a complete history of abuse and to explain the unfolding process of adjudication, serving legal as well as therapeutic objectives. Advocates can contribute to the accused woman's understanding of her legal options and rights, such as being informed on plea negotiations and the right to refuse pharmaceutical treatment.

Alternatives to Jail

Women who cannot make bail are in a disadvantaged position. Awaiting trial in custody makes everything more difficult for the battered woman defendant and leaves her vulnerable to the inappropriate use of psychotropic medications. A mother will see her children placed with her family, the family of the deceased batterer, or in foster care. As the adult most closely bonded to her children, a battered woman's concerns center around the well-being of her children with whom she will have little or no contact. A battered woman defendant lacking a history of criminal or violent behavior is not a danger to the community and poses no flight risk. They are excellent candidates for alternatives to jail, which would cut the costs of pre-trial detention, leave space for more dangerous defendants, and allow families to begin the healing process.

Recommendation:

A battered woman defendant should be released on her own recognizance so that she can provide financially for herself and maintain her household throughout the adjudication process. Otherwise, she and her children could be housed in the secure therapeutic environment of a battered woman's shelter where she and her children would receive counseling for what they have endured. The use of psychotropic medications on battered women defendants without proper medical and psychological evaluations is a serious human rights violation and must be discontinued.

Community-Based Corrections

State and federal governments spend millions of dollars each year to imprison convicted survivors, the least likely of felons to repeat their crimes. As inmates, women homicide offenders are "model prisoners," complying with institutional rules and parole board mandates. Before the homicide, these women were well-socialized by societal norms, thus, they pose no risk to the community. They can readily become productive members of society, as tax paying workers, members of families, contributors to their communities, and as advocates for family violence victims. If the criminal justice system believes that women must remain under correctional control, female community-based residential and nonresidential programs, already in existence, could be made available to them.

Recommendation:

Convicted survivors should be placed in community-based programs that allow women to support themselves and permit mothers to live with their children. This move would save millions of correctional dollars as well as millions of social service dollars spent to address the needs of children with mothers in prison.

Post-Trial Efforts

Battered women homicide defendants are treated harshly by the criminal justice system. With each unduly harsh penalty, patriarchal attitudes are reinforced—attitudes that remind women that their proper place is in the home where men are to hold a monopoly of power and control. Sexism in the legal system dictates that women fulfill gender role expectations or face severe consequences, the same message communicated to women by their abusive mates. Patriarchy will not tolerate women's use of force in response to their male intimate's violence. Following a battered woman's conviction, she enters yet another world of absolute control.

Recommendation:

Battered women who kill should be deemed eligible for parole and released. The institutionalized sexism as seen in sentencing and parole practices must be unmasked and discontinued. The possibility of retrials or early release for women imprisoned for killing their batterers needs exploration. Women serving life without parole must be allowed the opportunity for release. Executions of women on death row must cease and their cases must be revisited to explore what role domestic violence may have played in the homicide. While incarcerated, convicted survivors should be permitted, even encouraged, to organize themselves in support groups for education, growth, advocacy, and self-esteem. All correctional institutions should facilitate the formation of and support such groups. Further, advocacy groups for battered women convicted of homicide are needed to address issues of parole, resentencing, and clemency.

> We were and remain good mothers, daughters and grandmothers who were trapped in a desperate situation. To understand us, one must understand the key words, fear, threats, control, isolation, emotional and physical abuse, all of which are directed not only toward ourselves, but our loved ones...As long as one single battered woman, who did not receive a full and fair trial, remains in prison, the law has failed all who seek justice.

The eloquent and poignant voices of incarcerated women survivors give us unique insights concerning cases of battered women who kill to save their lives. The brutality, humiliation, and terror inflicted upon them by violent male intimates echo the experiences of the many women who die each year at the hands of men who say, "If I can't have you, nobody can." In essence, they are the voice of all the women who did not survive that final violent assault.

References

American Bar Association/National Bar Association. (2001). *Justice by gender: The lack of appropriate prevention, diversion and treatment alternatives for girls in the justice system* [On-line]. Available: Http://www.abanet.org/crimjust/juvjus/girls.html.

American Medical Association. (1992). *Diagnostic and treatment guidelines on domestic violence*. Chicago: American Medical Association.

American Psychiatric Association. (1994). *Diagnostic and statistical manual of mental disorders* (4th ed.). Washington, DC: American Psychiatric Association.

Amnesty International. (1999). *Not part of my sentence: Violations of the human rights of women in* custody. New York: Amnesty International.

Andersen, S. M., Boulette, T. R., & Schwartz, A. H. (1991). Psychological maltreatment of spouses. In R. T. Ammerman & M. Hersen (Eds.), *Case studies in family violence* (pp. 293–327). New York: Plenum Press.

Auerhahn, K., & Leonard, E. D. (2000). Docile bodies? Chemical restraints and the female inmate. *The Journal of Criminal Law and Criminology*, 90 (2), 599–634.

Bachman, R. (1994). *Violence against women*. Washington, DC: U.S. Department of Justice.

Bachman, R., & Saltzman, L. E. (1995). *Violence against women: Estimates from the redesigned survey*. Washington, DC: U.S. Department of Justice.

Bannister, S. A. (1991). The criminalization of women fighting back against male abuse: imprisoned battered women as political prisoners. *Humanity and Society*, 15 (4), 400–416.

Bannister, S. A. (1993). Battered women who kill their abusers: Their courtroom battles. In R. Muraskin & T. Alleman (Eds.), *It's a crime: Women and justice* (pp. 316–333). Englewood Cliffs, NJ: Regents/Prentice Hall.

Bannister, S. A. (1996). *Battered women who kill: Status and situational determinants of courtroom outcomes.* Ph.D. dissertation, Department of Sociology, University of Illinois-Chicago.

Belknap, J. (1995). Law enforcement officers: Attitudes about the appropriate responses to woman battering. International *Review of Victimology*, 4: 47–62.

Belknap, J. (2001). The *invisible woman: Gender, crime, and justice* (2nd ed.). Belmont, CA: Wadsworth.

Belt, K., & McDonald, E. (2000). *Battered defendants: Victims of domestic violence who offend* (Preliminary paper No. 41). Wellington, New Zealand: Law Commission.

Bergen, R. K. (1999). *Marital rape* [On-line]. Available: http://www.vawnet.org/vnl/library/general/libraryrecord1095.htm.

Block, C. R., & Christakos, A. (1995). Intimate partner homicide in Chicago over 29 years.*Crime and Delinquency,* 41 (4), 496–526.

Bloom, B. Chesney-Lind, M., & Owen, B. (1994). *Women in California prisons: hidden victims of the war on drugs.* San Francisco: Center on Juvenile and Criminal Justice.

Bourg, S., & Stock, H. V. (1999). A review of domestic violence arrest statistics in a police department using a pro-arrest policy. In J. M. Makepeace (Ed.), *Family violence: Studies from the social sciences and profession* (2nd ed., Vol. 2). New York: Primus Custom Publishing.

Browne, A. (1987). *When battered women kill.* New York: Free Press.

Browne, A. (1992). Violence against women: Relevance for medical practitioners. *Journal of the American* Medical *Association,* 267(23), 3184–3189.

Browne, A., & Williams, K. R. (1989). Exploring the effect of resource availability and thelikelihood of female-perpetrated homicides. *Law and Society Review,* 23 (1), 75–94.

Brownstein, H. H., Spunt, B. J., Crimmins, S., Goldstein, P. J., & Langley, S. (1994). Changing patterns of lethal violence by women: A research note. *Women and Criminal Justice, 5* (2), 99–116.

Buzawa, E., Austin, T. L., & Buzawa, C. G. (1995). Responding to crimes of violence againstwomen: Gender differences versus organizational imperatives. *Crime and Delinquency,* 41 (4), 443–466.

Buzawa, E. S., & Buzawa., C. G. (1993). The impact of arrest on domestic violence: Introduction. *American Behavioral Scientist,* 36 (5), 558–574.

Buzawa, E. S., & Buzawa, C. G. (1996). *Domestic violence: The criminal justice response.* Thousand Oaks, CA:Sage.

Campbell, J. C. (1992). If I can't have you, no one can: Power and control in homicide of femalepartners. In J. Radford & D. E. H. Russell (Eds.), *Femicide: The politics of woman killing* (pp. 99–113). New York: Twayne.

Campbell, J. C. (1995). Prediction of homicide of and by battered women. In J. C. Campbell (Ed.), *Assessing dangerousness: Violence by sexual offenders, batterers, and child abusers* (pp. 96–113). Thousand Oaks, CA: Sage.

Caringella-MacDonald, S. (1997). Women victimized by private violence. In A. P. Cardarelli (Ed.), *Violence between intimate partners* (pp. 144–153). Boston: Allyn and Bacon.

Casenave, N. A., & Zahn, M. (1992). Women, murder and male domination: Police reports of domestic violence in Chicago and Philadelphia. In E. Viano (Ed.), *Intimate violence: Interdisciplinary perspectives* (pp. 83–97). Washington, DC: Hemisphere Publishing.

Castel, J. R. (1990). Discerning justice for battered women who kill. *University of Toronto Faculty of Law Review*, 49 (2), 229–258.

Chesney-Lind, M., & Shelden, R. (1998). *Girls, delinquency and juvenile justice.* Thousand Oaks, CA: Sage.

Collins, K. S., Schoen, C., Joseph, S., Duchon, L., Simantov, E., & Yellowitz, M. (1999). *1998 survey of women's health.* New York: Commonwealth Fund.

Crary, D. (2001, June 16). In the gender wars, another flashpoint: Battered men. *The associated press* [On-line]. Available: http://www.vachss.com/help_text/archive/battered_men.html.

Crowell, N. A., & Burgess, A. W. (Eds.). (1996). *Understanding violence against women.* Washington, DC: National Academy Press.

Culliver, C. C. (1993). *Female criminality: The state of the art.* New York: Garland.

Diaz, K. (1996). *Pathfinder on domestic violence with emphasis on the criminal justice system*[Online]. New York: Center on Crime, Communities, and Culture. available:http://www.soros.org/crime/dvpath.html.

Dobash, R. E., & Dobash, R. (1977). Love, honor, and obey: Institutional ideologies and the struggle for battered women. *Contemporary Crises*, 1 (June/July), 403–415.

Dobash, R. E., & Dobash, R. (1979). *Violence against wives.* New York: Free Press.

Dobash, R. E., & Dobash, R. (1988). Research as social action: The struggle for batteredwomen. In K. Yllo & M. Bograd (Eds.), *Feminist perspectives on wife abuse* (pp. 51–74). Newbury Park, CA: Sage

Dobash, R. E., & Dobash, R. (1992). *Women, violence and social change.* London: Routledge.

Dressler, J. (1997). Battered women, sleeping abusers, and criminal responsibility. *Chicago Policy Review*, 2 (1), 1–16.

Duncan, J. W., & Duncan, G. M. (1978). Murder in the family. In I. Kutash, S. Kutash, & L.Schlesinger (Eds.), *Violence: Perspectives on murder and aggression* (pp. 171–186). Chapel Hill: University of North Carolina.

Eigenberg, H. M., Scarborough, K. E., & Kappeler, V. E. (1996). Contributory factors affecting arrest in domestic and non-domestic assaults. *American Journal of Police*, 15 (4), 27–54.

Ellis, D., & DeKeseredy, W. S. (1997). Rethinking estrangement, interventions, and intimate femicide. Violence *Against Women*, 3 (6), 590–609.

Ewing, C. P. (1990). Psychological self-defense: A proposed justification for battered women who kill. *Law and* Human *Behavior*, 14 (6), 579–594.

Ewing, C. P. (1997). *Fatal families.* Thousand Oaks, CA: Sage.

Fagan, J. (1996). The *criminalization of domestic violence: Promises and limits.* Washington, DC: U. S. Department of Justice.

Ferraro, K. J. (1989). Policing woman battering. *Social Problems*, 36 (1), 61–74.

Ferraro, K. J. (1993). Cops, courts, and woman battering. In P. B. Bart & E. G. Moran (Eds.),*Violence against women: The bloody footprints* (pp. 165–176). Newbury Park, CA: Sage.

Ferraro, K. J. (1997). Battered women: Strategies for survival. In A. P. Cardarelli (Ed.), *Violence between intimate partners* (pp. 135–153). Boston: Allyn and Bacon.

Ferraro, K. J. (2001). Woman battering: More than a family problem. In C. M. Renzetti & L. Goodstein (Eds.), *Women, crime, and criminal justice* (pp. 135–153). Los Angeles:Roxbury.

Flitcraft, A. H. (1995). Clinical violence intervention: Lessons from battered women. *Journal of Health Care for the Poor and Underserved*, 6 (2), 187–195.

Fox, J. A., & Zawitz, M. W. (1999). *Homicide trends in the United States*. Washington, DC: U. S. Department of Justice.

Gagne, P. (1998). *Battered women's justice*. New York: Twayne.

Genders, E., & Player, E. (1987). Women in prison: The treatment, the control, and the experience. In P. Carlen & A. Worrall (Eds.), *Gender, crime, and justice* (pp. 161–175). Philadelphia: Open University Press.

Gibbs, N. (1997). Til death do us part. In J. H. Skolnick & E. Currie (Eds.), *Crisis in American institutions* (pp. 229–239). New York: Longman.

Gillespie, C. K. (1989). *Justifiable homicide*. Columbus, OH: Ohio State University Press.

Goelman, D., & Valente, R. (1997). When *will they ever learn? Educating to end domestic violence*. Chicago: American Bar Association.

Goolkasian, G. A. (1986). The judicial system and domestic violence—An expanding role. *Response*, 9 (4), 2–7.

Greenfeld, L. A., Rand, M. R., Craven, D., Klaus, P. A., Perkins, C. A., Ringel, C., Warchol, G.,Maston, C., & Fox, J. A. (1998*). Violence by intimates*. Washington, DC: U. S. Department of justice.

Hamby, S. L. (1998). Partner violence: Prevention and intervention. In J. L. Jasinski & L. M.Williams (Eds.), *Partner violence* (pp. 210–258). Thousand Oaks, CA: Sage.

Hart, B. (1988). Beyond the 'duty to warn': A therapist's 'duty to protect' battered women and children. In K. Yllo & M. Bograd (Eds.*), Feminist perspectives on wife abuse* (pp. 234–248). Beverly Hills, CA: Sage.

Hart, B. (1990a). Assessing whether batterers will kill [On-line]. Available: http://www.mincava.umn.edu/hart/lethali.htm.

Hart, B. (1990b). Domestic violence intervention system: A model for response to woman abuse [On-line]. Available: http://mincava.umn.edu/hart/dvinter.htm.

Hart, B. (1992). Battered women and the criminal justice system. *American Behavioral Scientist*, 36 (5), 624–638.

Hart, B. (1996). Battered women and the criminal justice system. In E. S. Buzawa & C. G. Buzawa (Eds.), *Do arrests and restraining orders work?* (pp. 98–114). Thousand Oaks, CA: Sage.

Healey, K., Smith, C., & O'Sullivan, C. (1998). *Batterer intervention: Program approaches and criminal justice strategies*. Washington, DC: U. S. Department of Justice.

Heise, L. L. (1994). *Violence against women: The hidden health burden*. Washington, DC: The World Bank.

Hofford, M., & Harrell, A. V. (1993). *Family violence: Interventions for the justice system*.Washington, DC: Bureau of Justice Assistance.

Jacobs, M. S. (1998). Requiring battered women die: Murder liability for mothers under failure to protect statutes. *Journal of Criminal Law and Criminology*, 88 (2), 579–660.

Jacobson, N., & Gottman, J. (1998). *When men batter women*. New York: Simon & Schuster.

James, W. H., West, C., & Deters, K. E. (2000). Youth dating violence. *Adolescence*, 35 (139), 455–65.

Johnson, B., Li, D., & Websdale, N. (1998). Florida mortality review project: Executive summary. *Legal Interventions in Family Violence: Research Findings and Policy Implications*. Washington, DC: U. S. Department of Justice.

Jones, A. (1994). *Next time she'll be dead*. Boston: Beacon.

Jones, A. (1996). *Women who kill*. Boston: Beacon.

Jurik, N. C., & Martin, S. E. (2001). Femininities, masculinities, and organizational conflict: women in criminal justice occupations. In C. M. Renzetti & L. Goodstein (Ed.), *Women, crime, and criminal justice* (pp. 264–281). Los Angeles: Roxbury.

Kantor, G. K., & Jasinski, J. L. (1998). Dynamics and risk factors in partner violence. In J. L.Jasinski & L. M. Williams (Eds.), *Partner violence: A comprehensive review of 20 years of research* (pp. 1–43). Thousand Oaks, CA: Sage.

Langan, P. A., & Dawson, J. M. (1995). *Spouse murder defendants in large urban counties.*Washington, DC: U. S. Department of Justice.

Leonard, E. D. (2000). Convicted survivors: A California study of women imprisoned for killing abusive spouses. *Women, Girls, and Criminal Justice*, 1 (1), 5–6, 15.

Leonard, E. D. (2001). Convicted survivors: Comparing and describing California's battered women prisoners. The Prison Journal, 18 (1), 73–86.

Leonard, E. D. (2002). Convicted survivors: *The imprisonment of battered women who kill.* New York: State University of New York Press.

Lott, B. (1994). *Women's lives: Themes and variations in gender learning*. Pacific Grove, CA:Brooks/Cole.

Maguire, K., & Pastore, A. L. (Eds.). (1996). *Sourcebook of criminal justice statistics 1995*. Washington, DC: Government Printing Office.

Makepeace, J. M. (1999). Courtship violence among college students. In J. M. Makepeace (Ed.), *Family violence. Studies from the social sciences and professions: Vol. 2. Relationship violence* 2nd ed., (pp. 56–60). New York: McGraw-Hill.

Mann, C. R. (1992). Female murderers and their motives: A tale of two cities. In E. C. Viano (Ed.), *Intimate Violence: Interdisciplinary Perspectives*, (pp. 73–82). Washington: Hemisphere Publishing.

Marcus, M. L. (1981). Conjugal violence: The law of force and the force of law. *California Law Review*,69 (6), 1657–1733.

Marvin, D. R. (1997). The dynamics of domestic abuse. *Annual editions: Criminal justice 98/99*. Guilford, CT: Dushkin.

McCorkel, J. A. (1996). Justice, gender, and incarceration: An analysis of the leniency and severity debate. In J. A. Inciardi (Ed.), *Examining the justice process* (pp. 157–174). Fort Worth, TX: Harcourt Brace.

McLeer, S. V., & Anwar, R. (1989). A study of battered women presenting in an emergency department. *American Journal of Public Health*. 79 (1), 65–66.

Miller, S. L. (1993). Arrest policies for domestic violence and their implications for batteredwomen. In R. Muraskin & T. Alleman (Eds.), *It's a crime: Women and justice* (pp. 334–359). Englewood Cliffs, NJ: Prentice Hall.

Moracco, K. E., Runyan, C. W., & Butts, J.D. (1998). Femicide in North Carolina, 1991–1993. *Homicide Studies*, 2 (4), 422–446.

National Center for Women and Policing. (2001). *Police family violence fact sheet* [On-line].Available: http://www.feminist.org/police/violenceFS.asp.

O'Dell, A. (1996). Domestic violence homicides. *The Police Chief*, 63 (2), 21–23.

O'Shea, K. (1993). Women on death row. In B. R. Fletcher, L. D. Shaver, & D. Moon (Eds.),*Women prisoners: A forgotten population* (pp. 75–89). Westport, CT: Praeger.

Osthoff, S. (1991). Restoring justice: Clemency for battered women. *Response*, 14 (2), 2–3.

Pagelow, M. D. (1985). The 'battered husband syndrome': Social problem or much ado about little? In N. Johnson (Ed.), *Marital violence* (pp. 172–196). London: Routledge & Kegan Paul.

Rebovich, Donald J. 1996. Prosecution response to domestic violence: results of a survey of large jurisdictions. In E. S. Buzawa & C. G. Buzawa (Eds.), *Do arrests and restraining orders work?* (pp. 176–191). Thousand Oaks, CA: Sage.

Rennison, C. M., & Welchans, S. (2000). *Intimate partner violence.* Washington, DC: U. S.Department of Justice.

Richie, B. E. (1996). *Compelled to crime: The gender entrapment of battered black women.* New York: Routledge.

Roth, R. (2000). Adding insult to injury: New York charges battered mothers with neglect [On-line]. Available: http://www.salon.com/mwt/feature/2000/09/14/battered_mothers/ index.html.

Schafran, L. H. (1990). Overwhelming evidence: Reports on gender bias in the courts. Trial, *26* (2), 28–35.

Schafran, L. H. (1991). Update: Gender bias in the courts. *Trial, 27* (7), 112–118.

Schmidt, J. D., & Sherman, L. W. (1996). Does arrest deter domestic violence? In E. S. Buzawa & C. G. Buzawa (Eds.), *Do arrests and restraining orders work?* (pp. 43–53).Thousand Oaks, CA: Sage.

Schneider, E. M. (2000). *Battered women and feminist lawmaking.* New Haven, CT: Yale University Press.

Schneider, E. M., & Jordan, S. B. (1981). Representation of women who defend themselves inresponse to physical or sexual assault. In E. Bochnak (Ed.), *Women's self defense cases:theory and practice* (pp. 1–39). Charlottesville, VA: The Michie Company Law Publishers.

Schuller, R. A., & Hastings, P. A. (1996). Trials of battered women who kill: The impact of alternative forms of expert evidence. *Law and Human Behavior*, 20 (2), 167–187.

Sengupta, S. (2000, July 8). Tough justice: Taking a child when one parent is battered. *New York Times* [On-line]. Available: http://www.sanctuaryforfamilies.org/index16a.htm.

Siegel, L. J. (1998). *Criminology.* Belmont, CA: Wadsworth.

Silverman, J. G., Raj, A., Mucci, L. A., & Hataway, J. E. (2001). Dating violence against adolescent girls and associated substance use, unhealthy weight control, sexual risk behavior, pregnancy, and suicidality. *Journal of the American Medical Association, 286* (5), 572–579.

Stanko, E. A. (2001). Women, danger, and criminology. In C. M. Renzetti & L. Goodstein (Eds.), *Women, crime, and criminal justice* (pp. 13–26). Los Angeles: Roxbury.

Stark, E. (1990). Rethinking homicide: Violence, race, and the politics of gender. *International Journal of Health Services*, 20 (1), 3–27.

Stark, E. (1996). Mandatory arrest of batterers: A reply to its critics. In E. S. Buzawa & C. G.Buzawa (Eds.), *Do arrests and restraining orders work?* (pp. 115–149). Thousand Oaks, CA: Sage.

Stark, E., & Flitcraft, A. (1996). *Women at risk*. Thousand Oaks, CA: Sage.

Steffensmeier, D., & Allan, E. (1998). The nature of female offending: Patterns and explanation. In R. T. Zaplin (Ed.), *Female offenders: Critical perspectives and effective interventions* (pp. 5–29). Gaithersburg, MD: Aspen.

Steffensmeier, D., & Broidy, L. (2001). Explaining female offending. In C. M. Renzetti & L.Goodstein (Eds.), *Women, crime, and criminal justice* (pp. 111–134). Los Angeles: Roxbury.

Stinchcombe, J. B., & Fox, V. B. (1999). *Introduction to corrections* (5th ed.). Upper Saddle River, NJ: Prentice Hall.

Stout, K. D., & Brown, P. (1995). Legal and social differences between men and women who kill intimate partners. *Affilia*, 10 (2), 194–205.

Sugg, N. K., Thompson, R. S., Thompson, D. C., Maiuro, R., & Rivara, F. P. (1999). Domestic violence and primary care. *Archives of Family Medicine, 8* (July/August), 301–306.

Tjaden, P., & Thoennes, N. (1998). Prevalence, incidence, and consequences of violence against women: Findings from the national violence against women survey. Washington, DC: U. S. Department of Justice.

Tjaden, P., & Thoennes, N. (2000). *Full report of the prevalence, incidence, and consequences of violence against women*. Washington, DC: U. S. Department of Justice.

Totman, J. (1978). *The murderess: A psychosocial study of criminal homicide*. San Francisco:R & E Research Associates.

United Nations Children's Fund. (2000). Domestic violence against women and girls. *Innocenti Digest* No. 6, (May). Florence, Italy: Innocenti Research Centre.

United States Commission on Civil Rights. (1982). *Under the rule of thumb: Battered women and the administration of justice*. Washington, DC: U. S. Government Printing Office.

United States Conference of Mayors. (1998). *A status report on hunger and homelessness inAmerica's cities: 1998*. Washington, DC: U. S. Conference of Mayors.

United States Department of Justice, Office of Justice Programs, National Institute of Justice, United States Department of Health and Human Services, and National Institute of Mental Health. (1996). *The validity and use of evidence concerning battering and its effects in criminal trials*. Washington, DC: U. S. Department of Justice.

Violence Against Women Grants Office. (1997). *Domestic violence and stalking: The second annual report to congress under the violence against women act*. Washington, DC: U. S. Department of Justice.

Walford, B. (1987). *Lifers: The stories of eleven women serving life sentences for murder*. Montreal, Canada: Eden Press.

Walker, L. E. (1989). *Terrifying love: Why battered women kill and how society responds*. New York: Harper and Row.

Walker, L. E. (1992). Battered women syndrome and self-defense. *Notre Dame Journal of Law, Ethics and Public Policy*, 6 (2), 321–334.

Welling, B. L., Biren, A., Johnston, M., Kuehl, S., & Nunn, D. (1990). *Achieving equal justice for women and men in the courts: The draft report of the judicial council advisory committee on gender bias in the courts.* San Francisco: Judicial Council of California.

Wilson, M., & Daly, M. (1992). Till death us do part. In J. Radford & D. E. H. Russell (Eds.),*Femicide* (pp. 83–98). New York: Twayne.

Wilson, N. K. (1993). Gendered interaction in criminal homicide. In A. V. Wilson (Ed.), *Homicide: The victim-offender connection* (pp. 43–62). Cincinnati, OH: Anderson.

Wolfgang, M. E. (1957). *Victim precipitated criminal homicide. Journal of Criminal Law,* Criminology, and Police Science, 48 (1), 1–11.

Wolfgang, M. E. (1967). *Studies in homicide.* New York: Harper and Row.

Zawitz, M. W. (1994). *Domestic violence: Violence between intimates.* Washington, DC: U. S. Department of Justice.

Zorza, J. (1997). Battered women behave like other threatened victims. *Focus*: Los Angeles County Domestic Violence Council News Quarterly, 3 (2), 7.

CHAPTER 6

Cross-Sex Supervision of Incarcerated Women and the Dynamics of Staff Sexual Misconduct

Christine E. Rasche

Concern about the cross-sex supervision of correctional inmates, especially the supervision of female inmates by male correctional staff, has increased tremendously over the past decade. Some of this concern has been due to a few spectacular scandals. Other concerns have been raised as a result of independent investigations into the sexual abuse of female prison inmates, most notably by Amnesty International and Human Rights Watch. For students of women's prison history, this recent concern about cross-sex supervision of female offenders sounds like "deja vu all over again." Over one hundred years ago there was a movement to separate women convicts from their male counterparts and put them into all-women's prisons staffed entirely by women, which was a novel idea at the time (Freedman, 1981; Rafter, 1985). Much of the concern then was generated by evidence that women prisoners were routinely, and sometimes savagely or repeatedly, sexually assaulted or otherwise abused by male prison guards. The new concerns being raised today sound like echoes of a distant past.

Though the separate women's prison did eventually become the standard corrections practice throughout much of America for most of this past century, dramatic changes in employment law since 1970 have created a return to a correctional dilemma which pioneer prison reformers thought they had solved in the 1870s. The cross-sex supervision problems being faced now by virtually all state correctional systems, as well as by the federal government and local lock-ups, has brought the peculiarities of women's corrections into sharper focus than ever before. Some correctional administrators, who traditionally have been much less concerned about the special needs of female inmates because they needed to worry about the overwhelming needs of ten times as many male inmates, have now found their women's prisons the source of expensive lawsuits and/or embarrassing scandals. Though male inmates have also sued over cross-sex supervision issues, and despite the fact that inmate rape seems to be a much larger issue in men's' prisons, the particular intersections of cross-sex supervision and staff sexual misconduct toward inmates seems to be most serious in women's institutions.

The problems associated with cross-sex supervision of female inmates are numerous and reflect not only the management challenges posed by incarcerated female offenders in particular, but also the traditional difficulties of gender relations in our society. Some of these problems are related to ongoing concerns about violence and sexual assault inside prisons, while others are connected to the specific dilemma of correctional staff misconduct. The fact that these problems are reemerging in women's prisons after a century of presumed resolution is both fascinating and appalling to many scholars interested in women offenders and the problems they face during incarceration.

This chapter will briefly trace the historical demise of cross-sex supervision of female offenders in the late nineteenth and early twentieth centuries, and the legal changes of the 1970s and 1980s, which prompted its return. It will briefly describe the methodological difficulties of investigating this phenomenon, which will help to explain why some cases do not come to light until they explode into scandal. However, the overall focus of this chapter is a discussion of the forms and dynamics of staff sexual abuse of female inmates in cross-sex supervision situations, and then some possible remedies are presented for correctional authorities to consider.

In the final analysis, the problems of staff sexual abuse of female prison inmates can be seen to encompass the unrelenting challenges of gender relationships, the inevitable temptations of power, and at least one irony of unintended consequences.

The Historical Demise of
Cross-Sex Supervision

When incarceration became the standard form of punishment in America for criminal wrongdoing at the beginning of the nineteenth century, little thought was initially given to the conditions of confinement. Optimistic penal reformers had assumed that incarceration in and of itself would be sufficient to induce rehabilitation, since it would provide the time required for a miscreant to repent his or her evil ways (Roth, 1971).

That the goals of incarceration did not quite work as intended became clear relatively quickly. As early as 1826, Reverend Louis Dwight of Boston wrote about sexual assaults inside prison walls, which he decried as "this dreadful degradation" (Donaldson, Dumond, Knopp, Struckman-Johnson, & Thompson, 2000). In that same year, a woman prisoner by the name of Rachel Welch was impregnated while in solitary confinement, and died after receiving a flogging shortly after giving birth (Kurshan, 2000). That the conditions of confinement in the early prisons were often more harsh for women than men, and that such harsh conditions seemed to routinely include sexual assault and harassment, is now quite thoroughly documented (Lewis, 1965; Feinman, 1979; Freedman, 1981; Rafter, 1985; Freeman, 1997; Johnson, 1997; Kurshan, 2000). Up to the late 1800s, all prisoners were kept in the same facilities, but since the male prisoners vastly outnumbered the few women prisoners, and since all guards at the time were male, opportunities for misconduct toward women inmates were frequent. Johnson (1997) summarizes the situation as follows:

> Sexual abuse was disturbingly common in custodial prisons run by men. Women might well be fondled at intake…and later raped in their cells by their male keepers. On other occasions, guards would make sport of their sexual encounters with their female captives (see, for example, Anonymous 1871). The impression one gains from this literature is that the women relegated to custodial institutions, from the penitentiary onward, had little or no choice but to submit to the predations of their keepers (pp. 43–44).

In some cases, sexual misconduct in the nineteenth century went beyond abuses inflicted by individuals. Kurshan (2000) reports that the Indiana state prison ran a prostitution service with the female prisoners for the male guards. But even when such *organized* forms of sexual abuse were not present, *individual* misconduct was apparently widespread and routine. In some cases, prison conditions were known to be so abysmal that judges refused to send white women to prison, though they gave considerably less concern to the fate of black women (Johnson, 1995). Because so few women were imprisoned in the first place, those that were confined were regarded as unnatural and vile, "the dregs of the state prisoner population" (Rafter, 1990, p. 21).

As both Freedman (1981) and Rafter (1985; 1990) have so ably described, these abuses were key to the campaign which developed in the mid-1800s to remove women prisoners from the otherwise all-male institutions and separately house them in new, all-female facilities, which would also be staffed by female "warders" (Freeman, 1997). Though the campaign was hard-fought and took longer than early reformers expected, the first truly separate prison for women was opened in Indiana in 1873. It was followed in the next three decades by one separate facility for women in Massachusetts, and two additional women's reformatories in New York, for a total of four institutions in three states by the turn of the century. However, the idea caught on and 14 separate women's institutions were opened in 13 additional states in the years up to the Great Depression. There was a bit of a slump in the movement during the 1930s and 1940s, with four new separate institutions opening in the 1930s, and only two were added during the war years. Another three facilities in three more states opened during the 1950s, but the 1960s and 1970s saw another surge in the creation of separate prisons for women, with 15 new institutions being opened (Rafter, 1985). By 1980, only a dozen states still housed women in units within existing male prisons, or in separate institutions in other states. One of these, Idaho, opened its first separate prison for women as late as 1996. Even while these last separate prisons for women were being constructed, however, other changes were occurring in corrections, which served to undermine some of the original goals of separation and set the stage for a major unintended consequence of workforce integration.

The Re-emergence of Cross-Sex Supervision

It is perhaps ironic that the movement to end segregated supervision of prison inmates began in the 1970s with the concerns of women who were working in the field of corrections in women's facilities. The idea of gender-segregated corrections had taken hold so strongly by the mid-1900s that some states had even passed legislation which prohibited the employment of males in women's prisons (Freeman, 1997). Women, of course, were not permitted to work as correctional officers in men's prisons, though apparently the idea was so unthinkable that no legislation was needed to prevent it.

By the 1960s, however, some of the laws prohibiting male employment in women's prisons were repealed, allegedly due to a perceived shortage of qualified women to serve as wardens (Pollock-Byrne, 1990). Men began to be appointed to serve as the wardens and superintendents of women's prisons, though this was often regarded as virtual punishment in male correctional circles, or at least the basis for sympathy and consolation (Turnbo, 1993). Men in corrections viewed women's prisons as being simultaneously, "not real corrections," but yet more difficult to manage because women prisoners were so problematic.

As the second wave of feminism began to take hold in the United States in the mid-1970s, women working in corrections realized that not only were men moving into the most senior positions available in women's corrections, but that upward mobility for women in correctional service was capped at the level of warden of a women's facility. While men could become the wardens of women's facilities, women managers were not assigned to men's facilities. Even the most able female manager was denied further upward mobility because she had not served at a maximum-security men's prison, and such a position was denied to her on the basis of her sex. All that began to change with the passage of Title VII of the Civil Rights Act of 1964, which said that "an employer may not discriminate on the basis of sex unless an employee's sex is a bona fide occupational qualification (BFOQ), i.e., a qualification that is 'reasonably necessary' to perform the specific job. In the absence of unusual circumstances, United States federal courts have been unwilling to characterize a person's sex as a BFOQ (Human Rights Watch, 1996, pp. 20–21). Framing the issue this way set in motion a flurry of lawsuits in which women's right to equal employment was pitched against male inmates' rights to privacy. Male inmates, who claimed that their right to privacy was jeopardized by having female correctional officers supervise them, filed most of the initial lawsuits contesting cross-sex supervision. Though some cases prior to 1982 recognized the concerns of inmates for privacy from the scrutiny of the opposite sex, especially in bathrooms and sleeping areas, the bulk of the cases found that inmate privacy was not an overwhelming and compelling reason to deny equal opportunity in employment. In some cases, the courts explicitly told states to "balance the equal employment opportunities of the corrections officers with the need to protect the prisoners' right to privacy" (Human Rights Watch, 1996, p. 243). In other cases, the courts bluntly dismissed any notion that the prisoner had a "right under the Constitution against being viewed while naked by corrections officers of the opposite sex" (Human Rights Watch, 1996, p. 243, citing *Griffin v. Michigan Department of Corrections,* 654 F. Supp 690, E.D. Mich. 1982).

In essence, the legal dispute over equal opportunity in employment for women working in corrections opened the door for states to employ men as staff at every level in women's prisons. While advocates for the advancement of women working in corrections could see the benefit of dismantling segregated correctional employment, they could also see that the inevitable, albeit unintended, consequence of that dismantling would be some cross-sex supervision of female offenders. However, given that women's corrections was never viewed as a sure route to advancement in the field, and given that female prisoners are almost universally disliked by correctional officers, it was not expected that the increase in cross-sex supervision of female offenders would be so great so fast (Rasche, 2000). It is surprising to most observers to learn that in the United States today male correctional staff now constitute at least 40 percent of all correctional officers working in women's prisons over-all, and they constitute the *majority* of correctional officers in many women's facilities (Hill, 1997). For example, men make up 70 percent of the correc-tional officers in U.S. federal prisons for women (Amnesty International, 1999), and they are also the vast majority of guards at women's prisons in Cal-ifornia, Georgia, Illinois, Michigan, and the District of Columbia, just to name a few (Human Rights Watch, 1996). In short, it is virtually impossible for a woman prisoner in the United States today to avoid contact supervision by a male correctional officer.

In retrospect, we probably should *not* be surprised by this development. Cor-rectional institutions must be staffed 24 hours a day, 365 days a year, regardless of holidays or catastrophic events. From the point of view of correctional man-agement, it is infinitely easier to deploy staff *without* regard for gender issues. And since upward mobility in the profession still requires a variety of experi-ences, particularly at male institutions, women correctional staff today do not want to be constrained to service in women's prisons any more than their sisters did in the 1970s. Furthermore, many women in corrections share the dislike and disdain for women offenders that characterize their male counterparts and would not seek service in women's prisons for that reason (Rasche, 2000). In short, duty at a women's facility is increasingly likely to be an assignment for a new correctional officer right out of the academy who is not in a position to choose a desirable duty location. Since men entering correctional service outnumber women, it is only a matter of mathematics and deployment convenience that men now frequently outnumber women supervising female offenders.

According to some investigators, this is where the problem of staff sexual misconduct begins. As Human Rights Watch (1996) has noted:

One of the clear contributing factors to sexual misconduct in U.S. prisons for women is that the United States, despite authoritative rules to the contrary, allows male correctional employees to hold con-tact positions over prisoners, that is, positions in which they serve in constant physical proximity to the prisoners of the opposite sex. Under the United Nations Standard Minimum Rules for the Treat-ment of Prisoners (Standard Minimum Rules), which constitute an authoritative guide to international law regarding the treatment of prisoners...male officers are precluded from holding such contact posts. However, since the passage of the Civil Rights Act of 1964, U.S. employers have been precluded from denying a person a job solely on

the basis of gender unless the person's gender was reasonably necessary to the performance of the specific job. In the absence of unusual
circumstances, U.S. federal courts have been unwilling to recognize
a person's gender as meeting this standard with respect to correctional
employment. As a result, most restrictions on male officers working
in women's prisons…have been removed and, by some estimates,
male officers working in women's prisons now outnumber their female counterparts by two and, in some facilities, three to one (p. 2).

Problems in Investigating
Staff-Inmate Sexual Abuse

There are significant methodological difficulties in investigating the problem of staff sexual misconduct toward female inmates, difficulties, which have
often rendered the problem essentially *invisible*. This invisibility is peculiar in
some ways, because there was extensive early documentation about male rape
in prison (Karpman, 1948; Patterson & Conrad, 1950; Clemmer, 1958; Shaw,
1966; Davis, 1968; Roth, 1971; Sykes, 1971) and because some of the first
studies of female prison life focused disproportionately on the tendency of
women prisoners to form consensual homosexual liaisons and family networks
(Ward & Kassebaum, 1965; Giallombardo, 1966). By comparison, little discussion of female victimization by male staff seems to have developed. While
it is true that male inmate-on-inmate rape and female inmate homosexuality
seem to be much more pervasive than staff sexual misconduct, there are a
number of other reasons for the disparity in the reporting and analysis of this
phenomenon compared to those other forms of prison sexual misconduct.

> First, as Bowker (1980) has noted, information on staff victimization
> of inmates: …is beset by definitional problems. How does one sep-
> arate the victimization of prisoners by individual staff members from
> the "fair" application of institutional policies by correctional officers?
> This problem is particularly severe when dealing with historical ma-
> terial for which institutional standards of appropriate treatment are
> not available (p. 101).

Analyses of historical accounts of prison victimization are difficult to interpret within the context of modern American corrections, where humane standards of treatment are the norm. With this in mind, however, Bowker (1980)
asserts that staff victimization of inmates "is generally thought of as consist-
ing of acts committed by individuals and groups that go beyond the condi-

tions imposed upon prisoners by official institutional policies and state laws" (p. 102). While all jurisdictions in the U.S. today prohibit staff-inmate sexual contact, by virtue of either departmental policy or state law (Smith, 1998), there may still be matters of interpretation regarding which kinds of touches are "inappropriate" or might constitute "misconduct," and what kinds of activities constitute "sexual contact." Needless to say, prisons are not the only settings where these terms are definitionally problematic, as demonstrated in recent American politics.

Second, unlike male inmate-on-inmate rape or female prisoner consensual homosexuality, custodial sexual misconduct has remained out of the focus of scholarly scrutiny because it is much more likely to be *deliberately hidden* by all parties concerned. In men's prisons, male rapes serve a variety of purposes unrelated to sex, such as domination and control, which makes knowledge of their occurrence important; incidents are often widely known by both other inmates and staff even when inmate victims do not cooperate with authorities. In women's prisons, public displays of affection between inmates are often common and partnerships (sexual or not) are frequently a matter of public knowledge, both among other inmates and staff alike. By comparison, reports of staff-prisoner victimization "are almost always limited to the views of one of the participants or observers, with no corroboration from others. Even when reports are written by social scientists, they usually consist of second- and third-person accounts derived from interview rather than direct observation by the scientists" (Bowker, 1980, p. 101).

Clearly, staff members who are engaged in prisoner victimization have many incentives for keeping the activity hidden, since most correctional departments officially and explicitly forbid such victimization. Such staff are unlikely to acknowledge their activity to outside researchers. Furthermore, they are in a position to threaten inmates with retaliation if they say anything. Such threats can be extremely believable in the context of the prison. For example, Human Rights Watch (1996) reports on one allegation by a woman prisoner who claimed that she was forcibly assaulted by a correctional officer who then threatened her into silence by saying that he would harm her son if she told anyone. The officer named the town where the inmate's son lived, which terrified her. "It scares me because I don't know what he can do," she reported. "It's hard to avoid [an officer] around here" (pp. 189–190).

It can be difficult to get information about staff sexual misconduct even from staff who are not themselves engaged in it. Though there is some debate about whether there is a true correctional officer subculture inside prisons (Philliber, 1987), problems in finding out about staff sexual misconduct do appear to arise from staff subcultural allegiances. This comes partly from staff perceptions that correctional work is already less dignified or appreciated than police work or other related occupations; therefore, group protection norms tend to be invoked any time misconduct of any kind is alleged. It may also follow from staff perceptions that inmates are soliciting such misconduct or otherwise deserve such victimization, attitudes which will be explored in more detail below. In any case, even staff that are not engaged in misconduct—and do not approve of it—may choose to remain silent when asked about it.

Their superiors are not necessarily any more likely to be forthcoming. While correctional officials and authorities are often very vocal about trying to eradicate inmate-on-inmate rape or voluntary inmate sexual misbehavior—in fact, some observers of women's prisons have argued that authorities have been virtually preoccupied with detecting and penalizing lesbianism—there are few incentives for authorities to publicize the problem of staff sexual misconduct even when they know about it. After all, under the Constitution, imprisonment imposes certain responsibilities on the government, the least of which is the duty to protect the prisoner. It is difficult to reconcile inmate protection with staff sexual misconduct, and acknowledging the problem publicly threatens to open a floodgate of lawsuits. In a number of cases, legal action has been required before the problem was publicly acknowledged. For example, Human Rights Watch (2000) noted that in Georgia and the District of Columbia:

> Only after being sued did the departments of corrections admit that the problem of custodial sexual misconduct existed in their facilities for women and that reforms were needed. Sexual misconduct is often so entrenched that, in those correctional systems where class action suits have not yet occurred or have only recently been initiated, such abuse is still largely an invisible problem or one that the respective correctional systems flatly deny (pp. 4–5).

Denial of staff misconduct may even extend to the point of suppressing some kinds of information. For example, Human Rights Watch (1996) noted that when an independent Women's Commission investigated the status of women in the jails and prisons of Michigan, an open-ended question in the prisoner interviews reaped all kinds of inmate reports of sexual harassment and abuse by staff. These accounts were used to create a final chapter in the Commission's Report, but this chapter was "ultimately deleted from the published report...[and] the chapter has never been made public in any form" (Human Rights Watch, 1996, pp. 235–236). While the Michigan Department of Corrections argued that the disputed chapter contained nothing but unsubstantiated inmate allegations, Human Rights Watch seemed to believe that these allegations were being suppressed rather than investigated.

The problems associated with trying to study staff sexual misconduct would be difficult enough if correctional staff and authorities were the only ones responsible for stifling information about it. As it turns out, however, inmates also appear to be responsible for concealing staff misconduct, and not always in the face of threatened retaliation. Explicit threats are clearly a disincentive for inmates to report even the most assaultive forms of staff sexual misconduct. More subtle disincentives, however, exist in the form of penalties, which the inmates *perceive* to exist, even if they don't. For example, Human Rights Watch (1996) reported on a Georgia woman inmate who became involved in a sexual relationship with a correctional officer. When the affair came to the attention of officials at the prison, the inmate "repeatedly denied any sexual involvement with the officer because she feared that she would be disciplined if she told the truth" (p. 143). Other inmates deny such relationships because they are using them to obtain goods and services, which will stop if the relationship is exposed. Still other inmates are using sexual relationships with staff to satisfy emotional needs, or they believe themselves to be involved in true love relationships with staff and therefore, they vigorously deny staff misconduct.

In short, almost everyone involved in staff misconduct has reasons for keeping silent about it, which makes scientifically investigating or researching it extremely difficult. Bowker (1980) concluded that documentation on staff-prisoner victimization is "extensive but shallow" in that "incidents tend to be mentioned only in passing (or as part of a polemical piece of writing) and they are not presented or analyzed in any great detail" (p. 101). In recent years, investigations by Amnesty International, Human Rights Watch, and various prisoner advocates have shed more light on the subject than was previously true. However, even these investigations are often composed primarily of inmate allegations, which are difficult to substantiate. Lawsuits which have involved substantiated allegations, or which have resulted in out-of-court settlements, may be more compelling. In the final analysis, however, Bowker (1980) has noted that even the superficial accounts, which comprise the bulk of the literature, mostly describe incidents in institutions for men or delinquent boys, with "very little information on staff-prisoner victimization in institutions for females" (p. 101).

Forms of Staff-Inmate Sexual Victimization

Because of the difficulty in studying the phenomenon, as noted above, the scientific literature on staff sexual misconduct with inmates is extremely limited. One of the first to deal with the subject is Bowker (1980), who explored staff-inmate victimization in general. He noted that there are at least four different forms of staff-inmate victimization in prison:

1. psychological victimization, which may include threats, intimidation, or harassment
2. economic victimization, which includes providing illicit goods at highly inflated prices
3. social victimization, which includes favoritism, racial discrimination, or failure to protect some inmates from others
4. physical victimization, which includes sexual victimization
   (pp. 103–120).

While these forms of victimization may be discrete, many may also overlap.

One of the most comprehensive assessments specifically of staff risk of sexual misconduct towards female inmates was conducted by Calhoun (1996), who surveyed correctional employees in Hawaii about their attitudes on a variety of factors related to perceptions of female offenders, rape myths and other attributes hypothesized as likely to increase risk of inappropriate behavior. An important first consideration in the analysis of this phenomenon, as noted by Calhoun, is the distinction between: (a) *non-consensual sexual misconduct*, which is no different than any sexual assault in the outside world since it involves the use or threat of force to engage in sex against the victim's will; and (b) *pseudo-consensual sexual misconduct*, which may appear on the surface to involve consenting behavior on the part of the victim and may even involve some degree of collusion on the part of the inmate.

Non-consensual sexual abuse of female prisoners would appear to be the most egregious form of staff sexual misconduct, since it is essentially undifferentiated from rape as commonly understood but it takes place in an environment where the parties are, if anything, *more* disproportionately related to each other in terms of power differentials than is often the case in the outside world. That is, though the stereotypical image of rape involves a drooling male misfit brutally attacking a virginal female innocent, more recent research on rape suggests that most acts occur between dating couples, acquaintances, or individuals hierarchically related to each other, such as bosses and employees, teachers and students, etc. (Szymanski, Devlin, Christer, & Vyse, 1993). Such relationships, usually referred to as *acquaintance rapes*, are often marked by disproportionate power relations and/or assumptions about implied protection to be provided, which are used by the rapist to take advantage of the victim. A disproportionate power relationship and presumption of protection is even more clearly skewed in prison settings, where inmates are typically highly vulnerable to staff demands and first-timers may hold certain assumptions about the degree to which staff are supposed to shield them from harm.

However, Calhoun (1996) further divides non-consensual inmate sexual abuse into two subcategories which are useful for understanding the dynamics of such situations in prison settings. While the first of Calhoun's subcategories, *Brutal Rape*, involves the use of explicit force to sexually assault a woman prisoner as described above, most authorities acknowledge that this is probably the least common form of staff sexual misconduct in prison settings, particularly regarding women prisoners. Indeed, it is probably because most staff sexual misconduct does not involve *Brutal Rape* that the literature about rape in prison to date mostly focuses on male rape and has not made much mention of women prisoners (Bowker, 1980).

It is the second form of non-consensual inmate sexual abuse, which Calhoun (1996) refers to as *In the Line of Duty Abuse*, which is undoubtedly much more common with regard to female offenders. This second form involves abuses, which occur "during routine procedures involving necessary body contact or exposure" (Calhoun, 1996, p. 6). Such abuse includes inappropriate viewing, touching, caressing, or other forms of harassment which may occur during apparently routine staff inspections of bathrooms, strip or visual searches of inmates, pat searches of inmates, or medical procedures where appropriate viewing of the inmate or handling of parts of the inmate's body would be ordinarily expected. Just as with similar incidents of sexual harassment in the outside world, staff can clearly misuse conventional situations in the prison during which non-sexual contacts with the inmates' bodies might be expected but the boundary between appropriate and inappropriate touching or commentary might be more difficult to draw. Increased complaints by female prisoners over the last decade about such routine non-consensual sexual abuse, particularly during pat searches and other security procedures, have led many correctional systems to institute more explicit policies and training about the proper conduct of such routine actions, in an effort to both prevent abuses and evade liabilities when they occur.

And there are increasing liabilities when sexual misconduct does occur. Both U.S. federal and most state correctional systems now appear to have explicit policies, which not only prohibit, but also criminalize such behavior by staff (Amnesty International, 1999). The degree of protection varies. While all states and the federal government criminalize rape and other forms of *coerced* sexual contact, it is not so clear that *non-coerced sexual abuse* is prohibited or criminalized everywhere. In a 1999 survey, Amnesty International found that 36 states, the District of Columbia, and the U.S. federal government, all explicitly outlawed "sexual relations between staff of jails and prisons and inmates (p. 49)." Of these, 13 states plus the District of Columbia make it a crime even when the inmate consents, while three states penalize both inmates and staff members who sexually interact with each other even consensually (Amnesty International, 1999).

This last provision for holding the inmate also criminally accountable in cases of staff sexual misconduct reflects a limited understanding of such apparently consensual relationships. Indeed, in referring to this second form of sexual misconduct, Calhoun (1996) labels it *pseudo-consensual sexual abuse*. This is an important naming decision. Logically, any division of types, which calls one form of sexual misbehavior "non-consensual," implies that the other should be referred to as "consensual." Certainly, that is how this second category of misconduct has often been perceived because, as noted earlier, such sexual behavior may superficially appear to involve consent—even collusion or instigation—on the part of the inmate. But, as Calhoun (1996) clearly explains:

> The qualifier "pseudo" is used to indicate that, although the inmate may have actively participated in the sexual contact, this participation cannot be considered true consent. Counseling and security, the two roles performed by the correctional worker...produce an inherent inequality in the worker-inmate relationship. The counseling role establishes a fiduciary association. A defining quality of this type of relationship is that one individual trusts and relies on another on the basis of that other's knowledge, training, experience, or access to resources...In a fiduciary relationship, regardless of colluding or even seductive behavior by the client, it is entirely the responsibility of the counselor to ensure that the relationship is free of sexual contact... The power discrepancy in the worker-inmate relationship is intensified by the correctional worker's security function...The worker's uniform, badge, and access to weapons are constant reminders to the inmates of the correctional worker's authority over much of their day-to-day behavior...The extreme circumstances accompanying incarceration therefore preclude an adult's presumed capacity to consent to sexual activity (pp. 7–8).

In short, an incarcerated person is by definition not capable of giving consent under the law. Thus, there is legally no such thing as "consensual sexual interaction" between inmates and prison staff. According to this logic, all sexual staff-inmate interaction might well be referred to as coercive.

But this defies the subtleties of the situation. Anyone experienced in working with women prisoners knows that they frequently engage in forms of apparently voluntary sexual innuendo and banter, or explicit sexual propositions and seductions, with staff members. Overt sexual and affectionate displays, even elaborate fictive kinship relationships, *between* female inmates is a long-established feature of women's prisons, which sets them apart from male prisons to this day (Ward & Kassebaum, 1965; Giallombardo, 1966; Pollock-Byrne, 1990). The fact that the early literature on women's separate prisons did not mention staff-inmate sexual abuse is probably not because it completely disappeared in the all-female environments of the early separate prisons, but rather is due both to the invisibility of homosexual staff misconduct and truly lower levels of such abuse by women staff members. The reasons for possibly lower levels of sexual abuse by women staff will be addressed later in this discussion. For now, however, it suffices to say that most observers have long acknowledged patterns by female inmates of sexualized or seductive behavior towards, and apparently willing participation in sexual activity with, male staff or visitors.

Calhoun (1996) argues that an understanding of *pseudo-consensual sexual situations* is assisted by also dividing them into two subcategories. First, there is what Calhoun labels *Sexual Bartering*, which involves situations in which "correctional staff trade valued items or preferred treatment for sexual contact with the women prisoners" (p. 9). Such bartering may also involve the obtaining of extra privileges and information, or the avoidance of penalties normally administered by staff. It may be a one-time event or involve an ongoing relationship. The staff member, who is in a position to "extort" sex for access to certain goods or privileges, may initiate it or the inmate who "offers" sex in pursuit of such goods and privileges may initiate it. However it is started and whatever might be traded, the relationship clearly includes *apparently willing* inmate involvement in sexual activity for the explicit purposes of obtaining desired things.

By comparison, the second subcategory of *pseudo-consensual sexual misconduct* is what Calhoun (1996) refers to as *Pseudo Love Situations*, which she defines as situations in which "sexual contact with an inmate is achieved concurrent with the development of what is thought to be a mutual love relationship between the correctional staff member and the incarcerated female (pp. 9–10)." Though the exact degree to which such situations are truly *mutual* is difficult to ascertain, such relationships often involve passionate expressions of love on both sides and the conspicuous lack of explicit bartering behavior. This is not to say that "gifts" are not exchanged, which sometimes makes such situations difficult for outside observers to differentiate from *Sexual Bartering* episodes. But usually the language used by the inmate and/or staff member to describe the relationship has a distinctively romantic quality, in which one or both parties talk about loving the other and may even fantasize about being together on the outside. The fact that there are isolated cases of staff members actually continuing such relationships after the inmates have been released only adds fuel to the fantasy. Most such relationships do not seem to survive either official discovery or the inmate's release.

Not surprisingly, in an earlier analysis of actual sexual contacts between correctional personnel and female inmates, Calhoun (1993) found that the most common forms of staff-inmate sexual contact involved either *Sexual Bartering* or *Pseudo Love* relationships. This is consistent with anecdotal information about staff sexual contacts with female inmates, though evidence of various forms of *Non-consensual Sexual Misconduct* usually dominates news stories and the legal literature.

Causes of Staff Sexual Misconduct Towards Inmates

Whether it is non-consensual or pseudo-consensual, the persistence of staff sexual misconduct or abuse toward inmates in the light of the criminal penalty which can now result in most jurisdictions, may seem problematic. In a truly volitional and rational world, such as that envisioned by Cesare Beccaria, the prospect of severe penalties—which may include not only loss of employment but criminal prosecution and possibly incarceration—should be highly deterrent to otherwise conforming individuals. The fact that such prospects do **not** seem to deter some prison staff from entering into sexual contacts with inmates deserves further examination.

A review of the literature on staff victimization of inmates in general, and staff sexual victimization of female inmates in particular, reveals that there are at least four (4) major schools of thought which have developed over time in attempting to account for the persistence of this behavior. These are the following:

1. The *Blame the Men Models*, which take their starting point from the fact that most staff sexual misconduct appears to be heterosexual and that normal gender relations and training in the United States create peculiar adaptations in the unnatural world of the prison.
2. The *Blame the Staff Models*, which point primarily to negative or inadequate attributes of correctional staff themselves, regardless of sex, either in terms of their inherent qualities or their attitudes.

3. The *Blame the Inmate Models*, which point mostly to the negative attributes of the female inmates, either in terms of their inherent qualities or their situational dilemmas.
4. The *Blame the Institutional Context Models*, which view such interpersonal misconduct between staff and inmates as fundamentally flowing from the unnatural situation in which they both find themselves.

While there is undoubtedly overlap among these four strands of thought, they are conceptually distinct in terms of what they see as the *primary* causation of staff sexual misconduct. A further elaboration of each of these models can be briefly sketched.

Blame the Men Models

The fact that the increase in reports of, and lawsuits about, sexual misconduct toward female inmates seems to have corresponded with the increased deployment of *male* correctional staff inside women's prisons has led some writers to adopt a *Blame the Men Model* of the problem. This approach asserts that the early separate women's prisons were explicitly created precisely because female inmates were routinely sexually abused by the male guards inside the non-segregated prisons of the early nineteenth century (Freedman, 1981; Rafter, 1985; Feinman, 1994). According to this model, it is not hard to understand the dynamics and causes of inmate sexual victimization by male correctional staff because most, if not all, men will take advantage of situations in which they can have sex with women when they are faced with few negative consequences.

Some evolutionary biologists have recently given scientific support for this viewpoint (Thornhill & Palmer, 2000), arguing that male humans are hard-wired through evolution to be predisposed to attempting to spread their seed as far and wide as possible. While individual volition can override such predispositions and usually does, these evolutionary biologists argue that the predisposition of the male of our species is nonetheless genetically oriented toward sexual opportunism. According to this perspective, putting any male correctional officers into supervisory situations over female inmates would seem to be tantamount to putting the fox in charge of the henhouse. This certainly seemed to be the view of the early advocates of the separate system of women's prisons.

Unfortunately, the problem is probably not quite as simple as the all-men-are-genetic-sexual-opportunists approach would suggest, or *most* male correctional employees would attempt to sexually abuse female inmates and there is no evidence to support that this is the case. It may not even be as clear-cut as the similar but more complex assertion of feminist criminologists that all-men-are-rapists (Brownmiller, 1975), which uses more of a social learning approach than a genetic one. The feminist perspective, though it sounds analogous to the all-men-are-genetic-sexual-opportunists view, quite differently argues that because most men have the *capacity* to physically overpower women, and because some men do commit rape, women *learn* to regard all men as potential sexual predators. For this reason, women are carefully trained to be simultaneously watchful and manipulative in their relationships with men. They must be watchful in order to guard against sexual violence, but they must also be manipulative in order to exert control in situations where they are physically out measured. Males, by contrast, are socially trained to adopt a dominant and aggressive approach to the world in general, and towards women in particular, and are also trained to respond positively to women who indicate their sexual willingness. The fact that most men apparently do not sexually abuse women merely disguises the fact that women are almost always unequal in their relationships with men, both physically, in many cases, but certainly socially in most. Women may be mollified by the protection that some men attempt to extend toward them, believing that the men who protect them will not abuse them, not-withstanding the evidence of domestic violence. But men are more likely to be at the top of the social hierarchy, particularly where power is wielded, and have dominant positions in social life relative to women. Women therefore learn to appease and manipulate men, while men learn to protect some women (classified as "Madonnas") and take advantage of others (classified as "whores") (Feinman, 1994). According to this view, since women in prison may be perceived to fall into the "whore" class of women, men who were trained to social life in the United States are likely to see female inmates as individuals who may deserve to be abused rather than protected, regardless of the duties accompanying the correctional roles those men have taken on. As one male correctional staff member once quipped, "I'm here to protect the people on the outside from them, not to protect them from us" (Kelchner, 2000).

Since most of the empirical evidence of sexual misconduct by male staff against female inmates has surfaced within the past decade and in response to lawsuits or investigative inquiries such as those by Amnesty International, it is difficult to determine whether there is actually any real disparity in the sexual misconduct of male or female correctional employees. There is certainly disparity in the *reports* of sexual misconduct, most of them being brought by female inmates against male correctional staff. However, it is possible that female correctional staff are subtler in their abuse of female offenders, or that male inmates are less likely to complain about sexual interactions with female staff. The only empirical study to examine the problem directly was that of Calhoun (1993), who found that "...the participant's gender was not a statistically significant explanatory variable in the models predicting general risk, risk for perpetrating non-consensual inmate sexual abuse, or risk for perpetrating pseudo-consensual inmate sexual abuse" (cited in Calhoun, 1996, p. 41). However, Calhoun's 1996 follow-up study found that the gender relationship was actually more complex:

> The results indicated that gender was not a significant predictor of correctional worker risk for perpetrating pseudo-consensual sexual abuse but was a significant predictor of risk for perpetrating non-consensual sexual abuse. Males were found to have significantly greater risk for non-consensual abuse than female correctional workers. That males and females were at equal risk for pseudo-consensual sexual abuse but males were at greater risk than females for non-consensual sexual abuse contributes to the sparse literature regarding female perpetration of various forms of sexual abuse (p. 89).

According to Calhoun (1996), the heightened male risk for perpetrating non-consensual forms of inmate abuse, both *Brutal Rape* and *In the Line of Duty* offenses, led her to tentatively conclude that prison sexual abuse by males was probably etiologically similar to rape in the outside world. This would be consistent with the feminist all-men-are-rapists theory, in that gender can be seen to mediate the peculiar context of prison where female correctional employees are also in a position of dominance over female offenders but are apparently at less risk of sexually assaulting them. However, the fact that Calhoun found that like male staff, female staff are at *equal* risk for involvement in pseudo-consensual sexual abuse leaves questions remaining. If the problem of inmate sexual abuse was merely a problem of men, female staff should have displayed little to no risk of any form of abuse. Clearly there is more involved.

Blame the Staff Models

Because prison inmates, by definition, cannot legally consent to sexual relations with staff, *Blame the Staff Models* fix the blame for any sexual misconduct squarely on staff, regardless of gender, for personally failing to act appropriately on their responsibilities and legal duties. Even prior to the recent increase in correctional system concern about explicitly training staff to better understand those responsibilities and duties, some analyses of staff misconduct saw the genesis of that misconduct in general attributes such as the following:

Negative Attitudes Toward Female Inmates

There is a rich literature on how prison staff have tended to negatively view female prisoners over the last two centuries of incarceration. Though factors such as type of institutional assignment, race and gender can influence staff perceptions of inmates (Riley, 2000), there are some dominant patterns relevant to our discussion here.

For example, one prominent view of female offenders is to see them as less than human, as "utterly depraved" (Zedner, 1991), "spoiled goods" (Johnson, 1997), or "monstrous" (Lombroso & Ferrero, 1885/1980). Such attitudes can mean that staff come to define whatever happens to inmates in prison as acceptable, and staff mistreatment of inmates thereby comes to be viewed as what inmates deserve. A related attitude is to view female inmates, like all inmates, as essentially untrustworthy and manipulative (Riley, 2000). This view would tend to account for some staff misbehavior being defined as a sort of in-kind manipulation, or at least a form of excusable retaliation ("I take advantage of them before they take advantage of me" or "I use them because they use me").

Another related attitude is to view women inmates as largely responsible for their own victimization (Philliber, 1987), especially in the light of their sexually provocative behavior in prison. Such a *blame-the-victim* attitude is, of course, common in general public attitudes toward rape victims, but here it seems to operate more like a classic "neutralization" (Sykes & Matza, 1957), serving to nullify the rules regarding proper staff behavior in advance of their violation.

Similar, but distinct, from direct blame-the-victim attitudes is another view which sees female inmates simply as victims, a view which is facilitated by the actual horrific biographies of many female offenders. However, this view can lead to staff seeing the female offender as not entirely responsible for her criminal behavior and therefore in need of "rescue" from her horrible situation. Some observers argue that such a sympathetic view of female offenders can lead, in turn, to staff over-involvement with inmates (Calhoun, 1996).

Positive Attitudes Toward Rape Myths

Staff attitudes and sexual misconduct toward female inmates may be influenced by staff members' degree of acceptance of common rape myths. It has been argued repeatedly that sexual assault is facilitated by belief in rape myths (Brownmiller, 1975; Burt, 1980; Harney & Muehlenhard, 1991), such as the myth that women can fight off assailants if they *really* want to (so there really is no such thing as rape), or that it would do some women good to be raped (so it is really a favor to force sex on some women). Calhoun (1996) found that increased levels of Rape Myth Acceptance were a factor in heightened risk for perpetuating non-consensual sexual abuse by correctional officers.

Dissatisfaction With, or Alienation From, the Job

Calhoun (1993) found some evidence that staff sexual abuse of inmates may reflect job dissatisfaction and alienation, in that "correctional workers who experienced a sense of alienation from the administrative and supervisory hierarchy were at risk for turning to the female inmates as sources of support" (Calhoun, 1996, p. 103). There is anecdotal evidence that prison staff who feel alienated from their co-workers or supervisors may indeed come to fill the void with stronger emotional ties to inmates. The concern here is that attitudes, which facilitate inappropriate staff emotional dependency on inmates, might eventually facilitate a pseudo-consensual sexual relationship with inmates.

Individual Staff Qualities

Sexual misconduct by correctional staff has often been attributed to bad qualities of the individuals themselves, either inherent, or situationally induced. Of course, the stereotypical sadistic and evil prison guard is a staple of TV dramas and B-rated movies, and good correctional staff sometimes despair of living down that stereotype. But the fact that some unsuitable staff members are hired in every prison system is undeniable, though more advanced screening and training efforts may have reduced that likelihood. The huge growth of corrections as a sector of the service economy means that many prison systems are hard-pressed to find sufficient numbers of highly-qualified staff, and a robust economy means that the relatively non-competitive salaries of some correctional jobs have left penal systems re-evaluating hiring standards in order to fill positions. That some correctional staff may be persons who were unable to compete successfully for better-paying jobs, either because of lack of skills or personal flaws, leaves the door open for accusations of staff deficiency.

Even otherwise suitable staff, however, may harbor individual personal qualities, which have been indicted as conducive to staff sexual misconduct. For example, one personality trait thought to be related to sexual misconduct, especially among male staff, is *hypermasculinity*, which Calhoun (1996) describes as "the 'macho personality constellation' that includes…an acceptance of the use of verbal or physical aggression to express dominance and a belief that sexual intercourse is a means to 'establish masculine power and the submission of women'" (Calhoun, 1996, p. 35, citing Zaitchik & Mosher, 1993, p. 232). Clearly, the hypothesis is that men (or even women) who display the personality trait of *hypermasculinity* would be more threatened by deviant and uncooperative female inmates, more inclined to use force and aggression to solve problems, and more likely to see sex as a tool for reasserting control, especially over defiant inmates.

Another personal attribute, which has been thought to contribute to inappropriate sexual staff behavior, is an inability to deal with female inmate emotionalism and neediness. Both Pollock (1986) and Calhoun (1996) found that male correctional workers in particular were sometimes "less capable of dealing with the emotional needs of female inmates and more vulnerable to their sexual manipulation than female workers" (Calhoun, 1996, p. 93). Precisely for this reason, perhaps, some female offenders have been reported to express a preference for male staff (Owen, 1998; Kelchner, 2000), since female staff are presumably (though not necessarily) less likely to be manipulated by inmate emotionalism or vulnerable to inmate seduction attempts. The hypothesis is that individual lack of personal skills in managing female offenders, perhaps in conjunction with a personal attribute such as *hypermasculinity*, might result in inappropriate staff sexual contact with inmates.

In short, the *Blame the Staff Models* of staff sexual misconduct toward inmates sees correctional staff personality attributes or attitudes, regardless of gender, as primary factors facilitating sexual abuse. That these attributes might only flower in the unusual social setting of the prison is a contextual issue, which does not diminish the fact that the fundamental problem is seen as lying in the flawed staff person.

Blame the Inmate Models

Blame the Inmate Models point mostly to attributes of female inmates as the causal factors in staff-inmate sexual misconduct, either in terms of the female inmates' inherent qualities or their situational dilemmas. Among the most common attributes of female inmates which are mentioned in this regard are:

Female Inmates as Especially Vulnerable or Responsive to Sexual Abuse

While there is some evidence that no one group of female inmates is more likely than others to experience sexual misconduct by staff (Human Rights Watch, 2000), there is evidence that some types of inmates may be more frequently targeted. Among those most likely to be targeted are women in prison for the first time, those who are young and/or naive, the mentally ill, those who are emotionally weaker or with lower self-esteem, and lesbian or trans-gendered prisoners (Human Rights Watch, 1996; Amnesty International, 1999; Human Rights Watch, 2000). Koss and Dinero (1989) described "a very high risk profile" for victimization among college women, which consisted of attributes such as, among other things, a history of sexual abuse in childhood. Since there is abundant evidence that women in prison are disproportionately likely to have suffered prior sexual abuse in childhood or young womanhood (Widom, 1989; McClellan, Farabee & Crouch, 1997; Harlow, 1999), this factor is now used widely as a marker for sexual abuse vulnerability. It is also now understood that childhood sexual victimization, in particular, may lead to inappropriate adult sexual behaviors (Finkelhor, 1984). It is interesting to note that one survey found that, for this very reason, information about inmate prior sexual abuse and other vulnerability factors was noted in the inmate's file—which staff could easily access (Human Rights Watch, 1996); thus, while gathering such information may have been done with the good intentions of identifying and helping inmates who were prior victims, the fact that some staff could access this information and use it to target the most vulnerable inmates is clearly an unintended consequence. The main hypothesis here is that staff are being put in contact with inmates who are highly likely to engage in inappropriate sexual behaviors because of their prior victimization.

Another possible product of prior sexual victimization may be an attitude on the part of some female inmates that sexual victimization is normal, or that they are at least accustomed to it (Human Rights Watch, 1996). Abusive behavior, when it is defined as normal, tends not to be defined as rape or sexual harassment, and therefore not reported as such. Furthermore, the fact that some women prisoners are also emotionally fragile, or mentally ill, means that their ability to define, resist or report sexual abuse may be limited. In addition, corrections authorities have been accused of inadequately informing women prisoners of the risk of staff sexual misconduct or how to report and seek remedies for it, which would contribute to any ignorance women prisoners might have about the appropriateness of what is happening to them (Human Rights Watch, 1996).

Female Inmate Manipulativeness and Seductiveness

For advocates concerned about staff misconduct towards female inmates, one of the most frustrating aspects of the problem is that female prisoners often seem to actively *solicit* sexual relations, usually for the purposes of obtaining goods and services otherwise not available to them (Human Rights

Watch, 1996). As noted above, *Sexual Bartering* is perhaps one of the most common forms of staff-inmate misconduct (Calhoun, 1996). While this can certainly be initiated by staff in a thinly disguised form of extortion, it can be—and apparently often is—initiated by female inmates, who may see nothing abusive about such exchanges (Human Rights Watch, 1996). Every prison has an underground economy, and staff sexual contact may become a tacit part of that underground economy. Illicit goods, ranging from drugs to chewing gum, may be obtained from staff in return for sexual acts, which women offenders may view as normal for this purpose. Though some inmates clearly have found these relationships extortive and coercive, it is also apparent that women inmates can and do enter them "willingly" and even initiate them for their own purposes (Human Rights Watch, 1996). This tends to have the corollary effect of affirming staff views of female inmates as manipulative and whore-like. It is also consistent with public attitudes that prison rape is just "part of the price criminals pay for wrongdoing" (Struckman-Johnson, Struckman-Johnson, Rucker, Bumby, & Donaldson, 1996, p. 68). The hypothesis here is that female inmates are bad to begin with and solicit a lot of the sexual misconduct, which occurs for simple economic motives, and therefore have no one to blame but themselves.

Female Inmate Desire for Attention and Intimacy

Women inmates may also initiate or enter into sexual relationships with staff "willingly" in order to obtain less tangible resources, such as staff attention, feelings of being desirable, heterosexual companionship, loving intimacy, and/or sex (Human Rights Watch, 1996). Although such staff-inmate relationships are clearly abusive from the point of view that the inmate is legally incapable of consenting to such behavior, this is certainly not how these inmates see their situations. Such inmates have described themselves as willing participants in such relationships, and may deny any abusive or coercive qualities (Human Rights Watch, 1996).

Of course, offering personal attention, intimacy and protection may be a staff ploy to draw an already vulnerable inmate into sexual activity in which she does not really wish to participate. There are extreme cases of sexual misconduct in which the most egregious behavior by staff started out with what appeared to be a loving, attentive concern for inmates. For instance, the infamous case of widespread sexual misconduct and sexual assault in women's prisons in the state of Georgia in the early 1990s provided many examples of such attentiveness being used to lure women inmates into sexual activity: "[Correctional Lieutenant] Philyaw appeared to follow a pattern. He would approach certain prisoners, compliment them by telling them how pretty they were and offer them assistance" (Human Rights Watch, 1996, p. 138). Another Georgia inmate involved with Philyaw reported that she "liked the feeling that I had of being special and important to someone, and he made me believe that I was special...He made me feel like I was the only person that he was involved with, by telling me so many things...that made me think it was special" (Human Rights Watch, 1996, p. 141). That staff can take advantage of vulnerable and emotionally needy inmates is unquestioned. But the fact that inmates readily admit attempting to seduce staff, or successfully do so, in order to get their attention and purported love demonstrates that female inmates may be the sexual initiators in more than a few instances of staff misconduct. Indeed, as noted previously, Calhoun (1996) found that *Pseudo Love* was among the most frequent forms of sexual staff misconduct. The hypothesis here, of course, is that women prisoners crave love and sex, and will turn either to each other in homosexual pairings or to male staff in search of heterosexual bonds.

In short, the *Blame the Inmate Models* of staff-inmate sexual misconduct see female offenders as the willing participants in, and often the seductive initiators of, such sexual relationships because of their own vulnerabilities, desires for illicit goods and/or services, or need for love and companionship. The fact that female inmates may contribute in some way to their own sexual abuse is disconcerting to advocates. As Calhoun (1996) notes:

> It is imperative to avoid victim blaming when examining sexual exploitation of female inmates by correctional personnel. However, it also seems important to acknowledge that the circumstances under which prison personnel work—including the characteristics of the populations for whom they are responsible—may contribute to their likelihood of committing sexual abuse (pp. 25–26.)

Blame the Institutional Context Models

The fourth school of thought about the genesis and dynamics of staff sexual misconduct toward inmates dismisses the individual attributes of staff and inmates alike and focuses instead on the highly unusual social context in which both find themselves. Some of the earliest studies of prison staff misconduct tested the idea that the situational context of prisons could turn otherwise psychologically healthy persons into petty tyrants capable of misusing power and authority (Zimbardo, 1972). Zimbardo's famous Stanford Prison Experiment, in which a mock prison was created in the basement of a building at Stanford University, had to be halted prematurely after less than a week due to overenthusiastic and increasingly abusive behavior by the pretend guards, roles played by randomly selected but carefully screened and apparently normal male college students. This outcome, along with the cowering and depressed effect which playing the prisoner roles had on another group of randomly selected but carefully screened and apparently normal students, has long been used to demonstrate that it is the roles and the situation—and not the attributes of the individuals in the situation—that matter (Bowker, 1980).

Literature from the various helping professions, which may involve more solicitous but still unequal relationships, show that clergy, psychotherapists, attorneys, professors, and medical professionals are all at risk of crossing professional boundaries with their clients because of the relationship between power and sex (Fortune, 1995; Benowitz, 1995; Friedman & Boumil, 1995). Furthermore, the fact that such professionals are highly educated and extensively trained for their professions undermines the arguments made by some experts that correctional personnel are susceptible to sexual abuse only because they are inadequately trained to avoid it. If education and training were the only issue, psychiatrists should never fall prey to sexual abuse of their patients. But, clearly, sometimes they do.

Instead, this model asserts that *inadequate* training merely exacerbates an existing problem inherent to the structure of prisons and staff-inmate relationships. It may be possible to train staff to avoid the pitfalls common to unequal dominant-submissive social relationships, but the inequality of the situation and the peculiar context of prison is what can lead even good people into bad behavior. After all, this perspective argues, correctional staff are asked to spend their entire workdays locked up behind the same bars as the inmates, being vastly outnumbered by the inmates, and forced into repeated contact with criminal offenders who are frequently socially immature at best, and vicious or disgusting, at worst. Staff efforts to do their jobs well and with kindness may be repaid with verbal or physical abuse from inmates who are in prison precisely because they have demonstrated their inability to abide by the law on the outside. It would actually be surprising, according to this perspective, if all correctional employees were able to maintain a perfectly professional response to inmates under these circumstances. From a purely human standpoint, the strange inner world of the prison is bound to breed periodic contempt for some inmates and a desire to harm others in even the best staff. Such feelings, in the structurally induced massive inequality of the prison, are bound to result in abuses of all kinds against inmates, even by staff who are not personally marred by negative personality traits or warped social attitudes. This is similar to the argument that hierarchically structured social relationships of unequal power, especially those maintained through coercive authority, are likely to breed abusive behaviors in the outside world (Hooks, 1984). Prisons clearly exhibit the qualities of a rigidly hierarchical structure in which dominant-submissive relationships are fostered every day. They are the epitome of Goffman's (1961) concept of *total institutions*, in which the inmate finds all spheres of life contained within one physical space managed totally by others over whom the inmate has little or no control. According to this model, such settings may "contribute to the creation of an environment in which females, as well as males, are at risk for abusing inmates" (Calhoun, 1996, pp. 40–41).

The situation of dramatically unequal power in a difficult work environment is made all the more problematic if staff are not, in fact, trained to handle it. As poet Percy Shelley asserted, "Power, like a desolating pestilence, pollutes whatever it touches" (Shelley, 1993). By this measure, correctional staff should be—and supposedly are—specially screened and trained to use the enormous power granted to them. However, a wide range of studies found that inappropriate coercion is frequently used in corrections to control inmates (Bowker, 1980; Marquart, 1986; Baro, 1994; Hamm, Coupez, Hoze & Weinstein, 1994). Furthermore, Calhoun (1993) found that while "very few correctional personnel are able to use power appropriately all the time...a recurrent inability to use power appropriately in managing the behavior of inmates under his or her care may be related to a prison worker's increased risk of perpetrating sexual abuse" (Calhoun, 1996, p. 31). This is consistent with the argument by Groth, Burgess and Holmstrom (1978), whose pioneering analysis of rapists asserted that sexual aggression may actually have little to do with satisfying sexual drives and a great deal to do with meeting power-related needs.

That abusive sexual behavior may be symptomatic of other disguised needs fits with another argument, that some forms of prison sexual misconduct may be byproducts of social support deprivation (Calhoun, 1996). In essence, this hypothesis asserts that correctional workers, already exposed to a stressful and difficult work setting, may begin to experience social support deprivation if their outside social world collapses for any reason. Divorce, illness, death, or other losses may severely impact the prison staff member's ability to cope with job stresses; correctional work, which often has large amounts of overtime attached to it, may even be the precipitating cause of such social support collapses. Under these circumstances, the inmates with whom the correctional staff member spends most of his or her days may incrementally become a replacement support system, with staff receiving more and more emotional sustenance from inside than outside the prison. Like most oppressed persons, prison inmates become highly attuned to the emotional status of their keepers, a survival skill left over from early childhood (Lipman-Blumen, 1984). As a survival mechanism, their ability to detect an emotionally needy staff person and respond solicitously to this need can be enormous.

In short, the various *Blame the Institutional Context* theories of staff sexual misconduct sees inherent attributes of the prison and its power differentials as the essential basis for misconduct, especially if staff are not adequately prepared to handle power in this context and recognize their own vulnerabilities.

Reconciling the Differences and Finding Solutions

It is clear from the review of these four competing models of the origins of staff sexual misconduct that potential solutions for the problem of staff sexual misconduct toward inmates vary considerably.

Some advocates, such as Human Rights Watch (1996), clearly recommend the removal of male correctional staff from contact supervision over female inmates; while they explicitly base this recommendation on international prisoner treatment guidelines, it seems to come primarily from a *Blame the Men* type of model of causation. In this regard, they echo the rhetoric of the pioneer prison reformers of the nineteenth century who worked so hard to create the separate women's prison system in the first place. This also puts them at odds, of course, with current interpretations of the U.S. Constitution, and this recommendation is therefore unlikely to be implemented in the United States any time soon. For better or worse, equal employment laws at present seem to prevent the discretionary deployment of only same-sex staff in women's prisons. It is not clear that same-sex deployment would solve the problem in any case. While complaints about sexual misconduct have clearly increased since the re-introduction of male staff to women's prisons, there are good reasons to think that female staff are every bit as vulnerable to misconduct as their male counterparts. In fact, as noted earlier, Calhoun (1996) found that when compared to male staff, female staff were also at *equal* risk for involvement in pseudo-consensual sexual abuse. The fact that such abuse has not come to light as frequently as cross-sex abuse may reflect nothing more than the larger hidden nature of pseudo-consensual relationships in particular or the relative invisibility of female homosexuality in general.

By comparison, the *Blame the Staff* model would suggest that the problem of misconduct would be eliminated if a better class of staff persons, male or female, were hired in the first place. While screening procedures have certainly improved in correctional recruitment over the past several decades, correctional systems have not always been in a position to be extremely selective about new staff. As noted earlier, the robust economy and full employment of the past decade have left some correctional systems scrambling for employees and utilizing large amounts of overtime to cover all the shifts. Under these circumstances, being more selective in the hiring of correctional staff may be desirable but may not be practical.

Those who invoke the *Blame the Inmate* approach to understanding staff misconduct might seem to have no solutions to offer, since it is unlikely that prisons can be more selective in choosing their inmates. Indeed, in the past, some state officials have sought to dismiss concerns about prison conditions on the basis of the undeniably bad attributes of the inmates. For example, Georgia Governor Lester Mattox, when confronted with prison atrocities in the 1970s, allegedly responded to newspaper reporters that "There is nothing wrong with our prisons that wouldn't be solved by a better grade of clientele." This does not address the question. Implicit in the *Blame the Inmate* model is the notion that staff need to be prepared for the inevitable seductions and manipulations of inmates, and that male staff might need to be especially prepared for working with female inmates who often regard them as particularly vulnerable to such tactics. This concurs with the solutions inherent in the *Blame the Institutional Context* model, which mostly argues that, since it is the prison situation and not the people who are primarily to blame for the problem, even good staff need to be specially trained for the unique situation in which they will find themselves. Most correctional training required for new recruits tends to focus on institutional rules and procedures, and also tends to have a predominantly male-inmate focus (Rasche, 2000). This is not unreasonable, since most inmates in any correctional jurisdiction will be males. However, it is widely acknowledged that women prisoners "do time" very differently than do male prisoners, and a real appreciation of the differences is unlikely to be incorporated into routine new recruit training. This is unfortunate, since a certain proportion of each new recruit class will be assigned to women's facilities immediately out of academy training. Not only will these new correctional officers be initiates in their jobs, but also they are likely to be completely *un*prepared for the unique aspects of working in a women's prison.

As noted earlier, training cannot solve all problems of sexual misconduct by staff. But most staff working in women's prisons have never been specifically trained in the unique aspects of working with women prisoners. For example, a 1998 survey of prisons in 40 states found that in over half of them, there was no special training required of staff working with female prisoners (Hill, 1997; Amnesty International, 1999). Even for those states, which claimed some kind of specialized training, the quality of that training is highly variable and sometimes questionable. In some states training seems to consist of only a few hours of discussion about the ways in which female offenders differ from male offenders, with little background to help staff understand the underlying gender dynamics involved. In other states training appears to primarily focus on admonitions against sexual misconduct, as if reprimands were sufficient. Some states are using self-study programs, which focus on women offenders, sexual misconduct, or both (Miller, 1998). At present it appears that only Michigan and Pennsylvania have implemented full-fledged 40-hour specialized academy training programs that are mandatory for all staff employed in women's facilities. While even this extensive specialized training will not prevent all cases of staff sexual misconduct, it at least offers the prospect of preparing staff to understand the dynamics involved and to make choices which are more likely to avoid such misconduct.

In the final analysis, it is probable that all four models of the origins of staff sexual misconduct toward female offenders have something to contribute to our understanding of the phenomenon. Reliance on only one of them to explain the recent increase in staff sex scandals or lawsuits seems inadequate to the task, and potentially misleading in terms of developing solutions. But until correctional systems are willing to admit that staff sexual misconduct does occur, and that all staff working in women's prisons require specialized training for their jobs, the problem of sexual misconduct by staff is likely to continue unabated.

References

Amnesty International. (1999). *"Not part of my sentence": Violations of the human rights of women in custody* (AI Index AMR 51/19/99). New York, NY: Author.

Baro, A. L. (1994). Political culture and staff violence: The case of Hawaii's prison system. In M. C. Braswell, R. H. Montgomery, & L. X. Lombardo (Eds.), *Prison violence in America* (pp. 123–144). Cincinnati, Ohio: Anderson Publishing Co.

Benowitz, M. (1995). Comparing the experiences of women clients sexually exploited by female versus male psychotherapists. In J.C. Gonsiorek (Ed.), *Breach of trust: Sexual exploitation by health care professionals and clergy* (pp. 213–224). Thousand Oaks, CA: Sage.

Bowker, L. (1980). *Prison victimization.* New York: Elsevier North Holland, Inc.

Brownmiller, S. (1975). *Against our will: Men, women and rape.* New York: Simon & Schuster.

Burt, M. R. (1980). Cultural myths and supports for rape. *Journal of Personality and Social Psychology, 38,* (2), 217–230.

Calhoun, A. (1993). *Needs assessment report: Working with the female offender.* Unpublished Manuscript

Calhoun, A. (1996). *Correctional worker risk for perpetrating sexual abuse of female inmates.* Unpublished doctoral dissertation, University of Hawaii, Honolulu, Hawaii.

Clemmer, D. (1958). *The prison community.* Boston: Christopher Publishing House.

Davis, A. J. (1968). Sexual assault in the Philadelphia prison system and sheriff's vans. *Transaction,* 8–16.

Donaldson, S., Dumond, R. W., Knopp, F. H., Struckman-Johnson, C., & Thompson, L. (2000). Training Americans to rape: The role of our jails, prisons, and reformatories. *USA Today.* Retrieved April 10, 2000, from http://www.spr.org/docs/usatoday.html.

Feinman, C. (1979). Sex role stereotypes and justice for women. *Crime & Delinquency, 25* (1), 87–94.

Feinman, C. (1994). *Women in the criminal justice* system (3rd ed.). Westport, CT: Praeger.

Finkelhor, D. (1984). *Child sexual abuse: New theory and research.* New York: The Free Press.

Fortune, M. M. (1995). Is nothing sacred? When sex invades the pastoral relationship. In J. C. Gonsiorek (Ed.), *Breach of trust: Sexual exploitation by health care professionals and clergy* (pp. 18–28). Thousand Oaks, CA: Sage.

Freeman, R. (1997). Management and administrative issues. In J. Pollock (Ed.), *Prisons: Today and tomorrow* (pp. 294–299). Gaithersburg, MD: Aspen.

Freedman, E. B. (1981). *Their sisters' keepers: Women's prison reform in America, 1930–1930.* Ann Arbor, Michigan: The University of Michigan Press.

Friedman, J., & Boumil, M. M. (1995). *Betrayal of trust: Sex and power in professional relationships.* Westport, CT: Praeger.

Giallombardo, R. (1966). *Society of women: A study of a women's prison.* New York: John Wiley and Sons, Inc.

Goffman, E. (1961). *Asylums.* Garden City, NY: Doubleday.

Groth, A. N., Burgess, A. W., & Holmstrom, L. L. (1978). Rape: Power, anger and sexuality. *American Journal of Psychiatry, 134* (11), 1239–1243.

Hamm, M. S., Coupez, F. E. H., Hoze, F. E., & Weinstein, C. (1994). The myth of humane imprisonment: A critical analysis of severe discipline in maximum security prisons, 1945–1990. In M. C. Braswell, R. H. Montgomery, Jr., & L. X. Lombardo (Eds.), *Prison violence in America* (2nd ed., pp. 167–200). Cincinnati, OH: Anderson Publishing Co.

Harlow, C. W. (1999). *Prior abuse reported by inmates and probationers.* Bureau of Justice Statistics Selected Findings (NCJ 172879). Washington, DC: Government Printing Office.

Harney, P. A., & Muehlenhard, C. L. (1991). Rape. In E. Grauerholz & M. A. Koralewski (Eds.), *Sexual coercion: A sourcebook on its nature, causes and prevention* (pp. 3–15). Lexington, KY: Lexington Books.

Hill, G. (1997). Correctional officer traits and skills. *Corrections Compendium, 22* (8), 1–16.

Hooks, B. (1984). *Feminist theory: From margin to center.* Boston, MA: South End Press.

Huffman, A. (1948). Sex deviation in a prison community. *Journal of Social Therapy,* 6 170–181.

Human Rights Watch Women's Rights Project. (1996). *All too familiar: Sexual abuse of women in U.S. state prisons.* New York: The Ford Foundation.

Johnson, P.C. (1995). At the intersection of justice. *Journal of Gender and the Law, 4* (1), 1–76.

Johnson, R. (1997). Race, gender and the American prison. In J. Pollock (Ed.), *Prisons: Today and tomorrow* (pp. 26–51). Gaithersburg, MD: Aspen.

Karpman, B. (1948). Sex life in prison. *Journal of Criminal Law and Criminology, 3,* 475–486.

Kelchner, D. (2000). (personal communication, September 15, 2000).

Koss, M. P., & Dinero, T. E. (1989). Discriminant analysis of risk factors for sexual victimization among a national sample of college women. *Journal of Consulting and Clinical Psychology, 57* (2), 242–250.

Kurshan, N. (2000). *Women and imprisonment in the U.S.: History and current reality* {online}. Available: http://prisonactivist.org/women/women-and-imprisonment.html.

Lewis, D. W. (1965). *From Newgate to Dannemora: The rise of the penitentiary in New York, 1796–1848.* Ithica, NY: Cornell University Press.

Lipman-Blumen, J. (1984). *Gender roles and power.* Englewood Cliffs, NJ: Prentice Hall, Inc.

Lombroso, C., & Ferrero, W. (1980). *The female offender.* Littleton, CO: Fred Rothman & Company. (Original work published 1885).

Marquart, J. W. (1986). Prison guards and the use of physical coercion as a mechanism of prisoner control. *Criminology, 24* (2), 347–366.

McClellan, D. S., Farabee, D., & Crouch, B. M. (1997). Early victimization, drug use, and criminality. *Criminal Justice and Behavior, 24* (4), 455–476.

Miller, B. (1998). Different, not more difficult: Gender-specific training helps bridge the gap. *Corrections Today, 60* (7) 142–144.

Owen, B. (1998). *"In the mix:" Struggle and survival in a women's prison.* New York: State University of New York Press.

Patterson, H., & Conrad, E. (1950). *Scottsboro boy.* New York: Doubleday.

Philliber, S. (1987). Thy brother's keeper: A review of the literature on correctional officers. *Justice Quarterly, 4* (1), 9–37.

Pollock, J. (1986). *Sex and supervision: Guarding male and female inmates in prison.* Westport, CT: Greenwood.

Pollock-Byrne, J. (1990). *Women, prison, & crime.* Pacific Grove, CA: Brooks/Cole Publishing Company.

Rafter, N. H. (1985). *Partial justice: Women in state prison, 1800–1935.* Boston: Northeastern University Press.

Rafter, N.H. (1990). *Partial justice: Women, prison and social control* (2nd ed.) New Brunswiek: Transaction Publishing.

Rasche, C. (2000). The dislike of female offenders among correctional officers: A need for specialized training. In R. Muraskin (Ed.), *It's a crime: Women and justice* (2nd ed., pp. 237–252) Upper Saddle River, New Jersey: Prentice Hall.

Riley, J. (2000). Sensemaking in prison: Inmates identity as a working understanding. *Justice Quarterly, 17* (2), 359–376.

Roth, L. H. (1971). Territoriality and homosexuality in a male prison population. *American Journal of Orthopsychiatry, 41,* 510–513.

Shaw, C. R. (1966). *The jack roller.* Chicago: University of Chicago Press.

Shelley, P. B. (1993). Quotation from Queen Mab. *The Columbia Dictionary of Quotations.* Columbia University Press.

Smith, B. V. (1998). *An end to silence: Women's prisoners' handbook on identifying and addressing sexual misconduct.* Washington, DC: National Women's Law Center.

Struckman-Johnson, C., Struckman-Johnson, D., Rucker, L., Bumby, K., & Donaldson, S. (1996). Sexual coercion reported by men and women in prison. *The Journal of Sex Research, 33* (1), 67–76.

Sykes, G. M. (1971). *Society of captives.* Princeton, New Jersey: Princeton University Press.

Sykes, G. M., & Matza, D. (1957). Techniques of neutralization: A theory of delinquency. *American Sociological Review, 22* (6), 667–70.

Szymanski, L. A., Devlin, A. S., Christer, J. C., & Vyse, S. A. (1993). Gender roles and attitudes toward rape in male and female college students. *Sex Roles, 29* (1–2), 37–57.

Thornhill, R., & Palmer, C. T. (2000). *A natural history of rape: Biological bases of sexual coercion.* Cambridge, MA: MIT Press.

Turnbo, C. (1993). Differences that make a difference: Managing a women's correctional institution. In American Correctional Association (Ed.), *Female offenders: Meeting the needs of a neglected population* (pp. 12–16). College Park, MD: Author.

Ward, D., & Kassebaum, G. (1965). *Women's prison: Sex and social structure.* Chicago: Aldine Publishing Co.

Widom, C. S. (1989). Child abuse, neglect, and violent criminal behavior. *Criminology, 27* (2), 251–271.

Zedner, L. (1991). Women, crime and penal response: A historical account. *Crime and Justice, 14,* 307–362.

Zimbardo, P. (1972). Pathology of imprisonment. *Society, 9* (6), 4–8.

CHAPTER 7

GENDERED IMPLICATIONS OF SENTENCING AND CORRECTIONAL PRACTICES: A LEGAL PERSPECTIVE

Myrna S. Raeder[1]

Introduction

A primary goal of the criminal justice system is to mete out justice according to the prevailing norms of the day. As a result, criminal laws and correctional policies are typically written assuming equality of the sexes and gender and race blindness. Yet, in a world where gender and race affect and often reinforce cultural expectations and stereotypes, attempts to legislate equality have backfired on women, particularly single mothers whose lives are defined by their gendered reality. Over time, we have compounded our bad sentencing choices with equally shortsighted refusals to fund community correctional facilities so mothers can reside with their children while obtaining the treatment and skills that are necessary for them to live productive lives. At the same time, changes in social policy have made it more difficult for single mothers to avoid losing their children or to successfully reunify with them upon release from incarceration.

In addition to addressing the impact of sentencing on women offenders and child-related issues, this chapter will provide an overview of other correctional policies and practices that have gendered consequences despite their alleged

---

1. This chapter relies heavily on my writings. The statistics are from the Bureau of Justice Statistics or General Accounting Office reports unless otherwise indicated.

neutrality.[2] Topics will include unequal access to programs, services, and facilities, cross-gender supervision and sexual misconduct. The author suggests that in the present negative litigation environment, legislation may be the best route to obtaining gendered justice. To the extent that policies can be changed within the current legal framework, advocates on behalf of women offenders should focus on educating the legal and correctional communities about negative gender consequences and suggesting appropriate responses.

Federal Sentencing Policy Ignores the Realities of Womens' Lives and the Nature of Their Crimes

The war on drugs has often been viewed as a war on women and minorities. As in other wars, women and children are not the intended targets, but casualties of policy decisions aimed at violent men. It is the hardening of the American publics' attitude towards punishment rather than any increase in female criminality that has fueled the burgeoning population of female inmates (Chesney-Lind, 1997). The federal system now has the third largest female inmate population in the United States, housing more than 10,000 women who comprise 10 percent of all incarcerated females. In 1980, the Bureau of Prisons (BOP) operated five prisons for women. By 1998, there were fifteen federal prisons for women and ten administrative facilities housing both male and female inmates, with women's prisons exceeding the rated capacities by a higher percentage than federal prisons housing males.

Women are typically neither violent nor repeat offenders. In 1999, 77 percent of federally sentenced women fell within criminal history category I. Similarly, in 1997, less than 7 percent of female federal inmates were incarcerated for violent offenses. Instead, women typically commit property offenses such as larceny, fraud and embezzlement, or drug offenses. Twenty-five years ago, the courts routinely sentenced women to community sanctions (e.g., probation) when they committed nonviolent crimes. Other countries still adhere to this less punitive sentencing model. For example, Western Europe incarcerates one-tenth of the women incarcerated in the United States even though it has approximately the population (Amnesty International, 1999). Poland reduced its imprisonment of women by one-half without experiencing an in-

---

2. This chapter is intended as an introduction, not an exhaustive discussion of legal topics with gender consequences.

crease in the rate of crime committed by women. Thus, incapacitation and deterrence appear questionable as reasons to imprison nonviolent women. It is even arguable that women are more easily rehabilitated than men, and children appear to be a positive factor in such rehabilitation (Immarigeon & Chesney-Lind, 1992). This leaves revenge and uniformity of sentencing as the primary policies justifying the incarceration of such women.

Today, harsh mandatory-minimums and the federal sentencing guidelines help ensure not only that more women are confined, but that they also spend more time in custody. While the brunt of this sentencing policy falls on drug offenders, the guidelines have also resulted in higher rates of imprisonment for economic crimes, where women have always been overrepresented. Undoubtedly, some females commit economic crimes in order to support their children. Current sentencing guidelines require some incarceration for women, who pre-guidelines, would have been sentenced to straight probation. In addition, although average sentences for property crimes have decreased since 1986, the average percentage of sentence served to first release has increased. As a result, while a pre-guidelines sentence may have been longer, the availability of parole resulted in less time being served. This pattern also exists in state sentencing schemes, through the application of truth in sentencing laws, which extend the amount of time offenders serve, and repeat offender laws that turn misdemeanor economic crimes into felonies.

Prisons and jails have become the social services agencies of last resort for women. The operational challenges imposed upon the correctional staff do not simply revolve around security. Instead, key issues include providing adequate physical and mental health care, including treatment for substance abuse and trauma, and dealing with the impact of women's relationships inside as well as outside the prison, which ultimately affects the success of their programming. For example, large numbers of sentenced women have histories of profound physical and sexual abuse, entrenched histories of drug and alcohol dependence, and serious physical and mental health disorders. Forty percent of women in federal prisons have suffered physical or sexual abuse (Harlow, 1999). They also have higher rates of mental illness and HIV infection than male inmates (United States General Accounting Office, 1999). Commentators and service providers posit that a correlation exists between girls' and women's victimization and specific high-risk behaviors such as serious polydrug abuse (National Symposium on Women Offenders, 1999). It is likely that some segment of female offenders resort to substance abuse to self-medicate depression resulting from abuse or mental illness. It should come as no surprise that these problems are totally alien to a correctional philosophy based on command and control.

Moreover, many women who are sentenced, particularly in drug conspiracies, are the wives or girlfriends of male defendants, and may find themselves involved in criminal activity because of social and cultural pressures, or occasionally, as a result of more obvious means of coercion such as battering. Lengthy mandatory-minimums combined with the inflexible guidelines regime results in lengthy incarceration of such women whose actual role in drug cases is often quite limited. While not all women offenders are passive participants or victims, it is important to remember that many females turn to crime as a way to support themselves when escaping from their own victimization. In addition, some come from backgrounds that encourage them to be dependent on males. Feminists may justly fear that recognizing the importance of women's pathways to crime reinforces stereotypical thinking about female offenders. However, ingrained patterns of socialization cannot be dismissed by wishful thinking. Yet suggesting that these women be sentenced so they can reside with their children in the community while under correctional supervision is greeted with opposition. Such differential treatment is viewed by some feminists as being paternalistic, or even a violation of equal protection, while the knee-jerk response from the traditional legal community is to complain that women obtain a sexist benefit in sentencing.

Gender Neutrality in a Male-Oriented Sentencing Regime

Section 5H1.10 of the federal sentencing guidelines explicitly mandates that sex is not relevant in the determination of a sentence. However, such legislated equality poses difficulties for many women whose criminal behavior and history, as well as family responsibilities, cannot easily be shoehorned into a punitive pro-prison model for sentencing males who are assumed to be violent and/or major drug dealers. Female offenders are often mothers who have sole or primary responsibility for the care of their children, a consideration ignored by the current guidelines. Not surprisingly, fitting all offenders into the same Procrustean bed without regard to their individual characteristics imposes a hardship on female offenders whose lives are shaped by their gender roles and expectations. Male offenders are also dehumanized by the guidelines sentencing grid, but females are defined by their relationships and ties to their children to a much larger degree than are males in our current social structure.

Even under the federal guidelines, women are assumed to receive a break in sentencing, however, the existence and/or extent of any leniency in the sentencing of women offenders is unclear since the empirical data is not consistent. Recent data comparing male and female guidelines sentences still finds that women are given shorter sentences than men (Mustard, 2001). Putting aside explanations of paternalism or chivalry, the work of criminologist Kathleen Daly (1995) raises the intriguing suggestion that direct comparison of similar sounding crimes often reveals that the woman is less blameworthy than her male counterpart. Daly evaluated the "gestalt of the harm", which considers such factors as the relationship between victim and offender, the manner in which the crime was committed, as well as the mix of offense and offender biography. Daly concluded that even in an equality based model of sentencing, lighter sentences for females may be justified, although a statistical analysis would not reveal the nuances or textured reasoning which explain away any sentencing differential. As a result, simply controlling for easily compared factors such as prior record appears to be insufficient to detect legitimate differences in sentencing that are now considered as gender bias favoring females (Daly & Bordt, 1995). Thus, the seemingly principled imposition of across the board gender equality in sentencing may result in an unwarranted harshness, even before children are entered into the equation. Moreover, women were originally disadvantaged by the blending of male and female sentences to create the sentencing grid, because pre-guidelines, women served shorter sentences than men. Ironically, few notice when men sometimes benefit from lower sentences as a result of high crowding levels in male prisons, despite the reality that women's prisons are actually more overcrowded (Stolzenberg & D'Alessio, 1997).

Assuming that women do receive consideration because of their children, this result does not necessarily signify gender bias favoring women, because it is due to their role as caregiver. In other words, empirical studies have typically not controlled for the presence of young children. As a practical matter, before the adoption of the federal guidelines, judges considered children at sentencing. For example, Judge Merritt in his dissent in *United States v. Brewer* (1990), questioned why the fact that the defendant is a young mother who must raise several small children is no longer relevant to her sentence, now for the first time, when such facts, alone and in combination, have heretofore been considered highly relevant by sentencing judges and jurors. This type of favoritism may pose a dilemma for feminists who favor strict gender equality, as well as for those who fear that it encourages stereotypical thinking about the role of women in society. Yet while such sentencing can reinforce traditional family roles, jettisoning any consideration of children puts the family units of single mothers at risk. As Daly (1989) has aptly recognized, "equal treatment of defendants whose responsibilities for others vary and differ by gender may not be justice" (p. 12). In the case of childrearing, this task is primarily allocated to the mother in today's society. Therefore, why should the judiciary blindly impose equal treatment on parents with different primary caretaking responsibilities when the rest of society does not? The disadvantage to children whose lives are disrupted by their mothers' incarceration has societal costs that can outweigh any sentencing advantage (Parisi, 1982).

To the extent that sentencing preferences exist, it has also been viewed by feminists as a double-edged sword since any leniency in sentencing for female offenders may be intertwined with the exclusion of women from the economic process. Steffensmeier and Kramer (1995) have observed "the prime structural mainstay of male dominance lies in the continued assignment of females [to] the home and to the nurturant homemaker role...[which] helps eliminate labor competition" (p. 301). However, sentencing practices that further familial stability have great benefits for mothers, their children, and the community at large. As has been suggested in another context, feminists must devise a reliable approach to reckon with generalizations that are largely true either because of biology or highly successful socialization (Littleton, 1987). In the sentencing arena, such methodology must integrate gender assumptions concerning the predominantly nonviolent nature of female crime and parental role of female offenders. Merely denouncing sexism in sentencing without examining the effects of so-called gender neutral sentencing ultimately operates to the detriment of women whose lives are shaped by the existing gendered social structure and their children.

Family Ties Departures are Discouraged by the Guidelines

Section 5H1.6 of the Sentencing Guidelines states that "family ties and responsibilities and community ties are not ordinarily relevant in determining whether a sentence should be outside the applicable guideline range." This policy statement has posed great difficulty for pregnant offenders and women who are the sole or primary caretakers of their children. Before the sentencing guidelines, offender characteristics were traditionally taken into account in sentencing, and overt consideration of children was unnecessary because approximately two-thirds of all female offenders were given probation. Although the sentencing guidelines specified in section 5H1.6 permit offender characteristics including family ties to be considered for sentencing within the appropriate range, the quest for uniformity in sentencing resulted in family ties being relegated to factors that are not "ordinarily relevant." The downplaying of offender characteristics was intended to deter judges from giving longer sentences for minority males who lacked family and community ties and substantial employment histories. Yet it often results in unrealistically long sentences for all offenders because it disregards a basic tenet of sentencing, that punishment should be individualized.

Moreover, given the relatively few offenders that could benefit from a single parent departure, implementation would not result in untoward disparity, particularly when compared to acknowledged disparities inherent in the guidelines caused by prosecutorial discretion and regional sentencing differences. Indeed, the problem is not disparity per se, but *unwarranted* disparity. Taking children into account in sentencing is warranted. What is unwarranted and uncivilized is ignoring the plight of children unnecessarily severed from their sole parents.

Why Single Moms Are Not Ordinary for Purposes of Section 5H1.6

The current pro-prison model of sentencing has a dramatic impact on the children of federal women offenders that is not experienced by children of male offenders. There is absolutely no indication that pregnancy and single parenting were ever considered by the U.S. Sentencing Commission, let alone the lopsided gender effect that imprisoning single mothers has on their children. Yet the empirical data points to the gendered nature of single parenthood. A recent U.S. Census report (1999) recognized that the vast majority of all single parents are female. The single parenting problem disproportionately falls upon all female offenders as opposed to male offenders, but the problem may affect minority women offenders more severely than white female offenders. While almost two-thirds of single parents are white, single parenting is much more prevalent among Blacks than whites, with almost 63 percent of Black family groups with children being maintained by a single parent as compared with 23 percent of whites. Single parenting among Hispanics of all races has also increased, now comprising about one-third of Hispanic family groups with children. Presently, 92.6 percent of Black single parents are female, compared to 86.7 percent who are Hispanic and 83.7 percent who are white (U.S. Bureau of the Census, 1999).

It may be that the 'feminization of poverty,' in combination with the relative hopelessness of their lives is largely responsible for the increasing number of female offenders who are single mothers. Single mothers are disproportionately an impoverished group. For example, recent census statistics concerning poverty note that despite the drop in child poverty, children under age six living with single mothers experienced a poverty rate of 50.3 percent, more than five times the rate for children under six in married-couple families (U.S. Bureau of the Census, 1999). The effect is more dramatic for Black and Hispanic single mothers with children under 18 than for white single mothers, with 32 percent, 47 percent and 46 percent of those mothers, respectively, falling below the poverty level.

Just as the deletion of gender from alimony decisions had the unforeseen result of plunging children of divorced mothers into poverty, the deletion of gender from sentencing decisions often causes the complete disruption of the lives of children of female offenders who are single mothers. In divorce, the deletion of gender assumes the existence of equal economic opportunities contrary to the actual lower earning capabilities of most females. In sentencing, the deletion of gender assumes a world in which men and women have equal custody of children and where the non-custodial parent is willing and able to take responsibility for the care of their children. The reality is that single parents are disproportionately mothers. When fathers are incarcerated, their wives or former wives overwhelmingly care for their children. In contrast, when mothers are incarcerated, surveys confirm that their former husbands rarely have custody of the children.

Unlike a male parent whose children continue to live with their mother, a single mother's imprisonment is likely to lead to the total disruption of her children's lives. Of the 60 percent of female federal prisoners who have minor children, 84 percent of them lived with those children before entering prison (U. S. General Accounting Office, 1999). Yet less than 30 percent of the children having an incarcerated mother live with their fathers (Mumola, 2000). In fact, it is likely that the many of the children of male offenders who do not remain with their mothers, are separated because both parents are imprisoned. In other words, imprisonment of the mother shatters the family unit, placing the children in new home settings and often separating siblings. Approximately 45 percent of the children of federal women offenders live with grandparents, 34 percent with other relatives, 12 percent with friends and 3 percent are placed in foster care (U. S. General Accounting Office, 1999). It is likely that the foster care placement is understated, since many children in foster care are placed with relatives, and it is possible that affirmative foster care responses indicate that children are placed with non-relatives. Furthermore, many of these situations are temporary, resulting in multiple placements, or separation of siblings that are even more disruptive to the children. Indeed, the fact that the total percentage exceeds 100 percent is an indication of this effect.

Can we really doubt that these women's family ties are cut asunder in ways that drastically impact the lives of their children beyond what is endured by children of male inmates? All children of incarcerated parents face the stigma of their parent's imprisonment, lose their financial support and have their parental relationship impaired, but "children of single mothers" lose the emotional support and guidance of the only parent they live with, are often plucked from their family surroundings, torn from their siblings, and shuffled between relatives and friends to avoid total disintegration of the family by court ordered placements with non-relatives. In *United States v. Concepcion* (1992), Judge Weinstein recognized that "[r]emoving the mother in such a matriarchal setting destroys the children's main source of stability and guidance and enhances the possibility of their engaging in destructive behavior," and later themselves becoming offenders. In determining the appropriateness of a family based departure, he noted that the policy statement of section 5H1.6 is not useful because

> [i]t tells us that a defendant mother is not generally entitled to credit for her motherhood. It does not address the more critical problem of whether the court can consider the welfare of her child or children in determining the sentence…Insofar as the absence of the mother may have profoundly deleterious effects on her child or children, their care must be relevant in considering whether there should be incarceration or other forms of punishment (p.19).

Judge Weinstein has generally referred to the current family ties policy as "so cruelly delusive as to make those who have to apply the guidelines to human beings, families, and the community want to weep" (Weinstein, 1996). Yet many circuits have been cavalier in disregarding the effect that incarceration has on the children of single mothers. *United States v. Brand* (1990) epitomizes the classic justification for refusing departures to single mothers whose children will be placed with strangers:

> But such a situation is not extraordinary. A sole, custodial parent is not a rarity in today's society, and imprisoning such a parent will by definition separate the parent from the children. It is apparent that in many cases the other parent may be unable or unwilling to care for the children, and that the children will have to live with relatives, friends, or even in foster homes (p.4).

Brand concluded that the defendant's "situation, though unfortunate, is simply not out of the ordinary," despite the District Judge's conclusion that "[t]he carrying forward of the guideline range of imprisonment…would have a devastating impact upon the emotions, minds and the physical well-being, just every aspect, of two very innocent youngsters…." (p. 33). Until recently, the Second Circuit stood virtually alone in its willingness to affirm family ties departures for single parents, (Ellis & Shummon, 1999; Shoenberg, 1997). In *United States v. Johnson* (2d. Cir. 1992), the court recognized that the "sentencing guidelines do not require a judge to leave compassion and common sense at the door to the courtroom" (p. 125). Yet, even within the Second Circuit, the guidelines mandate that such departures remain the exception, not the norm.

The disallowance of family departures is particularly disturbing after the Supreme Court held in *United States v. Koon* (1996) that trial judges decisions concerning sentencing should be given deference and reviewed by an abuse of discretion standard. The Ninth Circuit is one of the few that has clearly rejected its pre-*Koon* disapproval of single-parent departures. In *United States v. Aguirre* (2000), the Court affirmed a departure for a mother whose common-law husband died during her incarceration, leaving her eight-year-old son without a custodial parent. *Aguirre* distinguished its previous case law precluding such departures by noting that they had been decided prior to *Koon's* shift in the standard of review. Under the new standard, the Court held, "[b]ecause district courts are 'particularly suited' to determine whether a given factor makes a case unusual, we will not second guess the district court's determination that this case involved an unusual family situation." This flexible approach should be adopted in all circuits, where it would ensure that pre-*Koon* negative case law no longer requires trial judges to reject single parent departures.

Even those who question the legitimacy of family ties departures recognize that women are disadvantaged in relation to men in sentencing because they are often housed farther from their families (Segal, 2001; Berman, 2001). Since it is too costly to build facilities in every state given the relatively small number of female federal inmates, 30 percent of them are assigned to facilities more than 500 miles from their release residences. When prisoners in Alaska and Hawaii are included, these distances are even greater (U. S. General Accounting Office, 1999). Although the figure of 500 miles may not sound so imposing, it is sufficiently large to make frequent visits impossible, particularly given the lack of accommodations in most prisons for families or for overnight visits (U. S. General Accounting Office, 1999). Research indicates that parent-child visits are important not only to maintain relationships that will increase the chance of successful family reunification after incarceration, but also to allow both individuals to deal with their reactions to separation and loss (U. S. General Accounting Office, 1999; Gabel & Johnston, 1995). The average distance from home for women prisoners exceeds that of men, despite the BOP attempts to lessen the disparity. The BOP is now responsible for housing District of Columbia inmates and has agreed to locate them within

500 miles of the District, but these women are still at a particular disadvantage because they formally would have been housed much closer to family members. Distant facilities also impact women incarcerated in state prisons, since there is usually only one such facility in each state.

Single mothers are less likely to receive visits from their children because substitute caregivers and foster care parents must arrange visitation and make the long journey with the children. When each child has a different family placement, as is not uncommon, separate arrangements must be made for each to visit. In the case of male offenders, wives and girlfriends may be more inclined to visit the prisoner, and they often bring the children along. For all of these reasons, distance is a burden imposed on female prisoners differently than on males, and this deserves consideration in the departure calculus. In *Froehlich v. Wisconsin Department of Corrections* (1999), the children of a female state prisoner sued the Department of Corrections to keep their mother in Wisconsin. In this matter, Judge Posner wrote that while such an accommodation is not constitutionally imposed upon prison officials, "it may be a moral duty." Yet in *United States v. Thomas* (1999), the court did not view the absence of a halfway house near the defendant's residence as a legitimate reason for a downward departure.

Single mothers also face a host of collateral consequences that are much more onerous than those endured by their male counterparts (Jacobs, 2001). Beyond the automatic loss caused by the incarceration itself, single mothers face the real danger of losing their children permanently. Under the Adoption and Safe Families Act of 1997 (ASFA), women who are incarcerated for more than fifteen months face early termination proceedings if their children are placed in foster care with non-relatives. While it is difficult enough for single mothers with substance abuse problems to meet ASFA's requirements when they live in the community, the short deadline has especially severe consequences for mothers who are incarcerated. Yet placement of the children with relatives, which would avoid ASFA's harsh mandates, is discouraged by state policies that provide less financial aid for family members compared to the amount awarded if the child were to be placed with a stranger. To further complicate matters, in some states, extended incarceration by itself is a sufficient reason for termination (Genty, 2001).

Laws impose an additional burden on single mothers who have been convicted of drug or drug-related offenses. For example, even if a single mother avoids termination of parental rights, she may still be denied federal cash assistance and food stamps if she lives in a state that has not opted out of the provision of the Personal Responsibility and Work Opportunity Reconciliation Act that bars anyone with a drug-related felony conviction from receiving such aid. She may face the lifetime five-year limit for receiving Temporary Assistance for Needy Families, or be hampered in obtaining work if she requires drug treatment or cannot obtain childcare. Her drug conviction may affect her ability to obtain public housing or assistance to pay for private housing. She may be deported as a result of her conviction, regardless of whether her children are citizens. Her educational opportunities may also be limited by the Higher Education Act of 1998, which denies eligibility for students convicted of drug offenses. Since a single mother bears the primary burden of caring for her children, these laws impose a special burden on her.

It appears that the drafters of the sentencing guidelines never contemplated the impact of this type of separation and loss on single mothers, which by its very nature is not "ordinary" when compared to the impact on the average male inmate. Even adding in the few males similarly situated as single parents whose children will not remain with their mothers during incarceration, the total universe of single parents in prison is clearly less than 5 percent of all inmates. Such a small proportion of offenders should be considered outside the "heartland." The present quandary over the feasibility of granting departures to pregnant women and single mothers ultimately results because the circuits have unnecessarily limited their interpretation of the 5H1 factors by defining the opposite of "ordinarily" as "extraordinarily," which conjures up images of unique circumstances, rather than circumstances which are infrequent in the larger offender population, although typical within a given population such as single mothers (Farrell, 2001). Yet, in a commentary concerning departures, the Commission itself uses language such as atypical and unusual as antonyms for ordinary. Single mothers are atypical of the majority of offenders being sentenced. Moreover, the effects of pregnancy and sole or even primary parenting responsibilities on women are not ordinary when considered in relation to the total offender population. Women still comprise less than 20 percent of federal offenders and less than 8 percent of the total federal inmate population. The percentage of single mothers, or pregnant offenders, is obviously even smaller, as is the number of such females whose family units would be disrupted by their incarceration. The disruption of a family unit is an extraordinary event in the lives of those affected, even if the number of single mothers who are being incarcerated is growing.

No doubt, some of the hostility toward more humane sentencing of single mothers is based on the unstated assumption that children are better off without bad mothers. In other words, the Pollyanna view holds that children have better alternatives. However, neither adoption, nor foster care is a panacea. Adoption is typically a realistic alternative for only young children. Other terminations simply cut ties to relatives without creating any new families. Many of the children of offenders are likely to be placed in unstable settings with family or friends, and it is not uncommon for siblings to be separated. Children that are placed in foster care may also find that contact with former family members is cut off, a result that is rarely in the child's best interest. Although some foster care arrangements are surely better for children than the option of remaining in a dysfunctional family, it would be naive to think that being shuttled among strangers is always preferable to remaining with their family. Numerous surveys, many of which were conducted as part of civil lawsuits against a particular jurisdiction's foster care system, reveal astoundingly high incidences of abuse or neglect within foster care when compared to abuse in the general population (Chaifetz, 1999). In addition, multiple placements and failure to adequately provide for a child's medical, psychological, and emotional needs are widespread problems in the foster care system (Chaifetz, 1999). A Bureau of Justice Statistics survey found that 87 percent of female prisoners who spent their childhood in foster care or institutions reported being physically or sexually abused (Harlow, 1999). Exposure to physical and sexual abuse may put children in greater jeopardy than staying with a parent who is obtaining supervised treatment.

Because judges can be unaware of the myriad of issues that should inform the sentencing of women offenders, the National Association of Women Judges in conjunction with the National Institute of Corrections, has published a curriculum for Sentencing Women Offenders, which can be adopted for use in state as well as federal trial courts.

A Pro-Family Ties Departures

Although some courts creatively interpret the guidelines to avoid Draconian results, it is time to recognize sex-based anomalies in sentencing, and where necessary, to modify the guidelines to encourage single parenting departures and permit pregnancy and primary parenting responsibilities to be considered in granting departures. I have advocated revision of section 5H1.6 as follows:

> A downward departure shall be granted to single parents and pregnant offenders who committed nonviolent crimes, unless good cause exists for denying it. Single or primary parenting responsibilities and pregnancy can ordinarily be considered in granting a family ties de-

parture. The absence of an appropriate facility for the parent within 150 miles of the child's home is also a factor that can be considered in granting a family ties departure.

As revised, this provision would help to erase the disproportionate impact of current sentencing practices on the children of single mothers. At present, the total disruption of the lives of such children makes a mockery of gender neutrality in sentencing. What we currently have is a facially sex neutral departure rule that ignores children and does not neutrally operate when applied to male and female offenders.

Why the Federal Safety Valve Has Gender Consequences

The Safety Valve provision adopted by 18 U.S.C. §3553(f) and contained in guidelines section 5C1.2 was enacted because of the generally acknowledged unfairness of punishing first-time, low-level drug offenders more severely than high-level conspirators who had information they could trade in exchange for substantial assistance departures. The provision permits the judge to depart below the applicable mandatory-minimum, and it was granted to 30 percent of drug offenders in 1999 (U. S. Sentencing Commission, 1999). However, this provision has not solved the over-incarceration of women offenders.

To be eligible for safety valve consideration, a defendant must commit specified drug-related crimes, which disqualifies women who are incarcerated for property crimes. The defendant can only have one criminal history point, eliminating a number of low-level offenders. In addition, defendants must also truthfully provide the Government with all the information and evidence they have concerning the offense they committed. Ironically, the women who participate in drug conspiracies with their male intimates often express an undivided loyalty toward their partner, and they are often hesitant to betray their partner by providing the authorities with information, even if it would help them receive a sentencing break. This reality hits hardest for women whose intimates deal drugs from the home. Families can be isolated from crime committed by males in a business or public setting, but not from drug-dealing at home. To be crime-free, the woman in this setting must be willing to leave the male who is often the father of her children. If not, the socialization that leads her to facilitate his criminal activity by answering the phone, taking packages, or counting money, also inhibits her from willingly disclosing his crimes to the authorities. Her bad choices in relationships are often compounded by unrealistic expectations of low sentences.

Even if a female offender satisfies the criteria for safety valve relief, the amount and type of drugs involved in the conspiracy could easily result in a substantial sentence, despite the ability of the judge to disregard the applicable mandatory-minimum. Thus, while a family ties departure cannot trump a mandatory-minimum, it is still necessary to fashion more equitable sentences for single and primary parents than the safety valve provision can accomplish alone. An amendment should be enacted to reach more offenders with minor criminal histories. To eliminate the gendered impact of the disclosure requirement, it should be deleted from the safety valve.

Other Departures with Gendered Implications: Coercion, Duress and Mental Difficulties

Section 5K2.12 of the guidelines, which provides that coercion or duress not amounting to a complete defense, may be a reason for the court to grant a downward departure. However, "ordinarily," coercion will be sufficiently serious to warrant departure only when it involves a threat of physical injury. In practice, departures for mental and emotional conditions, diminished capacity, and coercion, are more significant for females than for males. In addition, there appear to be some racial distinctions among females such that white women use coercion more frequently.

The Ninth Circuit dealt with several issues concerning coercion of female defendants in *United States v. Johnson* (9th Cir. 1992). *Johnson* recognized that "there are sets of circumstances in which gender is also a factor to be considered" in determining coercion. *Johnson* permitted the defendant's vulnerability to fear, not produced by the people causing the defendant's criminal action to be taken into account at the sentencing stage. Therefore, the fact that a defendant met the battered woman syndrome could be considered as an affirmative defense of duress for acts of distribution that are included as relevant conduct under section 1B1.3, and as evidence of incomplete duress for which the court could grant a discretionary downward departure.

Johnson also recognized that a downward departure for coercion could be granted in cases where the female defendant could have made efforts to escape. A downward departure based on incomplete duress was also discretionary if a defendant had "frozen fright," which made her an easy victim of powerful manipulative and violent men. In such cases, the court could consider the subjective vulnerability of the female offender as such coercion related not merely to entering a conspiracy, but also to failing to leave it. Coercion could also be considered in determining whether to grant a downward departure for acceptance of responsibility after the trial so long as the defendant admitted guilt.

Similarly, *United States v. Gaviria* (1992) ordered a downward departure for a woman whose history established a pattern of dependence due to male control from a combination of physical and psychological abuse, cultural norms, economic dependence and other factors. As Judge Weinstein noted in *Gaviria* "[n]owhere in the Guidelines' formulaic mechanism is there room to consider how the facts of the life of a woman abused in this fashion should bear upon her sentence" (p. 479). Justification for the departure was alternatively based upon the authority of sentencing guidelines in section 5K2.12, or independently upon Congress's directives in 18 U.S.C. §3553, or upon both. *Gaviria* also recognized that women in traditional cultures are particularly susceptible to patterns of dependence, domination and victimization, and noted that the Commission's statement on bias found in section 5H1.10 should not be interpreted expansively to deny the effects of gender on relevant and appropriate sentencing criteria.

United States v. B. Roe (1992) held that a female's extraordinary history of childhood neglect, physical, sexual and emotional abuse and neglect, could justify a downward departure from the sentencing guidelines. Therefore, where the medical experts agreed that the defendant's abuse was exceptional, turning her into "virtually a mindless puppet," it was an error for the trial court to find that her abuse was *not* extraordinary. Obviously, not every exhortation to dominance or battered woman status will result in a departure. First, the decision to depart is discretionary. Second, a factual predicate will have to be established before the court exercises its discretion. Similarly, not every circuit is eager to accept departures for other mental difficulties. For example, in *United States v. Vela* (1991), the Fifth Circuit upheld the trial court's refusal to depart on the basis of a female's childhood incest.

In addition, Policy Statement 5K2.13 restricts the ability to depart for diminished capacity unless the defendant committed a non-violent offense while suffering from significantly reduced mental capacity not resulting from voluntary use of drugs or other intoxicants. For example, a battered woman who was convicted of killing her abuser would not be able to claim diminished capacity. While most battered women accused of homicide are convicted in state court, women who kill their abusers on federal lands, such as reservations and military posts, face federal sentencing.

Alternative Sentencing
to Obtain Gendered Justice

Ultimately, a better world for nonviolent women offenders and their children requires innovative approaches to sentencing and correctional policy in both state and federal court that focus on gender-specific treatment, community corrections, and social services in the community (National Institute of Corrections, 2000). The goal should not merely be to mete out equal sentences to females, but rather to guarantee that they receive just sentences which reflect their dissimilar patterns of criminality and family responsibilities. The lofty goal of gender neutrality has backfired, wrecking havoc on the lives of female offenders and their children who are forgotten by the sentencing guidelines structure. It is time to establish a federal task force focusing on female offenders so that a rational sentencing policy concerning women and their children can be created and integrated into the guidelines structure. However, until Congress reconsiders the severe sentences dictated by mandatory-minimum drug statutes, over-incarceration will remain the norm, not the exception.

Until sentences are revised downward, facilities that would permit incarcerated mothers to live with their children should be available. To date, most jurisdictions that operate mother-child facilities have few beds and short-term placements. In 1994, recognizing that such residences should be available to inmates sentenced to a term of not more than seven years, Congress enacted the Family Unity Demonstration Project, 42 U.S.C. § 13882, whose stated purpose was to evaluate the effectiveness of community correctional facilities in encouraging family unity and reducing recidivism. The act was intended to house eligible offenders and their children under seven years of age in residential facilities that were not within the confines of a jail or prison, yet would provide a safe, stable, environment for children. Eligible parents included nonviolent offenders who had acted as a primary caretaker of the child prior to incarceration or had just given birth and were willing to assume a primary caretaking role. Parents guilty of neglect or convicted of crimes against their children were explicitly excluded. The residential facilities were designed to improve the stability of the parent-child relationship, provide alcoholism and drug addiction treatment, and offer services to enable inmates to find adequate housing, education, employment, and childcare upon their release. Unfortunately, despite a funding schedule in the legislation, money was never allocated for the Project. Congress is currently considering legislation to build residential treatment centers for mothers and their children, but this will only be effective if money is appropriated so that grants can be awarded. Similarly, legislation to provide mentoring programs for children of incarcerated parents has recently been enacted, but is not fully funded. The BOP is currently considering the option of permitting eligible pregnant offenders to reside with their child in a community correctional facility until the child is eighteen months old, and the creation of a prison nursery for more high-risk prisoners. While this is an appropriate beginning, it would apply to only a fraction of all federally incarcerated mothers, and may take several years to implement. Ultimately, we need better social policy to ensure that neither mothers nor their children are disproportionately punished when a female offender is incarcerated.

Correctional Policy and Practices with Gender Consequences: The Unfavorable Litigation Context: *Turner* and the Prison Litigation Reform Act (PLRA)

The Deferential *Turner* Standard

Since *Reed v. Reed* (1971), gender issues have typically received heightened scrutiny in equal protection analysis. Classifications must be reasonable, not arbitrary, and must rest upon some fair and substantial relation to the goals of the legislation, so that all persons similarly circumstanced shall be treated alike. In a correctional setting, this can be satisfied by showing that the classification serves important governmental objectives and that the discriminatory means employed are substantially related to the achievement of those objectives.

However, it is unclear how *Reed* and its progeny apply to prisons because the Supreme Court has eschewed any standard other than reasonableness for evaluating prison regulations that affect constitutional rights, which would otherwise require strict scrutiny. *Turner v. Safley* (1987) rejected strict scrutiny analysis even though the right to marry at issue was fundamental because the application of that standard would seriously hamper the ability of prison officials to anticipate security problems and adopt innovative solutions. *Turner* held that "when a prison regulation impinges on inmates' constitutional rights, the regulation is valid if it is reasonably related to legitimate penological interests" (p. 89). Therefore, some courts have abandoned mid-level scrutiny of gender claims. *Turner* makes it harder for women to challenge existing practices because it lowers the burden on the government to justify the discrimination. *Turner* applied the following criteria in determining constitutionality:

1. Is there a valid rational connection between the prison regulation and the legitimate governmental interest?
2. Are there alternative means of exercising the right that remains open to inmates?
3. What impact will accommodation of the constitutional right have on guards, other inmates, and the allocation of prison resources?
4. Is there an absence of ready alternatives that may evidence the reasonableness of the regulation?

A regulation is invalid if the logical connection between it and the asserted goal is so remote as to render the policy arbitrary or irrational. In other words, the governmental objective must be legitimate and neutral. When accommodation will have a significant ripple effect on inmates or staff, *Turner* mandates that courts should be particularly deferential to the correctional defendant. However, the existence of an obvious easy alternative at *de minimis* cost may be evidence that the regulation is not reasonable, but an exaggerated response. In the last fifteen years, the Supreme Court has consistently deferred to prison officials: *Turner's* rationale for the extreme deference accorded to correctional administrators is

> [s]ubjecting the day-to-day judgments of prison officials to an inflexible strict scrutiny analysis would seriously hamper their ability to anticipate security problems and to adopt innovative solutions to the intractable problems of prison administration. The rule would also distort the decision making process, for every administrative judgment would be subject to the possibility that some court somewhere would conclude that it had a less restrictive way of solving the problem at hand (p. 89).

Turner held that the stated penological objectives restricting the right to marry did not satisfy a rational relationship test. Interestingly, both had gender connotations. The first was to prevent love triangles that might lead to violent confrontations, which could easily be accommodated by banning marriages that present a security threat. The second was a rehabilitative concern that female prisoners might marry other inmates or ex-felons. The Court stated that this demonstrated excessive paternalism and a lopsided rehabilitation policy that could not justify the rule. Thus, even after *Turner*, stereotypical views of women may suffice to reject a regulation. Moreover, there is room to argue that laws or regulations that are intentionally discriminatory should be evaluated under heightened scrutiny. In other words, even if *Turner* applies to a facially neutral law or regulation that has a disparate impact, heightened scrutiny should apply to laws that facially classify individuals on the basis of their sex.[3] Whether *Turner* applies to jail regulations is unclear, because *Bell v. Wolfish* (1979) held that due process prohibits punishment of pretrial detainees. However, restrictions are constitutional due to an incident of some other legitimate governmental purpose, such as to assure that the individual will be present for his trial, or to maintain security and order at the institution. To the extent that a jail houses both pretrial detainees and convicted inmates, the appropriate standard of review becomes even thornier.

The PLRA Drastically Restricts Prison Litigation

The Prison Litigation Reform Act (PLRA) was enacted because of the perception that prisoners were bringing many frivolous actions. This legislation governs all civil litigation, whether in federal or state court, with respect to conditions in a federal, state, or local prison that are alleged to violate a Federal right. It provides that a court shall not grant or approve any prospective relief unless it is narrowly drawn, extends no further than necessary to correct the violation of the Federal right, and is the least intrusive means necessary to correct the violation of the Federal right (18 U.S.C. § 3626(a)(1)(A)). The act also limits attorneys' fees.

The PLRA also requires prisoners to exhaust their remedies before they can sue. In *Booth v. Churner* (2001), a unanimous Supreme Court held that under 42 U.S.C. § 1997e(a), an inmate seeking only money damages must complete any prison administrative process capable of addressing the inmate's complaint and providing some form of relief, even if the process does not make specific provision for monetary relief. The PLRA imposes another substantial restriction on obtaining relief by conditioning any recovery for mental or emotional injury on a showing of physical injury. Finally, the PLRA requires prisoners to pay filing fees and prohibits prisoners from proceeding in *forma pauperis* if they have brought three prior frivolous actions or appeals.

The combined effect of the deferential *Turner* standard and the PLRA drastically limits both the ability of prisoners to litigate, and the effectiveness of any relief they receive. As a result, legal advocates for women offenders must redirect their efforts to legislation and education of correctional officials in order to effect change. In other words, rather than lamenting about the absence of viable prison litigation, advocates should attempt to educate prison administrators about the benefits of gender-responsive programming, and

---

3. See *United States v. Virginia*, 518 U.S. 515, (1996).

ways to limit cross-gender supervision with the least resistance from correctional staff.

Equal Protection and Title IX Issues in Correctional Policy

The Fourteenth Amendment guarantees equal protection of the laws. This amendment is directly applicable to the states, and applies to the federal government and District of Columbia through the Fifth Amendment Due Process Clause. Because facilities for females are fewer and typically smaller than male facilities in every jurisdiction, equivalent access to programs and services is a significant issue from both a fairness and legal perspective. Such claims can arise in a variety of contexts, including educational and vocational training, availability of and payment for work, treatment for substance abuse, psychological and physical healthcare, sentencing and correctional alternatives such as boot camps, work furloughs, and community based facilities, court access, and placement in inadequate institutions that are virtually inaccessible for family visitation. Some equal protection claims directly implicate gendered discrimination, while others do so indirectly. In addition, statutory rights, particularly under Title IX, as well as constitutional rights, may be applicable (Collins & Collins, 1996).

The pre-*Turner* equal protection case law was quite favorable towards claims of incarcerated women. Cases found male and female inmates to be similarly situated for equal protection analysis, and courts applied the heightened scrutiny test by comparing programs for male and female offenders and typically found substantial disparities. Financial arguments were rejected as a reason justifying poorer conditions and programming for women due to their smaller numbers. Relief was afforded based on concepts of parity, substantially equivalent in substance, if not form.

In contrast, the post *Turner* case law has raised a number of unresolved issues:

1. Must women inmates make a threshold showing of being "similarly situated" to male inmates for constitutional and Title IX claims?
2. Is the threshold question or the entire equal protection claim measured, by mid-level scrutiny or *Turner's* reasonably related test? Is the standard different for a Title IX claim?
3. Does the standard of review depend on whether the regulation is facially discriminatory?
4. Is the remedy for an equal protection violation "equality" or "parity?" How does this differ from the Title IX remedy?

Several post-*Turner* cases have required a threshold showing that women are similarly situated to the male population based on prison population, security classification level, types of crime committed, length of sentence and special characteristics. In addition, the rational relationship test is applied unless the plaintiff shows purposeful or intentional discrimination because of the plaintiff's gender. Such cases reject any burden on the state to provide a gender-neutral basis for the discrepancy. If policy is neutral, disparate impact alone does not suffice to invalidate classification without a showing of discriminatory purpose. The focus is on the process by which programming decisions are made. Therefore, program comparisons are rejected. The anomalous result is that the more unequal the men's and women's prisons are, the less likely it is that courts will consider the differences in men and women's prison experiences as being unconstitutional.

While no litigants have challenged sex-segregated prisons, it should not follow that women may be segregated into unequal facilities. Because the Supreme Court has not addressed unequal treatment of women in prison, it is unclear whether heightened scrutiny for gender discrimination survives *Turner*. It has been suggested that the determination of substantial similarity be based on the purpose of programming, which is directed at preparing both populations for release into the community. Therefore, appropriate factors would include custody levels, length of sentence, purpose of incarceration, and ability to benefit from a program, not the number of inmates at the institution and their special characteristics, which are dictated by sex segregation.

One case that has received widespread attention is *West v. Virginia Department of Corrections* (1994), which held that the absence of any equivalent to placement in a male boot camp that could result in a shorter sentence violates equal protection. *West* applied a heightened scrutiny standard in analyzing the equal protection claim. This accords with decisions that view purposeful discrimination as requiring a higher level of scrutiny. However, even if *Turner's* standard is not applied, that does not ensure a positive decision. For example, *Pittsburg v. Thornburgh* (1989) upheld a regulation resulting in women serving their time at a distant location, because it satisfied a substantial governmental interest of alleviating overcrowding in men's institutions.

On occasion, men raise equal protection arguments that female prisoners are treated more favorably. This poses a challenge to administrators who desire to upgrade facilities and services for women, but are concerned that by doing so, they risk litigation that would require them to disproportionally expend greater resources for their vastly larger population of males. However, this fear appears unwarranted. First, trial and appellate courts have routinely granted the extreme deference to correctional judgment envisioned by

Turner. Second, the trend away from program-to-program analysis for purposes of establishing that male and female populations are similarly situated has resulted in equal protection litigation being virtually unwinnable in several circuits, despite even blatant disproportionality. Thus, until and unless the Supreme Court reverses this approach, differences in programming may not implicate equal protection unless the differences themselves evidence facial gender discrimination. Third, the PLRA has dramatically reduced the feasibility and efficacy of both prison reform litigation and litigation by individual prisoners. Thus, the innovation mentioned by *Turner* as a prime reason for deference can continue to benefit women by the introduction of gender-specific programming that is the most effective way to rehabilitate and treat women.

In addition to equal protection, Title IX, 20 U.S.C. §1681a, prohibits sex discrimination in any educational program or activity receiving Federal assistance. By definition it does not apply to the Federal Bureau of Prisons, but only to states and local governments. Title IX provides several advantages for female inmates. In contrast to equal protection litigation, the trend of Title IX litigation has been to reject a threshold showing that female and male populations are similarly situated. Moreover, some courts have applied strict scrutiny to Title IX claims, which is even more demanding than the heightened scrutiny test applied to gender-based discrimination. In addition, Title IX requires equality of programs, rather than parity. This difference is somewhat elusive. While women must have reasonable opportunities for similar studies, and equal opportunity to participate in programs of comparable quality, judges have not required gender-integrated classes in prisons, or strict one-for-one identity of classes, or as many classes in a small women's prison as in the larger men's prisons. The extension of Title IX to recreation and paying jobs has met mixed success, depending on the relationship between the educational and vocational programs in question. *Jeldness v. Pearce* (1994) held that the award of merit pay to men, but not to women, participating in the same vocational training course in the same location violated Title IX.

However, *Alexander v. Sandoval* (2001) recently held that there is no private right of action to enforce disparate-impact regulations promulgated under Title VI of the Civil Rights Act of 1964. The Court interpreted prior Title IX case law as providing private actions only in cases of intentional discrimination. As a result, it is possible that private claims would also be barred in disparate impact cases under Title IX. Such a restriction would virtually eliminate the use of Title IX in prison cases, since disparate treatment, rather than intentional discrimination is the usual problem.

Gender-Responsive
Programming and Policies

It is ironic, that while women have traditionally been placed in a prison system based on a male model for facilities, programs and services, providing them with gender-responsive programming is viewed by some as inappropriate from an equal protection perspective. In other words, they are doubly disadvantaged by their gender. First, women receive fewer resources, and the resources they are given often are not directed towards their needs. Second, when they seek gender-responsive programs and accommodations, they are told that women cannot be treated differently than men. The irrationality of this position should be self-evident. For example, there are valid biological reasons why women do not use urinals or why one-piece jumpsuits are a great inconvenience for women. Further, when women offenders have histories that demonstrate severe physical and sexual abuse, substance abuse, and more mental illness than male offenders, those factors should also be considered in determining differences in policies and programs for the two genders. Physiological differences are emerging in addiction and sexual trauma research that also suggests the need for men and women to be given distinct programming. Similarly, women's pathways to crime and their biological and cultural parenting ties to their children should be considered when attempting to determine how to create programming that will best enable women to succeed when they are released from custody.

Advocates for women offenders must continue to remind the correctional and legal communities that the current correctional system is not gender neutral, but is gender responsive to male inmates. Gender responsiveness to female needs is not a request for special treatment, but simply a response to unequal treatment in a system based on male risks and needs. Without gender-responsive programming and facilities, correctional systems will fail to ensure successful reintegration of females into the community because their programming is not designed in the most effective way to promote rehabilitation and deter recidivism.

Even if heightened scrutiny is applied to evaluating gender-responsive programming, it can be sustained by showing that this type of programming serves important governmental objectives such as ensuring a better likelihood of rehabilitating women, and is substantially related to the achievement of these objectives. So long as the basis of the programming is not based on a stereotypical view of women, and supportable reasons justify why such programming works, it should survive any challenge. For example, the underlying reason for many women to engage in substance abuse often flows from their previous sexual or physical abuse. Thus, the response to an equal protection challenge based on gender-responsive substance abuse treatment is that until the underlying causes for substance abuse are addressed in programming, such women are unlikely to forsake drugs.

The Supreme Court's recent decision in *Nguyen v. I.N.S.* (2001) lends support to providing gender-specific programming for women offenders. *Nguyen* upheld a statute that distinguished proof of citizenship based on whether the citizen parent was the child's mother or father. The biological differences between men and women concerning birth justified the statutory distinction that required fathers to acknowledge paternity in a way not required of mothers. The Court noted that "[t]he issue is not the use of gender specific terms instead of neutral ones," rather "that the difference does not result from some stereotype, defined as a frame of mind resulting from irrational or uncritical analysis." In other words, justification based on penological research and rehabilitative goals should survive claims of stereotyping. Thus, it is unlikely that courts will attempt to second-guess prison administrators concerning gender-specific programming based on rational distinctions, particularly in light of the difficulties posed by the PLRA in initiating prisoner litigation. Female offenders may also be able to attack some programming that is based on a male model. For example, boot camp programming that is centered on a view of male criminal personality traits that has no relationship to the profile of women offenders, and their pathways to crime may be open to challenge.

Concerning programs available only to women, *Smith v. Bingham* (1990) denied a claim of sex discrimination brought by a male inmate who was precluded from attending vocational classes only open to females. Security claims dictated the result. *Smith* noted that the challenge would have failed applying either *Turner* or heightened scrutiny. In *Oliver v. Scott* (2002), the court rejected an equal protection challenge, where female inmates were accorded more privacy, because the men were not similarly situated to the women. Differences in the population included the fact that there were six times as many men as women. Unlike the women, the men were convicted of violent crimes, and many males were involved in gang activity and were sexual predators. As *Oliver* noted: "All of the facts that justified round-the-clock surveillance by guards of both sexes applied uniquely to men (p. 747).

If a job description for a gender-responsive program specifies that only women are qualified for certain positions, staff members or their union may challenge the restriction. For example, if a female therapist is designated because administrators have found that women prisoners relate better to them, particularly in the early stages of treatment, litigation may result. The same type of issue has arisen when prisons have attempted to limit the role of male officers in female institutions to avoid cross-gender supervision and sexual misconduct. Such employee complaints are based on Title VII, which prohibits sexual discrimination in employment.

However, *Tharp v. Iowa Department of Corrections* (1995) held that a prison employer may, without violating Title VII, adopt a reasonable gender-based job assignment policy that is favorable to women employees if it imposes only minimal restrictions on male employees. Similarly, *Robino v. Iranon* (1998) also held that a policy of assigning only females to certain posts imposed a *de minimis* restriction on male employees. To the extent that a colorable Title VII claim was raised, *Robino* held that gender was a bona fide occupational qualification (BFOQ) to accommodate the privacy interests of female inmates. *Torres v. Wisconsin Department of Health and Human Services* (1988) also held that the state could exclude male guards from its female prisons in order to promote female prisoners' rehabilitation without violating the male staff's employment rights if it could show that the BFOQ was "reasonably necessary to furthering rehabilitation." *Torres* indicated that the state is not required to show objective evidence, either from empirical studies or otherwise displaying the validity of their theory. Proper evaluation is on totality of the circumstances as contained in the entire record. In other words, the decision of penal administrators is entitled to substantial weight when the product of a reasoned decision-making process is based on available information and experience. The fact that the program is considered a reasonable approach by other professional penologists is a significant consideration.

In the therapist example, there are several responses to a Title VII challenge by male staff. First, the restriction is *de minimis* because it affects only one or two slots in a prison system that includes many such slots (for these purposes slots in male facilities can be included, since the focus is job opportunity within the correctional setting). Second, gender is a BFOQ because effective therapy for the women to aid their rehabilitation is dependent upon the therapist's gender. However, BFOQs are difficult to justify and must be carefully considered. In addition, a BFOQ may ultimately disadvantage female staff in the overall correctional system if the same arguments regarding gender-responsiveness apply to male prisoners. For example, in *Dothard v. Rawlinson* (1977), the Supreme Court upheld gender restrictions that prohibited the hiring of female guards in contact positions for an all male maximum-security prison, finding that gender was a BFOQ based on the need to protect women guards from assaults by male prisoners. To date, lower courts have interpreted this decision narrowly when considering whether women correctional personnel should be excluded from supervising men.

Courts Give Female Inmates More Privacy Rights than Males

Courts apparently think that women have a greater expectation of privacy than men. Thus, cases in which women complain about cross-gender supervision have a greater probability for success. In *Forts v. Ward* (1980), female inmates challenged male guards' placement in their housing units during nighttime shifts. The court took as a given that women had a constitutional expectation of privacy. Women would be provided suitable sleepwear and would be permitted to cover their cell windows for 15-minute intervals. *Lee v. Downs* (1981) upheld a jury verdict on behalf of a female inmate who had been forced to disrobe in the presence of male guards. *Torres v. Wisconsin Department of Health and Human Services* (1988) *cert. denied* (1989) held that the state could exclude male guards from its female prisons in order to promote female prisoners' rehabilitation without violating the male staff's employment rights if it could show that the BFOQ was "reasonably necessary to furthering rehabilitation." Privacy was a key concern in reassignments, however, the law is not settled in this area. For example, *Cain v. Rock* (1999) upheld a cross-gender guarding policy, and rejected liability pursuant to 42 U.S.C. § 1983 where the plaintiff failed to establish that the policy was the direct cause of her alleged sexual assault.

In contrast, *Jordan v. Gardner* (1993) held that a Washington state policy that allowed male guards to conduct a pat search on female inmates violated the women's Eighth Amendment right to be free from cruel and unusual punishment where the cross-gender searches were random, nonemergency, suspicionless, and conducted on women offenders who had prior histories of abuse and would likely feel revictimized by the intimate contact of their breasts and genitals by male guards. *Colman v. Vasquez* (2001) refused to dismiss Fourth and Eighth Amendment claims on qualified immunity grounds where males conducted pat searches on female inmates who were assigned to special units for victims of sexual abuse. However, in *Carlin v. Manu* (1999), officers were entitled to qualified immunity for strip searches performed by female officers in the presence of male guards because this practice was not clearly unlawful at the time.

Most courts find that a strip search of arrestees charged with a minor offense is permissible only if an official has individualized suspicion that the arrestee is hiding weapons or contraband.[4] Thus, in *Foote v. Spiegel* (1997), a

---

4. See *Kelly v. Foti*, 77 F.3d 819, 822 (5th Cir. 1996); *Skurstenis v. Jones*, 236 F.3d 678 (11th Cir. 2000).

correctional officer was denied qualified immunity for strip searches of female jail inmates without reasonable suspicion.

Human rights organizations have suggested that there be no cross-gender supervision of women offenders. This eliminates privacy concerns and also minimizes the opportunity for sexual misconduct. However, single-sex supervision meets resistance on Title VII grounds. For example, *Carl v. Angelone* (1995) held that summary judgment on the BFOQ defense was precluded because there were no factual findings that a large percentage of female prisoners would suffer psychological pain or harm upon being physically searched by men, or that a prison's security was not dependent upon cross-gender-clothed body searches. The employer's single-sex supervision decision had been based solely on an interpretation of *Jordan v. Gardner* (1993), which held that cross-gender searches were illegal in all situations. *Carl* pointed to the factual underpinnings in the *Jordan* case, demonstrating that a very large percentage of the female population in the prison in question were victims of prior abuse and would suffer psychological harm from random searches. Moreover, *Carl* indicated that the employer must demonstrate why it cannot reasonably rearrange job responsibilities within the prison in order to minimize the clash between privacy interests of the inmates, the safety of the prison employees, and the non-discrimination requirement of Title VII, before the prison will be entitled to the BFOQ exception.

While a policy of single-sex pat downs, searches, or close supervision, can be justified in many female prisons, reference to the specific population held in a given prison is key. Therefore, discussions with prison psychologists, as well as security officers, produce evidence supporting single-sex close supervision. Ironically, such policies have the potential of limiting the employment opportunities of female correctional staff, and should be formulated so they do not unduly disadvantage employees of either sex. Establishing a gender sensitive policy that addresses potentially litigious issues requires thought to balance a number of interests, including security, rehabilitation, simple decency, past trauma of women inmates, and affirmative action considerations for female staff. Often female staff members who are not in correctional roles can be called in to search women inmates, rather than requiring correctional staff to be female.

Sexual Misconduct

Sexual misconduct cannot be tolerated in any correctional setting, regardless of whether it involves violence on the part of any correctional official. Sexual misconduct violates the Eighth Amendment of the United States Constitution, which provides that "cruel and unusual punishment shall not be inflicted." The Fourteenth Amendment makes this provision applicable to the states. *Farmer v. Brennan* (1994), a case in which a transsexual prisoner was raped in a male prison, clearly established that "being violently assaulted in prison is simply not part of the penalty that criminal offenders pay for their offenses against society." Increasingly, statutes and case law recognize that employees have a duty not to engage in any sexual activity with inmates, even if the inmate initiated the contact, because such liaisons cannot be deemed voluntary in light of the employee's position of authority in the institution.

The existence of sexual misconduct in female institutions in the United States can no longer be dismissed as an isolated phenomenon, and it has been condemned by several human rights organizations as well as in the case law (U. S. General Accounting Office, 1999; Amnesty International, 1999). Undoubtedly, the explosive growth of the female inmate population, and the prevalence of male employees in most female institutions, has contributed to the increased incidence of sexual misconduct. Sexual misconduct can result in discipline or criminal charges being brought against the staff member accused of improper behavior. In addition, civil litigation may be instituted against the particular staff member, other staff members, supervisors and even the municipality. Beyond the legal context, sexual misconduct implicates the culture of the institution and hinders the ability of administrators to achieve rehabilitative goals. Explicit prohibition of all sexual contact between staff and inmates, regardless of who initiates it, or whether it is arguably consensual, must be enacted to send a message of zero tolerance. Only if all such conduct is treated as abusive and warranting termination, can the safety of the inmates and the integrity of the institution be ensured. Supervisors must reinforce the message that any sexual contact will not be tolerated.

In 2001, Amnesty International published a follow-up report entitled, "Abuse of Women in Custody: Sexual Misconduct and Shackling of Pregnant Women," which condemned "the continuing lack of laws prohibiting custodial sexual misconduct in some states; [and] the failure of existing laws to provide adequate protection...." (p. 1). Amnesty International (2001) focuses on six problem areas:

- That an inmate could be held criminally liable for sexual contact with guards, which: could have the effect of making retaliation for complaints of custodial sexual misconduct lawful and sanctioned, and lead to violations of the right to an effective remedy as well as the equal protection of the law.

- That all forms of sexual contact by staff is not covered by statute, although it is inherently abusive.
- That a statute may consider the consent of an inmate to sexual acts a mitigating factor, despite the inherently abusive professional misconduct.
- That state laws fail to cover all staff (including contractors and volunteers), which could result in those not covered by the statute committing sexual misconduct without facing criminal charges.
- That laws may not cover all locations where an inmate could be abused, such as a local jail, resulting in the inability to bring charges for the abuse.
- That the level of the penalty meet the nature of the harm, whether felony, misdemeanor, or administrative penalty (pp. 1–2).

Amnesty International also proposed that effective policies and procedures for reporting and investigating allegations of misconduct must be introduced, along with educational programs on custodial sexual misconduct for staff and inmates. At least one of its suggestions is likely to conflict with Title VII, in that it would require females to be guarded by female officers and that any male providing services in female institutions should always be accompanied by a female officer.

When civil litigation is brought, usually under 42 U.S.C. § 1983, a favorable outcome for the female litigant is not assured, because the standard for establishing an Eighth Amendment violation is extremely difficult to prove. For example, in *Adkins v. Rodriguez* (1995), a jail deputy made comments to a female inmate about "her body, his own sexual prowess, and his sexual conquests." Because an Eighth Amendment violation only occurs in the prison context when the deprivation is "objectively, 'sufficiently serious,' " and the prison official acts with " 'deliberate indifference' to inmate health or safety," the "outrageous and unacceptable" conduct of the guard did not reach the level of an Eighth Amendment violation (p. 1037). In other words, it is not sufficient that the injury was grave enough that the official should have known of the risk, if that individual did not subjectively know of the risk. Thus, *in United States v. Sanchez* (2000), because an inmate did not tell the guards she was offended and harassed by their verbal abuse, they did not have the requisite culpable state of mind. Due to the actual notice requirement, on occasion even undisputed claims of sexual intercourse will not result in liability against the State.[5]

Bringing class actions to stem Eighth Amendment violations has become quite difficult, whether aimed at sexual misconduct or inadequacies in facilities, programming or medical care. The PLRA limits the extent of interfer-

5. See *Daniels v. Delaware*, 120 F.Supp.2d 411 (D. Del. 2000).

ence in which a court can mandate in the normal operation of a facility, and provides that a court shall not grant or approve any prospective relief unless it is narrowly drawn, extends no further than necessary to correct the violation of the Federal right, and is the least intrusive means necessary to correct the violation of the Federal right (18 U.S.C. §3626(a)(1)(A)). The act also limits attorneys' fees and limits the amount of time that an injunction is valid.

Some call for the application of international law to protect women against sexual violence in prison. For example, the Declaration on the Elimination of Violence Against Women (1993) defines violence against women as "any act of gender-based violence that results in, or is likely to result in, physical, sexual or psychological harm or suffering to women, including threats of such acts, coercion or arbitrary deprivation of liberty, whether occurring in public or in private life" (Article I). The Universal Declaration of Human Rights (1948) and the Convention Against Torture and Other Cruel, Inhuman or Degrading Treatment or Punishment (1987) arguably applies to rape of a female inmate by correctional staff. Under the International Covenant on Civil and Political Rights (ICCPR), sexual abuse may violate the right to be accorded human dignity and the right to privacy. The Standard Minimum Rules for the Treatment of Prisoners also has applicable provisions (Geer, 2000; Springfield, 2000). However, courts in the United States are likely to refuse to provide greater rights under international law, than are currently accorded prisoners under the United States Constitution.

As a result, the most effective role for legal advocates for women offenders may be to keep the glare of publicity on sexual misconduct issues, so that prison systems will be forced to respond. In a relatively short time after the initial barrage of negative media publicity due to reports by human rights organizations concerning sexual abuse of female prisoners, nearly all states have enacted laws criminalizing sexual misconduct. Drafting model legislation and lobbying for its passage may be equally, if not more critical than, litigation in the current legal environment. In this regard, including provisions for the reporting of abuse is key to eliminating improper conduct. Thus, legal advocates must ensure the existence of an appropriate inmate grievance procedure that establishes punishment for retaliatory conduct against inmates who report abuse. For example, *Women Prisoners v. District of Columbia* (1996) prohibited retaliatory acts, which included disciplining the inmates, changing their work or program assignments, transferring them to another facility, or placing them under involuntary protective custody. However, discipline of an inmate who fabricates a charge of sexual harassment, or otherwise acts in bad faith in connection with such a charge, was permitted.

In addition, legal advocates should be willing to work with the legal and correctional community to provide education in order to elicit support for reform by changing attitudes and explaining the legal consequences of inaction. Demonizing the entire correctional community ignores the reality that many individuals within the system currently desire change, and others will follow when they realize that change provides more rewards than doing nothing. While the result of litigation may not always establish liability, correctional officials recognize that claims of sexual abuse can result in bad publicity and costly litigation. Ironically, the threat of litigation, rather than its success, appears to provide motivation to correct the most glaring defects of prison administration.

Conclusion

While this chapter paints a fairly bleak legal portrait of gender issues affecting female offenders, there are hopeful signs for the future. First, the current interest in children of incarcerated parents may provide a context in which decarceration of nonviolent offenders becomes a system wide priority. Any swing of the pendulum towards community corrections and nonpunitive sentencing will benefit most female offenders and their children. For example, several states have started to favor treatment and retreat from lengthy sentences for drug offenses. A few states have even started to pull back from lengthy sentences in order to decrease correctional budgets. In addition, the benefits of rehabilitation in prison are starting to be appreciated again as communities recognize that some 600,000 prisoners are returning each year. Second, the hands-off attitude of the courts towards prison litigation can provide innovative correctional officials with latitude to create gender-responsive programs that are more likely to rehabilitate women offenders. Third, public attention on sexual misconduct will ultimately prove to be more effective than litigation in changing correctional attitudes. Indeed, such publicity has generated public questions concerning why many of these women are incarcerated at all.

Cases Cited

Adkins v. Rodriguez, 59 F.3d 1034, (10th Cir. 1995)
Alexander v. Sandoval, 532 U.S. 275 (2001)
Bell v. Wolfish, 441 U.S. 520 (1979)
Booth v. Churner, 532 U.S. 731(2001)

Cain v. Rock, 67 F.Supp.2d 544 (D. Md. 1999)

Carl v. Angelone, 883 F.Supp. 1433 (D. Nev. 1995)

Carlin v. Manu, 72 F.Supp.2d 1177 (D. Or. 1999)

Colman v. Vasquez, 142 F.Supp.2d 226 (D. Conn. 2001)

Daniels v. Delaware, 120 F.Supp.2d 411 (D. Del. 2000)

Dothard v. Rawlinson, 433 US 321 (1977)

Farmer v. Brennan, 511 U.S. 825 (1994)

Foote v. Spiegel, 118 F.3d 1416 (10th Cir. 1997)

Forts v. Ward, 621 F. 2d 1210 (2d Cir. 1980)

Froehlich v. Wisconsin Department of Corrections, 196 F.3d at 800, 802 (7th Cir. 1999)

Jeldness v. Pearce, 30 F.3d 1220 (9th Cir. 1994)

Jordan v. Gardner, 986 F. 2d 1521 (9th Cir. 1993) (en banc)

Kelly v. Foti, 77 F.3d 819, 822 (5th Cir. 1996)

Lee v. Downs, 641 F. 2d 1117 (4th Cir. 1981)

Nguyen v. I.N.S., 533 U.S. 53 (2001)

Oliver v. Scott, 276 F.3d 736 (5th Cir. 2002)

Pitts v. Thornburgh, 866 F.2d 1450 (D.C. Cir. 1989)

Reed v. Reed, 404 U.S. 71 (1971)

Robino v. Iranon, 145 F.3d 1109 (9th Cir. 1998)

Skurstenis v. Jones, 236 F.3d 678 (11th Cir. 2000)

Smith v. Bingham, 914 F.2d 740, 742 (5th Cir. 1990), *cert. denied*, 499 U.S. 910 (1991)

Tharp v. Iowa Department of Corrections, 68 F.3d 223 (8th Cir. 1995), *cert. denied*, 517 U.S. 1135 (1996)

Torres v. Wisconsin Department of Health and Human Services, 859 F. 2d 1523 (7th Cir. 1988), *cert. denied*, 489 U.S. 1082 (1989)

Turner v. Safley, 482 U.S. 78 (1987)

United States v. Aguirre, 214 F.3d 1122, 1127 (9th Cir. 2000), *cert. denied*, 121 S. Ct. 408 (2000)

United States v. Brand, 907 F.2d 31 (4th Cir 1990), *cert. denied*, 498 U.S. 1014 (1990)

United States v. Brewer, 899 F.2d 503, 512 (6th Cir. 1990), *cert. denied*, 498 U.S. 844 (1990)

United States v. Concepcion, 795 F. Supp. 1262, 1282 (E.D.N.Y. 1992)

United States v. Gaviria, 804 F.Supp. 476, 479–80 (E.D.N.Y. 1992)

United States v. Johnson, 964 F.2d 124, 125 (2d Cir. 1992)

United States v. Johnson, 956 F.2d 894 (9th Cir. 1992)

United States v. Koon, 518 U.S. 81 (1996)

United States v. B. Roe, 976 F.2d 1216 (9th Cir. 1992)

United States v. Sanchez, 53 M.J. 393 (2000)

United States v. Thomas, 181 F.3d 870 (7th Cir. 1999)

United States v. Vela, 927 F.2d 197 (5th Cir. 1991), *cert. denied*, 502 U.S. 875 (1991)

United States v. Virginia, 518 U.S. 515 (1996)

West v. Virginia Department of Corrections, 847 F. Supp. 402, 407 (W.D. Va. 1994)

Women Prisoners v. District of Columbia, 93 F.3d 910 (D.C. Cir. 1996), *cert. denied*, 520 U.S. 1196 (1997)

References

Amnesty International. (2001). *Abuse of women in custody: Sexual misconduct and shackling of pregnant women.* New York: Author.

Amnesty International. (1999). *Not part of my sentence: Violations of the human rights of women in custody.* New York: Author.

Berman, D. A. (2001). Addressing why: Developing principled rationales for family-based departures. *Federal Sentencing Reporter, 13*, p. 274–280.

Chaifetz, J. (1999). Listening to foster children in accordance with the law: The failure to serve children in state care. *New York University Review of Law and Social Change, 25* (1), 6–7.

Chesney-Lind, M. (1997). *he female offender.* Thousand Oaks, CA: Sage.

Collins, W. C., & Collins, A. W. (1996). *Women in jail: Legal issues.* Washington, DC: National Institute of Corrections.

Daly, K. (1989). Rethinking judicial paternalism: Gender, work-family relations, and sentencing. *Gender and Society, 3*, 9–36.

Daly, K., & Bordt, R. L. (1995). Sex effects and sentencing: An analysis of the statistical literature. *Justice Quarterly, 12*, pp. 141–177.

Ellis, A., & Shummon, S. A. (1999). Let judges be judges! *Post-Koon* downward departures.Part 7: Family ties and responsibilities. *Criminal Justice, 14*, pp. 48–52.

Farrell, A. (2001). Distinguishing among the "unhappys:" The influence of cultural gender norms on judicial decisions to grant family ties departures. *Federal Sentencing Reporter, 13*, pp. 268–273.

Gabel, K., & Johnston, D. (Eds.). (1995). *Children of incarcerated parents.* San Francisco, CA: Jossey-Bass.

Genty, P. M. (2001, November). Incarcerated parents and the adoption and safe families act: A challenge for correctional services providers. *International Community Correctional Association Journal*, pp. 42–47.

Harlow, C. W. (1999). *Prior abuse reported by inmates and probationers* (NCJ 72879). Washington, DC: U.S. Department of Justice.

Immarigeon, R., & Chesney-Lind, M. (1992). *Women's prisons: Overcrowded and overused.* San Francisco, CA: National Council on Crime and Delinquency.

Jacobs, A. L. (2001). Give 'em a fighting chance: Women offenders reenter society. *Criminal Justice, 16*, pp. 44–47.

Littleton, C. A. (1987). Reconstructing sexual equality. *California Law Review, 75*, 1279–1337.

Mumola, C. J. (2000). Bureau of justice statistics special report: Incarcerated parents and their children (NCJ 182335). Washington, DC: U.S.Department of Justice.

Mustard, D. B. (2001). Racial, ethnic, and gender disparities in sentencing: Evidence from the U. S. Federal courts. *Journal of Law and Economics, 44*.

National Institute of Corrections. (2000). *Topics in community corrections: Responding to women offenders in the community.* Washington, DC.

Parisi, N. (1982). Are females treated differently? In N. H. Rafter & E. A. Stanko (Eds.), *Judge,lawyer, victim, thief.* Boston, MA: Northeastern University.

Segal, J. A. (2001). Family ties and federal sentencing:A critique of the literature. *Federal Sentencing Reporter, 13*, 258–267.

Shoenberg, D. L. (1997). Departures for family ties and responsibilities after *Koon*. *Federal Sentencing Reporter, 9*, 292–297.

Steffensmeier, D. & Kramer, J. H. (1995). Sex-based differences in the sentencing of adult criminal defendants, an empirical test and theoretical overview. *Sociology and Social Research, 66*, 289–304.

Stolzenberg, L., & D'Alessio, S. J. (1997). Impact of prison crowding on male and female imprisonment rates in Minnesota: A research note. *Justice Quarterly, 14*, 793–809.

United States General Accounting Office. (1999). Women in prison: Issues and challenges confronting U. S. Correctional systems. Report to the Honorable Eleanor Holmes Norton House of Representatives. Washington, DC, December.

United States Office of Justice Programs. (1999). National symposium on women offenders.Washington, DC.

United States Sentencing Commission. (1999). Annual Report. Washington, DC.

Weinstein, J. B. (1996). The effect of sentencing on women, men, the family and the community. *Columbia Journal of Gender and Law, 5*, 169–181.

CHAPTER 8

PROFESSIONALS' ASSESSMENTS OF THE NEEDS OF DELINQUENT GIRLS: THE RESULTS OF A FOCUS GROUP STUDY

Joanne Belknap,
Erica J. Winter, and
Bonnie Cady[1]

Both studies of and responses to delinquent youth in the United States were almost exclusively male-specific until the 1980s. That is, until recently, with few exceptions, it was assumed that "delinquent" was synonymous with "male." The increase in both feminist scholarship and feminist professionals working with delinquent girls since the 1970's has resulted in unprecedented pressure to examine the processing and treatment of delinquent girls (Belknap, 2001; Chesney-Lind & Shelden, 1998; Daly & Chesney-Lind, 1988). In addition to the increased attention brought to girl delinquents by both feminist scholars and professionals in the juvenile justice system, responses to delinquent girls received unprecedented attention due to government statistics and publications pointing to the increase in the number of girl delinquents. These publications suggested that delinquent girls are becoming more aggressive as well as numerous (Budnick, 1998; Poe-Yamagata & Butts, 1996). A recent report by the Office of Juvenile Justice and Delinquency Prevention (OJJDP), "What

1. The authors are grateful to all of the members of Colorado's Young Women's Research Group who helped guide every phase of this project, from the design and implementation to interpreting the results. Additionally, the authors thank the Colorado Division of Youth Corrections for funding this study.

about the Girls?," documents the nationwide problem of the increasing numbers of delinquent girls, and also addresses the challenge across the United States in the "demand for comprehensive needs assessments that identify gaps in the provision of services for girls" (Budnick, 1998, p. 2).

The third significant occurrence leading to an unprecedented questioning of how female offenders are treated was the 1992 re-authorization of the Juvenile Justice and Delinquency Prevention (JJDP) Act of 1974.[2] This re-authorization, as a result of convincing testimony from professionals who worked with delinquent girls, established the need to create what the Act referred to as "gender-specific treatment" for delinquent girls' "gender-specific needs." To this end, the re-authorization legislation proclaimed that each state should

1. conduct an analysis of the need for, and assessment of, existing treatment and services for delinquent girls
2. develop a plan to provide the appropriate gender-specific services necessary for the prevention and treatment of juvenile delinquency
3. provide assurance that youth in the juvenile system are treated fairly regarding their mental, physical, and emotional capabilities, as well as on the basis of their gender, race, and family income
(Belknap, Dunn, & Holsinger, 1997).

Despite these gains, it is important to proceed cautiously in determining what "gender-specific" means, how it is measured, and some potentially negative consequences of labeling behaviors and programs as "gender-specific." For example, could some gender-specific programs actually reinforce sexist norms and gender role expectations? One way to proceed in asking about girls' needs in both deterrence from offending or effective treatment once processed as delinquents, is to ask the professionals who deal with them on a daily basis. To date, little research has taken this approach. The study reported in this chapter is the result of five focus groups with over 50 individuals across the State of Colorado who work with delinquent girls.

A Review of the Literature

There is some disagreement concerning research on the rates of delinquency. While it is clear that both boys and girls' arrest rates are increasing, it

---

2. The original JJDP Act of 1974 was the federal implementation of a law mandating that status offenders could not be incarcerated.

is less clear that girls are becoming more aggressive and violent than they used to be. One recent report on U.S. statistics evaluating girls' percentage of juvenile arrests between 1980 and 1995 indicates that girls' rate of arrests has increased from about one-in-five to about one-in-four of total juvenile arrests (Belknap & Holsinger, 1998). Another analysis of juvenile arrest changes between 1989 and 1998 indicates boys' arrests for property crimes *decreased* by the same percentage that girls' arrests for property crimes *increased* (Belknap, 2001, p. 86). This same study found a much faster paced increase in girls' arrests for violent offenses than that for boys. Thus, although boys constitute the majority of juvenile arrests, girls' rates appear to be increasing at a faster rate than boys'.

Now turning to the causes of delinquency, a major contribution of the more recent delinquency research addressing gender is the recognition that girls and boys have some similar, but also, some different "pathways" to offending. Significantly, the traditional theories failed to measure these events. For example, traditional strain theory never measured childhood abuse by parents as a source of strain that might lead to delinquency for either girls or boys. However, three studies published in the 1970s and 1980s reported high rates of prior victimization, in particular child abuse, in offending girls' and women's lives (Chesney-Lind & Rodriguez, 1983; James & Meyerding, 1977; Silbert & Pines, 1981). Since the late 1980s, numerous other studies report that childhood victimization, such as incest, is not only related to the subsequent offending of girls and women (Arnold, 1990; Browne, Miller, & Maguin, 1999; Chesney-Lind & Shelden, 1992; Coker, Patel, Krishnaswami, Schmidt, & Richter, 1998; Gilfus, 1992; Klein & Chao, 1995; Lake, 1993; Owen, 1998), but these traumatic childhood events are also precursors for boys' likelihood of offending (Dembo, Williams, Wothke, Schmeidler, & Brown, 1992; Dodge, Bates, & Pettit, 1990; Widom, 1989a, 1989b; Widom & Maxfield, 2001).

An important aspect of this research is the understanding that while both girls' and boys' traumatic childhood events are often high-risk factors for the onset of delinquency, many of these traumas are "gendered." More specifically, there is considerable indication that while childhood sexual abuse is high for boys, it is significantly higher for girls (Finkelhor & Baron, 1986; Holsinger, Belknap, & Sutherland, 1999; Kann, Kinchen, Williams, Ross, Lowry, Grunbaum, Kolbe, & State and Local YRBSS Coordinators, 2000). One recent report states that while childhood victimization increases the likelihood of subsequent arrests for violent offenses among both females and males, it does so "in different ways" (Widom & Maxfield, 2001, p. 4). More specifically, females who survived childhood abuse were at a far greater risk of committing *any* future violent offenses (as measured by arrest), while for males, childhood victimization increased the *frequency* with which they had future violent offense arrests.

Given the research that suggests that many delinquent girls' and delinquent boys' lives are both fraught with traumatic events, including abuse, and that many of these victimizations are gendered, with girls experiencing higher rates than boys, it is to be expected that delinquent girls' programming would "look" different than boys. Although little research exists addressing this in detail, one recent study points to the problem of not addressing abuse histories. Specifically, a study on the effect of women's childhood traumatic events on their current state of psychological well-being (measured as dissociation), found that those who experienced child sexual abuse had significantly greater dissociation (Butzel, Talbot, Duberstein, Houghtalen, Cox, & Giles, 2000). Another study evaluating a program for delinquent youth where they participated in four weeks of family therapy, parent groups, educational sessions, community service projects and empathy building exercises, reported that participation in this multi-pronged program reduced recidivism (Myers, Burton, Sanders, Donat, Cheney, Fitzpatrick, & Monaco, 2000). The sample size was not sufficient to examine gender differences, but the sample was 63 percent female.

Clearly an important aspect of treating delinquent youth entails responding to chemical dependency. For example, one study of delinquent girls and boys reported that substance abuse is more prevalent among those youth with psychiatric disorders (Milin, Halikas, Meller, & Morse, 1991). Another study found that both female and male childhood sexual abuse survivors report higher rates of substance use than their non-abused counterparts (Rohsenow, Corbett, & Devine, 1988). Consistent with past research, a recent study found that although self-reported polydrug use was higher among boys than girls, it is an issue for both, and the sexes' rates became more similar in a two-year follow-up (Epstein, Botvin, Griffin, & Diaz, 1999). Also consistent with existing research, white youth reported the most polydrug use, and within each racial/ethnic grouping (white, Black, Asian, Hispanic) boys tended to report more polydrug use, although, again, the gender differences tended to become less pronounced in the two-year follow-up. Given the high rates of polydrug use, this study advocated for prevention and treatment programs that target multiple substances (Epstein et al., 1999).

The issue of illegal substance use may be particularly important for girls, who often "self-medicate" the pain of their victimization histories through drug and alcohol use (Arnold, 1990; Briere & Runtz, 1987; Inciardi, Lockwood, & Pottieger, 1993). The drug and alcohol use itself is typically considered illegal, and drug and alcohol use is also often a precursor to other offending, such as drug selling, prostitution, robbery and burglary (Belknap & Holsinger, 1998).

Recent research in Ohio (Belknap, Dunn, & Holsinger, 1997; Belknap, Holsinger, & Dunn, 1997) and California (Owen & Bloom, 1998) employing focus groups with both girls and professionals who work with them in order to better understand delinquent girls' issues, had many overlapping findings. For example, both studies reported that in problematic families, environments, and schools from which many of these girls originate, there is a prevalence of substance abuse problems, extensive abuse and victimization histories, serious mental and physical health problems, lack of access to adequate health care, and a general lack of respect in girls' lives in and out of institutions (Belknap, Dunn, & Holsinger, 1997; Belknap, Holsinger, & Dunn, 1997; Owen & Bloom, 1998). Similarly, Greene, Peters, and Associates (1998) OJJDP report on delinquent girls' needs highlighted 20 issues, including: addressing the need for better education, skills training, positive development programming, relationship building, culturally relevant activities, career opportunities, health services, recreational activities, mentoring, family involvement, community involvement, and better re-entry programming.

A recent research overview of treatment for delinquent girls conducted by a family therapist and juvenile justice consultant, criticizes the current mental health treatment in girls detention facilities for (1) limited access to comprehensive counseling to address their victimization, and (2) the need for strength-based treatment planning to facilitate delinquent girls' "ability to self-advocate within a support network" (Pepi, 1997, p. 86). To this end, Pepi (1997) advocates for restorative justice models to most effectively respond to delinquent girls:

> Treatment based on a feminist model of intervention that, in essence, assists the young woman in 'finding her voice,' can lead to a systemic homeostatic response in her family, and, consequently, the greater society. This response supports the re-parenting of the child and the self-identification of her strengths and competencies. Participation in a process of accountability for offending behavior based on restorative justice principles can help create a sense of belonging rather than alienation from community. Systemic work with the family or alternate support network and the young woman's efforts to move into responsible living can significantly reduce the incidence of recidivistic crime (p. 99).

Thus, the findings to date, and the policies emanating from these findings, suggest that girls at risk for delinquency have some serious needs. While many of these needs are similar for boys, the nature and frequency of the needs is often gendered. One study in a co-educational youth detention facility found that the implementation of an all-girls group was first useful in "challenging the invisibility of the girls in detention" (Tuesday, 1997, p. 130). But it was also useful in the girls feeling "special" and learning about how to respect themselves and other girls, and address sexism in their worlds both within and outside of the detention facility.

Method

Concern over the availability of gender-specific services and treatment in the Colorado Division of Youth Corrections (CDYC) led to the formation of a task force in the Spring of 2000, the Young Women's Research Group (YWRG), charged with recommending how to best assess delinquent girls' unique needs and improve responses to these girls. Members of the YWRG included two researchers (the first two authors) and a number of professionals who were selected based on their experience with delinquent girls and interest in gender-specific needs and programming. The third author, Bonnie Cady, is currently a Client Manager and Parole Officer in the Colorado Division of Youth Corrections, and has been working in criminal justice in Colorado for 24 years. She is responsible for putting together the YWRG, which is a collaborative researcher-practitioner team. After several monthly meetings, the researchers, in conjunction with the task force, concluded that a modified replication of an Ohio focus group study (Belknap et al., 1997a) would best provide a preliminary exploration of gender-specific needs and issues of delinquent girls in Colorado. Under the guidance of the YWRG, the researchers extended the scope of the Ohio study by distinguishing between *committed* and *pre-adjudicated* girls in an effort to identify girls' pathways to delinquency. Additionally, the researchers wanted to ascertain the needs of both girls who have yet to be officially judged as delinquent (the pre-adjudicated girls), and of those who have been officially adjudicated as delinquent and placed in treatment facilities or other correctional institutions (the committed girls).

Information often surfaces through focus groups that might not otherwise be easily obtained using other methods (see Knodel, 1993). Focus groups were thus chosen for their ability to yield richer, more diverse perceptions and insights. A professional facilitator was hired to administer the focus groups, while the first author of this chapter took notes, audiotaped, and transcribed all of the sessions into a computer. A total of 15 focus groups were completed for this study between June and November 2000. One focus group with *committed* delinquent (adjudicated) girls, one with *pre-adjudicated* (at-risk) girls, and one with professionals in each of the five regions of the state (Western, Northeastern, Central, Denver and Southern). The intention of sampling the various areas of Colorado was to more accurately capture not only regional differences in correctional goals and/or girls' experiences, but also to assess whether girls face different stresses and problems depending on whether they are from a rural, suburban, or urban location. This chapter will focus on the results obtained from the focus groups conducted with the CDYC professionals who work with girls.

The number of professionals participating in each focus group ranged from seven to 17, adding up to 56 total for all the groups across the state. A variety of occupations from within the juvenile justice system were represented, including residential treatment center executive directors, client managers, attorneys, a Department of Youth Corrections regional director, parole officers, program coordinators, probation officers, security officers, program managers for alternative or unique programs, therapists, group living coordinators, placement supervisors, interns, and drug and alcohol counselors. Three-quarters (76.8%, n=43) of the 56 professionals were women. Given the awkwardness of asking the participants to identify their race/ethnicity, they were not asked to do so. However, the researchers estimate that approximately two-thirds were white, with the remainder mostly Latino/a and four African Americans.

The focus group participants were contacted either by a member of the task force or a CDYC worker. The focus groups were conducted at juvenile correctional facilities or in community buildings in each of the five regions. The sites where groups took place were Gilliam (Denver), Daybreak (Denver), Spring Creek (Colorado Springs), Platte Valley (Greeley), Mount View (Denver), Teen Quest (Denver), Ft. Morgan Diversion, and Grand Mesa (Grand Junction). Participation in the focus groups was voluntary and confidential. To this end, each individual signed a confidentiality agreement and consent form before the focus groups took place. In addition, the participants were advised that if they at any time did not feel comfortable or wished to terminate their participation, they were free to leave, however, no one in any of the groups chose to do so. Those present during the focus groups were the professionals themselves, the facilitator, and one of the researchers who was taking notes. None of the committed, or pre-adjudicated girls, was ever present during the focus groups with the professionals.

The questions used for all the focus groups were based on the original questions from the Ohio study (Belknap, Holsinger, and Dunn, 1998), and the YWRG task force suggested several additional topics not addressed in the Ohio questions, such as spirituality, educational involvement and success, cultural issues, recreational activities, and participation or support in the local community. The format of the questions was not formal or rigid, but rather allowed the facilitator and the participants for each group to expand upon or delve deeper into topics of particular concern. The facilitator was requested to insure that each topic of discussion was at least put forth for consideration. The following set of questions was presented to the professionals working with girls in each of the various regions of the Colorado youth corrections system who volunteered to participate in the focus groups:

Focus Group Questions for the Professionals

Background about Participants

- How long have you been working in the Colorado Youth corrections system? Have you worked in similar systems in other states? Was there a difference?
- Describe your current job.

Information about Participants' Clients

- Describe the young people you work with. Describe the demographics of your clients.
- What aspects of girls' lifestyles or backgrounds do you think have the most impact on the quality of their lives? What aspects have the most influence on their tendency to engage in delinquent activity?
- What is your greatest frustration in working with young women? What do you find most rewarding?
- How would you describe the most significant differences between delinquent girls and delinquent boys?
- Who would you say the girls you work with look up to? Whom do they admire?

Treatment Strategies and Services

- What are the issues you most commonly deal with in working with young women? How are they different from those of young men? How are they the same?

- What are the health issues young women face?
- Do you think the system should differentiate more between the needs of young men and young women in the services and programs it offers? If so, in what ways?
- Do you believe girls have special needs in the system? Are there special programs and services that should be available to young women?
- What type of life skills do girls need? Is that different from what boys need?
- What are the types of programs you find most helpful for young women? To what types of programs do young women respond best?
- What types of programs or services are missing for young women? Which ones should be made available sooner?
- Do you think young women and young men are treated differently? Do you think the system does a better job of meeting the needs of one or the other?

Needs and Beliefs of Professionals in the System

- Do you believe professionals working with delinquent girls need specialized training? What kind?
- Is there a difference in how professionals who work only with young girls are treated in the system?
- If you had a choice would you prefer to work with young men, young women, or both? Why?

The focus group participants were invited to sit around a long conference table, with the facilitator and the researcher at the head. At the inception of each focus group, the facilitator first introduced herself, explained the procedure for focus groups and their purpose, and set the ground rules. For example, she explained that since there is a significant amount of material to cover she must move the group rather swiftly from topic to topic, that everyone must act respectfully toward one another (being careful not to interrupt) and that there were no right or wrong answers. She then discussed the note taking and audiotaping, the guarantee of confidentiality, and asked the participants to sign the consent forms. Next, the participants introduced themselves, followed by the facilitator starting the questions. Most participants were eager to share their experiences and insights, however a few needed some prompting. Rarely did anyone need to be asked to allow others to speak.

The focus groups were scheduled for and completed in an hour and a half. After each focus group, the facilitator and the research team debriefed, considered what needed further attention in future groups, and identified the themes that had arisen. After all three focus groups were completed in a particular region, the key findings were then synthesized and organized for compilation into a monograph presented to the Director of the CDYC. The following presents a summary of the findings from the focus groups with professionals.

Findings

The five focus groups conducted in Colorado during the summer and fall of 2000 with the Division of Youth Corrections professionals yielded a significant amount of data, from which numerous themes emerged. Below, direct quotes from the participants follow a description of each theme, powerfully illustrating and lending voice to the topics discussed in the focus groups. The verbatim selections from the transcripts are presented in an effort to accurately portray professionals' perceptions of how girls experience the corrections system, the needs of committed and pre-adjudicated adolescent girls, and the steps they believe should be taken to improve or reform juvenile services and facilities to better meet those needs. In total, twelve main themes emerged and are reported. The first four themes are those that emerged in both the focus groups with the girls and the focus groups with the professionals. The remaining eight main themes are those that emerged in the professional focus groups, but did not emerge from the focus groups with the girls.

Four Main Themes That Were Common in Both the Professionals and Girls' Focus Groups

Main Theme Number 1:
Girls Often Must Get Committed before
They Receive Help

Many of the girls and professionals alike perceived that girls often have to get incarcerated to receive the help they need, and once in the system, they may actually be better off. The correctional facility frequently becomes "home" to them in a sense, perhaps even a home environment they have never experienced before with clear rules and structure, predictable meals, and the opportunity to establish nurturing relationships with parent figures. Related to the observation that detained or pre-adjudicated girls receive fewer services than committed girls, it appears that the deeper into the system a girl progresses, the more help—in the sense of treatment and services—she can receive. Regardless of their needs, the girls with the more severe charges tend to get the most treatment and receive more funding and program options.

- Girls—it's like they're home—they're safe, with their homeys, they get food, told when to go to bed. They have structure, expectations, consistency, they know what's going to happen, who's there, and they can build relationships with staff.
- (Girls) have to come into the system to get good health care.
- Detained girls don't get the services that committed girls do.
- Girls have to get committed to get substance abuse services.
- Some girls are running away over and over—it's their way of saying, "commit me! Take control." They need help and need treatment and don't know how to get it.

Main Theme Number 2: Girls Want and Need More Health Education and Services

Repeatedly, both girls and professionals mentioned the acute need for girls to increase their knowledge of their own physical health, hygiene, and development. Some girls may not even know how to wash, what is normal or symptomatic, or about how their bodies function. Furthermore, girls would like more nutritional information and access to meals created for girls, rather than being served a male diet that often far exceeds their calorie requirement. A diet packed with calories, in addition to getting little exercise, leaves many girls unhealthy and with a tendency to gain weight while in the system. Such a change in their physical state can often produce the secondary effect of decreased self-esteem, which may put girls at even greater risk for adopting damaging behavioral patterns. Many girls and professionals recognized this cycle, and in addition to a more nutritious, appropriate diet, they suggested that girls need more opportunities to participate in a greater variety of sports and exercise routines. In most facilities, boys receive more exercise time and access to better and more diverse recreational options than girls.

- There are all kinds of issues with feminine things they have to have. They don't know their bodies. And touching—playing with each other's hair—knowing what's sexual.
- The girls are fed too much, and have to fight for gym time.
- Nutrition, eating disorders, self-image issues are dramatically higher for girls.

- (Girls) need to be taught about sex and their own bodies—it goes hand in hand with self-esteem. So many don't even know how to wash themselves properly! They are locked on—they feel respected when you teach them.
- Girls get the most bizarre ideas. It affects general health issues. Not having the knowledge, not knowing about their body or what to expect.
- Girls want interaction with kids from other facilities.
- They're not used to having that much food available to them, and their body image is already so poor, so their self-esteem plummets.
- They really don't know about their bodies.
- That sports issue is really important. Girls are physical, and they do like to play sports. We give them pictures and makeup, but they need an outlet.

Main Theme Number 3:
Some Girls in the Corrections System
Should Be Getting Help Elsewhere

A number of girls may be entering the corrections system due to charges that would likely be better handled through other means such as within the community, public school system, or the family, with the help of counselors or social services. The concern seems to be that the corrections system is somewhat akin to a dumping ground in the sense that problem children, when other resources are not available, are incarcerated rather than managed through other less radical means. Consequently, contact with more severe delinquency may transform what perhaps was a relatively minor teenage problem into a long-term struggle.

- A girl hit a teacher with a tootsie roll, and now she's in the system. The things we lock girls up for are not the same as boys. We're starting to see girls in here who should be back in the community—they aren't going to benefit from being locked up.
- Boys get committed for new crimes, whereas girls get committed for parole violations. Technical violations—running away, doing drugs.
- They'll send us truancy girls. Instead of dealing with that in the school, they throw them to us! Public schools need to come up with ways to deal with it—community service, something. Instead we monitor them in jail.
- People don't understand how to use the services, and assessment might not support what they're doing. (Girls) might need foster care rather than incarceration.

Main Theme Number 4:
Girls Receive Fewer Opportunities and
Less Funding Than Boys

Girls plainly have fewer placement options and less funding than boys who are in the system. This difference may well be linked to the fact that there are fewer girls, and since they are a minority, their needs may be viewed as lower priority. A significant number of the girls were frustrated at how long they had been waiting for placements, and both girls and professionals lamented the dearth of funding and other resources available to girls. As noted above, this is even more the case with pre-adjudicated girls. They likely receive even fewer programs and resources, despite the fact that many of them are detained for months at a time while they await sentencing or their release date. The scarcity of programs and funding for girls often translates into limited opportunities to individualize treatment plans to meet each girl's specific needs. Interestingly, though, while girls do not appear to receive the same opportunities as boys for appropriate programs and services, life skills, or vocational training, they do tend to receive more focus in the area of treatment and therapy.

- The boys have a number of vocational programs, and can have access more to different placements. Girls don't get nearly as much. Boys even have more clothing.
- We do not have anything for (female) criminal sex offenders. Is that clear? We do not!
- There is no place for girls to receive (drug and alcohol treatment) where they're secure and safe while they're investing in a program.
- There are even less services for young women than young men.
- We promote that they need to develop pro-social skills and get involved in positive activities in the community, but we don't have a lot of avenues for them to do that.
- When you ask for resources for a girl, bring things to administration's attention, they say we don't have as many girls. Since they're a minority they get minority time, minority money, minority responses.
- Girls need vocational training. They don't get as much as boys. Not nursing and secretarial training—it needs to be more broad and build on her interests. Guys can get certificates in culinary arts, and come out with a career.
- Systematically girls are treated differently. They have longer lengths of stay; their behaviors are viewed as symptomatic, not normal.

- Boys get more opportunities to get skills for emancipation and independent living.
- Girls are automatically treated differently and sometimes people see their abilities as different. It's coming around—traditionally things like wilderness programs and things like that were initially developed only for boys, and now there's the new idea to provide that opportunity to girls.

Eight Main Themes That Were Unique to the Professional Groups

Main Theme Number 1:
Professionals Need to Establish Trusting Relationships with the Girls, Many of Whom Are Emotionally Needy

Recognition of girls' critical need to establish relationships added to professionals' frustration with the lack of resources available for girls, including insufficient funding for extended treatment, as well as a shortage of appropriate programs and services to meet their specific needs. The awareness that girls need time to connect with staff and develop trust before they can fully engage in treatment and work toward their goals was reiterated continually by the professionals participating in the groups. The rewards of working with girls were largely associated with the successful formation of a bond, such that through the safety of a positive, nurturing relationship, girls could make progress toward creating healthy relationships with others, and look forward to promising futures.

Interestingly, some of the greatest frustrations experienced by professionals working with girls in the corrections system also center on girls' need to continuously work through the dynamics of relationships. Professionals report feeling frustrated with girls' behavior, at times, because often there exists a very emotional, occasionally manipulative component to their routine interactions with each other and with staff. When generalizing about girls, professionals often characterized girls' behavior or relationship skills in a stereotypical, if not sexist, manner. Professionals often used words such as "hysterical," "histrionics," "erratic," and "soap opera" to describe the sometimes unpredictable, dramatic, and agitated elements of girls' interpersonal exchanges. While clearly the intention of most professionals was to present an accurate, descriptive representation of the nature of girls' needs and experiences in the system, some recognized that such perceptions of girls are to a degree based on labels that may translate into expectations of girls' behavior. Even the "common knowledge" that girls invest much of their effort in and need close connection with others, may potentially frame professionals' work with girls and their response to both girls and boys in the system.

- There are not enough resources. It takes a lot longer to develop rapport with girls to the point that they can tell you what their needs are. By that time they're in a pretty desperate situation.
- Males—you know when they're mad. Females are very emotional, erratic.
- Girls are so extremely verbal, too. They say one thing and do the other the next five minutes.
- They expect a pill or something to solve a problem. They have no problem-solving skills.
- They get too involved in what others are doing.
- Histrionics. They're so incredibly contagious. You have 12 girls, everyone's crying, holding hands; even the people who started it don't know why it started. They pass that on to staff, too. "Oh God, they're going to run tonight."
- They think unless they're hysterical nothing will be done—nobody cares. So it's a problem-solving situation.
- Sometimes if everything is not in turmoil, (girls think) "what's the point? If it's not all stirred up then I'm going to damn well stir it up." The "soap opera" syndrome.
- (With girls) it's more on the level of someone is drowning—versus most the guys will respond to a show of force—it's cool. The girls will escalate.
- It's all about relationship. Until they get invested in the relationship you won't get anywhere with them.
- Working with girls, first you have to establish a relationship before you can make any progress. You can't just solution-focus or brainstorm. They want to see who you are up front.
- They're looking for a connection, a way to be connected with something bigger than themselves, which often the gang fills that need.
- They need positive regard so much, unconditional love. Girls will shoot themselves in the foot—do anything—to have a relationship that gives them that regard.
- They need to look into themselves, what are their strengths, but they don't know how to do that. It's really getting a good connection with these girls—making sure they know they're genuinely cared for.
- Girls are much more emotional and relationship-based. Girls will talk, especially about their relationships, and unfortunately a lot of the programming has been more focused on what males need and it hasn't worked for girls.

- Girls will base their self-image on their relationships to develop, whereas boys will base their image on accomplishments, status, and what they have materially.
- Assessments with girls are very gender-biased. There isn't anything specifically for girls and their needs.
- (Like racism), it's the same with girls. They're automatically treated differently and sometimes people see their abilities as different.
- Girls are scary. Bad things are going to happen—somebody's going to cry, and it's probably going to be me!
- Finding people who want to work with girls is difficult. They're needy, demanding, take too much time. It's hard to find people who are willing and eager to work with females who don't say they're whiney, emotional. That's the preconceived notion, but they may not be. It's a generality, but the label's there.
- Some of the trainings almost perpetuate stereotypes, that girls are this, etc.
- (The reward is) the success—when they come back and they've made it, and maybe they're contributing something to the community.
- (The reward is) to find relationships that are healthy for them.
- Sometimes the reward is greater with girls because you spent so much more on them—invested more in them.
- Once you establish a relationship with girls it's very close. With boys, they're easier to work with, but it's surface. But when you actually manage to break through to a girl that relationship stays there.
- It's a lot more rewarding working with girls. If you engage her and build a relationship you can get a lot done. Because they like to process so much I've seen girls do things I never thought any person could do in therapy. Work out some serious issues. Some boys do that, but not many. They usually touch the surface, but girls go really deep, to the core of who they are.
- I think working with girls sometimes is very rewarding. You can see them develop and move on with their lives, but it gets real frustrating because there isn't the programming and services for girls.
- I love them. I've worked with both (boys and girls), but with girls there's a connection, and I'm really happy when they can express things, whereas with boys it's pulling it out of them. (Girls) are often people who have been ignored for a long time, so it's rewarding to work with them.

Main Theme Number 2:
Girls Need Treatment Separate from Boys

As evidenced above, much of what girls need appears to revolve around the significance of relationships in their lives, according to the view of professionals in the system. Since girls are often quite focused on the dynamics of relationships, they may become easily distracted when placed in a treatment environment with boys. In such situations they have the tendency to concentrate more heavily on their self-presentation and the intricacies of a relationship or potential relationship rather than focusing their energy and attention on their own personal growth and self-awareness. In order to encourage girls to more fully engage in and focus on their own lives and current treatment issues, professionals suggest that girls should participate only in gender-specific therapy groups and reside separately from boys. Furthermore, they need to be encouraged to focus on their own progress in the program as well as on their development as individuals, as the protagonists of their own lives, rather than concentrating so heavily on the dynamics of a relationship.

- Girls kind of lose themselves in other people.
- They get too involved in what others are doing.
- Girls can't focus on their own issues because they're focused on their friends, Aunt Susie, etc.
- They want that relationship with their dad and they might not have it. Even if the relationship isn't good they seek that out.
- Girls do well in groups alone. They benefit from gender-specific groups. Girls don't benefit from having boys with them—they're distracted by them.
- Treatment needs to be separate from boys! No mixed groups! Total interest goes to the males. Grooming, preening, the goal changes for (girls).
- The girls shouldn't be over there in school with the boys. They flash each other, pass notes...the way they dress, walk. Then (girls) could just focus on themselves. They won't even wear a coat! They say a boy might see them.
- There needs to be separation. It's setting them up.
- Girls and boys should be completely separate for girls' sake. Then girls find their power. They would be able to say what they need to say.
- Girls compete with girls no matter what, but they will compete harder if there are boys present, because that's what they're competing for.
- When they are getting treatment, above all, they should be separated. Then there needs to be a lot of education about how to interact with the

opposite sex. They need some exposure, and understanding of how to interact with males, otherwise once they leave they'll relapse. Teaching girls to interact with each other is really important, too.

- Male/female contact needs to be structured. They need to learn how to have fun without having sex.
- Initially a girls-only environment is good because boys can be a distraction. Again, girls being relationship-based, their focus goes directly to the boys. It takes the focus off some of their other needs. They can't think about themselves if they're thinking about a relationship with a significant other. So if you can take them away long enough they will be more confident, more self-efficacious, learn their internal strengths.
- A lot of girls are in this situation because of a boy. A lot of them are doing it to get approval or attention from a man.
- As a society we train girls to seek approval from others, to show they're there, visible, and whether they're good or bad. Whereas males are taught to be more within themselves. Girls, in an effort to find out who they are, will do anything to seek approval or continue a relationship even if it impacts them negatively. You'll see them take charges for boyfriends who have three or four other girls. They'll go to jail...repeatedly. Whereas boys, at some point will go, "well that was wrong that somebody set me up and I'm not doing that."

Main Theme Number 3:
Girls Need to Develop Respect for Women and Girls

Professionals in the focus groups observed that girls need connection with strong female role models. They noted that girls often appear to value and identify with males in an attempt to feel powerful and respected. At the same time, they desire to connect with others and establish relationships, so they often end up feeling conflicted about who they are and who they want to be. They find it difficult to value themselves, and thus need to see strong women who are respected, powerful, and in control of their emotions and personal lives in order to understand that they, too, are capable of such qualities and skills. Along these lines, girls need exposure to female staff who they can identify with, who understand them and their life experiences, and can bond with them at a level that makes a girl feel connected to the world and confident in herself as a woman. The professionals felt strongly that having correctional staff that is self-aware, balanced in their own personal lives, and experienced in working with girls can better provide young women with a role model to look up to, and they can serve as a mentor to help them develop respect for themselves and to find value in their own strengths and skills.

- Girls are trying to straddle the fence—they're having real issues with being female. They're trying to be intimidating, hard, but on the other hand they are trying to look pretty enough to catch a boy. Boys can just be boys.
- They always say, "I don't get along with girls".
- Girls can't ever appreciate being girls. They're always trying to act like guys...shave their heads to look hard on the streets. They have no appreciation for being female.
- When you're young, it's a thrill [to be a girl], but when you get older it becomes something to be ashamed of.
- Girls are really judgmental and harsh on each other. They're always labeling each other negatively.
- Everything goes back to the self-esteem thing. They will be exploited, do whatever it takes to feel good about themselves.
- They need to connect to someone who understands them.
- (Girls need) to see women in roles that they feel are powerful. They look up to women who appear to have their stuff together.
- Most of our girls are very male-identified because that's where the power is.
- I think that they are looking for a positive role model but aren't used to having a positive female role model. They despise females when they come in, though, so it takes a long time to establish trust. They are very submissive to males. Listening to a female is very hard for them. They need constant approval, positive strokes, and if they do not get that they act out—they'll do anything to get that attention.

Main Theme Number 4:
Girls Need Arenas Where They Learn to Develop Appropriate Boundaries with Men

Again, related to girls' relationships with others, many of the professionals recognize that a significant proportion of the girls have little or no history interacting with males, particularly men who set appropriate boundaries with them. Girls need to learn how to interact appropriately with males and establish healthy relationships with them. To many of these professionals, the solution is to ensure that there are male staff who can show girls that men can be there to help them, not just to exploit them. For this reason, professionals mentioned that male staff who can model appropriate male/female interactions are a critical asset to girls' facilities. Girls can observe positive, non-sexual relationships between staff from male role models, as well as learn to interact with males who maintain healthy emotional boundaries and teach the girls to do the same.

- Male staff has to know how to handle it. If he can tell her to look at her behavior, she might listen. But we don't get that many men that apply. But I do think it can be very positive. The problem is they don't know—they don't even see it. And they're scared to be on the pod with the girls. And it throws the whole house off—girls don't know how to interact with them.
- Girls will say inappropriate things to male staff.
- The girls don't understand the age thing, either. They come on to 35-year-old men.
- The whole mail [from males] thing is really annoying. These older men are allowed to write them—it's solicitation of a minor. They were literally sending the girls checklists—"How do you like to do it?" "How's your body?"
- They shouldn't be allowed to write anyone in an adult facility or any adult men.
- Many of the girls are looking for a caretaker. Someone to listen, give them advice. That's their excuse—the draw. Some guy tells them, 'Oh, Baby, I love that picture you sent me. You're so beautiful!' They just suck it up when they're just sitting in their rooms feeling yucky about themselves.
- Many of the girls are dealing with domestic violence issues at 16. Show me their burns, marks, but they wouldn't acknowledge that in the group. They expect to be hit. They're just getting beat up, because they think when you commit to a relationship you commit to getting your head beat up.
- They think they're going to have a man for everything—a man who pays for my nails, one for my hair—they've got a little ring of men to pay for things. It's the dependency factor.
- They will be exploited, do whatever it takes to feel good about themselves.
- A lot of the girls are in this situation because of a boy. A lot of them do it to get approval or attention from a man.
- It's related to the lack of a father figure. As a man [staff member], it's difficult because you have to establish really difficult boundaries.
- We have difficulty hiring men to work at our girls facility because they're afraid of being accused of some type of sexual impropriety. Girls do not have a healthy image of men—I wish we could develop a sensitivity training so more men would feel comfortable.

Main Theme Number 5:
Girls Need Access to Cultural and
Spiritual Practices

Many of the professionals pointed out girls' need to connect with the parts of themselves that are shaped by their cultural heritage and spiritual or religious background and beliefs in order to create a positive identity, and perhaps even a healthy means of rebelling against the status quo. They reported, however, that girls often have access to few options for gaining cultural and spiritual pride while in the youth corrections system, often largely due to the lack of coordination with, or availability of community resources.

- Without a connection to their cultural base you'll continue seeing them in the system.
- They only have the street mentality. The only thing that appeals to them is to learn about themselves, where they came from, self-pride, the contributions of their people—anything positive you can hook into—then you can go on to show them how they have a responsibility to their community.
- The cultural piece—across cultures…because of the confinement, kids are always trying to find who they are within their own cultural base. When there is only one African American or one Asian, that person finds it difficult to find their place. Ethnicity is a huge issue. How much does knowledge of one's culture play into your ability to be successful? It's a nurturing piece, and sometimes our kids don't have that.
- It's all symptomatic of the lack of cultural awareness. Once they are (aware), they don't have those cultural issues. They need to identify with someone they perceive as powerful, because they see that as (an) attempt to reject the system in a positive way.
- Latina women are built completely different from the women in magazines. We have girls who faint from not eating, trying to put themselves into some little body they're never going to be in. We have to stop the lesson (in class), and talk to her. You have to take the time to deal with the issue—right now, everybody. Time to talk about it so they all can learn—talk to them about what reality is for them.
- It's hard to know if they want to go to Bible study because they're interested or because they want to get off. Although, since we don't have the ability to offer it to all 180 students here, the ones who tend to go consistently do have a real high interest. We offer religious services to all, but we can only have so many in a room with one staff. And they're fully attended.

- The Vietnamese/Cambodian population has a strong affiliation with the Buddhist religion. Those are the only kids I've really seen express a religious preference and actually act on it.
- [Are all services Christian-based?] Most facilities don't offer a variety of different services each week. That's probably because the services being conducted are by volunteers from the community, so it depends on the community you're in. So if you get more minority religions, you'd have to find people. It becomes one of those difficult dynamics. It's difficult to offer different services if the volunteers aren't in the community.
- Ritual things are really important. We need more programs that do more spiritual kinds of things. The girls want it.
- All of these children have a real need to have some kind of spiritual understanding. They have to have some kind of spiritual connection—they have to have a choice—a chance to explore to find out what fits for them. They understand a lot more than what people give them credit for. [The girls'] connecting with spiritually really works. If they don't connect to that [spirituality], they will connect to something else.

Main Theme Number 6:
Staff Working with Girls Need Special Training
and Awareness of Girls' Issues

Professionals agree that staff needs special training to work with girls in correctional facilities. The training issues most emphasized revolve around creating a positive peer culture among staff, empowering and educating staff to be able to address girls' specific needs and issues, and providing access to information about girls' unique life experiences: their pathways to delinquency, how girls move through and view the world in general, the diversity of their personalities and backgrounds, the type of environment they need, and specific information regarding adolescent girls' normal developmental stages in order to avoid confusing normal behavior with deviance or acting out. Additionally, staff need assistance in learning how to become aware of and work through their own issues that may surface and affect how they interact with the girls, knowing how to maintain boundaries, gathering information on stress reduction techniques and strategies for increasing patience and tolerance. Comments were also made regarding the potentially detrimental effects of the hierarchical, formalistic structure of staff positions within correctional facilities. When staff is overburdened and their job description too rigidly delimited, their ability to meet girls' day-to-day needs may be constrained. The professionals clearly possessed a great deal of insight and felt very strongly about staff relations and development:

- You can't even come to work and breathe...everyone is so under the gun for reports and stuff that the real stuff gets pushed aside. One-on-one with kids, training new staff, helping people along....
- Things like girls' cycles, physiological differences, get skipped over a lot during training.
- You can't empower kids if you don't empower your staff.
- The weight thing is interesting—if staff say, "I'm trying to lose weight" or "my big butt", things like that—it's constant role modeling. (The girls) pick up on everything...what staff say to each other, how they present (themselves) around men....
- For a lot of staff (working with girls) brings up lots of adolescent issues. I wish they could see that they're not alone—a third of the women helping them have been victims. They're not alone.
- Staff needs knowledge of normal developmental stages.
- You need to have staff that want *to work with girls—male or female.*
- It's adversarial for us as professionals, and so we're modeling competition, gossiping, criticizing. We're set up in the hierarchy model—your title is your rank. It doesn't work unless you're a general! If you're on the bottom you aren't allowed to say—you're a level—you become an automation. You're told to do this, this, and this...well, what lower level people have to do is impossible in a single shift.
- Specialized training is one thing, but on-the-job experience is invaluable. To get into a program where you're working with good staff and the support of the administration, understanding what a positive peer culture is you've got to get in there at the direct care level and get your hands dirty. You have to be supported by experienced staff so you learn and keep an open mind to things.
- You've got to retain staff because girls are relationship-based. Otherwise you're doomed.
- [Working with girls relative to boys] is a time and effort thing. You try not to have preconceived notions, but you know you're going to get more phone calls, more time with that client one-to-one. You have to spend more time listening to things that have very little to do with the criminal justice system. Just listening.
- Each girl is 3 boys. As far as my caseload, as far as total time. It's much more of a challenge, but it's also much more rewarding in many cases, too. Percentage-wise, there's not so many girls going on to the adult system as boys.
- It's hard to know when to draw the line as to where to be empathetic and where you need to be a little more firm. A lot of times with guys

you just say 'cut that crap out. Stop!' You try to say that with girls, and it's like 'ooh'—the emotional piece—and it's like "Oh god! What did I just do?"

- Working with girls brings up issues for the professional more with girls.
- So much comes down to a personnel issue. We need to look at the things a person can bring to a facility that you can't learn in college—that are not things you put on a resume. [For example, hiring] the elderly with experience, people with integrity, etc. We need to redesign the hiring process.
- You have this police system that has been developed where you have to have a certain amount of your staff for safety and security, and we anoint this one person as counselor who's going to take care of all the issues for the kids, and then the people who are *walking on the floor* having human relationships, then no, you can't trust that because (they) don't have the skills—(they're) not a counselor, (they're) safety and security. To keep it separate is ridiculous. Everyone else is supposed to keep hands off. We need to not differentiate the roles to that degree.

Main Theme Number 7:
Girls Need More Transition Services

One of the main components of the treatment cycle that professionals deemed inadequate or entirely missing was transitional services. Again, considering that girls place a high value on connection with others, it follows that they would benefit from continuity of services and stability in their relationships as they transfer between facilities and eventually make the move from an institution back to the home environment. The current reality appears to be far from ideal in that girls are bounced around within the system with little or no preparation or continuity as they transfer between facilities from one program or placement to the next. Then, when it is time to go home, there is little follow-up care or help with re-adjustment. Some professionals also noted that as girls get into treatment, their needs in terms of security fluctuate, but that the programming cannot always address these fluctuating needs.

Many professionals lament that they are not able to provide such ongoing support for the girls, but emphasize that they already experience an overload of duties on their shift such that adding transition efforts to their list of responsibilities would prove problematic and so time-consuming they would have to neglect their regular tasks. Some suggested having special staff or mentors specifically charged with accompanying girls from one site or program to the next, providing them with the means to meet their specific needs at each new phase of their treatment. Others suggested that a particular counselor or case manager should follow them consistently, so girls might maintain a sense of stability in at least one key relationship in their lives. As it now stands, girls commonly spend time at numerous placements or facilities during the duration of their contact with the corrections system. Adjustment to so much change—of residence, relationships, routines, and opportunities—may well consume emotional energy better spent on treatment issues.

- Having their therapist follow them for a while—that's really important.
- We're cheating them. It's like fairyland for a year, then the system says it's time to go home, and we betrayed them. Then what we're doing is institutionalizing them to that setting. Where we're missing it is in the transition. They need to be able to succeed in that less-than-desirable situation with their own strengths.
- Girls blossom in treatment, during incarceration. The heartbreak is, when time's up—the pocket's empty—you can set your watch by it, three months and they're back. You have something fixed, and then they get bowled down like bowling pins.
- We can't just take youth and dump them into the system and then back out. They need an easier transition—more collaborative, with preventive types of services.
- There needs to be a continuity of care. They need to go from less secure to more secure, and back and forth.
- Transitional services are really missing. It needs to be a more gradual transition. They're building relationships—they need time to do that at the new place. That would cut down on the running away a lot. Girls need to overlap for a few weeks, so when they actually do leave one program, they've already formed some relationships in the new program.
- Having continuity with an individual is really important for some of these girls. Being able to have one person they can build a relationship with makes all the difference in the world.
- Usually their family life is pretty poor—no support system—so they come to a facility where they build relationships then we push them away, and we can't have any more contact with them. It makes me sick.
- We should set them up with outside resources.
- Almost every single committed girl thinks it's so scary with less structure—they go directly from (a facility) to home. They're overwhelmed. They freak out the first time they go into Safeway.
- A slower, more gradual transition into new programs is critical.

- Any facility needs to work with the facility that's detaining them so they're ready.
- There need to be specific staff that only deals with transitional kids. Take them to the high school, set up their classes. There need to be staff to deal with only that. We are surrogate parents. We would love to do it, but we're not paid well, we're already doing overtime…we can't.
- It seems to be one of the most effective pieces of transitioning kids, is having a mentor follow them out. Instead of saying "go to a drug and alcohol group" someone will help them get there. We demand a lot, but I don't know that we provide a lot of the support system for them to be able to follow through, and then when they don't, they've violated their parole because they didn't follow through with our expectations.

Main Theme Number 8:
The Girls are Seriously Lacking in Appropriate Parenting Experiences

Many of the professionals voiced concerns about girls' lack of exposure to positive parenting. Clearly, professionals feel that much of the instability girls experience in their childhoods stems from difficult family arrangements or dynamics. Professionals expressed frustration that girls often return to these environments after treatment, and communicated the difficulties they encounter in attempting to work with girls' families and get beyond the parents' view that the child is the only problem. Professionals clearly felt that children who enter the corrections system often lack a parental figure in their lives, either due to death, substance abuse, or emotional unavailability. It is often the case that the parent simply does not possess the skills to know how to manage the child's behavior and meet her needs for nurturing and discipline.

- A lot of mothers are intimidated by their children. We have to tell them they are the parent, they are the boss. You have to go back and work with the parent—teach them they are the ones who are supposed to have control. You should have more control over your kids than someone out on the streets who's going to sell them drugs.
- My biggest frustration is dealing with families. Dealing with dysfunctional families, families that abuse their children, families that neglect their children.
- Families want to see the client [delinquent girl] as the identified problem and don't want to take a look at their own stuff and only want to identify the kid as the problem. Then we return the girls to that same environment that they left, from looking pretty good [here], in a secure,

community facility. The parents will say how wonderful that their child has changed, but three weeks later they're back. They really haven't identified the stressors in the family.

- A lot of times the families are more delinquent than the kids.
- There are a lot of parentless kids in our system. They feel they want you to parent them—like when they get off your caseload they panic a little, because their parent is leaving, and it's pretty pathetic and sad as far as what their future holds.
- The absent mother piece is huge with these girls. I haven't had one girl who didn't have a mother who left at an early age, or they're just emotionally unavailable or drug addicted or whatever during those early formative years, and that—'mommy factor'—is huge. Girls spend a lot of time trying to recover that.
- The girls look up to older boyfriends, even though they may be abusive, because a lot of times, that's the transference over from the dad or step-dad.

Conclusions and Policy Recommendations

The findings reported in this chapter are consistent with previous focus groups in Ohio (Belknap et al., 1997a, 1997b) and California (Owen & Bloom, 1998), and the OJJDP Report on responding to delinquent girls (Greene, Peters & Associates, 1998). A unique characteristic of the study reported herein was that it also included issues for pre-adjudicated girls. Although this chapter focuses on the findings from the professionals (not the girls), the findings suggest similarities with the previous research.

According to the professionals in this focus group study, girls who come into contact with the Department of Youth Corrections in Colorado receive less funding and fewer appropriate services than boys. Some professionals noted that this may well be due to the fact that girls are often viewed as minorities in the juvenile system, considering that there are comparatively fewer girls than boys, and such demographic information is frequently used to determine and/or justify funding and policy decisions. Girls' needs, in other words, may be seen as less pressing because they represent a smaller portion of the delinquent population, and because they may be perceived as presenting less of a threat to the public (see Chesney-Lind & Shelden, 1998; Wells, 1994). Pre-adjudicated girls who have not formally entered the corrections system pose even less of a threat in society's view, perhaps since they have yet to be formally charged with delinquent behavior, and thus professionals observed that pre-adjudicated girls receive even less funding for services than delinquent girls. However, given the growing number of girls who have come to the attention of the juvenile justice and human services systems, and taking into account their abuse histories and the unique circumstances surrounding their criminal and/or self-destructive behaviors, this explanation is clearly becoming unsatisfactory.

Furthermore, the professionals participating in this study argued that delinquent girls in juvenile correctional facilities need more in the form of gender-specific treatment and services than has typically been available. Interestingly, many of the girls' needs, as perceived by the professionals, center on relationships. Professionals lament not having enough time or resources to tend to girls' emotional and psychological development on an individual, daily (or perhaps even hourly) basis, in addition to meeting their physical needs. They feel that girls need access to relationships with both male and female staff that are capable of modeling appropriate relationships for them and can also help them develop self-respect and confidence. In addition, they voiced concern over the lack of transition services available to girls when they move from one facility to the next, or from a facility back home. Again, this speaks to girls' need for continuity in their lives and stability of key relationships. As they take steps to become independent and avoid high-risk behaviors, girls need the reassurance that they can depend on the support of someone whom they trust. Finally, the professionals recognized that girls need the opportunity to establish a connection to their chosen spiritual, religious, and/or cultural base, to provide them with a greater sense of their own identity and a broader connection to the community, as well as helping them create a potential support system upon which they might draw in their future efforts to avoid involvement in delinquent behavior.

The key to being able to provide services to meet girls' needs is funding for gender-specific programs and for training and retaining skilled, experienced staff. Throughout their comments, professionals in Colorado insist that a key component to empowering girls and curbing recidivism is providing pre-adjudicated and committed girls with programming that fosters self-efficacy by helping girls create mastery and confidence in their own strengths and skills, and provides continuing access to options beyond delinquent behavior. Also essential to this end, staff needs to be chosen for their desire, experience, and competence in working with girls, trained according to a gender-specific model of child development, educated in girls' pathways to delinquency, and supported and empowered in their effort to establish and maintain connections with girls such that:

- Girls learn how to develop positive, supportive relationships in their own lives.
- Girls learn to value themselves as women, members of society, and unique individuals.
- Girls feel supported in their efforts to move forward in their lives and are provided with the resources to do so.
- Girls feel empowered to avoid relationships that are antagonistic to their own life goals or personal aspirations.

While recognizing that there are many complex components involved in the treatment of juvenile offenders, professionals clearly voiced the opinion that girls need to receive services and participate in programs that account for gender-specific pathways to delinquency and acknowledge the unique developmental stages, perspectives, and experiences of girls and young women. In effect, the CDYC professionals argue girls should receive treatment separate from boys that takes into account their unique circumstances and needs in a trusting environment where they can learn to master the skills, perhaps previously unavailable to them in their own families, necessary to create positive relationships and lifestyles. Clearly, many of the institutions and programs in Colorado appeared to be doing some cutting edge work in addressing girls' needs, however all facilities and programs serving girls throughout the country would do well to keep current their awareness of the issues and needs of delinquent girls, being sure to base policy and treatment decisions firmly on what is in girls' best interest rather than on their charges, pressure from the community, or what is most convenient or inexpensive.

References

Arnold, R. A. (1990). Women of color: Processes of victimization and criminalization of black women. Social Justice, 17(3), 153–166.

Belknap, J. (2001). *The invisible woman: Gender, crime, and justice* (2nd ed.). Pacific Grove, CA: Wadsworth Publishing Company.

Belknap, J., Dunn, M., & Holsinger, K. (1997). *Moving toward juvenile justice and youth serving systems* that *address the distinct experience of the adolescent female.* A Report to the Governor. Office of Criminal Justice Services, Columbus, Ohio.

Belknap, J., Holsinger, K., & Dunn, M. (1997). Understanding incarcerated girls: The results of a focus *group* study. *The Prison Journal, 77* (4), 381–404.

Belknap, J., & Holsinger, K. (1998). An overview of delinquent girls: How theory and practice have failed and *the* need for innovative changes. In R. T. Zaplin (Ed.), *Female crime and delinquency: Critical perspectives and effective interventions,* (pp. 31–64). Gaithersburg, MD: Aspen Publishers.

Briere, J., & Runtz, M. (1987). Post sexual abuse trauma. *Journal of Interpersonal Violence, 2* (4), 367–379.

Browne, A., Miller, B., & Maguin, E. (1999). Prevalence and severity of lifetime physical and sexual victimization among incarcerated women. *International Journal of Law and Psychiatry, 22,* 301–322.

Budnick, K. J. (1998). *What about girls?* U.S. Department of Justice, Office of Juvenile Justice and Delinquency Prevention Fact Sheet, June, 2pp. Washingon, DC: OJJDP.

Butzel, J. S., Talbot, N. L., Duberstein, P. R., Houghtalen, R. P., Cox, C., & Giles, D. E. (2000). The relationship between traumatic events and dissociation among women with histories of childhood sexual abuse. *The Journal of Nervous and Mental Disease, 188* (8), 547–549.

Chesney-Lind, M., & Rodriguez, N. (1983). Women under lock and key. *Prison Journal, 63*(3), 47–65.

Chesney-Lind, M. & Shelden, R. G. (1992). *Girls, delinquency and juvenile justice.* Belmont, CA: Wadsworth Publishing Company.

Chesney-Lind, M., & Shelden, R. G. (1998). *Girls, delinquency and juvenile justice* (2nd ed.). Belmont, CA: Wadsworth Publishing Company.

Coker, A. L., Patel, N. J., Krishnaswami, S., Schmidt, W., & Richter, D. (1998). Childhood forced sex and cervical dysphasia among women prison inmates. *Violence Against Women, 4* (5), 595–608.

Daly, K., & Chesney-Lind, M. (1988). Feminism and criminology. *Justice Quarterly, 5*(4), 497–535.

Dembo, R., Williams, L., Wothke, W., Schmeidler, J., & Brown, C.H. (1992). The role of family factors, physical abuse, and sexual victimization experiences in high-risk youths' alcohol and other drug use and delinquency: A longitudinal model. *Violence and Victims, 7,* 245–266.

Dembo, R., Williams, L., & Schmeidler, J. (1993). Gender differences in mental health service needs among youth entering a juvenile detention center. *Journal of Prison and Jail Health, 12* (2), 73–101.

Dodge, K. A., Bates, J. E., & Pettit, G. S. (1990). Mechanisms in the cycle of violence. *Science, 250* (April), 1678–1683.

Epstein, J. A., Botvin, G. J., Griffin, K.W., & Diaz, T. (1999). Role of ethnicity and gender in polydrug use among a longitudinal sample of inner-city adolescents. *Journal of Alcohol and Drug Education, 45* (1), 1–12.

Finkelhor, D., & Baron, L. (1986). High risk children. In D. Finkelhor (Ed.), *A sourcebook on child sexual abuse* (pp. 60–88). Beverly Hills, CA: Sage.

Gilfus, M. E. (1992). From victims to survivors to offenders: Women's routes of entry and immersion into street crime. *Women and Criminal Justice, 4* (1), 63–90.

Greene, Peters, & Associates. (1998). *Guiding principles for promising female programming: An inventory of best practices.* Washington, DC: Office of Juvenile Justice and Delinquency Prevention.

Holsinger, K., Belknap, J., & Sutherland, J. (1999). *Assessing the gender specific program and service needs for adolescent females in the juvenile justice system.* Final Report to the Office of Criminal Justice Services, Columbus, OH.

Inciardi, J., Lockwood, D., & Pottieger, A. E. (1993). *Women and crack-cocaine.* New York: Macmillan.

James, J., & Meyerding, J. (1977). Early sexual experiences and prostitution. *American Journal of Psychiatry, 134* (12), 1381–1385.

Kann, L., Kinchen, S. A., Williams, B. I., Ross, J. G., Lowry, R., Grunbaum, J., Kolbe, L. J., & State and Local YRBSS Coordinators. (2000). Youth risk behavior surveillance-United States, 1999. *Journal of School Health, 70* (7), 271–285.

Klein, H., & Chao, B. (1995). Sexual abuse during childhood and adolescence as predictors of HIV-related sexual risk during adulthood among female sexual partners of drug users. *Violence Against Women, 1* (1), 55–76.

Knodel, J. (1993). The design and analysis of focus group studies: A practical approach. In D. L. Morgan (Ed.), *Successful focus groups: Advancing the state of the art* (pp. 35–50). Newbury Park, CA: Sage.

Lake, E. S. (1993). An exploration of the violent victim experiences of female offenders. *Violence and Victims, 8* (1), 41–51.

Milin, R., Halikas, J. A., Meller, J. E., & Morse, C. (1991). Psychopathology among substance abusing juvenile offenders. *Journal of American Academy of Child and Adolescent Psychiatry, 30* (4), 569–574.

Myers, W. C., Burton, P. R. S., Sanders, P. D., Donat, K. M., Cheney, J., Fitzpatrick, T. M., & Monaco, L. (2000). Project back-on-tract at 1 year: A delinquency treatment program for early-career juvenile offenders. *Journal of the American Academy of Child and Adolescent Psychiatry, 39* (9), 1127–1134.

Owen, B. (1998). In the mix: Struggle and survival in a women's prison. New York: State University of New York Press.

Owen, B., & Bloom, B. (1998).*Modeling gender-specific services in juvenile justice: Policy and program* recommendations. Final Report to the State of California Office of Criminal Justice Planning, Sacramento, CA.

Pepi, C. (1997). Children without childhoods: A feminist intervention strategy utilizing systems theory and restorative justice in treating adolescent female offenders. *Women and Therapy, 20* (4), 85–101.

Poe-Yamagata, E., & Butts, J. A. (1996). *Female offenders in the juvenile justice system: Statistics summary*. Washington, DC: Office of Juvenile Justice and Delinquency Prevention.

Rohsenow, D., Corbett, R., & Devine, D. (1988). Molested as children: A hidden contribution to substance abuse? *Journal of Substance Abuse Treatment, 5* (1), 13–18.

Silbert, M. H., & Pines, A. M. (1981). Sexual child abuse as an antecedent to prostitution. *Child Abuse and Neglect, 5* (April), 407–411.

Tuesday, V. J. (1997). Girls in jail. *Women and Therapy, 21* (1), 85–101.

Wells, R. H. (1994). America's delinquent daughters have nowhere to turn for help. *Corrections Compendium* (November):4–6.

Widom, C. S. (1989a). The cycle of violence. *Science, 244* (490), 160–166.

Widom, C.S. (1989b). Child abuse, neglect, and adult behavior: Research design and findings on criminality, violence, and child abuse. American Journal of Orthopsychiatry 59(3):355–367.

Widom, C. S., & Maxfield, M. G. (2001). *An update on the 'cycle of violence'*. Washington, DC: National Institute of Justice, Office of Justice Programs.

CHAPTER 9

GENDER MATTERS:
PATTERNS IN GIRLS'
DELINQUENCY AND GENDER
RESPONSIVE PROGRAMMING[1]

Meda Chesney-Lind and
Scott K. Okamoto

Girls in the juvenile justice system were once "dubbed" the "forgotten few" (Bergsmann, 1989). That construction of female delinquency has rapidly faded as increases in girls' arrests have dramatically outstripped those of boys for most of the last decade. Girls now account for one out of four arrests, and attention is being called to the fact that their arrests for non-traditional, even violent, offenses are among those showing the greatest increases. These shifts and changes all bring into sharp focus the need to better understand the dynamics involved in female delinquency and the need to tailor responses to the unique circumstances of girls growing up in the new millennium.

This article examines the prevalence of female juvenile delinquency and reviews the literature from a sociological and practice perspective. Specifically, we focus attention on girls' aggression and violence and argue that close analysis of the data indicates that changes in arrests of girls for certain violent offenses reflect complex changes in the policing of girl's aggression (including the arrest of girls for minor forms of family violence) rather than actual changes in girls' behavior. Following this review, we consider more traditional themes in girls' delinquency: status offenses, larceny theft and drug use, that

---

1. This article originally appeared in the Journal of Forensic Psychology Practice, Vol. 1 (3) 2001.

still account for the bulk of girls arrests. Finally, we briefly review trends in the treatment of girls by the juvenile justice system, and we discuss the emerging literature

Patterns in Girls' Delinquency: Are Girls Closing the Gender Gap in Violence?

Between 1989 and 1998, for example, girls' arrests increased 50.3 percent compared to only 16.5 percent for boys (Federal Bureau of Investigation, 1999). Concomitant with these arrest increases are increases in girls' referral to juvenile courts; between 1987 and 1996, the number of delinquency cases involving girls increased by 76 percent compared to a 42 percent increase for males (Stahl, 1999). Arrests of girls for serious violent offenses increased by 64.3 percent between 1989 and 1998; arrests of girls for "other assaults" increased by an even more astounding 125.4 percent (Federal Bureau of Investigation 1999, 215). The Office of Juvenile Justice and Delinquency Prevention (1999) found that the female violent crime rate for 1997 was 103 percent above the 1981 rate, compared to 27 percent for males. This prompted them to state that "increasing juvenile female arrests and the involvement of girls in at-risk and delinquent behavior has been a pervasive trend across the United States" (pg. 2). Discussions of girls' gang behavior and, more recently, girls' violence have also been extremely prevalent in the media (see Chesney-Lind 1999 for a review).

Girls' Aggression and Violence

With reference to what might be called girls' "non-traditional" delinquency, it must be recognized that girls' capacity for aggression and violence has historically been ignored, trivialized or denied. For this reason, self-report data particularly from the seventies and eighties has always shown higher involvement of girls in assaultive behavior than official statistics would indicate. As an example, Canter (1976) reported a male versus female, self-reported delinquency ratio of 3.4:1 for minor assault and 3.5:1 for serious assault. At that time, arrest statistics showed much greater male participation in aggravated assault (5.6:1, Federal Bureau of Investigation, 1980) and simple assault (3.8:1, Canter, 1982). Currently, arrest statistics show a 3.54:1 ratio for "aggravated assault" and a 2.25:1 ratio for "other assaults" (Federal

Bureau of Investigation, 1999). Taken together, these numbers suggest the gap is closing between what girls have always done (and reported, when asked anonymously) and arrest statistics rather than a course change in girls' participation in serious violence.

Detailed comparisons drawn from supplemental homicide reports from unpublished FBI data also hint at the central, rather than peripheral way in which gender has colored and differentiated girls' and boys' violence. In a study of these FBI data on the characteristics of girls' and boys' homicides between 1984 and 1993, Loper and Cornell (1996) found that girls accounted for "proportionately fewer homicides in 1993 (6 percent) than in 1984 (14 percent)" (p. 324). They found that, in comparison to boys' homicides, girls who killed were more likely to use a knife than a gun and to murder someone as a result of conflict (rather than in the commission of a crime). Girls were also more likely than boys to murder family members (32 percent) and very young victims (24 percent of their victims were under the age of three compared to 1 percent of the boys' victims). When involved in a peer homicide, girls were more likely than boys to have killed as a result of an interpersonal conflict and were more likely to kill alone, while boys were more likely to kill with an accomplice. Loper and Cornell concluded that "the stereotype of girls becoming gun-toting robbers was not supported. The dramatic increase in gun-related homicides...applies to boys but not girls" (p. 332).

To further support this notion, other research on trends in self-report data of youthful involvement in violent offenses also fails to show the dramatic changes found in official statistics. Specifically, a matched sample of "high risk" youth (aged 13–17) surveyed in the 1977 National Youth Study and the more recent 1989 Denver Youth Survey revealed significant *decreases* in girls' involvement in felony assaults, minor assaults, and hard drugs, and no change in a wide range of other delinquent behaviors—including felony theft, minor theft, and index delinquency (Huizinga, 1994). Further, a summary of two more recent studies on self-reported aggression (see Table 1) also reflects that while about a third of girls reported having been in a physical fight in the last year, this was true of over half of the boys in both samples (Girls Incorporated, 1996). Girls are far more likely to fight with a parent or sibling (34 percent compared to 9 percent), whereas boys are more likely to fight with friends or strangers. Finally, boys are twice to three times more likely to report carrying a weapon in the past month (Girls Incorporated, 1996).

Table 1. Actual and Potential Involvement in Physical Violence

	Females %	Males %	Source
Involved In:			
Physical fight in past year	34	51	Adams et al.
	32	51	Kann et al.
Four or more physical fights in the past year	9	15	Adams et al.
Fought With:			
Stranger	7	15	Adams et al.
Friend	24	46	Adams et al.
Date/romantic partner	8	2	Adams et al.
Parent/sibling	34	9	Adams et al.
Other	4	6	Adams et al.
Several of the above	24	26	Adams et al.
Carried a Weapon:			
In the past month	7	17	Adams et al.
	9	34	Kann et al.

Adams et al. (1995: ages 14–17, 1992 data) and Kann et al. (1995: grades 9–12, 1993 data) in Girls, Inc. 1996.

The psychological literature on aggression, which considers forms of aggression other than physical aggression (or violence), is also relevant here. Taken together, this literature generally reflects that, while boys and men are more likely to be physically aggressive, differences begin to even out when verbal aggression is considered (yelling, insulting, teasing; Bjorkqvist & Niemela, 1992). Further, girls in adolescence may be more likely than boys to use "indirect aggression," such as gossip, telling bad or false stories, telling secrets (Bjorkqvist, Osterman, & Kaukiainen, 1992). When this broad definition of "aggression" is utilized, only about 5 percent of the variance in aggression is explained by gender (Bjorkqvist & Niemela, 1992).

Those who study aggression in young children and young adults also note that girls' aggression is usually within the home or "intrafemale" and, thus, likely to be less often reported to authorities (Bjorkqvist & Niemela, 1992). The fact that these forms of aggression have been largely ignored by scholars as well as the general public also means that there is substantial room for girls' aggression to be "discovered" at a time where concern about youthful violence is heightened.

Finally, girls' behavior, including violence, needs to be put in its patriarchal context. In her analysis of self-reported violence in girls in Canada, Artz (1998) has done precisely that, and the results were striking. First, she noted that violent girls reported significantly greater rates of victimization and abuse than their non-violent counterparts, and that girls who were violent reported great fear of sexual assault, especially from their boyfriends. Specifically, 20 percent of violent girls stated they were physically abused at home compared to 10 percent of violent males, and 6.3 percent of non-violent girls. Patterns for sexual abuse were even starker; roughly one out of four violent girls had been sexually abused compared to one in ten of non-violent girls (Artz, 1998). Follow-up interviews with a small group of violent girls found that they had learned at home that "might makes right" and engaged in "horizontal violence" directed at other powerless girls (often with boys as the audience). Certainly, these findings provide little ammunition for those who would contend that the "new" violent girl is a product of any form of "emancipation."

Indeed, what needs to be understood about girls' delinquency, particularly from a programmatic and policy standpoint, is the clear link between victimization, trauma, and girls' delinquency. The other major theme that must be addressed is the fact that most often this trauma produces not violent offenses but rather what have long been regarded as "trivial" or unimportant offenses like running away from home.

Relabeling Status Offenses

But what about dramatic increases, particularly in arrests of girls for "other assaults"? Relabeling of behaviors that were once categorized as status offenses (non-criminal offenses like "runaway" and "person in need of supervision") into violent offenses cannot be ruled out in explanations of arrest rate shifts, nor can changes in police practices with reference to domestic violence. A review of the over two thousand cases of girls referred to Maryland's juvenile justice system for "person-to-person" offenses revealed that virtually all of these offenses (97.9 percent) involved "assault." A further examination of these records revealed that about half were "family centered" and involved such activities as "a girl hitting her mother and her mother subsequently pressing charges" (Mayer, 1994).

More recently, Acoca's study of nearly 1000 girls' files from four California counties found that while a "high percentage" of these girls were charged with "person offenses," a majority of these involved assault. Further, "a close reading of the case files of girls charged with assault revealed that most of these charges were the result of nonserious, mutual combat, situations with parents." Acoca details cases that she regards as typical including: "father lunged at her while she was calling the police about a domestic dispute. She (girl) hit him." Finally, she reports that some cases were quite trivial in nature including a girl arrested "for throwing cookies at her mother" (Acoca, 1999, pgs. 7–8).

In essence, when exploring the dramatic increases in the arrests of girls for "other assault," it is likely that changes in enforcement practices have dramatically narrowed the gender gap. As noted in the above examples, a clear contribution has come from increasing arrests of girls and women for domestic violence. A recent California study found that the female share of these arrests increased from 6 percent in 1988 to 16.5 percent in 1998 (Bureau of Criminal Information and Analysis, 1999). African American girls and women had arrest rates roughly three times that of white girls and women in 1998: 149.6 compared to 46.4 (Bureau of Criminal Information and Analysis, 1999).

Relabeling of girls' arguments with parents from status offenses (like "incorrigible" or "person in need of supervision") to assault is a form of "bootstrapping," has been particularly pronounced in the official delinquency of African American girls (Robinson, 1990; Bartollas, 1993). This practice also facilitates the incarceration of girls in detention facilities and training schools—something that would not be possible if the girl were arrested for non-criminal status offenses.

In essence, it has long been known that arrests of youth for minor or "other" assaults can range from school yard tussles to relatively serious, but not life threatening assaults (Steffensmeier & Steffensmeier, 1980). These authors first noted a increasing tendency to arrest girls for these offenses in the seventies and commented that "evidence suggests that female arrests for 'other assaults' are relatively non-serious in nature and tend to consist of being bystanders or companions to males involved in skirmishes, fights, and so on" (Steffensmeier & Steffensmeier, 1980, p. 70). Currie (1998) adds to this the fact that these "simple assaults without injury" are often "attempted" or "threatened" or "not completed." At a time when official concern about youth violence is almost unparalleled and school principals are increasingly likely to call police onto their campuses, it should come as no surprise that youthful arrests in this area are up.

This observation is supported by recent research on the dynamics of juvenile robbery in Honolulu (another violent offense where girls' arrests showed sharp increases). In the last decade, Hawaii, like the rest of the nation, had seen an increase in the arrests of youth for serious crimes of violence[2] coupled with a recent decline. In Hawaii (murder, rape, robbery and aggravated assault) increased 60 percent from 1987–1996 coupled with an 8.6 percent decline between 1996 and 1997 (Crime in Hawaii, 1996, 1997).

---

2. In this report, "seriousness crimes of violence" will refer to the Federal Bureau of Investigation's index offenses which are used to measure violent crime: murder, forcible rape, aggravated assault and robbery.

Most of the change can be attributed to increases in the number of youth arrested for two offenses: aggravated assault and robbery. Between 1994 and 1996, for example, the number of youth arrested for robbery doubled in Honolulu.

These increases prompted a study of the actual dimensions of juvenile robbery in Honolulu (see Chesney-Lind & Paramore, 1999). In this study, police files from two time periods (1991 and 1997) that focused on robbery incidents resulting in arrest were identified. According to these data, in 1991, the vast majority of those arrested for robbery in Honolulu were male—114 (95 percent) versus 6 (5 percent). However, a shift occurred in 1997—83.3 percent were males. Thus, the proportion of robbery arrests involving girls more than tripled, between 1991 and 1997.

Taken alone, these numeric increases, along with anecdotal information are precisely why the "surge" in girls' violence has been made. However, in this study, we were able to carefully characterize of each of these "robberies" during the two time periods. Essentially, the data suggested that no major shift in the pattern of juvenile robbery occurred between 1991 to 1997 in Honolulu. Rather it appears that less serious offenses, including a number committed by girls, are being swept up into the system perhaps as a result of changes in school policy and parental attitudes (many of the robberies occurred as youth were going to and from school). Consistent with this explanation are the following observable patterns in our data: during the two time periods under review, the age of offenders shifts downward, as does the value of items taken. In 1991, the median value of the items stolen was $10.00; by 1997, the median value had dropped to $1.25. Most significantly, the proportion of adult victims declines sharply while the number of juvenile victims increases. Finally, while more of the robberies involved weapons in 1997, those weapons were less likely to be firearms and the incidents were less likely to result in injury to the victim. In short, the data suggest that the problem of juvenile robbery in the City and County of Honolulu is largely characterized by slightly older youth bullying and "hi-jacking" younger youth for small amounts of cash and occasionally jewelry and that arrests of youth for these forms of robbery accounted for virtually all of the increase observed.

Girls' Troubles and Trauma—
Non-Aggressive Offenses and Drug Use

While the media has focused attention on girls' violent, non-traditional delinquency, most of girls' delinquency is not of that sort at all. Examining the types of offenses for which girls are actually arrested, it is clear that most are arrested for the less serious criminal acts and status offenses (non-criminal offenses for which only youth can be taken into custody like "running away from home" or curfew violation). In 1998, roughly half of girls' arrests were for either larceny theft (21.5 percent) much of which, particularly for girls, is shoplifting (Shelden & Horvath, 1986) or status offenses (22.1 percent). Boys' arrests were far more dispersed.

Status Offenses

Status offenses have always played a significant role among the offenses that bring girls into the juvenile justice system. They accounted for about a quarter all girls' arrests in 1998, but only ten percent of boys' arrests—figures that remained relatively stable during the last decade. In 1998, over half (58.7 percent) of those arrested for one status offense—running away from home— were girls (Federal Bureau of Investigation, 1999). Running away from home and prostitution remain the only two arrest categories where more girls than boys are arrested, and despite the intention of the Juvenile Justice and Delinquency Prevention Act in 1974, which, among other things, encouraged jurisdictions to divert and deinstitutionalize youth charged with status offenses, arrests for these have remained stable or have actually been climbing in recent years. Between 1989 and 1998, for example, the number of girls arrested for runaway remained about the same (decreasing by 1.2 percent), and arrests of girls for curfew violations increased by an astonishing 238.5 percent (Federal Bureau of Investigation, 1999).

Why are girls more likely to be arrested than boys for running away from home? There are no simple answers to this question. Studies of actual delinquency (not simply arrests) show that girls and boys run away from home in about equal numbers. As an example, Canter (1982) found in a National Youth Survey that there was no evidence of greater female involvement, compared to males, in any category of delinquent behavior. Indeed, in this sample, males were significantly more likely than females to report status offenses. There is some evidence to suggest that parents and police may be responding differently to the same behavior. Parents may be calling the police when their daughters do not come home, and police may be more likely to arrest a female than a male runaway youth.

Finally, research on the characteristics of girls in the CYA system reveals that while these girls cannot be incarcerated in the Youth Authority for status offenses, nearly half (45 percent) had been charged with status offenses prior to their incarceration in the CYA for more serious offenses (Bloom & Campbell, 1998). Focus groups with program staff working in a variety of settings in California also indicated that these individuals felt that girls in that state were chiefly involved in the juvenile justice system for offenses such as "petty theft, shoplifting, assault and battery, drug violations, gang activity and truancy, lying to a police officer, and running away" (Bloom & Campbell, 1998).

Sexual and Physical Abuse

Research illustrates the differences in the reasons that boys and girls have for running away. Girls are, for example, much more likely than boys to be the victims of child sexual abuse with some experts estimating that roughly 70 percent of the victims of child sexual abuse are girls (Finkelhor & Baron, 1986). Not surprisingly, the evidence is also suggesting a link between this problem and girl's delinquency—particularly running away from home.

Studies of girls on the streets or in court populations are showing high rates of both sexual and physical abuse. A study of a runaway shelter in Toronto found, for example, that 73 percent of the female runaways and 38 percent of the males had been sexually abused. This same study found that sexually abused female runaways were more likely than their non-abused counterparts to engage in delinquent or criminal activities such as substance abuse, petty theft, and prostitution. No such pattern was found among the male runaways (McCormack, Janus, & Burgess, 1986).

Detailed studies of youth entering the juvenile justice system in Florida have compared the "constellations of problems" presented by girls and boys entering detention (Dembo, Williams, & Schmeidler, 1993; Dembo et al., 1995). These researchers have found that female youth were more likely than male youth to have abuse histories and contact with the juvenile justice system for status offenses, while male youth had higher rates of involvement with various delinquent offenses. Further research on a larger cohort of youth (N=2104) admitted to an assessment center in Tampa concluded that "girls' problem behavior commonly relates to an abusive and traumatizing home life, whereas boys' law violating behavior reflects their involvement in a delinquent life style" (Dembo et al. 1995, 21).

More recent research confirms Dembo's insights; Cauffman, Feldman, Waterman, and Steiner (1998) studied the backgrounds of 96 girls in the custody of the California Youth Authority and compared these results with those garnered from a comparison sample of male youth (N=93) held by CYA. In this comparison, Cauffman et al. found that while boys were more likely to be traumatized as observers of violence, "girls were more likely to be traumatized as direct victims" (more than half the girls were the victims of either sexual or physical abuse). Perhaps as a result, girls were significantly more likely than boys to be currently suffering from post traumatic stress disorder; the levels of PTSD found in this population were "significantly higher than among the general adolescent female population" (11 percent compared to 65 percent, Cauffman et al., 1998). Interestingly, about two thirds of the girls in this sample were serving time for a violent offense (murder, assault, robbery), and 43 percent of the girls identified as gang members (Cauffman et al., 1998).

The Family Court and the Female Delinquent: A Legacy of Sexism

Girls on the run from these sorts of homes clearly need help. For many years, however, their accounts of abuse were ignored, and they were inappropriately institutionalized in detention centers and training schools as delinquents if they refused to stay at home. While girls have long been invisible to those who crafted theories of "delinquency," concerns about girls' immoral conduct were at the center, rather than at the periphery, of the movement that established the juvenile court (Platt, 1969; Odem, 1995; Kunzel, 1993). As a result, in the earliest years of the court, girls were frequently institutionalized for such offenses as "sexual immorality" or "waywardness" and well into the seventies, contemporary "status offenses" such as runaway often functioned as "buffer charges" for the court's concern about the sexual behavior of girls (see Chesney-Lind & Shelden, 1997, for a discussion of these issues).

Correctional reformers, concerned about abuse of the status offense category by juvenile courts (though not necessarily about girls), were instrumental in urging the U.S. Congress to pass the Juvenile Justice and Delinquency Prevention (JJDP) Act of 1974. This legislation required that states receiving federal delinquency prevention money begin to divert and deinstitutionalize their status offenders. Despite erratic enforcement of this provision and considerable resistance from juvenile court judges, girls were the clear beneficiaries of the reform. Incarceration of young women in training schools and detention centers across the country fell dramatically in the decades since its passage, in distinct contrast to patterns found early in the century.

National statistics on girls' incarceration reflect both the official enthusiasm for the incarceration of girls during the early part of this century and the impact of the JJDP Act of 1974. Girls' share of the population of juvenile correctional facilities (both public and private) increased from 1880 (when girls were 19 percent of the population) to 1923 (when girls were 28 percent). By 1950, girls had climbed to 34 percent of the total, and in 1960 they were still 27 percent of those in correctional facilities. By 1980, the impact of the JJDP Act was clear, and girls had dropped to only 19 percent of those in any type of correctional facility (Cahalan, 1986).

In 1997, though, the pattern appears to have reversed itself. Between 1989 and 1997, for example, the number of girls held in public detention and training schools actually increased by 33.1 percent (Krisberg, DeComo, & Herrera, 1992; Snyder & Sickmund, 1999). Girls comprised about 12 percent of those held in public detention centers and training schools (Snyder & Sickmund, 1999). Overall, girls were far more likely than boys to be detained or incarcerated in public facilities for a status offense or a technical violation of their conditions of probation or parole (32 percent compared to 13 percent of boys). Such a pattern is particularly stark among those held in detention. Statistics reveal that in 1993, nearly a quarter of girls (24 percent) were held for probation or parole violation, compared to only 12 percent of boys (Poe-Yamagata & Butts, 1996).

These figures likely reflect long-standing opposition to the deinstitutionalization mandates, and particularly, the implementation of judicial mechanisms to avoid the deinstitutionalization mandates in the original legislation. In 1980, the National Council of Juvenile and Family Court Judges was able to narrow the definition of a status offender in the amended act so that any child who had violated a "valid court order" would no longer be covered under the de institutionalization provisions (United States Statutes at Large, 1981). This change effectively gutted the 1974 JJDP act by permitting judges to reclassify a status offender who violated a court order as a delinquent. This meant that a young woman who ran away from a court-ordered placement (a halfway house, foster home, etc.) could be re-labeled a delinquent and locked up.

Judges have long engaged in efforts like "violation of a valid court order" or issuing contempt citations to "bootstrap" status offenders into categories that permit their detention. They thereby circumvent the de institutionalization component of the act (Costello & Worthington, 1981). These judicial maneuvers clearly disadvantage girls. For example, Bishop and Frazier (1992) reviewed 162,012 cases referred to juvenile justice intake units in Florida during 1985–1987. The researchers found only a weak pattern of discrimination against female status offenders compared to the treatment of male status offenders. However, when they examined the impact of contempt citations, the pattern changed markedly. They found that females offenders referred for contempt were more likely than females referred for other criminal type offenses to be petitioned to court, and substantially more likely to be petitioned to court than males referred for contempt. Moreover, the girls were far more likely than boys to be sentenced to detention. Specifically, the typical female offender in their study had a probability of incarceration of 4.3 percent, which increased to 29.9 percent if she was held in contempt. Such a pattern was not observed among the males in the study. The authors concluded, "the traditional double standard is still operative. Clearly neither the cultural changes associated with the feminist movement nor the legal changes illustrated in the JJDP Act's mandate to de institutionalize status offenders have brought about equality under the law for young men and women" (p. 1186).

Much the same pattern has been observed in Canada where well over a quarter of all the girls (27.3 percent) brought youth courts in 1995–96 were charged with "failure to comply" compared to only 5.7 percent in 1980 (Reitsma-Street, 1999). In fact, the situation could well be worse for Canadian girls than their US counterparts with Canadian courts increasing the rate of incarceration of female youth at a significant and alarming rate. As an example, the number of girls placed in "secure custody" increased in just the space of four years (1991–1995) by an alarming 55 percent. This increase was virtually all explained by the incarceration of girls for "administrative" offenses (like violating the conditions of probation or being held in contempt of court) and other violations of court rules rather than criminal acts (DeKeseredy, 1999).

Gender-Specific Services for Girls

On the legislative front, things initially seemed different and more positive for girls. Hearings held in 1992 in conjunction with the reauthorization of the Juvenile Justice and Delinquency Prevention Act, addressed for the first time the "provision of services to girls within the juvenile justice system" (United States House of Representatives, 1992). At this hearing, both the double standard of juvenile justice was discussed, as well as the paucity of services for girls. The chair of the hearing, Rep. Matthew Martinez noted the high number of girls arrested for status offenses, the high percentage of girls in detention as a result of violation of court orders, and the failure of the system to address girls' needs. He ended with the question, "I wonder why, why are there no other alternatives than youth jail for her?" (United States House of Representatives, 1992, p. 2).

As a result of this landmark hearing, the 1992 reauthorization of the act included specific provisions requiring plans from each state receiving federal funds to include "an analysis of gender-specific services for the prevention and treatment of juvenile delinquency, including the types of such services available and the need for such services for females and a plan for providing needed gender-specific services for the prevention and treatment of juvenile delinquency" (Juvenile Justice and Delinquency Prevention Act of 1992). Additional money was set aside as part of the JJDP Act's challenge grant program for states wishing to develop policies to prohibit gender bias in placement and treatment and to develop programs that assure girls equal access to services. As a result, 23 states embarked on such programs—by far the most popular of the ten possible challenge grant activity areas (Girls Incorporated, 1996). Finally, the legislation moved to make the "bootstrapping" of status offenders more difficult (United States House of Representatives, 1992).

Sadly, these changes, while extremely hopeful, were short-lived. Several recent sessions of congress sought major overhauls of the Juvenile Justice and Delinquency Prevention Act, and virtually all of the initiatives they considered were ominous for girls. The bills generally attempted to refocus national attention on the "violent and repeat juvenile offender" (read boys) while also granting states "flexibility" in implementing some if not all of four core mandates of the original JD Act. Key among these mandates, of course, is the deinstitutionalization of status offenders, though conservative lawmakers are also taking aim at efforts to separate youth from adults in correctional facilities, efforts to reduce minority over-representation in juvenile detention and training schools, and efforts to remove juveniles from adult jails (Schiraldi & Soler, 1998).

In a debate that featured "guns, the Ten Commandments, the Internet, video games and the movies" (Boyle, 1999), there was considerable emphasis on punishment (such as allowing the prosecution of 13 year olds as adults). Most ominous for girls are efforts loosen restrictions on the detention of status offenders. Here, conservative legislators were clearly influenced by juvenile court judges, who pushed for a recriminalization of status offenses. Judge David Grossman, who testified before Congress representing the National Council of Juvenile and Family Court Judges, contended that the deinstitutionalization was a "movement" whose time had passed: "All too often, it left the intended young beneficiaries of its advocacy adrift on the streets, fallen between the cracks" (Alexander, 1998, p. 46). He advocated, instead, that status offenders be returned to the court's jurisdiction.

Perhaps as a result of testimony of this sort, Senate Bill 254 calls for the National Institute of Justice to conduct a study "on the effect of on status offenders compared to similarly situated individuals who are not placed in secure detention in terms of continuation of their inappropriate or illegal conduct, delinquency or future criminal behavior, and evaluation of the safety of status offenders placed in secure detention." Even more worrisome, both current bills make it easier to hold youth in adult jails. The later provision is most disturbing, since girls were not infrequently held in such situations in the past (as de facto detention centers in rural America). Sadly, abuse is not uncommon in such settings. In Ohio, for example, a 15-year-old girl was sexually assaulted by a deputy jailer after having been placed in an adult jail for a minor infraction (Ziedenberg & Schiraldi, 1997). Due to the isolation and abuse in these settings, girls are also at great risk for suicide (see Chesney-Lind, 1988). At present, both house and senate versions are in conference committee (Boyle, 1999).

These initiatives should not surprise any student of the court's history, since they represent return to the court's backstopping the sexual double standard (and parental authority) at the expense of girls' freedom. Indeed, a careful review of the data on incarceration patterns (during deinstitutionalization) signaled the resilience of the court's bias against girls as well as the special meaning of this for girls of color. Specifically, recent research suggests that the impact of deinstitutionalization has produced a racialized, two track system of juvenile justice—one in which white girls are placed in mental hospitals and private facilities, while girls of color are detained and institutionalized.

Deinstitutionalization Under Siege: Rising Detentions and Racialized Justice

While DSO stressed the need to deinstitutionalize status offenders, we have seen that the numbers of girls and boys arrested for these non-criminal offenses continues to increase. Most worrisome are reports of increasing use of detention. National data indicate that between 1989 and 1993, detentions involving girls increased by 23 percent compared to an 18 percent increase in boys' detentions (Poe-Yamagata and Butts, 1996).

Some states are moving to make detention of girls easier as well. In 1995, the state of Washington passed "Becca's Bill" in the wake of the death of 13-year-old Rebecca Headman, a chronic runaway who was murdered while on the run. Under this legislation, parents can call the police and allege that their daughter has run away. Each time this happens, the girls can be detained in a secure "crisis residential center" for up to 5 days or up to 7 days for contempt if she violated court-ordered conditions. As a result of the passage of this bill, the number of youth placed in detention rose 835 percent between 1994 and 1997, and estimates are that 60 percent of the youth taken into custody under "Becca's Bill" are girls "for whom few long-term programs exist" (Sherman, 2000).

San Francisco researchers (Shorter, Schaffner, Schick, & Frappier, 1996) examined the situation of girls in their juvenile justice system and concluded that the girls in their system were "out of sight, out of mind" (p. 1). Specifically, girls would languish in detention centers waiting for placement, while the boy's were released or put in placement. As a result, 60 percent of the girls were detained for more than seven days, compared to only 6 percent of the boys (Shorter, Schaffner, Schick, & Frappier, 1996).

More recently, Acoca and Dedel interviewed 200 girls in county juvenile halls in California. They report "specific forms of abuse" experienced by girls including "consistent use by staff of foul and demeaning language, inappropriate touching, pushing and hitting, isolation, and deprivation of clean clothing." (Acoca, 1999, p. 6). Most disturbing, they report that "some strip searches of girls were conducted in the presence of male officers, underscoring the inherent problem of adult male staff supervising adolescent female detainees" (Acoca, 1999).

Turning to the situations of youth held in more long term settings, what has emerged is a complex, and not necessarily equitable system. Notably, over the last two decades, there has been a distinct rise in the numbers of youth confined in "private" facilities, and this trend in particular, has special meaning for girls, since girls comprise a larger proportion of those held in private facilities. In 1997, girls were 12 percent of those in public institutions, but about a fifth (18 percent) of those held in private institutions. Nearly half of the girls (45 percent) but only one in ten boys (11 percent) were being held in these facilities for status offenses. Ethnic differences are also apparent in the populations of these institutions; whites constituted about 33 percent of those held in public institutions in 1997, but 45 percent of those held in private facilities (Snyder & Sickmund, 1999). These data suggest that both race and gender play a role in the ultimate placement of youth in training schools or private institutions.

In fact, some suspect that deinstitutionalization may have actually signaled the development of a two-track juvenile justice system—one track for girls of color, and another for white girls. In a study of investigation reports from one area office in Los Angeles, Jody Miller (1994) examined the impact of race and ethnicity on the processing of girls' cases during 1992–1993. Reviewing the characteristics of the girls in Miller's group reveals the role played by color in the current juvenile justice system. Latinas comprised the largest proportion of the population (43 percent), followed by White girls (34 percent), and African American girls (23 percent; Miller, 1994). Predictably, girls of color were more likely to be from low-income homes, but this was especially true of African American girls (53.2 percent were from AFDC families, compared to 23 percent of white girls and 21 percent of Hispanic girls). Most importantly, Miller found that white girls were significantly more likely to be recommended for a treatment rather than a "detention oriented" placement than either African American or Latina girls. In fact, 75 percent of the white girls were recommended for a treatment oriented facility compared to 34.6 percent of the Latinas and only 20 percent of the African American girls (Miller, 1994).

Examining a portion of the probation officer's reports in detail, Miller found key differences in the ways that girls' behaviors were described—reflecting what she called "racialized gender expectations." In particular, African-American girls' behavior was often framed as products of "inappropriate 'lifestyle' choices," while white girls' behavior was described as resulting from low self-esteem, being easily influenced, and the result of "abandonment" (Miller, 1994). Latina girls, Miller found, received "dichotomized" treatment, with some receiving the more paternalistic care white girls received, while others received the more punitive treatment (particularly if they committed "masculine" offenses like car theft).

Robinson (1990) in her in-depth study of girls in the social welfare (CHINS) and juvenile justice system (DYS) in Massachusetts documents the racialized pattern of juvenile justice quite clearly. Her social welfare sample (N=15) was 74 percent white/non-Hispanic and her juvenile justice system sample (N=15) was 53 percent Black or Hispanic. Her interviews, though, document the remarkable similarities of the girls' backgrounds and problems. As an example, 80 percent of the girls committed to DYS reported being sexually abused compared to 73 percent of the girls "receiving services as a child in need of supervision" (p. 311). The difference between these girls was in the offenses for which they were charged; all the girls receiving services were charged with traditional status offenses (chiefly running away and truancy), while the girls committed to DYS were charged with criminal offenses. Here, though, her interviews reveal clear evidence of bootstrapping, such as the sixteen year-old girl who was committed to DYS for "unauthorized use of a motor vehicle." In this instance, Beverly, who is Black, had "stolen" her mother's car for three hours to go shopping with a friend. Previous to this conviction, according to Robinson's interview, she had been a "CHINS" for "running away from home repeatedly." Beverly told Robinson that her mother had been "advised by the DYS social worker to press charges for unauthorized use of a motor vehicle so that Beverly could be sent to secure detention whenever she was caught on the run" (p. 202).

Other evidence of this pattern is reported by Bartollas (1993) in his study of youth confined in juvenile "institutional" placements in a midwestern state. His research sampled female adolescents in both public and private facilities. The "state" sample (representing the girls in public facilities) was 61 percent black, while the private sample was 100 percent white. Little difference, however, was found in the offense patterns of the two groups of girls. Seventy percent of the girls in the "state" sample were "placed in a training school as a result of a status offense" (p. 473). This state, like most, does not permit youth to be institutionalized for these offenses; however, Bartollas noted that "they can be placed on probation, which makes it possible for the juvenile judge to adjudicate them to a training school" (p. 473). In the private sample, only 50 percent were confined for status offenses; the remainder were there for "minor stealing and shoplifting-related offenses" (p. 473). Bartollas also noted that both of these samples of girls had far less extensive juvenile histories than did their boy counterparts.

Issues in Working with Girls and Promising Practices

Nationally, there has been an increasing interest in programs that address "at-risk" girls' specific needs. The Office of Juvenile Justice and Delinquency Prevention, for example, has commissioned reports focused on examining practice principles in working with girls and outlining individual state efforts in gender-specific programming (Budnick & Shields-Fletcher, 1998). Despite the increased attention, much is still unknown with regards to specific skills or techniques in working with girls. This section will describe the unique characteristics in working with girls and the implications of these characteristics for practice. Promising programs for girls will then be reviewed.

Girls in the Intervention Setting

A developing body of research in the field of criminology has focused on the gender differences in working with girls. Much of this research has focused on youth practitioners from juvenile justice and mental health agencies in order to identify the unique characteristics in working with female clients. Three characteristics appear consistent throughout the studies on female youth clients—(1) girls are much more emotional than boys in the treatment setting, (2) Girls have distinctly different needs than boys in the areas of life skills training and education, and (3) Girls elicit unique countertransference reactions from practitioners. These issues have ramifications for gender-specific training and education of youth practitioners, and development of youth-serving programs.

Unlike their male counterparts, research has illustrated how girls are much more expressive with their emotions in the treatment setting (Baines & Alder, 1996; Chesney-Lind & Freitas, 1999). Using focus groups with youth-serving practitioners in Hawaii, Chesney-Lind and Freitas found that female clients were cited as being much more emotional than their male counterparts and had a strong need to verbally communicate their emotions to staff. Other studies similarly found that girls had a need to communicate their feelings and emotions to staff (Baines & Alder, 1996, Alder & Hunter, 1999). These needs, though, do not necessarily mean that girls are successful in connecting in meaningful ways with staff in conventional delinquency programs.

Research has found that many (but not all) people who work in the juvenile justice system typically prefer working with boys, and routinely stress the "difficulty" of working with girls. Belknap and her colleagues in Ohio reported, in their study of youth workers, that "most of the professionals, unless they worked exclusively with girls, had a difficult time not talking solely about the male delinquents" (Belknap, Dunn & Holsinger, 1997, p. 28). Likewise, Alder (1997) has noted that "willful" girls produce problems for a system initially devised to handle boys: girls in these systems get constructed as "hysterical," "manipulative," "verbally aggressive," and "untrusting" while boys are "honest," "open," and "less complex."

Taken together, these findings suggest that some practitioners find the expressive nature of girls to be more demanding and time-consuming (Baines & Alder, 1996). Other research, though, has indicated that because of their need to express emotions, girls have been described as easier to engage in the practice setting than boys (Chesney-Lind & Freitas, 1999). This suggests that programs for girls should have low staff to client ratios in order for staff to be able to address the complex emotional needs of female clients. Specifically, the typical model of residential treatment (i.e., one to two staff per eight youth) may not be suitable for working with girls. More intensive therapeutic foster care models may be a better "fit" for effectively working with girls. Further, youth workers should be trained in ways to promote positive methods of communication from their female clients.

Girls have specific needs in the areas of life skills training and education. Life skills training (e.g., training in cognitive-behavioral skills for building self-esteem, communicating effectively, and assertiveness) has been shown to be an effective intervention for substance abuse prevention for both Caucasian (Botvin, Baker, Dusenbury, Botvin, & Diaz, 1995) and minority (Botvin, Schinke, Epstein, & Diaz, 1994; Botvin, Schinke, Epstein, Diaz, & Botvin, 1995) youth. OJJDP (1998) has identified specific areas of skills training for girls, including self-defense training, assertiveness training, and self-esteem enhancement. Education in the areas of pregnancy, substance use, eating disorders and sexually-transmitted diseases has also been identified in the literature as important for girls (Chesney-Lind & Freitas, 1999; Belknap, Dunn, & Holsinger, 1997). Youth practitioners should be trained in the gender-specific areas of life skills training and the use of effective teaching techniques (e.g., behavioral rehearsal, feedback, and reinforcement) to train female clients in those specific areas.

Finally, research has suggested that practitioners experience unique countertransference feelings when working with girls, which in turn may impact their work with their clients. The term *countertransference* refers to the practitioners' emotional and behavioral reactions to a client's behavior (Brandell, 1992). Using observational research, Kersten (1990) described how workers in juvenile institutions enforced institutional policies more strictly with female inmates and used "time-out" facilities more frequently with girls. These findings suggest that female inmates elicit different (and perhaps stronger) emotions and behaviors from practitioners than their male counterparts. Some literature further suggests that countertransference feelings and behaviors appear strongest with male practitioners working with female clients. Baines and Alder (1996) found that male workers in their study had major concerns relating to physical proximity, physical touch, and maintenance of an appropriate professional relationship when working with female clients. Okamoto (2000) found that higher levels of male practitioners' fear of litigation was significantly related to higher levels of female clients on their caseload. These studies suggest that training and supervision of youth practitioners should incorporate ways to manage the feelings and perceptions in working with female youth, in particular with male practitioners working with female clients.

Promising Programs for Girls

In recent years, there has been much attention on identifying effective or promising interventions for delinquency. For example, articles have identified "empirically supported" treatments for conduct disorder (Brestan & Eyberg, 1998; Kazdin & Weisz, 1997) and "what works" in violence prevention (Tolan & Guerra, 1994). However, little is known about the applicability of these treatments for girls (Keenan, Loeber, & Green, 1999). Many of the published program evaluations describe the proportion of girls included in their sample; however, fail to examine the difference in outcome based on gender. Further, there are very few program evaluations that focus exclusively on girls. Nonetheless, the empirical literature suggests several types of programs as effective for girls, including cognitive-behavioral interventions, parent training interventions, and dialectical behavioral therapy.

Cognitive-behavioral interventions have been found to be effective for the reduction of aggressive or delinquent behavior in numerous studies (e.g., Feindler, Marriott & Iwata, 1984; Guerra & Slaby, 1990; Izzo & Ross, 1990; Lochman, 1992; Schlichter & Horan, 1981). Therefore, it would logically follow that these types of programs would be promising for girls. In their description of the ideal program for girls, Chesney-Lind and Shelden (1998) recommend the use of behavioral or skill-oriented approaches. These recommendations were further supported by a recent meta-analytic review on female offenders (Dowden & Andrews, 1999). In this review, stronger treatment effects were related to the use of behavioral-social learning programs versus non-behavioral treatment strategies. Their results further suggested that the use of behavioral-social learning interventions were associated with reductions in reoffending. While cognitive-behavioral interventions are promising for the prevention and treatment of female juvenile delinquency, little is still known as to the gender-specific ways in which to implement these programs.

Like cognitive-behavioral interventions, numerous studies have also supported behavioral parent training as effective in reducing aggressive or delinquent behaviors (e.g., Long, Forehand, Wierson, & Morgan, 1994; Serketich & Dumas, 1996; Webster-Stratton, 1984). Webster-Stratton (1996) examined the effect of gender on treatment outcome of parent training and found that girls' and boys' responses to treatment were similar (e.g., significant reductions in externalizing behaviors and noncompliance based on parent and teacher reports and home observations). Additionally, predictors of externalizing behavior problems at home were examined for both boys and girls. Family factors, including mother and father "negativity" and mother depression, predicted girls' externalizing behaviors 1–2 years post-treatment. No family factors predicted externalizing behaviors in boys. These findings not only highlight the efficacy of parent training for reducing girls' behavior problems, but also emphasize the overall impact of the caregiving environment on girls' emotional and behavioral development (Keenan et al., 1999).

Finally, one recent study has supported the use of dialectical behavior therapy (DBT) with incarcerated female juvenile offenders (Trupin et al., 1999). Typically used for the treatment of borderline personality disorder, DBT uses a combination of validation, problem solving strategies, and group skills training to address a series of negative behaviors (e.g., suicidal behaviors, behaviors interfering with the conduct of therapy, avoidance and escape behaviors; Linehan, 1993; Linehan & Wagner, 1990). Validation consists of emphasizing client strengths and motivating the client toward change. Problem solving strategies target problem behaviors by identifying the antecedents to those behaviors and developing a plan of alternative behaviors. Group skills training consists of training in psychosocial skills with six to eight members. DBT has been shown to be effective in reducing symptomatology related to borderline personality disorder (e.g., suicidal behaviors) in several studies (see Shearin & Linehan, 1994 for review). Trupin et al. (1999) applied the components of DBT to female juvenile offenders to evaluate client behavioral improvement and staff use of restrictive punitive actions against clients. While DBT was not shown to be effective with less emotionally and behaviorally disturbed female juvenile offenders, more severely disturbed female juvenile offenders demonstrated a significant reduction of behavior problems (i.e., aggression, parasuicidal behavior and class disruption) following the DBT intervention. Further, staff were found to utilize fewer restrictive punitive actions against clients during the DBT intervention. These findings suggest that principles of DBT may be efficacious with female juvenile delinquents.

Conclusion

Clearly, after decades of invisibility, girls and their issues have surfaced on the national agenda. Unfortunately, what has been served up is largely a mixed message, although Challenge grant activities across a number of states are providing much grassroots support for girls programming. Certainly, a lot remains to be done. Youth services all too often translate into "boys' services" as can be seen in a 1993 study of the San Francisco Chapter of the National Organization for Women. The study found that only 8.7 percent of the programs funded by the major city organization funding children and youth programs "specifically addressed the needs of girls" (Siegal, 1995). Not surprisingly, then, a 1995 study of youth participation in San Francisco after school or summer sports programs found only 26 percent of the participants were girls (Siegal, 1995). Likewise, problems exist with delinquency programming; in a list of "potentially promising programs" identified by the Office of Juvenile Justice and Delinquency Prevention, there were 24 programs cited specifically for boys and only two for girls. One program for incarcerated teen fathers had no counterpart for incarcerated teen mothers (Girls Incorporated, 1996). One student of these patterns called this, "throw away programs for throw away girls" (Wells, 1994).

The content of gender-specific programs formed within the juvenile justice system requires special vigilance, since the family court has a long history of sexism, particularly in the area of policing girls' sexuality. In fact, the one area where the GAO found evidence of gender difference was the focus on girls' sexuality. In addition to a fairly routine focus on girls' ability to get pregnant or be pregnant, the researchers reported that institutions that served girls exclusively included testing for sexually transmitted diseases while "at similar male-only facilities operated by the same organizations, such testing was not done unless requested by the males" (GAO, 1995, 5.2.3). As Kempf-Leonard (1998) has recently cautioned, the juvenile justice system's long history of paternalism and sexism makes it a problematic site for gender-specific services. Certainly, the existence of such "services" should not be used as justification for incarcerating girls, and girl-specific programming should never be an excuse to return to the good old days of girls' institutions where working class girls were trained in the womanly arts.

The major challenge to those seeking to address the needs of girls within the juvenile justice system remains the demonization of many girls, particularly girls of color, coupled with a considerable invisibility of these young women in the actual programming that either seeks to prevent or intervene in delinquent behavior. The short-lived congressional focus on girls has unfortunately been followed by a major retreat from such initiatives. Not only that, congress is apparently encouraging the recriminalization of status offenses, which suggests that without powerful, local advocacy, the nation could again see large numbers of young girls incarcerated "for their own protection." A girl centered response to this backlash, as well as continued pressure on the juvenile justice system to do more to help girls, are both essential. Much more, not less, work needs to be done to support the fundamental needs of girls on the margin.

References

Acoca, L. (1999). Investing in girls: A 21th century challenge. *Juvenile Justice, 6 (1) 3–13.*

Alder, C. (1997, March). *'Passionate and willful' girls: Confronting practices.* Paper presented to the Annual Meeting of Academy of Criminal Justices Sciences. Louisville, Kentucky.

Alder, C., & Hunter, N. (1999). *"Not worse, just different"?: Working with young women in the juvenile justice system.* Melbourne, Australia: The University of Melbourne, Criminology Department.

Alexander, B. (1998, October). Hatch quarterbacks sneak play for youth crime bill. *Youth Today,* pp. 46–47.

Artz, S. (1998). *Sex, Power and the Violent School Girl.* Toronto: Trifolium Books.

Baines, M., & Alder, C. (1996). Are girls more difficult to work with? Youth workers' perspectives in juvenile justice and related areas. *Crime & Delinquency, 42*(3), 467–485.

Bartollas, C. (1993). Little girls grown up: The perils of institutionalization. In C. Culliver (Ed.), *Female Criminality: The State of the Art.* (pp. 469–482). New York: Garland Press.

Belknap, J., Dunn, M., & Holsinger, K. (1997). *Moving toward juvenile justice and youth-serving systems that address the distinct experience of the adolescent female.* Cincinnati, OH: Gender Specific Services Work Group.

Bergsmann, I. R. (1989). The forgotten few: Juvenile female offenders. *Federal Probation, LIII*(1), 73–78.

Bishop, D., & Frazier, C. (1992). Gender bias in the juvenile justice system: Implications of the JJDP Act. *The Journal of Criminal Law and Criminology, 82*(4), 1162–1186.

Bjorkqvist, K., & Niemela, P. (Eds.). (1992). New trends in the study of female aggression. In *Of Mice and Women: Aspects of female aggression.* San Diego: Academic Press.

Bloom, B., & Campbell, R. (1998). Literature and policy review. In B. Owen & B. Bloom (Eds.)., *Modeling gender-specific services in juvenile justice: Policy and program recommendations.* Sacramento: Office of Criminal Justice Planning.

Botvin, G. J., Baker, E., Dusenbery, L., Botvin, E. M., & Diaz, T. (1995). Long-term follow-up results of a randomized drug abuse prevention trial in a White middle-class population. *JAMA, 273*(14), 1106–1112.

Botvin, G. J., Schinke, S. P., Epstein, J. A., & Diaz, T. (1994). Effectiveness of culturally focused and generic skills training approaches to alcohol and drug abuse prevention among minority youths. *Psychology of Addictive Behaviors, 8*(2), 116–127.

Botvin, G. J., Schinke, S. P., Epstein, J. A., Diaz, T., & Botvin, E. M. (1995). Effectiveness of culturally focused and generic skills training approaches to alcohol and drug abuse prevention among minority adolescents: Two-year follow-up results. *Psychology of Addictive Behaviors, 9*(3), 183–194.

Boyle, P. (1999, July/August). Youth advocates gear up to fight over the fine points. *Youth Today,* pp. 46–47.

Brandell, J. R. (Ed.). (1992). *Countertransference in psychotherapy with children & adolescents.* Northvale, NJ: Jason Aronson.

Brestan, E. V., & Eyberg, S. M. (1998). Effective psychosocial treatments of conduct-disordered children and adolescents: 29 years, 82 studies, and 5,272 kids. *Journal of Clinical Child Psychology, 27*(2), 180–189.

Budnick, K. J., & Shields-Fletcher, E. (1998). *What about girls?* (OJJDP Publication No. 84).Washington, DC: U.S. Department of Justice.

Bureau of Criminal Information and Analysis. (1999). *Report on arrests for domestic violence in California, 1998.* Sacramento: State of California, Criminal Justice Statistics Center.

Cahalan, M. (1986). *Historical corrections statistics in the United States, 1850–1984.* Washington, D.C.: Bureau of Justice Statistics.

Canter, R. J. (1982). "Sex differences in self-report delinquency." *Criminology, 20,* 373–393.

Cauffman, E., Feldman, S. S., Waterman, J., & Steiner, H. (1998). Posttraumatic stress disorder among female juvenile offenders. *Journal of the American Academy of Child and Adolescent Psychiatry, 31*(11), pp. 1209–1216.

Chesney-Lind, M. (1988). Girls in jail. Crime and Delinquency, 34(2), 150–168.

Chesney-Lind, M. (1997). *The female offender: Girls, women and crime.* Thousand Oaks: Sage.

Chesney-Lind, M. Media Misogyny: Demonizing 'Violent' Girls and Women. In J Ferrel & N. Websdale (Eds.), *Making trouble: Cultural representations of crime, deviance, and control* (pp. 115–141). New York: Aldine.

Chesney-Lind, M., & Freitas, K. (1999). *Working with girls: Exploring practitioner issues, experiences and feelings* (Rep. No. 403). Honolulu, HI: University of Hawaiÿi at Mänoa, Social Science Research Institute.

Chesney-Lind, M. and Paramore, V. (in press). Are girls getting more violent?: Exploring juvenile robbery trends. *Journal of Contemporary Criminal Justice.*

Chesney-Lind, M., & Shelden, R. G. (1998). Girls, delinquency, and juvenile justice *(2nd ed.).* Belmont, CA: Wadsworth.

Costello, J. C. & Worthington, N. L. (1981). Incarcerating status offenders: Attempts to circumvent the Juvenile Justice and Delinquency Prevention Act. *Harvard Civil Rights-Civil Liberties Law Review, 16,* 41–81.

Currie, E. (1998). *Crime and punishment in America.* New York: Metropolitan Books

DeKeseredy, W. (1999). *Women, crime and the Canadian criminal justice system.* Cincinnati: Anderson.

Dembo, R. S.C. Sue, P. Borden, and D. Manning(1995, August). *Gender differences in service needs among youths entering a juvenile assessment center: A replication study.* Paper presented at the Annual Meeting of the Society of Social Problems.Washington, D.C.

Dembo, R., Williams, L., and Schmeidler, J. (1993). Gender differences in mental health service needs among youths entering a juvenile detention center. *Journal of Prison and Jail Health, 12,* 73–101.

Dowden, C., & Andrews D. A. (1999). What works for female offenders: A meta-analytic review. *Crime & Delinquency, 45*(4), 438–452.

Federal Bureau of Investigation. 1999. *Crime in the United States 1998.* Washington, D.C.:Government Printing Office.

Feindler, E. L., Marriott, S. A., & Iwata, M. (1984). Group anger control training for junior high school delinquents. *Cognitive Therapy and Research, 8*(3), 299–311.

Finkelhor, D. & Baron, L. 1986. Risk factors for child sexual abuse. *Journal of Interpersonal Violence, 1,* 43–71.

Girls Incorporated. (1996). *Prevention and Parity: Girls in Juvenile Justice.* Indianapolis: Girls Incorporated National Resource Center.

Government Accounting Office. Juvenile Justice: Minimal Gender Bias Occurring in Processing Non-Criminal Juveniles. Washington, D.C.: Letter Report.

Guerra, N. G., & Slaby, R. G. (1990). Cognitive mediators of aggression in adolescent offenders: 2. Intervention. *Developmental Psychology, 26*(2), 269–277.

Hearings on the Juvenile Justice and Delinquency Prevention Act of 1974. Hearings Before the Subcommittee on Human Resources of the Committee on Education and Labor, House of Representatives, 102d Cong., (1992).

Huizinga, D. (1997). *Over-time changes in delinquency and drug-use: The 1970's to the 1990's.* University of Colorado: Research Brief.

Izzo, R., & Ross, R. R. (1990). Meta-analysis of rehabilitation programs for juvenile delinquents. *Criminal Justice and Behavior, 17*(1), 134–142.

Kazdin, A. E., & Weisz, J. R. (1998). Identifying and developing empirically supported child and adolescent treatments. *Journal of Consulting and Clinical Psychology, 66*(1), 19–36.

Keenan, K., Loeber, R., & Green, S. (1999). Conduct disorder in girls: A review of the literature. *Clinical Child and Family Psychology Review, 2*(1), 3–19.

Kempf-Leonard, K. (1998). Disparity based on sex: Is gender specific treatment warranted? University of Missouri-St. Louis. Unpublished paper.

Kersten, J. (1990). A gender specific look at patterns of violence in juvenile institutions: Or are girls really "more difficult to handle"? *International Journal of the Sociology of Law, 18,* 473–493.

Krisberg, B., DeComo, R., & Herrera, N. (1992). *National juvenile custody trends 1978–1989.* Washington, D.C.: Office of Juvenile Justice and Delinquency Prevention.

Kunzel, R. (1993). *Fallen women and problem girls: Unmarried mothers and the professionalization of social work, 1890–1945.* New Haven: Yale University Press.

Linehan, M. M. (1993). *Cognitive-behavioral treatment of personality disorder.* New York: Guilford.

Linehan, M. M., & Wagner, A. W. (1990). Dialectical behavior therapy: A feminist-behavioral treatment of borderline personality disorder. *The Behavior Therapist,13*(1), 9–14.

Lochman, J. E. (1992). Cognitive-behavioral intervention with aggressive boys: Three-year follow-up and preventive effects. *Journal of Consulting and Clinical Psychology, 60*(3), 426–432.

Long, P., Forehand, R., Wierson, M., & Morgan, A. (1994). Does parent training with young noncompliant children have long-term effects? *Behaviour Research and Therapy, 32*(1), 101–107.

Loper, A. B. & Cornell, D.G. (1996). Homicide by girls. *Journal of Child and Family Studies, 5,* 321–333.

Mayer, J. (1994,July). *Girls in the Maryland juvenile justice system: Findings of the female population taskforce.* Presentation to the Gender Specific Services Training. Minneapolis, Minnesota.

McCormack, A., Janus, M.D., & Burgess, A. W. (1986). Runaway youths and sexual victimization: Gender differences in an adolescent runaway population. *Child Abuse and Neglect, 10,* 387–395.

Miller, J. (1994). Race, gender and juvenile justice: An examination of disposition decision-making for delinquent girls." In M. D. Schwartz & D. Milovanovic (Eds.), *The intersection of race, gender and class in Criminology.* New York: Garland Press.

Odem, M. E. (1996). *Delinquent daughters.* Chapel Hill: University of North Carolina Press.

Office of Juvenile Justice and Delinquency Prevention. (1998, October). *Guiding principles for promising female programming* [On-line]. Available Internet: www.ojjdp. ncjrs.org/pubs/principles/contents.html

Okamoto, S. K. (2000). *Development and validation of the Youth Practitioner Fear Survey (YPFS).* Unpublished doctoral dissertation, University of Hawaii at Manoa.

Platt, A. M. (1969). *The childsavers.* Chicago: University of Chicago Press.

Poe-Yamagata, E. & Butts, J. A. (1995). *Female offenders in the juvenile justice system.* Pittsburgh: National Center for Juvenile Justice.

Public Law 96-509. 96d Cong., 2d Sess. (1981, December).

Reitsma-Street, M. (1999). Justice for Canadian girls. *Canadian Journal of Criminology,41*(4), 335–363.

Robinson, R. (1990). *Violations of girlhood: A qualitative study of female delinquents and children in need of services in Massachusetts.* Unpublished doctoral dissertation, Brandeis University.

Schiraldi, V. and Soler, M. (1998). *The will of the people? The public's opinion of the Violent and Repeat Juvenile Offender Act of 1997.* Washington, D.C.: Justice Policy Institute and Youth Law Center.

Schlichter, K. J., & Horan, J. J. (1981). Effects of stress inoculation on the anger and aggression management skills of institutionalized juvenile delinquents. *Cognitive Therapy and Research, 5*(4), 359–365.

Serketich, W. J., & Dumas, J. E. (1996). The effectiveness of behavioral parent training to modify antisocial behavior in children: A meta-analysis. *Behavior Therapy, 27,* 171–186.

Shearin, E. N., & Linehan, M. M. (1994). Dialectical behavior therapy for borderline personality disorder: Theoretical and empirical foundations. *Acta Psychiatrica Scandinavica, 89*(Suppl. 379), 61–68.

Shelden, R. and Horvath, J. (1986). Processing offenders in a juvenile court: A comparison of male and female offenders. Paper presented at the annual meeting of the Western Society of Criminology. Newport Beach, California.

Sherman, F. (1999). What's in a name? Runaway girls pose challenges for the justice system.*Women, Girls and Criminal Justice, 1*(2), 19–20, 26.

Shorter, A. D., Schaffner, L., Shick, S., & Frappier, N. S. (1996). Out of sight, out of mind: The plight of girls in the San Francisco juvenile justice system. San Francisco: Center for Juvenile and Criminal Justice.

Siegal, N. (1995, October 4). Where the girls are. *San Francisco Bay Guardian,* pp. 19–20.

Snyder, H. N., & Sickmund, M. (1999). *Juvenile offenders and victims: 1999 national report.* Washington, D.C.: Office of Juvenile Justice and Delinquency Prevention.

Stahl, A. L. (1999). *Delinquency cases in juvenile courts, 1996.* (OJJDP publication no. 109). Washington, D.C.: U.S. Department of Justice.

Steffensmeier, D. J., & Steffensmeier, R. H. (1980). Trends in female delinquency: An examination of arrest, juvenile court, self-report, and field data. *Criminology, 18,* 62–85.

Tolan, P., & Guerra, N. (1994). *What works in reducing adolescent violence: An empirical review of the field.* Boulder: University of Colorado, Boulder, Institute for Behavioral Sciences.

Trupin, E. W., Stewart, D., Boesky, L., McClurg, B., Beach, B., Hormann, S., & Baltrusis, R. (1999, February). *Evaluation of dialectical behavior therapy with incarcerated female juvenile offenders.* Paper presented at the 11th annual research conference, a system of care for children's mental health: Expanding the research base, Tampa, FL.

Webster-Stratton, C. (1984). Randomized trial of two parent-training programs for families with conduct-disordered children. *Journal of Consulting and Clinical Psychology, 52*(4) 666–678.

Webster-Stratton, C. (1996). Early-onset conduct problems: Does gender make a difference? *Journal of Consulting and Clinical Psychology, 64*(3), 540–551.

Wells, R. (1994, November). America's delinquent daughters have nowhere to turn for help. *Corrections compendium,* pp. 4–6.

Zeidenberg, J., & Schiraldi, V. (1997). *The risk juveniles face when they are incarcerated with adults.* Policy report. Washington, D.C.: Justice Policy Institute.

CHAPTER 10

A New Vision: Gender-Responsive Principles, Policy, and Practice

Barbara E. Bloom

Introduction

This chapter documents a need for a new vision for the criminal justice system—a vision that recognizes the behavioral and social differences between female and male offenders that have specific implications for gender-responsive policy and practice. It delineates guiding principles, general strategies, and steps for implementing the principles. The content of this chapter is drawn from a National Institute of Corrections (NIC) report, *Gender-Responsive Strategies: Research, Practice, and Guiding Principles for Women Offenders* (Bloom, Owen, & Covington, 2002).[1]

Developing gender-responsive policies, practices, programs, and services requires the incorporation of the following key findings:

- An effective system for female offenders is structured differently than a system for male offenders.
- Gender-responsive policy and practice target women's pathways to criminality by providing effective interventions that address the intersecting issues of substance abuse, trauma, mental health and economic marginality.

---

1. I wish to thank the National Institute of Corrections for sponsoring the research that provided the foundation for this chapter.

- Criminal justice sanctions and interventions recognize the low risk to public safety created by the typical offenses committed by female offenders.
- Gender-responsive policy considers women's relationships, especially with children, and their roles in the community when delivering both sanctions and interventions.

Being gender-responsive in the criminal justice system requires an acknowledgement of the realities of women's lives, including the pathways they travel to criminal offending and the relationships that shape their lives. In order to effectively and appropriately respond to this information, Bloom and Covington (2000) developed the following definition:

> Gender-responsive means creating an environment through site selection, staff selection, program development, content, and material that reflects an understanding of the realities of women's lives and addresses the issues of the participants. Gender-responsive approaches are multi-dimensional and are based on theoretical perspectives that acknowledge women's pathways into the criminal justice system. These approaches address social (e.g., poverty, race, class and gender inequality) and cultural factors as well as therapeutic interventions. These interventions address issues such as abuse, violence, family relationships, substance abuse and co-occurring disorders. They provide a strength-based approach to treatment and skill building. The emphasis is on self-efficacy (p. 11).

Guiding Principles and Strategies

Evidence drawn from a variety of disciplines and effective practice suggests that addressing the realities of women's lives through gender-responsive policy and programs is fundamental to improved outcomes at all criminal justice phases. The following principles offer fundamental building blocks to criminal justice policy and they can provide a blueprint for the development of gender-responsive practice.

Gender	Acknowledge that gender makes a difference.
Environment	Create an environment based on safety, respect, and dignity.
Relationships	Develop policies, practices and programs that are relational and promote healthy connections to children, family, significant others, and the community.
Services and Supervision	Address the issues of substance abuse, trauma, and mental health through comprehensive, integrated, culturally relevant services and appropriate supervision.
Economic and Social Status	Improve women's economic/social conditions by developing their capacity to be self-sufficient.
Community	Establish a system of community supervision and reentry with comprehensive, collaborative services.

General Strategies

To implement the guiding principles, the following overarching strategies can be applied to each of the principles:

Adopt	Each principle is adopted as policy on a system-wide and programmatic level.
Support	Principle adoption and implementation receive the full support of the administration.
Resources	An evaluation of financial and human resources is done to ensure that adequate implementation and allocation adjustments are made to accommodate any new policies and practices.
Training	Ongoing training is provided as an esential element of the implementation of gender-responsive practices.
Oversight	Oversight of the new policies and practices is included in management plan development.
Congruence	Procedural review is routinely conducted to ensure that procedures are adapted, deleted, or written for new policies.
Environment	Ongoing assessment and review of the culture/environment take place in order to monitor attitudes, skills, knowledge, and behavior of administration, management, and line staff.
Evaluation	An evaluation process is developed to consistently assess management, supervision, and services.

I. Acknowledge that Gender Makes a Difference

The first and foremost principle in responding appropriately to women is to acknowledge the implications of gender throughout the criminal justice system. The criminal justice field has been dominated by the "rule of parity," with equal treatment to be provided to everyone. However, this does not necessarily mean that the exact same treatment is appropriate for both women and men. The data are very clear concerning the distinguishing aspects of female and male offenders. They come into the criminal justice system via different pathways; respond to supervision and custody differently; have differences in terms of substance abuse, trauma, mental illness, parenting responsibilities, and employment histories; and represent different levels of risk within the system and the community. In order to successfully develop and deliver services, supervision and treatment for women offenders, these gender differences must first be acknowledged.

Key Findings

The differences between women and men are well documented across a variety of disciplines and practices. Increasing evidence shows that the majority of these differences are due to both social and environmental factors. While certain basic issues related to health, such as reproduction are influenced by physiological differences, many of the observed disparities are the result of gender-related differences such as socialization, gender roles, gender stratification and gender inequality. The nature and extent of women's criminal behavior and the ways in which they respond to supervision reflects such gender differences. These differences include:

- Women and men differ in levels of participation, motivation and degree of harm caused by their criminal behavior.
- Female crime rates, with few exceptions, are much lower than male crime rates. Women's crimes tend to be less serious than men's crimes. The gender differential is most pronounced in violent crime, where women's participation is profoundly lower.
- The interrelationship between victimization and offending appears to be more evident in women's lives. Family violence, trauma, and substance abuse contribute to women's criminality and shape their offending patterns.
- Women respond to community supervision, incarceration and treatment in ways that are different from their male counterparts. Women

are less violent while in custody, but have higher rates of disciplinary infractions for less serious rule violations. They are influenced by their responsibilities and concerns for their children, and also by their relationships with staff and other offenders.

Implementation

- Make women's issues a priority.
- Allocate both human and financial resources to create women-centered services.
- Designate a high-level administrative position for oversight of management, supervision and services.
- Recruit and train personnel and volunteers who have both the interest and the qualifications needed for working with women who are under criminal justice supervision.

II. Create an Environment Based on Safety, Respect, and Dignity

Research from a range of disciplines (e.g., health, mental health, and substance abuse) has shown that safety, respect, and dignity are fundamental to behavioral change. In order to improve behavioral outcomes for women, it is critical to provide a safe and supportive setting for supervision. A profile of women in the criminal justice system indicates that many have grown up in less than optimal family and community environments. In their interactions with women offenders, criminal justice professionals must be aware of the significant pattern of emotional, physical, and sexual abuse that many of these women have experienced, and every precaution must be taken to ensure that the criminal justice setting does not reenact those earlier life experiences. A safe, consistent, and supportive environment is the cornerstone of a corrective process. Because of their lower levels of violent crime and their low risk to public safety, women offenders should, whenever possible, be supervised with minimal restrictions required to meet public safety guidelines.

Key Findings

Research from the field of psychology, particularly trauma studies, indicates that environment cues behavior. There is now an understanding of what an environment must reflect if it is to impact the biological, psychological and social consequences of trauma. Because the corrections culture is influenced by punishment and control, it is often in conflict with the culture of treatment. The criminal justice system is based on a control model while treatment is based on a model of behavioral change. These two models must be integrated so that women offenders can experience positive outcomes. This integration should acknowledge the following facts:

- Substance abuse professionals and literature report that women require a treatment environment that is safe and nurturing, as well as a therapeutic relationship that is one of mutual respect, empathy, and compassion.
- A physically and psychologically safe environment produces positive outcomes for women.
- Studies in child psychology demonstrate that the optimal context for childhood development consists of a safe, nurturing, and consistent environment. Such an environment is also necessary for changes in adult behavior.
- Safety is identified as a key factor in effectively addressing the needs of domestic violence and sexual assault victims.
- Custodial misconduct has been documented in many forms including verbal degradation, rape, and sexual assault.
- Classification and assessment procedures often do not recognize the lower level of violence by women both in their offenses and in their behavior while under supervision. This can result in women's placement in higher levels of custody than necessary in correctional institutions and in an inappropriate assessment of their risk to the community.
- Low public safety risk suggests that women offenders can often be managed in the community, and their needs for personal safety and support suggest the importance of safe and sober housing.

Implementation

- Conduct a comprehensive review of the institutional or community environment in which the women are supervised to provide an ongoing assessment of the current culture.
- Develop policy that reflects an understanding of the importance of emotional and physical safety.
- Understand the effects of childhood trauma in order to avoid further traumatization.
- Establish protocols for reporting and investigating claims of misconduct.
- Develop classification and assessment systems that are validated on samples of women offenders.

III. Develop Policies, Practices, and Programs That Are Relational and Promote Healthy Connections to Children, Family, Significant Others and the Community

Understanding the role of relationships in women's lives is fundamental as the common theme of connections and relationships threads throughout the lives of female offenders. When the concept of relationship is incorporated into policies, practices, and programs, the effectiveness of the system or agency is enhanced. This concept is critical when addressing the following:

- reasons why women commit crimes
- impact of interpersonal violence on their lives
- importance of children
- relationships between women in an institutional setting
- process of women's psychological growth and development
- environmental context needed for programming
- challenges involved when reentering the community

Attention to the above issues is crucial to the promotion of successful outcomes for women in the criminal justice system.

Key Findings

A basic difference in the way women and men "do time" is in their ability to develop and maintain relationships. Studies of women offenders highlight the importance of relationships and the fact that criminal involvement often develops through relationships with family members, significant others, or friends. This is qualitatively different than the concept of peer associates, which is often cited as a criminogenic risk factor in assessment instruments. For many females, their connections with significant others are often key to their involvement in crime. Interventions must acknowledge and reflect the impact that these relationships have on women's current and future behavior. Important relationship findings include the following:

- Developing mutual relationships is fundamental to women's identity and sense of worth.
- Women offenders frequently suffer from isolation and alienation created by discrimination, victimization, mental illness, and substance abuse.
- Studies in the substance abuse field indicate that partners, in particular, are an integral part of women's initiation into substance abuse, contin-

uing drug use, and relapse. Partners can also influence the retention of
women in treatment programs.

- Theories that focus on female development, such as the relational model,
  posit that the primary motivation for women throughout life is the establishment of a strong sense of connection with others.
- The majority of women under criminal justice supervision are mothers
  of dependent children. Many women try to maintain their parenting responsibilities while under community supervision or while in custody,
  and many plan to reunite with one or more of their children upon release from custody or community supervision.
- Studies have shown that relationships among women in prison are also
  important. Women often develop close personal relationships and
  pseudo-families as a way to adjust to prison life. Research on prison staff
  indicates that correctional personnel are often not prepared to provide
  appropriate responses to these relationships.

Implementation

- Develop training for all staff and administrators in which relationship
  issues are a core theme. Such training should include the importance of
  relationships, staff-client relationships, professional boundaries, communication, and the mother-child relationship.
- Examine all mother and child programming through the eyes of the
  child (e.g., child-centered environment, context) and enhance the
  mother-child connection and the connection of the mother to child
  caregivers and other family members.
- Promote supportive relationships among women offenders.
- Develop community and peer-support networks.

IV. Address the Issues of Substance Abuse, Trauma, and Mental Health Through Comprehensive, Integrated, and Culturally Relevant Services and Appropriate Supervision

Substance abuse, trauma, and mental health are three critical, interrelated
issues in the lives of women offenders. These issues have a major impact on a
woman's experience of community correctional supervision, incarceration,
and transition to the community, in terms of both programming needs and
successful reentry. Although they are therapeutically linked, these issues have
historically been treated separately. One of the most important developments

in health care over the past several decades is the recognition that a substantial proportion of women have a history of serious traumatic experiences that play a vital and often unrecognized role in the evolution of a woman's physical and mental health problems.

Key Findings

The salient features that propel women into crime include family violence and battering, substance abuse, and mental health issues. The connections between substance abuse, trauma, and mental health are numerous. For example, substance abuse can occur as a reaction to trauma, or it can be used to self-medicate symptoms of mental illness; mental illness is often connected to trauma; and substance abuse can be misdiagnosed as mental illness. Other considerations include the following:

- Substance abuse studies indicate that trauma, particularly in the form of physical or sexual abuse, is closely associated with substance abuse disorders in women. A lifetime history of trauma is present in 55 to 99 percent of female substance abusers.
- Research shows that women who have been sexually or physically abused as children or adults are more likely to abuse alcohol and other drugs and may suffer from depression, anxiety disorders, and post-traumatic stress disorder (PTSD).
- Regardless of whether the mental health or substance abuse disorder is considered to be primary, co-occurring disorders complicate substance abuse treatment and recovery. An integrated treatment program concurrently addresses both disorders through treatment, referral, and coordination.
- Research by the National Institutes of Health has found that gender differences, as well as race and ethnicity, must be considered in determining appropriate diagnosis, treatment and prevention of disease.
- The substance abuse field has found that treatment programs are better able to engage and retain women clients if programs are culturally targeted.

Implementation

- Service providers need to be cross-trained in the three primary issues: substance abuse, trauma, and mental health.
- Resources, including skilled personnel, must be allocated.
- The environment in which services are provided must be closely monitored to ensure the emotional and physical safety of the women being served.

- Service providers/criminal justice personnel must receive training in cultural sensitivity so that they can understand and respond appropriately to issues of race, ethnicity, and culture.

V. Improve Women's Economic and Social Conditions by Developing Their Capacity to Be Self-Sufficient

Addressing both the social and material realities of women offenders is an important aspect of correctional intervention. The female offender's life is shaped by her socioeconomic status; her experience with trauma and substance abuse; and her relationships with partners, children, and family. Most women offenders are disadvantaged economically and socially, which is compounded by trauma and substance abuse histories. Improving outcomes for women requires providing them with preparation through education and training to support themselves and their children.

Key Findings

Most women offenders are poor, undereducated, and unskilled. Many have never worked, have sporadic work histories, or have lived on public assistance. Other factors that impact their economic/social condition include:

- Most women offenders are female heads of household. In 1997, nearly 32 percent of all female heads of households lived below the poverty line.
- Research from the domestic violence field has shown that such material and economic needs as housing and financial support, educational and vocational training, and job development are essential to women's ability to establish lives apart from their abusive partners.
- Research on the effectiveness of substance abuse treatment has noted that, without strong material support, women presented with economic demands are more likely to return to the streets and cease treatment.
- Recent changes in public assistance (e.g., Temporary Assistance for Needy Families) affect women disproportionately and negatively impact their ability to support themselves and their children. In approximately half the states in the nation, convicted drug felons are ineligible for benefits. When eligible, they still may not be able to apply for benefits until they have been released from custody or community supervision. They cannot access treatment or medical care without Medicaid. Additionally, their conviction can also preclude them from being eligible for public housing or Section 8 subsidies.

Implementation

- Allocate resources within both community and institutional correctional programs for comprehensive, integrated services that focus on the economic, social, and treatment needs of women. Ensure that women leave prison and jail with provisions for short-term emergency services (subsistence, lodging, food, health care, transportation, and clothing).
- Provide traditional and non-traditional training, education, and skill-enhancing opportunities to assist women in earning a living wage.
- Provide sober living space in institutions and in the community.

VI. Establish a System of Community Supervision and Reentry with Comprehensive Collaborative Services

Women offenders face specific challenges as they reenter the community from jail or prison. Women on probation also face challenges in their communities. In addition to the female offender stigma, they may carry additional burdens such as single motherhood, decreased economic potential, lack of services and programs targeted for women, responsibilities to multiple agencies, and a general lack of community support. Navigating through a myriad of systems that often provide fragmented services and conflicting requirements can interfere with supervision and successful reintegration. There is a need for wraparound services—that is, a holistic and culturally sensitive plan for each woman that draws on a coordinated range of services located within her community. The types of organizations that should work as partners in assisting women who are reentering the community include the following:

- mental health systems
- alcohol and other drug programs
- programs for survivors of family and sexual violence
- family service agencies
- emergency shelter, food, and financial assistance programs
- educational organizations
- vocational and employment services
- health care
- the child welfare system, child care, and other children's services
- transportation
- self-help groups
- consumer advocacy groups

- organizations that provide leisure options
- faith-based organizations
- community service clubs

Key Findings

Challenges to successful completion of community supervision and reentry for women offenders have been documented in the research literature. These challenges can include housing, transportation, child care, and employment needs; reunification with children and other family members; peer support; and fragmented community services. There is little coordination among community systems that link substance abuse, criminal justice, public health, employment, housing, and child welfare. Other considerations for successful reentry and community supervision include the following:

- Substance abuse studies have found that women's issues are different from those of men. Comprehensive services for women should include, but not be limited to, life skills, housing, education, medical care, vocational counseling and assistance with family preservation.
- Studies from fields such as substance abuse and mental health have found that collaborative, community-based programs that offer a multidisciplinary approach foster successful outcomes among women.
- Substance abuse research shows that an understanding of the interrelationships among the women, the program, and the community is critical to the success of a comprehensive approach. "Comprehensive" also means taking into consideration a woman's situation and desires related to her children, other adults in her family or friendship network, and her partner.
- Data from female offender focus groups indicate that the following needs, if unmet, put women at risk for criminal justice involvement: housing, physical and psychological safety, education, job training and opportunities, community-based substance abuse treatment, economic support, positive role models, and a community response to violence against women. These are all critical components of a gender-responsive prevention program.
- Research has found that women offenders have a great need for comprehensive, community-based wraparound services. This case management approach has been found to work effectively with women because it addresses their multiple treatment needs.
- Relational theory indicates that approaches to service delivery that are based on women's relationships and the connections among the differ-

ent areas of their lives are especially congruent with female characteristics and needs.

Implementation

- Create individualized support plans and wrap the necessary resources around the woman and her children.
- Develop a "one-stop shopping" approach for community services with the primary service provider also facilitating access to other needed services.
- Use a coordinated case management model for community supervision.

Developing Gender-Responsive Policy and Practice

The guiding principles proposed in this chapter are intended to serve as a blueprint for the development of gender-responsive policy and practice. These principles can also provide a basis for system-wide policy and program development. The following are scenarios based on a gender-responsive model for women offenders:

- The correctional environment or setting is modified to enhance supervision and treatment.
- Classification and assessment instruments are validated on samples of women offenders.
- Policies, practices, and programs take into consideration the significance of women's relationships with children, families and significant others.
- Policies, practices, and programs promote services and supervision that address substance abuse, trauma, and mental health and provide culturally relevant treatment to women.
- The socioeconomic status of women offenders is addressed by services that focus on their economic and social needs.
- Partnerships are promoted among a range of organizations located within the community.

A first step in developing gender-appropriate policy and practice is to address the following questions:

- How can correctional policy address the differences in behavior and needs of male and female offenders?
- What challenges do these gender differences create in community and institutional corrections?

- How do these differences affect correctional practice, operations, and supervision in terms of system outcomes and offender-level measures of success?
- How can policy and practice be optimized to best meet criminal justice system goals for women offenders?

Policy Considerations

As agencies and systems examine the impact of gender on their operations, policy-level changes are a primary consideration. A variety of existing policies developed by the National Institute of Corrections Intermediate Sanctions for Women Offender Projects, the Federal Bureau of Prisons, the American Correctional Association(ACA), the Minnesota Task Force on the Female Offender, and the Florida Department of Corrections contain elements of a gender-appropriate approach. Gender-responsive elements derived from this analysis are considered below:

Create Parity

As stated in the *ACA Policy Statement*, "Correctional systems should be guided by the principle of parity. Female offenders must receive the equivalent range of services available to male offenders, including opportunities for individual programming and services that recognize the unique needs of this population" (American Correctional Association, 1995, p. 2). Parity differs conceptually from 'equality' and stresses the importance of equivalence rather than sameness. Women offenders should receive opportunities, programs, and services that are equivalent, but not identical to those available to male offenders.

Commit to Women's Services

Executive decision-makers, administrators, and line staff must be educated about the realities of working with female offenders. Establishing mission and vision statements regarding women's issues and creating an executive-level position charged with implementing these statements are two ways to ensure that women's issues become a priority. A focus on women is also tied to the provision of appropriate levels of resources, staffing, and training.

The National Institute of Corrections has recognized the need for gender-specific training and has sponsored a variety of initiatives designed to assist jurisdictions in addressing issues relevant to women offenders. In Florida, a staff training and development program was mandated and will be imple-

mented for correctional officers and professionals who work with female offenders in institutions and community corrections. In the Bureau of Prisons,
training occurs at the local institution level. The Texas Division of Community Corrections has also created specific training for those who work with female offenders in the community.

Review Standard Procedures for Their Applicability to Women Offenders

Another key element of policy for women offenders concerns a review of
policies and procedures. While staff working directly with women offenders
on a day-to-day basis are aware of the procedural misalignment of some procedures in relation to the actual realities of women's lives, written policy often
does not reflect the same understanding of these issues. As stated in the ACA
policy, "Sound operating procedures that address the {female} population's
needs in such areas as clothing, personal property, hygiene, exercise, recreation and visitations with children and family" should be developed (American Correctional Association, 1995, p. 1).

Respond to Women's Pathways

Policies, programs and services need to respond specifically to women's
pathways in and out of crime and to the contexts of their lives that support
criminal behavior. Procedures, programs, and services for women should be
designed and implemented with these facts in mind. Both material and treatment realities of women's lives should be considered. For example, Florida's
policy states that

> emphasis is placed on programs that foster personal growth, ac-
> countability, self-reliance, education, life skills, workplace skills and
> the maintenance of family and community relationships to lead to
> successful reintegration into society and reduce recidivism (Florida
> Department of Corrections, 1999, p.1).

Florida's policy also states that the system must "ensure opportunities for female
offenders to develop vocational and job-related skills that support their capacity for economic freedom" (Florida Department of Corrections, 1999, p. 1).

Consider Community

Given the lower risk of violence and community harm found in female
criminal behavior, it is important that written policies acknowledge the actual
level of risk represented by women offenders' behavior in the community and

in custody. The recognition and articulation of this policy will enable the development of strong community partnerships, creating a receptive community for model reentry and transitional programs that include housing, training, education, employment, and family support services.

The ACA advocates for a range of alternatives to incarceration, including pretrial and post trial diversion, probation, restitution, treatment for substance abuse, halfway houses, and parole services. Community supervision programs need to partner with community agencies in making a wide range of services and programs available to women offenders. Community programs are better equipped than correctional agencies to respond to women's realities.

Include Children and Family

Children and family play an important role in the management of women offenders in community and custodial settings. Women offenders, more so than males, have primary responsibility for their children. However, female offenders' ties to their children are often compromised by correctional policy. ACA policy states that the system should "facilitate the maintenance and strengthening of family ties, particularly between parents and children" (American Correctional Association, 1995, p.1). In Florida, an emphasis on the relationships of women offenders with their children and other family members has potential rehabilitative effects in terms of motivation for treatment and economic responsibility (Florida Department of Corrections, 1999).

Implications for Practice

After policy development, the next step concerns the specific ways in which gender-appropriate policy elements can be incorporated into practice in order to improve service delivery and day-to-day operations and procedures. Identifying problems created by a lack of knowledge about women offenders and by gender-neutral practice is a critical step in addressing these issues.

The analysis of operational practice and procedures raises several questions that agencies and the criminal justice system need to consider when developing a systemic approach for women offenders. These questions are organized into categories that reflect specific elements of gender-responsive practice, as shown below:

Operational Practices

- Are the specifics of women's behavior and circumstances addressed in written planning, policy, programs, and operational practices? For example, are policies regarding classification, property, programs, and services appropriate to the actual behavior and composition of the female population?

- Does the staff reflect the offender population in terms of gender, race/ethnicity, sexual orientation, language (bilingual), ex-offender and recovery status? Are female role models and mentors employed to reflect the racial/ethnicity and cultural backgrounds of the clients?
- Does staff training prepare workers for the importance of relationships in the lives of women offenders? Does the training provide information on the nature of women's relational context, boundaries and limit-setting, communication, and child-related issues? Are staff prepared to relate to women offenders in an empathetic and professional manner?
- Are staff trained in appropriate gender communication skills and in recognizing and dealing with the effects of trauma and PTSD?

Services

- Is training on women offenders provided? Is this training available in initial academy or orientation sessions? Is the training provided on an ongoing basis? Is this training mandatory for executive-level staff?
- Does the organization see women's issues as a priority? Are women's issues important enough to warrant an agency-level position to manage women's services?
- Do resource allocation, staffing, training and budgeting consider the facts of managing women offenders?

Review of Standard Procedures

- Do classification and other assessments consider gender in classification instruments, assessment tools, and individualized treatment plans? Has the existing classification system been validated on a sample of women? Does the database system allow for separate analysis of female characteristics?
- Is information about women offenders collected, coded, monitored, and analyzed in the agency?
- Are protocols established for reporting and investigating claims of staff misconduct, with protection from retaliation ensured? Are the concepts of privacy and personal safety incorporated in daily operations and architectural design, where applicable?
- How do the policies address the issues of cross-gender strip searches and pat-downs?

- Do the policies include the concept of zero tolerance for inappropriate language, touching, other inappropriate behavior and staff sexual misconduct?

Children and Families

- How do existing programs support connections between the female offender and her children and family? How are these connections undermined by current practice? In institutional environments, what provisions are made for visiting and other opportunities for contact with children and family?
- Are there programs and services that enhance female offenders' parenting skills and their ability to support their children upon release? In community supervision settings and community treatment programs, are parenting responsibilities acknowledged through education? Through child care?

Community

- Are criminal justice services delivered in a manner that builds community trust, confidence, and partnerships?
- Do classification systems and housing configurations allow community custody placements? Are transitional programs in place that help women build long-term community support networks?
- Are professionals, providers, and community volunteer positions used to facilitate community connections? Are they used to develop partnerships between correctional agencies and community providers?

Building Community Support

Building community support is an important factor in effective community corrections. In order to improve the circumstances of women offenders and their children, a gender-responsive approach must emphasize community support for women. There is a critical need to develop a system of support within our communities that provides assistance to women who are returning to their communities in the areas of housing, job training, employment, transportation, family reunification, childcare, drug and alcohol treatment, peer support, and aftercare. Women transitioning from jail or prison to the community must navigate a myriad of systems that often provide fragmented services, and this can pose a barrier to their successful reintegration (Covington, 2002).

Prevention

Prevention is another aspect of building community support. In the series of focus groups that were conducted with women in the criminal justice system, participants identified the following factors when asked what they felt could help prevent them from criminal involvement:

- housing
- physical and psychological safety
- education, job training and opportunities
- community-based substance abuse treatment
- positive female role models
- an appropriate community response to violence against women (Bloom, Owen, & Covington, 2002)

Restorative Justice

Restorative justice is an important vehicle for building community support for criminal justice services. In keeping with female psychosocial developmental theory, the framework for restorative justice involves relationships, healing, and community. The focus is not on punishment and retribution, but rather on a variety of mechanisms that include victim-offender mediation, family conferencing, and community circles of support. This perspective is consistent with both the level of harm represented by women offenders and the need to target their pathways to offending. Social support is a key variable in a range of effective interventions and includes intimate relationships, social networks, and communities.

Women offenders are good candidates for restorative justice and community corrections. Because they commit far fewer serious or violent offenses and pose less of a risk to public safety than male offenders, they are in a preferred position to take the lead in participating in programs of restorative justice. Similarly, because of their suitability for community correctional settings, women offenders may be in a better position to model the significant benefits to the community that may be achieved through effective restorative justice programs.

Reentry and Wraparound Services

Reentry programs can serve as a model for enhancing community services. While all offenders must confront the problem of reentry into the community, many of the obstacles and barriers faced by women offenders are specifically related to their status as women. In addition to the stigma attached to a criminal conviction and a likely history of substance abuse, women carry additional burdens. These extra burdens are due to such individual-level characteristics as single motherhood, decreased economic potential, as well as to system-level characteristics such as the lack of services and programs targeted for women, responsibilities to multiple agencies, and the lack of community support for women in general. Often, non-offending women in the larger community confront many of the same harsh realities.

Clearly, there is a need for wraparound services—that is, a holistic and culturally sensitive plan for each woman that draws on a coordinated continuum of services within the community. As Jacobs (2001) notes, "[W]orking with women in the criminal justice system requires ways of working more effectively with the many other human service systems that are involved in their lives" (p. 47).

Integrated and holistic approaches, such as wraparound models, can be very effective because they address multiple goals and needs in a coordinated way and facilitate access to services (Reed & Leavitt, 2000). Wraparound models stem from the idea of "wrapping necessary resources into an individualized support plan" (Malysiak, 1997, p. 400). Both client-level and system-level linkages are stressed in the wraparound model. The need for wraparound services is highest for clients with multiple and complex needs that cannot be addressed by limited services from a few locations in the community.

For women leaving custodial environments, the program focus should be on planning for successful community reentry. Many types of reentry services for female offenders would also benefit women in the larger community. The development of more effective and comprehensive services for women in general, and women offenders specifically, could not only enhance community services, but could also help to prevent crime.

Considerations for Gender-Responsive Programs and Services

As highlighted in Chapter 1, there are a number of considerations for the development of gender-responsive programs and services. For women who are in the system, a gender-responsive approach would include comprehensive services that take into account the content and context of women's lives. Programs need to take into consideration the larger social issues of poverty, abuse, and race and gender inequalities, as well as individual factors that impact women in the criminal justice system (Bloom, 1996). Services also need to be responsive to women's cultural backgrounds (Bloom & Covington, 1998).

Programming that is responsive, in terms of both gender and culture, emphasizes support. Service providers need to focus on women's strengths, and they need to recognize that a woman cannot be treated successfully in isolation from her social support network (i.e., her relationships with her children, partner, family, and friends). Coordinating systems that link a broad range of services will promote a continuity-of-care model. Such a comprehensive approach would provide a sustained continuity of treatment, recovery, and support services, beginning at the start of incarceration and continuing through transition to the community.

Gender-Responsive Program Evaluation

Program evaluation is another step in building gender responsiveness. As the vision of gender-responsiveness evolves, documenting the effectiveness of practice addresses the need for empirical research on the outcomes of gender-responsive programs.

Process evaluation identifies the fit between the principles of gender responsivity and program implementation. This type of evaluation measures the environments within which programs operate. Process evaluation measures the unique "culture" of individual programs, such as the relationships between staff and women offenders, relationships between women, and rules and regulations, in order to determine how these factors may impact the program. Such evaluations must also involve the input of the participants so that their feedback on the services provided can be obtained.

Outcome evaluations describe measures of program success or failure, examining both the short- and long-term impacts of the interventions on program participants. Ideally, outcome measures used in evaluations should be tied to the program's mission, goals, and objectives. Also, outcome measures should go beyond traditional recidivism measures to assess the impact of specific program attributes on pathways to female criminality and rehabilitation.

Conclusion

This chapter documents the importance of understanding and acknowledging differences between female and male offenders and the impact of those differences on the development of gender-responsive policies, practices, and programs in the criminal justice system. This analysis has found that addressing the realities of women's lives through gender-responsive policy and practice is fundamental to improved outcomes at all phases of the criminal justice system. This review maintains that consideration of women's and men's different pathways into criminality, their differential responses to custody and supervision, and their differing program requirements can result in a criminal justice system that is better equipped to respond to both male and female offenders.

References

American Correctional Association. (1995). *Public correctional policy on female offender services.* Latham, MD: Author.

Bloom, B. (1996). *Triple jeopardy: race, class and gender as factors in women's imprisonment.* Riverside, CA: Department of Sociology, University of California, Riverside.

Bloom, B. & Covington, S. (2000, November). *Gendered justice: Programming for women in correctional settings.* Paper presented to the American Society of Criminology, San Francisco, CA.

Bloom, B. & Covington, S. (1998, November). *Gender-specific programming for female offenders: What is it and why is it important?* Paper presented to the American Society of Criminology, Washington, DC.

Bloom, B., Owen, B., & Covington, S. (2002). *Gender-responsive strategies: Research, practice and guiding principles for women offenders.* Washington, DC: National Institute of Corrections.

Covington, S. (2002). *A woman's journey home: Challenges for female offender.* Washington,DC: Urban Institute.

Florida Department of Corrections. (1999). *Operational plan for female offenders.* Tallahassee,FL: Florida Department of Corrections.

Jacobs, A. (2001). Give'em a fighting chance: Women offenders reenter society. *Criminal Justice Magazine, 16* (1), 44–47.

Malysiak, R. (1997). Exploring the theory and paradigm base for wraparound fidelity. *Journalof Child and Family Studies, 6* (4), 399–408.

Reed, B. & Leavitt, M. (2000). Modified wraparound and women offenders in community corrections: Strategies, opportunities and tensions. In M. McMahon (Ed.), *Assessment to assistance: Programs for women in community corrections* (pp. 1–106). Lanham, MD: American Correctional Association.

AUTHOR INDEX

Subject Index